Between Peril and Promise

Between Peril and Promise:

The Politics of International Law

J. Martin Rochester

University of Missouri–St. Louis

CQ PRESS

A Division of Congressional Quarterly Inc.
Washington, D.C.

CQ Press
1255 22nd Street, NW, Suite 400
Washington, DC 20037

Phone: (202) 729-1900; toll-free, 1-866-427-7737 (1-866-4CQ-PRESS)

Web: www.cqpress.com

Cover Design: Naylor Design Inc.

⊗ The paper used in this publication exceeds the requirements of the American
National Standard for Information Sciences—Permanence of Paper for Printed Library Materials,
ANSI Z39.48-1992.

Printed and bound in the United States of America

10   09   08   07   06   1   2   3   4   5

Library of Congress Cataloging-in-Publication Data

Rochester, J. Martin.
    Between peril and promise : the politics of international law / J. Martin
Rochester. — 1st ed.
        p. cm.
    Includes bibliographical references and index.
    ISBN 1-933116-49-8 (alk. paper)
    1. International law.   2. International relations.   I. Title.
KZ3410.R63 2006
341—dc22
                                    2005033850

For Ruth and our Tree of Life—

Shaya and Marisa, Sean and Carolyn, Leah and Mendy

Contents

Preface

INTERNATIONAL RELATIONS SCHOLARS, when given a choice between being labeled a "realist" or an "idealist," tend to prefer the former. Indeed, the idealist school of scholarship, which dominated the profession in the interwar period between 1919 and 1939, was so besmirched by the failure of the League of Nations to prevent World War II that the nomenclature itself was subsequently discarded in favor of a less utopian-sounding word: "liberal." Today, we find numerous schools in the international relations discipline—neorealist, neoliberal, neo-marxist, along with feminist, constructivist, and others—but none calling itself neoidealist. Practitioners and laypersons, too, no less than academics, like to think of themselves as "realistic" types, lest they be dismissed as wishful thinkers or, worse, idle dreamers.

Therefore, anyone who dares to write about the possibility of a new world order in international affairs grounded in the rule of law risks being accused of indulging in faith—what Mark Twain called "believin' in what you know ain't true"—rather than fact. However, the risk is worth taking, not only because of the normative imperative to work toward a more peaceful, stable, and just world order, but also because a solid body of evidence has shown convincingly that international law is an authentic, significant feature of international life, not an oxymoron.

No scholar is owed a greater debt in this regard than Louis Henkin, whose *How Nations Behave* was the main inspiration for this book. I do not pretend to bring the same level of legal erudition to my study that he demonstrated in his 1968 classic (revised in 1979). First, I am a political scientist, not a lawyer, and thus by training not as steeped in formal jurisprudence as a member of the bar (though perhaps a bit better positioned to observe the law in action). Second, I am writing here more for an undergraduate and graduate student audience and the general reader than attempting a treatise. What I do share in common with Professor Henkin is the objective of delineating the connection between international law and international politics—how law affects politics and vice versa. Although I trace the evolution of international law in various issue-areas, I am most concerned about its relevance to post–cold war politics.

Part One addresses some of the age-old questions surrounding international law, including whether it actually exists. Part Two focuses on the contemporary operation of international law in specific domains: human rights, war and peace, the international economy, the allocation of legal competences (on land and sea and in airspace and outer space), and the environment. Part Three attempts to pull together the threads of analysis in the first two sections and peers into the future, speculating on what the twenty-first century might hold for international law and politics. I should add that I examine international law in the larger context of "global governance," including how it relates to the development of international organizations, regimes, and institutions broadly defined.

The reader will find three appendixes designed to promote further reflection: Questions for Study and Discussion, Table of Cases, and Resources for Researching International Law: Web Sites, Casebooks and Reference Works, and Readings. These appendixes can also be found on the book's companion Web site: www.cqpress.com/cs/rochester. The site provides links to the full text of most cases listed in the Table of Cases and also links for further research. In addition, this site includes an engaging mock court simulation exercise, "The Great Tuna Boat Chase and Massacre," a fictitious case that serves as the basis for a moot court contest that applies the legal rules and principles discussed in this book.

I wish to acknowledge my mentor, Bill Coplin, who first interested me in the study of international law when I was a student at Syracuse University; my own students, who have provided great stimulation for my thinking and re-thinking about international law over the past thirty years at the University of Missouri–St. Louis; the very helpful proposal reviewers—Curtis G. Reithel (University of Wisconsin–La Crosse), Katie Verlin Laatikainen (Adelphi University), M. J. Peterson (University of Massachusetts–Amherst)—and manuscript reviewers—Remonda B. Kleinberg (University of North Carolina at Wilmington), R. Michael Collins (University of Memphis), and Juergen Kleiner (Boston University, retired)—whose constructive criticism improved the book considerably; and the outstanding staff at CQ Press, including editor Charisse Kiino, assistant editor Colleen Ganey, copyeditor Dan Conlon, and production editor Anna Schardt. Finally, I must pay special tribute to my family—Ruth, Shaya, Sean, Marisa, Carolyn, Leah, and Mendy—who have always provided emotional support for my writing endeavors and who are reason enough for me to want to see a better, safer, happier world.

J. Martin Rochester
St. Louis, Missouri

I

Introduction

Putting International Law in Proper Perspective, or Putting Your Legal Prototypes Aside

In my office and in my Department, we are, first of all, students of international law.

—Paul Martin, former Canadian Secretary of State for External Affairs

Law is to be found within nations rather than above them. There is no world state and therefore no world law.

—David Fromkin, The Independence of Nations, *1981*

International law . . . meets none of the tests we normally impose on "law."

—John Bolton, appointed U.S. ambassador to the United Nations in 2005, in an article he wrote in the January/February 1999 issue of Foreign Affairs.

The first time that states break a rule of international law, they apologize and claim that they were unaware the rule existed. The second time, they claim that the rule is ambiguous. The third time, they claim that the rule has changed.

—*Graham Allison, author of* Essence of Decision: Explaining the Cuban Missile Crisis, *based on an anecdote told to the author.*

1

International Law and
International Politics

THERE IS A JOKE THAT GOES AS FOLLOWS: Two close friends, Larry and Harry, are avid baseball fans and attend almost every home game at Yankee Stadium. One day, Larry asks, "Harry, do you think they play baseball in heaven?" whereupon Harry says, "That's a good question—I don't know." Several weeks go by without Harry being seen at the ballpark or anywhere else, and Larry gets worried. Finally, Harry turns up at the stadium. Larry says, "Harry, where have you been? I have been worried sick." Harry replies that he had been hit by a truck, had gone to heaven, and had good news and bad news. "The good news is, yes, there is baseball in heaven. The bad news is you're pitching next Tuesday."

On a more serious note, there is both good news and bad news about the state of the world. The good news is that people all over the globe are more interconnected than ever before, not only in terms of being "wired" but also in sharing a common destiny, which is also the bad news, in that problems which in the past might have been localized now are often globalized. Spurred by the arrival of the new millennium, forecasters are hard at work pondering what the twenty-first century holds for humanity. One can find both optimists and pessimists. It has been said that a pessimist is an optimist with experience. But experience itself can be an uncertain teacher whose lessons can be difficult to grasp. This is especially true for those trying to make sense of happenings in the realm of world politics, where the future of humanity will largely be determined.

On the hazards of trying to predict the future—even of five-year cycles—in international relations, allow me another anecdote, this one based on recent history. I can still vividly recall sitting in a paneled room at the International Studies Association annual meeting in Washington, D.C., in April of 1986, attending a session featuring two American diplomats engaging two Soviet diplomats in a speculative discussion about "The Future of U.S.-Soviet Relations." This was at a time when the cold war was still raging, when Soviet leader Mikhail Gorbachev had just come to power in the Kremlin, when U.S. President Ronald Reagan was continuing to characterize the USSR as the "evil empire," and when Reagan's own secretary of defense was quoted as saying that East-West tensions were such that "we are no longer in the postwar era but the prewar era." One of the Russian diplomats began his comments by uttering what he took to be an old Romanian proverb, that "it is always hard to predict anything, especially the future." Indeed, who in that room, or for that matter in any room anywhere that day, can claim to have predicted that within a half-decade the world would witness the end of the cold war and the end of the Soviet Union itself, with hardly a shot being fired?[1] It is fair to say that most people—scholars, practitioners, and laypersons alike—shared former Carter administration National Security Advisor Zbigniew Brzezinski's 1986 assessment that "the American-Soviet conflict is not some temporary aberration but a historical rivalry that will long endure."[2] Yet, by December 1989, the Berlin Wall that had symbolized the Iron Curtain separating the free and non-free worlds had collapsed, and the Soviet Red Army Chorus could be heard in Washington, D.C., leading Reagan's successor and a throng of dignitaries at a Kennedy Center gala in a stirring rendition of "God Bless America"; by December 1991, the USSR had dissolved into Kazakhstan, Tajikistan, Uzbekistan, and assorted other independent republics.

At that very moment, amidst much fanfare and jubilation, President George Bush declared a "New World Order" of peace and harmony and Francis Fukuyama of the U.S. State Department proclaimed "the end of history," arguing that the forces of Western liberal democracy and free-market capitalism had seemingly achieved their final triumph over all other competing ideologies.[3] The "holiday from history"[4] was short-lived, as was the jubilant mood. If 11/9 (the fall of the Berlin Wall on November 9, 1989) had been earthshaking, 9/11 was no less so: on September 11, 2001, some 3,000 people lost their lives in the attack by al Qaeda terrorists on the United States—abruptly ending the post–cold war era and ushering in the post–9/11 era. What had been euphoria turned to despair, and what had been advertised as the New World Order was renamed the "New World Disorder"[5] or, according to even gloomier pundits, the New Dark Age.

The moral of the story is that you should proceed at your own risk in making predictions about the direction in which the post–9/11 world is headed. The cold war lasted fifty years, the post–cold war era far less. It is hard to know how long the post–9/11 era will last and what the post–post–9/11 era might look like. Some predictions, however, are safer bets than others. When I said at the start that the future of humanity would largely hinge on what transpires in the realm of world politics, I was perhaps betraying my bias as a political scientist. Still, it seems a reasonable proposition to argue that developments in the political arena will inform developments in the economic, cultural, environmental, and other arenas. And it seems an equally reasonable proposition to argue that politics will continue to be mostly about governance, which in turn has to do mostly with the creation and functioning of rules, what most people think of as "laws." One of the safer bets is that there is likely to be little progress in international politics without progress in international law—"the law of nations," defined as "the body of rules which are binding upon states in their relations with one another."[6]

The purpose of this book is to examine and encourage further reflection on the nature of the relationship between international politics and international law, and the role that the latter might plausibly be expected to play in improving the former. In short, how does politics shape the development of international law,

"Don't get me wrong. Legality has its place."

How relevant is international law?

and how does international law shape politics? We need to examine not only what rules exist in the global polity but also how they are created, the extent to which they are obeyed and influence behavior, and how they "work" (or do not work). Most importantly, we need to consider whether international law "matters." In other words, as a recent symposium posed the question, "What good is international law?"[7] If we can answer that question and improve our understanding of the relationship between international law and international politics, we may then be in a better position to speculate, should we wish to, about what alternative world futures are possible and desirable. We begin our investigation here by looking at the current setting in which international law has to operate.

The Relevance of International Law

Judging by coverage in the mass media, international law would appear to matter quite a bit, although the media are more likely to report on major violations of law than on its routine observance. ("U.S. Troops Invade Iraq" or any other apparent act of aggression is front page news, while one would be surprised to see even buried in the back of a newspaper an article trumpeting "7 Billionth Piece of Mail

Is Delivered Safely Across National Boundaries This Year," a fact made possible only through the existence of the Universal Postal Union, an international organization created by a treaty that has established a single planet-wide postal territory.)

Among the headlines that have appeared in the world's newspapers in recent times are the following:

- "Biological Treaty, With the Goal of Saving Species, Becomes Law," referring to the 1992 Convention on Biological Diversity that obligates countries to protect the tropical rainforests and other habitats rich in biodiversity.

- "U.S. Germ Warfare Review Urges Pullback from Pact Trying to Limit Biological Weapons," referring to the George W. Bush administration's misgivings about certain provisions of a proposed treaty aimed at strengthening the 1972 Biological Weapons Convention that bans the development, production, and stockpiling of bacteriological agents that could be used in war and could potentially wipe out large segments of the human species itself.

- "Major Portion of Israeli Fence Is Ruled Illegal by World Court," alluding to the 2004 opinion (*Legal Consequences of the Construction of a Wall in the Occupied Palestinian Territory*) issued by the International Court of Justice that called upon Israel to dismantle the 400-mile barrier it was erecting as a response to Palestinian terrorist attacks, since the wall violated "humanitarian law" and other norms.

- "UN Investigator Faults Sudan for Atrocities," calling attention to the killing of over 70,000 black, non-Arab villagers by militias supported by the Sudanese government, which the United Nations charged with possible "crimes against humanity."[8]

Indeed, on almost any given day, if one were to read the *New York Times* or any comparable newspaper, one would likely find a number of stories that have some sort of "international law" angle, either reporting on arms control, environmental or human rights treaties, or dealing with more mundane but not insignificant matters, such as the regulation of trade in foodstuffs, overseas air travel, disease control, or countless other concerns—all of which have relevance to the life of the average citizen on the planet.

Yet many would question the relevance of international law in a world in which so much lawlessness and violence exist.[9] To be sure, order is not the only function to be served and value to be promoted by law. Others, as suggested above, include democracy, justice, economic prosperity, and ecological quality. However, order is the *sine qua non*, since it is hard to maximize any of the others in the absence of at least a modicum of stability (i.e., peace). Obviously, to even the most casual observer, the globe has not been a very peaceful place of late. As Charles Tilly has written, "More collective violence was visited on the world (in absolute terms, and probably per capita as well) in the twentieth century than in any century of the previous ten thousand years. . . . Between 1900 and 1999, the world produced about 250 new wars, international or civil, in which battle deaths averaged at least 1,000 per year. . . . Altogether, then, about 100 million people died in the twentieth century as a direct result of action by organized military units backed by one government or another."[10] The first decade of the new millennium does not seem any less violence-prone, although the primary security threat today arguably stems somewhat more from nongovernmental actors such as al Qaeda, that is, not so much from rogue, outlaw states as nonstates.

Jonathan Schell, in *The Fate of the Earth,* has eloquently captured the ultimate cataclysm that might possibly await us in the twenty-first century, the extinction of the human race:

> Only six or seven thousand years ago civilization emerged, enabling us to build a human world, and to add to the marvels of art, of science, of social organization, of spiritual attainment. But, as we built higher and higher, the evolutionary foundation beneath our feet became more and more shaky, and now in spite of all we have learned and achieved—or, rather, because of it— we hold this entire terrestrial creation hostage to nuclear destruction, threatening to hurl it back into the inanimate darkness from which it came. And this threat of self-destruction and planetary destruction is not something that we will pose one day in the future, if we fail to take certain precautions; it is here now, hanging over the heads of all of us at every moment."[11]

A similarly poignant reminder of how far we have come and how far we still have to go comes from the 1965 film *The War Game:* "Technically and intellectually we are living in an atomic age. Emotionally we are still living in the Stone Age. The Aztecs on their feast days would sacrifice 20,000 men to their gods in the belief that this would keep the universe on its proper course. We feel superior to them."[12] Former Governor Richard Lamm of Colorado has stated the problem more succinctly: "It has historically been one thing to die for your country. It is a different thing [in the event of major war today] to die *with* your country."[13]

One might be forgiven, then, for thinking it is the *worst* of times, a period that one would not ordinarily associate with the growth of world order and the rule of law. After all, for the first time in history we can now conceivably annihilate the entire *Homo sapiens* population, not only through the use of nuclear weapons but through other means as well. Atomic, biological, and chemical (ABC) weapons are all considered weapons of mass destruction (WMDs) and are on the brink of proliferating dangerously; biological and chemical weaponry—the "poor person's nuclear bomb"—are especially easy to develop and especially liable to end up in the hands of terrorists. As for poverty, the number of poor people in the world is increasing, partly as a function of an ongoing population explosion in many less developed countries and partly because of a growing rich-poor gap that finds over one-third of humanity living on less than two dollars a day.[14] If humanity is not exterminated by the arms buildup of WMDs, it may happen instead through the buildup of CO_2 and other greenhouse gases in the Earth's atmosphere that are contributing to global warming, which made the 1990s the warmest decade on record and 2002, 2003, and 2004 the second, third, and fourth hottest years ever.[15]

However, to borrow the oft-quoted words from Charles Dickens's *A Tale of Two Cities*, if it is the worst of times, it may also be the *best* of times. Alongside the potential for unprecedented planetary conflict and disaster is the potential for unparalleled planetary cooperation and well-being. It is worth reminding that the United Nations, for all its many flaws, is nonetheless the most ambitious attempt at global institution-building in the many millennia humanity has inhabited the Earth. Certainly, for most people, contemporary life is not nearly as "nasty, brutish and short" as it was when Thomas Hobbes was using those adjectives in *The Leviathan* to describe the human condition in the seventeenth century. Even with grinding poverty in parts of the world, life expectancy has increased almost everywhere in recent decades (except where the AIDS epidemic has decimated the populace), and the "globalization" of the international economy promises a better life for more consumers if economic growth with equity can be promoted. As the World Bank has noted, "the past 30 years . . . [have seen] considerable progress in improving human well-being. Average income per capita . . . in developing countries grew from $989 in 1980 to $1,354 in 2000. Infant mortality was cut in half, from 107 per 1,000 live births to 58, as was adult illiteracy, from 47 to 25 percent."[16] Regarding the global environment, notwithstanding global warming, tropical rainforest deforestation, and other problems, if one were to take the pulse of the biosphere in 2000 compared with that thirty years earlier on the first Earth Day, one could conclude that on many measures there has been environmental progress and "the environment is in a lot better condition in the U.S. [and elsewhere] today."[17] Some of the most impressive gains in recent decades have been made in the area of democratization; granted that human rights violations remain prevalent, Freedom House, in its recent survey entitled "Liberty's Expansion in a Turbulent World: Thirty Years of the Survey of Freedom," nevertheless reports that "there has been dramatic progress in the expansion of freedom and democratic governance over the life of the survey," with eighty-nine countries in 2003 rated "free," fifty-five "partly free," and forty-eight "not free" (with both the number of free countries and their proportion being the highest in the history of the survey).[18]

The move toward more open societies has been assisted by modern technology, which has created dramatic opportunities to enhance communication, travel, and information processing worldwide. A three-minute telephone call between New York and London (in current dollars) cost $300 in 1930; today it is practically free over the Internet.[19] The fastest mode of transportation prior to the twentieth century was the steam locomotive, which could reach a speed of 100 mph; jet planes can now fly over 2,000 mph and humans in capsules can exceed 18,000 mph in outer space. All of this is helping to create greater interdependence, which clearly cuts both ways: The same communications technology that disseminates democratic ideas and connects families and friends across national boundaries also can facilitate the growth of terrorist networks; likewise, the mere six hours it now takes to go between New York and London is matched in travel efficiency only by the mere minutes it would take if you caught a ride on an intercontinental ballistic missile hurtling through space between New York and Moscow.

The point is that it is the worst of times and best of times precisely because there is a double-edged sword quality to much that surrounds us, not only technology but other aspects of our existence as well. Even when it comes to the issue of violence, one can cite some positive trends amidst the nightmarish possibilities relating to WMDs. As noted above, substantial progress toward economic prosperity and other values is not possible without a degree of order; whatever progress has occurred, which has been considerable judging from the aforementioned statistics, can be attributed at least partly to some hopeful developments in world order. Few people alive today have had to cope with sustained crises of the magnitude experienced by my parents' generation, which in successive decades spent the flower of their youth suffering through World War I (1914–1918), the Great Depression (1929–1939), and World War II (1939–1945). For all its tensions, the cold war that followed WWII was just that, a non-hot, non-shooting war. In some important respects, the period since 1945 has been relatively peaceful, and has even been characterized as "the long peace"[20] insofar as the over half-century span is the longest continuous stretch of time since the beginning of the modern state system (in the seventeenth century) in which there has not been a single recorded instance of a direct great-power exchange of actual hostilities. It is not an exaggeration to say that the probability of a great-power war occurring today is closer to zero than at any point in history. That isn't to say it couldn't happen, only that it is a remarkably remote possibility. This is no small accomplishment. One wishes we could say the same for interstate wars between not-so-great powers, as well as intrastate (civil) wars and extrastate violence perpetrated by terrorists, all of which unfortunately remain major concerns, especially as the specter of WMD proliferation threatens to blur the distinction between who is or is not a "great power" capable of causing significant harm to its neighbors and the world as a whole.

The Challenge

So the world is not as civilized a place as one might hope, but not as savage as commonly thought. There is a space for rules to operate, however narrow. Amid the din of conflict that surrounds international relations, there does exist some degree of order. In fact, many kinds of transactions across national boundaries, such as mail and travel flows, tend to occur in such a routine, cooperative fashion that they generally go unnoticed by the average observer. The orderly nature of many international interactions is mainly a function of the mutual interests that states share in having at least some measure of stability in their day-to-day affairs. To this end, states have created a body of international law designed to help regulate relations between countries, as well as a network of intergovernmental organizations designed to facilitate conflict management along with collaboration in economic and social problem-solving at the regional and global level. The development of these institutions, primitive as they might be, is a manifestation of humanity's continual quest for order in a fragmented world of politically independent but economically, socially, and otherwise interdependent units that are inexorably being drawn ever closer by technological and other forces. The current globalization of the world economy is but the latest turn in a long-term evolutionary trend.

Institutional links among national governments have been increasing, with the growth of the United Nations system being the most visible symbol of the international organization phenomenon. Just as governments have been developing greater organized ties across national frontiers, so have private individuals and groups such as multinational corporations and nongovernmental organizations. There are far more nongovernmental international organizations than intergovernmental ones. There is some question whether the existing body of international legal rules and intergovernmental organizations are adequate to cope with the burgeoning volume of transnational activities and the expanding agenda of economic, environmental, and other international issues competing with traditional war-peace issues.

In an effort to address these problems, there is an ongoing challenge to develop what are called international *regimes*—sets of institutions "around which actor expectations converge in a given issue-area."[21] Hence, one hears references to the "nuclear proliferation regime" or the "trade regime." Regimes constitute widely accepted norms and principles ("soft law"), rules ("hard law"), and decision-making procedures and organizations, in other words "governing arrangements" that "regularize behavior and control its effects."[22] Regimes are an alternative to each country pursuing strictly its own unilateral foreign policies. The drafting of treaties and international agreements, the cultivation of shared norms, and the creation of international organization machinery are all part of regime-building. Our focus in this book is on rules—on international law—but law cannot be divorced from organizational and other regime elements.

Opinions about the effectiveness of international law and organization have traditionally ranged from extremely harsh cynicism to extremely naïve utopianism, and many observers today still tend to view international institutions in these Cassandra and Pollyanna terms. From this brief overview of the state of the world, it should be evident to the reader that we would be wise to refrain from both excessive pessimism and excessive optimism. To repeat, there is both good news and bad news. Ironically, it is the good news that somewhat undermines the prospects for further global institution-building and the rule of law, namely the absence of any singular, palpable system-wide crisis equivalent to World War I or II that might serve as the catalyst for the next stage of global organization. WWI and WWII, with all their destructiveness, motivated the formation of the League of Nations and the United Nations, while the cold war, having ended without a shot being fired, produced indifference toward constructing additional

"I really envy you your ability to think globally."

Building global relationships.

global architecture. Instead of a visible system-wide crisis, there is a general malaise and uneasy feeling "in the air," grounded in the vague sense that the next system-wide crisis may well be, as Schell warns, the last. Perhaps that bit of bad news might be sufficient to convince leaders and publics of the necessity for action. However, even if there is a compelling logic dictating a reformation in international governance arrangements—and a greater respect for international law—the question must be asked, as Stanley Hoffmann once put it, "Will the need find a way?" [23]

In order to grapple with this puzzle, it is not enough for the student of international law to be versed in the content of the law. Important as that is, the student must also seek to acquire an understanding of the law in a larger context. The portrait of international law that this book tries to paint combines broad strokes with sharp details, starting out with "big picture" generalities in Part One (outlining the nature of international politics and international law), filling in the specifics in Part Two (delineating the operation of international law in the security, economic, and other sectors), and putting the finishing touches on the canvas in Part Three (speculating about the future of global institution-building).

In contemplating both the opportunities and constraints surrounding the development of international law and organization in the contemporary international political system, it is useful first to examine the main competing schools of thought, or paradigms, that have guided thinking over the years about the essence of international relations and what makes the world go round. It is one thing to talk about "the politics of international law." It is another to talk about the "laws of international politics" and what variables drive the foreign policy behavior of states in their interactions with each other and other actors. We now turn to that analysis.

2

The Great Paradigm Debate:
Realism, Idealism, and Other Schools

PARADIGMS ARE "WAYS OF SEEING THE WORLD,"[1] or "comprehensive perspectives that organize our overall understanding"[2] of some set of phenomena we are trying to fathom. They perform an important function in any discipline, giving general direction to our observations at any moment—steering our attention toward some things and away from others. An example that is commonly cited is the evolution of the discipline of astronomy. The Ptolemaic paradigm, named after the second century philosopher who took an Earth-centric view of the universe, dominated thinking about astronomy until the sixteenth century when Copernicus posited that the sun was the center of the solar system, with all planets, including the Earth, revolving around it. Although paradigms are of particular importance to scholars, they have relevance for policy makers and laypersons as well. The Copernican system not only paved the way for the modern science of astronomy, but also fundamentally altered people's outlook about the cosmos.

As applied to the study of world politics, paradigms help us "tease meaningful patterns" out of "the welter of events, situations, trends, and circumstances that make up international affairs."[3] In the field of international relations, there have been two dominant paradigms. The first is known as the *realist* paradigm, which is the basis for the tradition of cynicism. The other is the *idealist* paradigm (also called the *liberal* paradigm), which is the basis for the tradition of utopianism. Whereas realists see international law and international organizations as simply additional instruments that great powers in world politics seek to use to maintain the status quo, idealists see these as representing noble experiments in institution-building possibly leading eventually to world government.[4]

The idealist paradigm can trace its roots at least as far back as Dante, the Italian poet of the fourteenth century who wrote of the "universality of man" and urged the unification of Europe. The idealist tradition also includes Hugo Grotius, the

13

Dutch jurist widely considered the father of international law, whose *On the Laws of War and Peace,* written in 1625 (shortly before the Peace of Westphalia in 1648 gave birth to the modern interstate system), suggested a body of rules that sovereign states might abide by; Emeric Cruce, the French monk and worldly thinker who died in 1648, having dreamed of the creation of a world court, a common meeting place for nations to work out their disputes, and the abolition of armies; and Immanuel Kant, whose *Perpetual Peace,* written in 1795, envisioned the possibility of a federation of democratic, pacific states sharing a harmony of interests.[5]

In the twentieth century this paradigm has been most closely associated with Woodrow Wilson and other thinkers who were prominent in the period between the two world wars. Idealists focus attention on legal-formal aspects of international relations, such as international law and organization, and on moral concerns such as human rights. It was out of the ashes of World War I that idealists claimed to have learned certain lessons about the workings of international relations and what had to be done to prevent another catastrophe. In their minds, a new world order had to be constructed based on a respect for law, the acceptance of shared universal values, and the development of international organizations such as the League of Nations.

It was the very failure of the idealists to anticipate and prevent World War II that gave rise to the dominance of the realist paradigm after 1945. Whereas the idealists argued that their ideas had not been fully implemented in the interwar period and hence had not been fully tested, observers such as E. H. Carr contended that they *had* been tested but could not stand up against armies marching across Europe and halfway around the world. Hans Morgenthau, in his classic 1948 work *Politics Among Nations,* became identified as the father of the realist school, even though Carr had been writing a few years earlier and the roots of realist thought could be traced as far back as the sixteenth century to Machiavelli's *The Prince* and even to Thucydides's accounts of the Peloponnesian War between Athens and Sparta in ancient Greece.[6] Realists are as interested as idealists in the problem of conflict management, but they claim to have learned their own lessons from World War II, namely that the way to prevent future wars was to rely not on legal-formal institutions or moral precepts but on "balance of power" alliances capable of deterring would-be aggressors, or on a "concert of powers" willing to police the world. Not surprisingly, realists have tended to focus on such topics as military strategy, the elements of national power, diplomacy and other instruments of statecraft, and the nature of national interests rather than such subjects as international law and organization.

Today, the realist-idealist divide can be seen in the fact that most international politics textbooks continue to give relatively little space to international law, while most international law textbooks give relatively little attention to international politics. The two sides talk past each other, if they talk at all.[7] As the title of this book suggests, it is the author's view that this needs remedying and that it is important to examine the *intersection* of international politics and international law. While politics shapes law, as realists would predict, law shapes politics, as idealists would maintain. Let us explore how the divide might be bridged by looking more closely at the basic assumptions of each paradigm.

The Realist Paradigm

Realists insist they are not cynics, only skeptics. To realists, the golden rule is "whoever has the gold rules." Power drives all politics, national or international, but especially the latter. This is so, according to realists, because of the inherent nature of the international system, whose most distinguishing feature is that it is a *decentralized* political system, lacking any central authoritative institutions of any consequence—a legislature, a court, or a police force—for making, adjudicating, and enforcing law. In other words, if one thinks of the over 6 billion human beings in the world today as constituting a single polity, there is no world government. Instead, people are organized into some 200 *nation-states*, demarcated by the dark borders on a world map. A nation-state is a political unit with a relatively well-defined set of territorial boundaries and population, over which a central government exercises *sovereign* rule through institutions based in its national capital. "Sovereignty" refers to the existence of a supreme authority that can claim the exclusive right to rule over that patch of real estate and people and recognizes no higher authority outside those boundaries (whether it is the United Nations, the pope, or any other body).

This has been the primary framework for human political organization for the past several centuries, as far back as the Peace of Westphalia that ended the Thirty Years' War in Europe in 1648, and that generally marks the origin of modern international relations. As Leo Gross observed, "The Peace of Westphalia . . . marks the end of an epoch and the opening of another. It represents the majestic portal which leads from the old world into the new world."[8] Prior to Westphalia, the main mode of political organization in Europe was feudalism, a crazy-quilt pattern of duchies, walled cities, landed manors, kingdoms, ecclesiastical territories, and assorted other entities tied together in a complex web of overlapping hierarchies of authority and multiple loyalties, with the Holy Roman Emperor on much of the continent having nominal control over all secular matters and the pope over all religious matters, but in reality neither having much power to regulate local rulers. In consolidating their power against local rulers and repudiating any allegiance to higher secular or religious authorities outside their territory, national monarchs in England, France, and elsewhere were countering the forces of both localism and universalism.[9] Westphalia "represented a new diplomatic arrangement—an order created by states, for states."[10] Later, with the French Revolution and democratic developments in the eighteenth and nineteenth centuries, sovereignty was to reside not in the monarch but in the *nation*, in the people. The Westphalian state system eventually was to spread out across the globe to North and South America, Asia, and Africa, where once-colonial possessions became sovereign states welcomed into the "community of nations."[11]

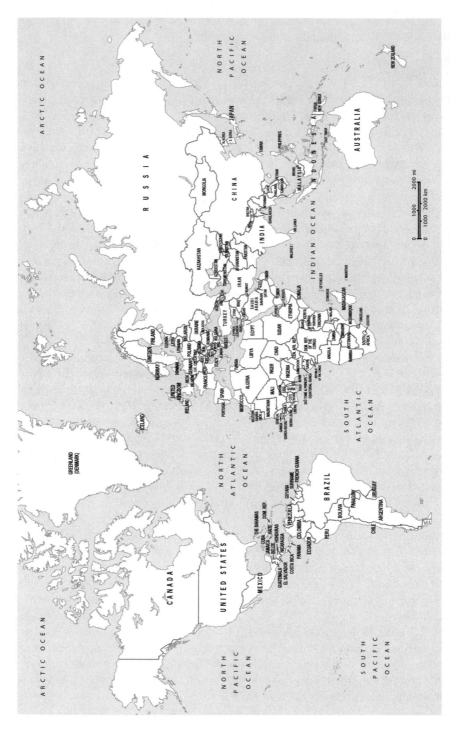

This is a standard map of the world, showing the Westphalian state system, which today has roughly 200 sovereign countries demarcated by distinct boundary lines.

Three key realist assumptions follow from the decentralized nature of the international system.

Realist Assumption 1

The first assumption is that *states* are the lead actors on the world stage. The world map with well-marked national boundaries, which is the main image most of us instantly reproduce in our head when we think about world politics, only reinforces this assumption. Many states, commonly labeled "third world" countries, may be "weak states" in terms of lacking economic and other resources that would confer a strong capacity to govern their populace; and, indeed, some states, such as Somalia and Haiti, may even be "failed states," whose governing institutions barely function at all. Nonetheless, the primacy of states in world politics is acknowledged even by writers who might resist the realist label, such as Oran Young: "Most contemporary discussions of world politics are based on the postulate that the state . . . is the fundamental political unit in the world system and that therefore it is possible to analyze world politics largely in terms of interstate relations."[12] Similarly, Hedley Bull: "The starting point of international relations is the existence of states, of independent political communities."[13] Also, Alexander Wendt: "States still are at the center of the international system, and as such it makes no more sense to criticize a theory of international politics as 'state-centric' than it does to criticize a theory of forests for being 'tree-centric.' "[14]

This state-centric view, according to realists, is justified not only because states enjoy sovereignty, which gives them legal control over all human beings on the planet, but, more importantly, because states—more precisely, their national governments and foreign policy establishments—exercise the most actual influence on what happens in world affairs. Obviously, although all sovereign states are technically, juridically equal, some states exercise far more influence than others, being "strong states" not merely in an internal sense but in terms of being able to project power externally through military or other means. The more powerful states have been known to ignore the sovereignty of less powerful states when it suits them.[15]

But what of *nonstate* actors—intergovernmental organizations, nongovernmental organizations, multinational corporations, and other *transnational* actors—that have developed alongside nation-states? Realists assume that they are no more than a supporting cast, playing bit roles in the drama of world politics. Realists treat *intergovernmental organizations* (IGOs) as mere extensions of nation-states or as peripheral to the major power struggles of world politics. IGOs are viewed as created by states (mainly through treaties) and for states, as organizations whose members are nation-states and that serve as forums for interstate diplomacy. Moreover, realists maintain that the decision-making apparatus in IGOs, particularly global IGOs, tends to reflect the power structure in the international system and ultimately serves the interests of the great powers, as suggested by the ability of the major victors in World War II, led by the United States, to acquire special voting privileges on the United Nations Security Council, including veto power. Realists predict that, when major powers find an IGO no longer serves their interests, they will become less involved in the organization and will reduce their commitment of resources to its operation, making it even more marginalized in world affairs. In short, the United Nations and other such institutions have "minimal influence on state behavior."[16]

Realists consider *nongovernmental organizations* (NGOs), such as Greenpeace or the International Council of Scientific Unions, even less important than IGOs in world politics—situated further out on the wings, since, by definition, these entities are composed of private individuals or groups that have organized across national boundaries and hence are even further removed from the centers of power in the Westphalian state system than are IGOs. Although many NGOs recently have been granted consultative status to participate in diplomatic conferences sponsored by the United Nations and other bodies, it is just that—merely consultative—and their capacity to form associations and to function in the international arena remains wholly dependent upon the permission of governmental authorities that can limit citizen activity if they so choose.

Multinational corporations (MNCs), such as British Petroleum or Toyota—"companies which have their home in one country but operate and live under the laws and customs of other countries as well"[17]—can be thought of as a special subset of NGOs, subject to the same constraints as other NGOs. Indeed, MNCs often have been depicted as agents of their home country and home government, with American-based MNCs especially criticized by many less developed countries over the years as an arm of U.S. imperialism and neocolonialism, under the control of Washington. Others see host governments recently exercising growing control relative to home governments. In any case, realists argue MNCs are hardly autonomous actors challenging nation-state dominance.[18]

Realist Assumption 2

The second assumption is that states behave as *unitary, rational* actors, pursuing their individual *national interests,* with the highest priority given to *national security* defined mainly in *military-strategic* terms. A hallmark of the realist paradigm is not only that nation-states are the only actors of consequence in the international system, but also that each can be conceptualized as a homogenous, coherent unit when it comes to the formulation and conduct of foreign policy. This realist view is one that most of us accept. Every day we hear references in conversations and news reports that "the United States" or "Washington" (or "Japan" or "Tokyo") has "decided" something or "done" something in the international arena. These are not just convenient shorthand expressions but a reflection of a natural tendency to reify the nation-state, to attribute human qualities to a collectivity. States are thought to be ego-driven rational actors concerned about maximizing their national interests in response to stimuli (hostile or friendly moves and other conditions) in their external environment outside their borders. A metaphor frequently used by state-centric analysts to characterize world politics is that of a set of *billiard balls* interacting on a pool table.[19] The balls are the nation-states; the table is the state system; and the collisions constitute inter-state relations.

A corollary of Assumption 2 is that the internal makeup of a state is not critical to how it behaves in international relations. No matter whether the state is a democracy or a dictatorship, or is led by a Saddam Hussein or a George Bush, "given the same external stimuli, all states will behave in a similar manner."[20] One could predict a hostile response by a country that had just discovered enemy troops encamped near its border regardless of whether its leaders were elected or self-appointed. Realists contend that, even with the rise of the welfare state and the growing visibility of economic and nonsecurity issues on national agendas, nation-states remain obsessed above all else with maintaining their physical security and territorial integrity against any outside threats.

Courtesy of Joshua Korenblat

The billiard ball paradigm.

There is a *hierarchy* of concerns states face, with military security at the top. If Assumption 1 discounts the importance of transnational actors, Assumption 2 discounts the importance of *subnational* actors—interest groups, political parties, bureaucratic agencies, public opinion, the mass media, and other domestic political elements—which are presumed to defer for the most part to the national leadership, at least on those issues of gravest concern to the nation. The reader will recognize the familiar adage that in foreign policy, as opposed to domestic policy, politics is supposed to "stop at the water's edge."[21]

Realist Assumption 3

The third assumption is that, given the decentralized, anarchic nature of the state system, where in the absence of any common authority to enforce agreements and maintain order there is inherent mutual distrust, relations between states tend to be characterized by *conflict,* often involving the *threat or use of armed force.*

Realists emphasize the profound implications that result from anarchy. Again, if "international politics, like all politics, is a struggle for power,"[22] it is a struggle whose signal feature is that it is unmediated by any referee. As Thucydides said about the Greek city-state system, "the strong do what they will and the weak suffer what they must."[23] Given the absence of any umpire to regulate the behavior of the members of the international system, even those states which are not interested in self-aggrandizement but only self-defense tend to feel a need to expand their power, if only for self-help purposes. As states sense that the best way to deter aggression and preserve peace is to arm to the teeth, they find themselves trapped in a "security dilemma" whereby the pursuit of security inevitably breeds greater insecurity. Agreements can be hard to reach since there is no central authority to ensure compliance. Hence, cooperation is difficult. Conflict is the norm. In fact, the constant threat of the use of armed force is endemic to the system, producing the pattern of state-to-state warfare documented by Charles Tilly and others. Peace is viewed as "a period of cheating between two periods of fighting."[24]

A contemporary variant of realism, the *neorealist* school, focuses especially on Assumption 3 and how the structure of the international system determines developments in world politics.[25] Neorealists draw on a body of literature called *game theory,* which assumes that many situations in international relations are analogous to games of poker or chess, in which the players (statesmen) seek to make moves based on a rational calculus of what strategies are likely to maximize their gains and minimize their losses. Although some games may be *zero-sum* in nature, where what one party wins the other automatically loses (for example, where two states claim the same parcel of land but obviously cannot both exercise sovereignty over it), many games can involve the possibility of all parties winning something, albeit not all benefiting equally (for example, where states sign an environmental treaty that improves air quality for all the parties but requires some to bear a greater share of the costs of pollution control). Neorealists argue that, because security remains the paramount concern, even when all states may benefit from an agreement (that is, even when negotiations offer *absolute* gains for all—a "win-win" outcome), cooperation may prove difficult if some states are perceived as winning more *relative* to others, since the former's improved capabilities could subsequently confer military advantage.[26] Neorealists posit that the prospects for international regime-building and getting agreement on the rules governing international relations are greatest when there is a *hegemon*—a single dominant power—capable of getting states to follow its lead through inducements or outright coercion.

All of this may seem somewhat simplistic, but realists consider their worldview an elegant, parsimonious representation of much that goes on in international relations. Suffice it to say, there seems little room for international law to grow in a purely realist world.

The Idealist (Liberal) Paradigm

Idealists, or liberal internationalists as they prefer to be called, believe that the realist paradigm is too simplistic and ignores much of reality. As Morton Kaplan and Nicholas Katzenbach have noted, "No one can observe the international political system without being aware of the fact that order does exist and that this order is related in important ways to . . . a body of law and to a process of law-government."[27] I alluded earlier to the fact that amid the din of conflict in international relations, there does exist some degree of order, based not entirely on the law of the gun but on more cooperative impulses which liberals emphasize. In contrast to the views expressed by Thucydides on the role of power, liberals quote Rousseau's famous line—"the strong are never so strong that they can be master of all," implying that even hegemons and superpowers need at times to rely on something other than brute force to achieve their objectives. What are the assumptions of the liberal paradigm?

Idealist Assumption 1

The first assumption is that states increasingly compete with *nonstate* actors in producing outcomes in the international arena. Although transnational actors have been around for a long time, they have especially proliferated since World War II. It is estimated that there are now more than 300 IGOs, 10,000 NGOs, and 35,000 MNCs in the world.[28] Such entities have not only increased in sheer numbers but have also gained in importance. One will not find al Qaeda or Microsoft on a world map, yet they arguably have far greater power to impact lives on the planet than many nation-states. One writer notes that "the state-centered view of world affairs, the interstate model which still enjoys so much popularity in the study of international relations," is open to question, mainly because "nation-states are not the only actors on the world scene. . . . Some NGOs probably have more power and influence in their respective fields than some of the smaller nation-states. The same applies to several IGOs and undoubtedly to many multinational business enterprises which have more employees and a larger production output than most countries."[29]

For example, one cannot fully understand the dynamics of the 1992 UN Conference on Environment and Development held in Rio de Janeiro (the "Earth Summit") unless one takes into account, in addition to the interplay between governments from the North and the South, the variety of nonstate actors involved: the secretariats of the United Nations, World Bank, and other IGOs (such as the UN Environmental Program, which organized the meeting), nongovernmental scientific research bodies ("epistemic communities") and global environmental advocacy groups, MNCs, and a host of other players. The point is not that nonstate actors played the decisive role in the conference, only that they were a not insignificant part of the equation that produced several new environmental agreements.[30]

The idealist tradition focuses special attention on IGOs, since they are seen as key vehicles for the development of international regimes, including international law. One scholar notes that, counting offshoots of existing IGOs, the number of IGOs grew 5,000 percent in the twentieth century, from only 37 in 1909 to 1,850 by 1997, with most of the growth occurring after 1980.[31] IGOs command attention, however, not because they are easily counted but because they appear to be part of an evolutionary process at work in world politics. Rather than being viewed as failed or at best marginal responses to the problem of war, as realists tend to see them, intergovernmental organizations may be more cogently seen as structures that are deeply embedded in historical forces. Inis Claude has said:

> The *expectation* of international organization, the *habit* of organizing, the *taking-for-granted* of international bodies . . . are permanent results of the movement [that began almost from scratch a century or so ago]. . . . We cannot ignore the successful implantation of the *idea* of international organization. International organization may not have taken over the system, but it has certainly taken hold in the system. The twentieth century has seen the establishment of the prescription that multilateral agencies are essential to the conduct of international affairs [italics mine].[32]

While broad, multipurpose IGOs such as the League of Nations and the United Nations were created as a direct reaction to war, functionally specific IGOs such as the International Civil Aviation Organization and other "specialized agencies" owe their existence to the expansion of interstate commerce and the need for new structures to assist national governments in promoting orderly economic relations in an emergent world capitalist economy. Regarding the latter IGOs (sometimes called "public international unions"), their arrival on the scene in the late nineteenth century—the Universal Postal Union dates back to 1878—coincided not only with the growth of an internationalist-oriented capitalist class but also with the beginnings of the welfare state and modern industrial society. The expansion of democracy gave rise to increased pressures on governments from mass publics demanding an improved standard of living. The welfare state increased the range of public policy concerns governments were expected to address, while the technological revolutions in communications and travel tended to internationalize these concerns and create incentives for intergovernmental cooperation.[33] While it is true that on some measures global interdependence today is not as great as it was on the eve of World War I, in most respects globalization is now "faster, cheaper and deeper" and "thicker"[34] than ever and is producing ever greater pressures for cooperation across national boundaries.

States today form intergovernmental organizations for the same practical reasons that have always provided the fundamental rationale behind IGOs—that is, problems exist that either cannot be handled unilaterally within the capabilities of a single state or can be dealt with more efficiently through collaboration with others.[35] When a problem arises, the first inclination on the part of the affected parties is ordinarily to try to address the concern simply through formation of an international regime (some set of written agreements or informal ad hoc arrangements) short of creating an organization, since the latter is more costly; however, if the problem is viewed as an ongoing one, more elaborate machinery may be found necessary and an IGO may be born. The pattern is for international law (treaties) to beget international organization, and for the latter (through sponsorship of conferences and other activities) in turn to beget further international law. Some problems may involve only two states and, hence, may call for merely a bilateral IGO (for example, the St. Lawrence Seaway Authority established by the United States and Canada), whereas other problems may be defined as requiring a regional approach (for example, the European Union) or a global approach (for example, the United Nations). Although there are more regional IGOs than global ones, liberal thinkers expect that economic globalization and related trends are likely to provide further impetus for global IGO growth.

Idealist Assumption 2

A second assumption of liberalism is that, since traditional national defense issues increasingly have to compete for attention on national agendas with welfare and other issues, states themselves should be conceptualized less as unitary, rational, security-obsessed actors single-mindedly driven by "national interests," and more as *pluralistic* collections of interests (farmers, bankers, chemical manufacturers, and other constituencies) seeking to affect the foreign policy process in their particular issue domain within and outside their respective political systems. Just as more and more societal interest groups are being impacted by international events and have a specific stake in foreign policy, so, too, has the governmental "foreign policy establishment" expanded in most states to include not only defense and foreign ministries but also agriculture, environmental, energy, and other executive branch agencies as well as counterpart legislative committees that had relatively little or no connection to foreign policy in earlier eras. These officials now turn up at diplomatic conferences in greater numbers than defense and foreign affairs officials; for example, in recent years, well over half the American delegates accredited to international meetings have come from outside the U.S. State Department.[36] Perhaps at the beginning of the Westphalian state system, a head of state could proclaim *"l'etat c'est moi"* ("I am the state"), as King Louis XIV of France did in the seventeenth century, but those days have long since passed, thanks not only to democratization but other developments.

One could argue that the "billiard ball" model has always been a simplistic depiction of nation-state behavior, insofar as foreign policy, even on national security matters, has always been subject to domestic political forces to some extent; but especially in an age of "complex interdependence," a "cobweb" model[37] would seem more appropriate. As Robert Keohane and Joseph Nye observe:

> *Multiple channels* connect societies, including: informal ties between governmental elites as well as formal foreign office arrangements; informal ties among nongovernmental elites . . . ; and transnational organizations (such as multi-national corporations). These channels can be summarized as interstate, transgovernmental, and trans-national relations. *Interstate*

relations are the normal channels assumed by realists. *Transgovernmental* applies when we relax the realist assumption that states act coherently as units;
transnational applies when we relax the assumption that states are the only
units. . . . The agenda of interstate relationships consists of multiple
issues that are not arranged in a clear . . . hierarchy. *The absence of hierarchy*
among issues means . . . that military security does not consistently dominate the agenda. Many issues arise from what used to be considered domestic policy, and the distinction between domestic and foreign issues
becomes blurred. . . . Different issues generate different coalitions, both
within governments and across them and involve different degrees of conflict. Politics does not stop at the water's edge.[38]

It was already apparent by the 1970s, as the cold war wore on, that we were witnessing "the move from a world dominated by a single chessboard—the strategic-
diplomatic one (which eclipsed or controlled all others)—to a world dispersed
into a variety of chessboards."[39] Staying with the game analogy, Robert Putnam has
argued that when national leaders meet, "the politics of many international negotiations can usefully be conceived as a *two-level game* [one pitched at an international audience and the other at a domestic audience]." He says, "Each national
political leader appears at both game boards. Across the international table sits his
foreign counterparts, and at his elbows sit diplomats and other international advisors. Around the domestic table behind him sit party and parliamentary figures,
spokespersons for domestic agencies, representatives of key interest groups, and
the leader's own political advisors [italics mine]."[40] Putnam quotes Robert Strauss,
the chief U.S. official at trade negotiations in the 1970s, as saying that "during my
tenure as Special Trade Representative, I spent as much time negotiating with my
domestic constituents [both industry and labor] and members of the U.S. Congress as I did negotiating with our foreign trading partners."[41]

Anne-Marie Slaughter speaks of "the disaggregated state," whose component
units are becoming more enmeshed in "transgovernmental networks" across national boundaries. She emphasizes that it is not only "terrorists, arms dealers,
money launderers [and] drug dealers . . . [who] all operate through global networks," but "so, increasingly, do governments. Networks of government officials—police investigators, financial regulators, even judges and legislators—
increasingly exchange information and coordinate activity to combat global crime
and address common problems on a global scale."[42] These transgovernmental relations may or may not be highly formalized. If one adds the representatives of
IGOs, NGOs, and other players that now frequently participate in diplomatic conferences, such as at the 1992 Earth Summit in Rio, then international gatherings
can be said to resemble *three-level games.*[43]

Idealist Assumption 3

The third assumption of the liberal paradigm is that "cooperation under anarchy,"[44]
while difficult, occurs more often than realists recognize, precisely because states

have *mutual interests* in finding ways to overcome distrust and *collective action* problems in those situations where all sides stand to gain. The Prisoner's Dilemma game is often used as an analytic tool to show how perfectly rational players can end up with an outcome neither side desires, because of lack of information and mutual suspicion. In this game, two prisoners are interrogated in separate rooms by the police, and each is told that he will receive the maximum sentence if he remains silent while the other confesses. However, he will go free if he confesses and implicates his partner in crime while the partner remains silent. If both parties confess, they will each receive intermediate sentences; if both remain silent, they will receive the minimum sentence. Although each could get off fairly easily by cooperating through joint silence, their problem is that neither can trust the other to keep quiet, and therefore there is a strong tendency for both to

Courtesy of Joshua Korenblat

The cobweb paradigm.

confess (to "defect"), thereby causing both to "lose." Realists note that many situations in international relations resemble a Prisoner's Dilemma game. Liberals agree, but are not as pessimistic about engineering ways around the problem.

So-called neoliberal institutionalists[45] point out that, even if one accepts the realists' state-centric view of the world, international regimes can help states realize their self-interests in reaching agreements since regimes generally reduce uncertainty, improve information, and contain built-in safeguards that help states monitor and, hence, dissuade "cheating" (defecting) on legal obligations. Moreover, if states expect that they will continually have to interact with other states in ongoing bargaining over issues—that is, if instead of a "game" being a one-shot affair, such as the Prisoner's Dilemma game, there is "a shadow of the future"[46] that states must worry about, as is the case with membership in international organizations—then they will be more likely to honor their commitments since constant noncompliance will make states untrustworthy and undermine their diplomacy.

Keeping in mind Keohane and Nye's statement that "different issues involve different degrees of conflict," it is useful here to note the distinction between *high politics* issues (having to do with vital, core interests) and *low politics* issues (having to do with not-so-vital, non-core interests). We have seen that the problems that give rise to IGOs can be of the high-politics or low-politics variety, with multipurpose organizations generally dealing with the former and functionally specific organizations dealing with the latter, which by definition tend to involve relatively narrow, technical, noncontroversial, routinized matters (although even setting international mail rates or sharing weather forecasting data can become considerably politicized). Clearly, developing new rules as part of a new arms control regime figures to be a more conflictual undertaking than developing a new postal regime.

There remains the question of just how much sovereignty, if any, nation-states are willing to surrender for a larger cause. Most liberals (other than the World Federalists and a few other idealists) stress for the foreseeable future not an end to sovereignty but instead a *pooling of sovereignty*. If one looks at the typical IGO, one will find a plenary assembly or conference in which all member governments discuss and vote on policies, as well as a smaller council that serves as a steering body, along with a secretariat or bureau that is responsible for implementing decisions and running the organization's administrative apparatus. However, IGOs differ considerably in the amount of decision-making power that states vest in the organization. A few IGOs approach a "supranational" model, where the organization is empowered to make decisions that are binding on the entire membership, requiring all member states to abide by the collective will no matter whether they are on the winning or losing side of a roll-call vote. Far more IGOs, though, are at the opposite extreme, empowered by member states merely to offer recommendations or resolutions of an advisory nature that each individual national government is free to accept or reject as it sees fit. Other IGOs fall somewhere in-between, respecting the sovereignty of individual members in most organizational matters but evidencing a degree of supranationalism in certain areas.

States generally have been more willing to cooperate robustly and entrust decision-making competence in organizations having narrow, well-defined goals (functionally specific IGOs) rather than in organizations having broader, more open-ended missions (multipurpose IGOs). A number of UN specialized agencies do approximate the supranational model in some respects. In the case of the Universal Postal Union and some other organizations, governments have even allowed officials in IGO bureaucracies ("technocrats") to exercise substantial discretion in making and implementing policies on behalf of the entire membership. The "higher" the politics, the less supranationalism that is likely and the more likely states will want to retain sovereignty, with the most powerful states in particular seeking to impose their will on the organization, although IGO secretaries-general and other IGO officials have been known at times to play an important independent role in situations involving war and peace and other volatile concerns.

One subset of liberal thinkers, the so-called functionalist school, hypothesizes that as states collaborate and surrender some measure of sovereignty to IGOs in low politics issue-areas, their governments will learn *habits* of cooperation that will slowly over time induce further collaboration and surrender of sovereignty in high politics issue-areas, all leading ultimately to a possible supranational community (a regional or world government).[47] Some functionalists emphasize that certain sectors of intergovernmental cooperation are more likely candidates for "spillover" than others because they create not only a desire but a need for ever more ambitious cooperation across issue-areas. (An example might be a group of countries discovering that the benefits they have derived from sharing a common fishing ground cannot be sustained without additional collaboration in environmental policy making pertaining to ocean pollution.) The European Union, the regional economic integration project that now includes twenty-five countries sharing a common currency (the Euro), is often cited as the best real-world example of an experiment that seems to have followed the logic of functionalist theory.

Where realists would counter that politics can never be completely divorced from even the most seemingly apolitical, technical set of issues and—more importantly—that there are obvious limits to the extent to which national governments can be expected to relinquish power to a higher authority in areas that bear on their very survival, liberals would simply reply that whether supranationalism materializes or not, international institutions *do matter,* that "to analyze world politics . . . [today] is to discuss . . . the rules that govern elements of world politics and the organizations that help implement those rules."[48]

Bridging the Realist-Idealist Divide

One of the major dramas being played out in the twenty-first century is the tension between the forces of *integration* (globalism) and *disintegration* (localism). Harold Jacobson has noted that "the tapestries hung in the *Palais des Nations* in Geneva [the former headquarters of the ill-fated League of Nations that preceded the United Nations] . . . picture the process of humanity combining into ever larger and more stable units for the purpose of governance—first the family, then the tribe, then the city-state, and then the nation—a process which presumably would eventually culminate in the entire world being combined in one political unit."[49] Alexander Wendt suggests "a world state is inevitable," noting that "in the year 1000 B.C. there were 600,000 independent political communities on the Earth . . . and today there are less than 200."[50] However, this depiction of the human story as one involving the steady, unilinear progression from small political units to bigger ones, with the timeline ultimately projecting out toward world government, is an inaccurate rendering of history. The tale is considerably more complicated. The history of humanity can more accurately be read as the search for the optimal political unit, with the pendulum swinging between two extremes: almost a single universal political order (such as the world empires of Alexander the Great and Rome) and a set of much tinier, highly fragmented polities (such as the series of walled cities and other entities that typified the Middle Ages in Europe).[51] We already noted that the nation-state created by the Peace of Westphalia was a halfway house between the universalistic tendencies of the Holy Roman Empire and papacy on the one hand and the localistic tendencies of the feudal fiefdoms on the other.

Hence, the competition between the forces of integration and disintegration today is nothing new, as centripetal and centrifugal forces have alternated with each other throughout history, although they seem to be occurring all at once today. It remains to be seen what the implications of the contemporary drama are for the nation-state as the primary form of human political organization. Alongside the explosive growth of IGOs, NGOs, and MNCs, the integration of the European Union, and other aggregation phenomena—what Benjamin Barber has called "McWorld"—are more parochial countertrends in the form of growing subnational ethnic conflict and the breakup of states such as the Soviet Union and Yugoslavia as well as demands for greater local autonomy in Wales, Quebec, and elsewhere—what he calls "Jihad."[52] Both these integrative and disintegrative forces pose challenges to the viability of the nation-state and the nation-state system, as "state authority has leaked away, upwards, sideways, and downwards."[53] Indeed, some observers speak of "the new feudalism" or call for a new "post-international politics" paradigm.[54]

Former UN Secretary General Boutros Boutros-Ghali captured the schizophrenic character of the contemporary international system when he wrote at the start of the post–cold war era:

> We have entered a time of global transition marked by uniquely contradictory trends. Regional and continental associations of states are evolving ways to deepen cooperation and ease some of the contentious characteristics of sovereign and nationalistic rivalries. . . . At the same time, however, fierce new assertions of nationalism and sovereignty spring up, and the cohesion of states is threatened by ethnic, religious, social, cultural, or linguistic strife.[55]

Boutros-Ghali reminds that, at least for the present, "the foundation-stone [of the international system] is and must remain the State."[56] Likewise, Yale historian Paul Kennedy: "The nation-state remains the primary locus of identity of most people; regardless of who their employer is and what they do for a living, individuals pay taxes to the state, are subject to its laws, serve (if need be) in its armed forces, and can travel only by having its passport."[57] He adds, "if there is to be coordinated action by the peoples of the world . . . to halt the destruction of the tropical rainforests or reduce methane emissions [or address other problems], then *international* agreements, negotiated by the participating governments, are clearly required."[58]

We come back to international law. As I indicated at the outset, humanity is at a crossroads, with the potential for either unprecedented global conflict and disaster or unparalleled global cooperation and well-being. In place of the "double-edged sword" imagery I used earlier, we might think of international relations as a two-sided coin. As realists point out, one side is *the struggle for power;* as idealists point out, the other side is *the search for order.*[59] This provides an opening not for world government but for improved *global governance,* meaning "the cooperative problem-solving arrangements . . . that states and other actors have put into place to deal with various issues and problems"[60]—in other words, the development of international regimes. Another way to think about international regimes is to equate them with "global public policy," what one writer has defined as "joint responses to common problems that . . . national governments work out with one another [which are] products of the international community as a whole."[61]

About the search for world order through the development of international regimes, specifically global bodies such as the United Nations, Inis Claude has written: "The international organization movement . . . can be interpreted as an attempt to perpetuate the multistate system by making its continued operation tolerable; it is not so much a scheme for creating world government as for making world government unnecessary."[62] To use Barry Buzan's felicitous phrase, the aim is a "more mature anarchy."[63] This pivotal moment in history occurs precisely when "central guidance" mechanisms for "pooling sovereignty" are less feasible in some respects than previously due to recent changes in the international system. It could be argued that, if comprehensive, global approaches to world order such as the League of Nations and the United Nations have failed or worked only marginally in the past, they are even less likely to succeed today, given the proliferation of states as well as nonstate actors clamoring to be at the global bargaining table (the original UN membership was only 51 states, compared to almost 200 today) and the equally unwieldy proliferation of items on the agenda (ranging from CO_2 emission reductions to intellectual property rights enforcement) that tax the financial and technical capacities of even the most well-heeled and well-intentioned states and greatly complicate reaching and implementing international agreements of wide scope.

Granted the obstacles to global institution-building are substantial. However, we have to be careful not to underestimate the possibilities. For example, we sometimes forget how close the world has come, with the UN Law of the Sea Treaty (discussed in chapter 7), to producing a single set of rules governing virtually every human activity on 70 percent of the Earth's surface. The upshot of all this is, to reiterate, we should try to avoid the twin traps of "bad idealism" (wishful thinking) and "bad realism" (resignation to failure).[64]

The Constructivist Paradigm and Other Schools of Thought

There is a need to mention at least briefly a few other paradigms that some have found superior to the realist or idealist paradigms as frameworks for understanding world politics. Both the realist and liberal paradigms, for all their differences, share essentially an interest-based explanation of international relations, that is, a "rationalist" perspective that treats actors as calculating, utility-maximizing agents (whether driven by national interests or mutual interests) coping with various *material forces* or *structures* that limit choice. In contrast, *constructivism* is a fairly new paradigm that takes a "reflectivist" perspective, stressing the power of *ideas* and putting emphasis on the *agents* more than the structures.[65] Constructivists study the emergence of new normative beliefs and new knowledge that become widely accepted and that can cause a redefinition of interests and changed behavior.

Constructivists go so far as to argue that there is no objective social reality whatsoever, so that, for example, they consider sovereignty simply a social construct rather than a given; it was a concept that began to be internalized by the seventeenth century and can be unlearned just as readily as it was learned.[66] The so-called English School, represented by scholars such as Hedley Bull and Martin Wight, "holds that the system of states is embedded in a society of states, which includes sets of values, rules, and institutions that are commonly accepted by states and which make it possible for the system of states to function."[67] The recently articulated norm of "humanitarian intervention," promoted by UN Secretary General Kofi Annan and others who argue that the international community has a right to intervene in the internal affairs of countries where genocide and gross human rights abuses are occurring, now threatens to play havoc with the norm of sovereignty. Constructivist theorists such as Martha Finnemore argue that "realist and liberal theories do not provide good explanations for this behavior," referring to interventions in Somalia and elsewhere since 1990.[68]

Likewise, other long-held ideas can give way to new ideas, based not merely on changed historical forces but on new thinking that renders the old ideas "bad." Slavery and colonialism, considered for centuries to be human institutions that would prevail forever, were eventually ended by the mid-twentieth century; although their passing might be tied partly to the fact that they were no longer as profitable as in earlier days, constructivists would attribute it more to normative progress.[69] "Free trade" is now widely accepted as the basis for international economic relations not merely because of changed constellations of interests but because it is considered a "good" idea, grounded in the collective memories of how protectionism contributed to the Great Depression and World War II.[70] Inis Claude has noted the power of the "idea" of international organization, something that did not fully become "taken for granted" until the twentieth century[71]; and Finnemore notes that "states are socialized to accept new norms, values, and perceptions of interest by international organizations."[72] Constructivists also point to the role of "epistemic communities"—climatologists and other scientific networks—in disseminating new knowledge that leads to a rethinking of environmental and other concerns.[73]

As applied to international law, constructivist theory focuses our attention not so much on the specific rules of international law as the rules that underlie the rules (sometimes called "meta-rules")—"a set of underlying implicit rules which create a framework that allows formal agreements between states to be meaningful and binding"[74] (for instance, the simple understanding that treaties should not be broken). Although constructivism suffers from a high level of abstraction and a paucity of empirical testing, it is considered a useful way to think about international politics in general and international law in particular.[75]

There are other schools of thought as well. One is *feminist theory*, which sees gender-based identities and beliefs as an overlooked set of variables that have affected world politics, for example the relationship between male-dominated, patriarchic societies and war-proneness.[76] Another is *marxist theory*, which focuses attention on the development and workings of the world-capitalist system, how it came into being, and how it might be changed; marxists and neo-marxists see not only multinational corporations but also international law and organization as products of the capitalist elites who control dominant states, and hence they are not as state-centric in orientation as realists and not as sanguine as liberals about the benefits of international institutions.[77] Although the marxist tradition has been somewhat discredited by the demise of communism in the Soviet Union and Eastern Europe, it still influences views of international politics, particularly international economic relations, in many parts of the less developed world. There are still other bodies of theory one could cite, such as postmodernism and various off-shoots of constructivism and marxism, but space does not permit discussion here.

All of these paradigms have something to offer in terms of enhancing our understanding of the relationship between international politics and international law. Because the realist and liberal schools dominate most scholarly discourse, it is that debate I have given the most attention to here, and it is those two viewpoints I have attempted to reconcile. In our investigation of whether "a more mature anarchy" in international relations is possible, we now are ready to concentrate more fully on the nature of international law and exactly how it operates.

3

Is International Law Really Law, or a Charade?

ON NOVEMBER 17, 1989, immediately following the fall of the Berlin Wall, the UN General Assembly declared the 1990s the "UN Decade of International Law," urging that the decade "should promote acceptance of and respect for the principles of international law; promote means and methods for the peaceful settlement of disputes between States, including resort to and full respect of the International Court of Justice; [and] encourage the progressive development and codification of international law."[1] The beginning of the new millennium has come and gone, and there has been questionable progress made toward the above goal.

In assessing the magnitude of this challenge, it is worth going back in time to a moment just ten years prior to the 1989 UN declaration. On November 4, 1979, sixty-six Americans in the U.S. Embassy in Tehran were seized by an angry mob of Iranian militants protesting Washington's grant of asylum to the recently deposed Shah. After a few escaped or were released, fifty-two remained imprisoned. The intent was to use the hostages to force the extradition of the Shah back to Iran to stand trial, an endeavor that had the blessing of the new regime in Iran headed by Ayatollah Khomeini. It was not until January 20, 1981, after 444 days in captivity, that the American diplomatic personnel were finally released by the Iranian government, coinciding that same day with the inauguration of President Ronald Reagan, who had warned of possible military action by his administration. Though a somewhat distant memory now, this event preoccupied the nation for over a year and raised interesting questions about the role of international law in international affairs.

To many, the Iranian hostage crisis seemed a vivid illustration of the lawless character of international relations. However, rather than reflecting the nonexistence or impotence of international law, the episode in some respects illustrated its general reliability. In particular, what made the incident such a *cause célèbre* was precisely the fact that it involved a virtually unprecedented violation of one of the most sacred rules of international conduct, namely, the immunity of diplomats from host government seizure and punishment. The actions of the Iranian government represented such a departure from the routinely honored canons of state practice that observers at the time feverishly searched through history books to determine the last time such a violation had occurred. (There was a certain irony in-

UN DPI/Photo

The photo shows the International Court of Justice at The Hague, on March 18–20, 1980, hearing arguments in the *United States v. Iran* case involving the seizure of U.S. diplomatic and consular staff in Teheran.

volved, too, because it was in Persia—in the land now called Iran—that the principle of "diplomatic immunity" first evolved a thousand years ago.) Although the timing of the release of the hostages perhaps reflected Iran's fear of U.S. military action, it may also have reflected Iran's concern about its growing isolation as a pariah nation, given the fact that when the United States brought suit against Iran before the International Court of Justice in 1979 (*The United States Diplomatic and Consular Staff in Iran*), Iran's blatantly illegal behavior resulted in the World Court issuing a rare unanimous judgment (15–0) in favor of the United States that included support even from the Soviet judge.[2] Iran chose to ignore the Court's verdict, but faced mounting international pressure to end the standoff, so that it might have eventually relented even if "Rambo" Reagan had not won election.

Still, long after the hostages were returned, questions remained as to what kind of legal system depended for its success upon the threat of retaliation by one party to a dispute, or would allow a court order to be ignored and a major violation of law to go unpunished. One might add, in regard to one of the news headlines cited in chapter 1, that the Israeli government likewise ignored the near-unanimous

World Court opinion in 2004 (*Legal Consequences of the Construction of a Wall in the Occupied Palestinian Territory*) calling for the dismantling of its security fence next to Palestinian territory.[3]

The believer in international law might ask a number of questions: Why, if international law is a farce, would the U.S. State Department's Office of the Legal Advisor maintain a staff of 130 international lawyers, and why would multinational corporations employ hundreds more?[4] Why would a Canadian secretary of state remark that "in my office and in my department, we are, first of all, students of international law"?[5] The skeptic might respond that much of international law is a charade in which states pick and choose to obey those rules that happen to coincide with their interests at a given moment; even if international law is grudgingly acknowledged to exist, it is considered to be feeble in those situations "that really count" and helpless altogether in the face of power politics.[6] Cynics could note, for example, that the United States, which was so quick to invoke international law in the Iranian hostage case, chose to flout it in 1986, when the Reagan administration refused to acknowledge that its mining of Nicaraguan harbors violated the rule against aggression despite widespread condemnation by international legal experts and a World Court ruling against the United States (*Case Concerning Military and Paramilitary Activities In and Against Nicaragua*).[7]

Hence, we are still left with the nagging question relating not only to whether the World Court is *really* a court but the much larger issue of whether international law is *really* law. In this chapter we examine the case for and against international law as a true legal system.

Is International Law Really Law?

To answer this question, we need first to define what *law* is. Law can be defined as a set of rules or expectations that govern the relations between the members of a society, that have an obligational basis, and whose violation is punishable through the application of sanctions by society.[8] It is the obligational character of law that distinguishes it from morality, religion, social mores, or mere protocol. The definition implies that at least three fundamental conditions must be present if law can be said to exist in a society: (1) a process for developing an identifiable, legally binding set of rules that prescribe certain patterns of behavior among societal members (a law-making process); (2) a process for punishing illegal behavior when it occurs (a law-enforcement process); and (3) a process for determining whether a particular rule has been violated in a particular instance (a law-adjudication process). These are the three conditions normally associated with domestic law within national societies. Certainly, such conditions exist in the United States or Japan or any other nation-state. Although some national legal systems might be much more effective than others—for example, in achieving compliance with the law—all have the basic elements noted above, as manifested by legislatures, law enforcement agencies, and courts. Even so-called failed states have these basic structures in place, at least on paper.

What about *international* law, traditionally defined as the body of rules which are binding upon states in their relations with one another? How does it compare with law in *national* political systems (commonly called *municipal* law)? The most obvious difference is that the central governmental institutions that are associated with law within nation-states simply do not exist in relations between nation-states. There is no world government, no supreme law-giver, no police squads patrolling international affairs and directing traffic, and no court (at least not one that has all of the normal attributes of a court). The standard, dictionary definition of law—"the principles and regulations established by a government and applicable to a people, whether in the form of legislation or of custom and policies recognized and enforced by judicial decision"[9]—does not apply to the international plane. To elaborate, international law does not meet what some consider the "Five Cs" test of law: Congress, Code, Court, Cop, and Clink:

> First, the rule must be produced by a centralized legislative body—a "Congress," or parliament, or whatever. Second, this legislative body must produce a written "Code." Anyone should be able to pull out a statute book and read precisely what the rule says. Third, there must be a "Court"—a judicial body with complete compulsory jurisdiction to resolve disputes about the rules or to determine culpability for violation of the rules. Fourth, there must be a "Cop," some centralized means of enforcing violations of the rule. Finally, there has to be a "Clink." There must be some kind of sanctions that will be imposed on those who choose to violate the rule.[10]

However, if one is willing to overlook the lack of strong central authoritative institutions in the international system—in other words, to abandon the stereotype of law as "a centralized constraint system backed by threat of coercive sanctions"[11] and to adopt instead the more relaxed definition of law I offered at the outset—then it would leave open the possibility of accepting international law as law. After all, one can find historically the functional equivalent of a legal system in any number of tribal and other societies lacking the standard institutional trappings correlated with law. One must still be prepared to demonstrate how law can operate in a decentralized political system such as the international system. One can rightly ask, "If international law is really law, who enacts, construes, and enforces it?"[12]

The Making of International Law:
Where Does the Law Come From?

In our earlier discussion of international regimes and global governance, it was suggested that one could think in terms of a global public policy process that provides grist for the development of international law. Those who study public policy in a national context, which is the usual context in which the term is used, commonly point to several sequential stages that comprise the policy process: (1) *agenda-setting* (identifying problems or issues and getting them at least on the radar screen of the political system, so that some collective action is possible); (2) *policy formulation* (consideration of a menu of various possible proposals for new rules or other responses that might address the problem or issue); (3) *policy adoption* (selection of a particular course of action); and (4) *policy implementation* (putting the chosen decision into effect). The public policy process in national political systems usually, although not always, revolves around some sort of legislative action.

As applied to the international political system, the policy process begins—agenda-setting occurs—when one actor or set of actors seeks to have a particular "demand" (concern) acted upon by the international community, whether it is a call for a coordinated response to the AIDS epidemic or the proliferation of landmines or nuclear weapons or some other matter. Again, some problems will be viewed as calling for more narrow, bilateral, or regional responses, but other problems will elicit multilateral, global ones. Few issues in any society, particularly one as diverse as the international society, are so noncontroversial that they can be labeled purely technical or nonpolitical, although, as previously noted, one can distinguish between low-politics and high-politics issues.

Nation-states have the primary access to the global political process, but demands for global policies can originate from a variety of sources, not only individual national governments but blocs of states, subnational and transnational interest groups, and officials of intergovernmental or nongovernmental organizations. As we will discuss later, many of these actors are increasingly being accorded a degree of "international legal personality" alongside states, meaning that they are being formally accommodated into the policy process and are treated as subjects of international law. The chief structures that receive and process global policy demands are the various United Nations organs and specialized agencies; as Marvin Soroos remarks, "these international bodies are the primary arenas in which global policies are made."[13] Some observers feel that the proliferation of international bodies at the global and regional levels in recent years has added enormously to an already dense web of IGOs that may be getting out of control, with the escalation of demands exceeding the capacity of many states and the system as a whole to function. As Harold Jacobson comments, "If the U.S. finds it [difficult] . . . to formulate constructive policies for the organizations to which it belongs, . . . what must the situation be like for countries that belong to proportionately more IGOs and have much smaller bureaucracies [and resources]?"[14]

Even where there may be widespread agreement about the existence of a problem and its rightful place on the global agenda, reaching agreement on a suitable solution can often be difficult. A number of mechanisms exist for facilitating the formulation and adoption of global policy. The UN General Assembly itself is a sounding board for articulating concerns and trying to mobilize the international community to act, although it functions not as a legislature but rather a forum for "parliamentary diplomacy," where debate and roll-call votes result mostly in "resolutions" that are merely expressions of world public opinion rather than mandatory rules; since, under the UN Charter, the General Assembly is the United

Nations' plenary body in which each state is treated equally and has one vote, and in which decisions are generally taken based on majority rule, there is reluctance on the part of the members, especially the more powerful ones, to permit the institution to operate in a "supranational" fashion whereby its decisions would have the status of "laws" binding on everyone.[15]

In chapter 2, I noted that some of the specialized agencies of the United Nations approach a supranational decision-making model that arguably is at least quasi-legislative in nature the closer to the "low-politics" end of the spectrum one moves. There are currently seventeen specialized agencies formally affiliated with the UN General Assembly and another UN organ, the Economic and Social Council, although each is essentially an autonomous IGO with its own charter, budget, membership, headquarters, and secretariat. These include the World Bank, the International Monetary Fund (IMF), the Food and Agriculture Organization (FAO), the World Health Organization (WHO), the International Civil Aviation Organization (ICAO), the Universal Postal Union (UPU), and the International Telecommunication Union (ITU), among others.

As just one example of the supranational character of some of these functional agencies, "the World Health Organization, acting through its Health Assembly, has express authority—acting by simple majority—to adopt regulations binding on all members except those that notify the director-general of rejection or reservations within a designated time. . . . [The International Health Regulations] are of major importance. The Health Regulations try to preclude the international spread of such diseases as cholera, the plague, and yellow fever."[16] (WHO recently was given authority to issue global alerts for international health threats such as the SARS virus and to send inspection teams to countries experiencing epidemics to insure that proper containment measures are being taken.)[17] As for the UPU, "changes in the rules and regulations governing letter post are effected by a simple majority of the membership, . . . and compliance with the rules is obligatory from the time of their entry into force, with loss of membership privileges as the sanction [for violations]."[18] Every five years, the "plenipotentiaries" representing each of the UPU's 190 member countries meet to review postal rules; the 23rd UPU Congress was held in Bucharest, Romania, in 2004, and considered a number of issues, including the adoption of a revised system for compensating countries for the reciprocal processing of international mail as well as the adoption of a "World Postal Strategy" for making global postal service more efficient. Sovereign states cannot be forced to join WHO or UPU or other IGOs, but, once they do, they often find their sovereignty somewhat compromised.

These and other UN bodies have sponsored numerous conferences over the past several decades on myriad agenda items ranging from deep seabed mining to the environment, from population to women's rights, from regulation of the Internet to placement of satellites in outer space, and countless others. The mushrooming growth of international conferences is captured in the following statistics: "Between 1838 and 1860 there were two to three a year, in the decade after 1900 there were about 100 per year, in the decade after 1910 there were about 200 a year, and [by] the 1970s, there were more than 3,000."[19] Many UN-sponsored gatherings since the 1970s have contributed to the formulation and adoption of global policy measures that add to the body of international law. The main outputs produced by some of these conferences, such as the women's rights conferences (held in 1975, 1985 and 1995), have been in the form of general norms and principles (what is sometimes called "soft law"), but other outcomes have included hard-and-fast rules. It is the latter we are most interested in here.

Clearly, the law-making process in the international political system is far more complicated and disjointed than that which is found typically in national political systems. If one were the legal advisor in the foreign ministry of a country involved in an international dispute over maritime boundaries, or a justice on a country's highest court hearing a case involving an international matter of some sort, there is no single body of world statutes that can be consulted to discover what the relevant law is. However, there is an identifiable set of rules accepted by states as legally binding, derived from "sources" of international law specified in Article 38 of the International Court of Justice (ICJ) Statute that is attached to the United Nations Charter. The officially recognized sources of international law include: (1) custom; (2) treaties; (3) general principles of law recognized by "civilized" nations (that are found in most legal systems of the world); (4) judicial decisions rendered by national and international tribunals; and (5) the writings of legal scholars. Since the latter two are viewed as secondary, "subsidiary" sources, and the third source is normally considered only when there is no relevant customary or treaty law to be found, we will limit the discussion here to custom and treaties.

Customary Law

Customary rules of international law are those practices that have been widely accepted as binding by states over time as evidenced by repeated usage. In the early life of the international system, custom was an especially important source of international law. Hugo Grotius, the seventeenth-century Dutch scholar, noted even in his day the development of certain common practices whose routine observance by governments led to their acceptance as required behavior in relations between states. One such custom, already referred to, was the practice of diplomatic immunity granted by a host government to a foreign government's ambassadors.[20] Another was the designation of a three-mile limit within which coastal states were assumed to exercise sovereignty over "territorial waters" adjacent to their land, beyond which there was to be "freedom of the sea"; the three-mile limit was based on the effective range of cannon fired from shoreline fortifications. Numerous other rules developed.

Rarely were any of these rules specifically written down, but they were nonetheless understood to constitute rules of prescribed conduct. Given the decentralized nature of the international system, a customary rule technically became binding only on those states that, through their compliance over time, indicated their willingness to be bound by the rule in question, so that a "persistent objector" generally was exempted from any such legal obligation. For example, Sweden long insisted on maintaining a four-mile territorial sea, whereas practically all other states observed the three-mile limit. That did not mean a state could make any legal claim to ocean space it wanted—early claims by Spain to the Pacific Ocean and Portugal to the Atlantic Ocean were not recognized by other states—only that it was not automatically bound by the behavior of a majority of states.

Today many customary rules continue to form part of the body of international law and the "persistent objector" concept still applies, although there is some controversy over whether the consensual basis of customary law applies to newly independent states, with some commentators arguing that acceptance of existing customary rules is the price of admission new states pay to join the international community and others arguing that sovereign states cannot be forced to abide by rules they had no hand in creating. There is also disagreement over what percentage of states in the international system must support a customary practice before it can be said to constitute a rule of international law, although it is assumed that the practice must be "nearly universal."[21]

Not surprisingly, those countries that have a special stake and play a pivotal role in a given issue-area will tend to exercise special influence over the development of customary law in that area, so that "for example, the practice of major maritime powers will have more significance in the formation of rules on the law of the sea than [say] that of landlocked Austria."[22] In some instances, "it may be that the persistent objector is such an important operator in a particular field that its continued objection prevents customary law developing for all states. . . . However, while in theory a persistent objector can opt out of evolving customary law, in practice there is very little evidence to suggest that the persistent objector can remain outside the scope of a new customary law for very long. The pressure to conform to the new standard, as well as the disadvantages of being outside the legal orthodoxy, ensure that the objecting state does not maintain a position contrary to the overwhelming practice of other states."[23] Once a state has demonstrated its acceptance of a customary rule by repeated observance, it is expected to continue to be bound by it; customary law is not something that can be arbitrarily adopted and rejected from one moment to the next.

An example commonly cited to illustrate the workings of customary law is the state practice that developed in immediate response to the first artificial satellite that was put into orbit around the earth on October 4, 1957—the Sputnik spacecraft launched by the Soviet Union—and the subsequent satellites launched shortly thereafter by the United States. The fact that no state for many years protested this as a violation of its air space, and hence there was general acquiescence to the claim by the US and the USSR that they had the right to place satellites over the territory of other states, effectively created customary law on this subject. Wherever one looked for "evidence"[24] of state practice, whether in the form of what countries *said* in their official governmental pronouncements or what they *did* in their actual behavior, the circling of objects overhead, as long as they were in outer space and not flying through national air space, was permitted (even if the exact boundary between outer space and national air space remained some-what uncertain).

An important point to add is that, in order for customary practice to be con-sidered customary law, it is not sufficient that the practice is widely conformed to. Customary rules of law are to be distinguished from rules of etiquette, known as *comity*. In the case of customary law, an established pattern of conduct (for ex-ample, diplomatic immunity) is based on a sense of legal obligation (*opinio iuris*) and invites legal penalties if breached, whereas in the case of comity, it is merely a matter of courtesy (for example, two ships saluting each other's flag while passing at sea). Admittedly, when states engage in certain standard practices toward each other, it is not always clear whether they do so out of a sense of legal obligation or simply out of politeness. Moreover, given the unwritten nature of customary law, there is great potential for ambiguity and misinterpretation of the rules. For these reasons, there has been a distinct trend in recent years to *codify* customary law, that is, to embody customary rules in more precise, written documents to which states can explicitly give or withhold consent.

Treaties

Written agreements between societies can be found from the beginnings of human history—"archeologists have discovered a treaty between the city-states of Umma and Lagosh written in the Sumerian language on a stone monument and concluded about 3100 B.C."[25]—and have grown in importance as the modern nation-state system has evolved. *Treaties* are formal written agreements between states, which create legal obligations for the governments that are parties to them. Treaties are binding only on those states that consent to be bound by them. A state normally in-dicates its consent by a two-step process in which its authorized representative *signs* the treaty and its legislature or other constitutionally empowered body *ratifies* the agreement.[26] For example, President Carter in 1977 signed a landmark human rights treaty, the International Covenant on Civil and Political Rights, but failed to win ratification by the U.S. Senate; the treaty was not approved by the Senate until 1992, when it finally became binding on the United States. The Convention on Bi-ological Diversity, referred to earlier (also known as the Biodiversity Treaty), was signed by President Clinton in 1993, but has yet to be approved by the U.S. Senate and, hence, is not yet technically binding on the United States.

Those international instruments called "conventions," "protocols," or "covenants" are essentially the same as treaties, at least in their binding quality. (Note that a "convention" here refers not to a conference but to a paper docu-ment.) Once a state becomes a party to such an agreement, it is expected that its government will honor the fundamental principle associated with treaties—*pacta sunt servanda,* which means that treaties are to be obeyed. Many treaties are simply bilateral agreements between two states seeking, for example, to establish trade relations or an alliance, or regarding the use of each other's air space or the extra-dition of criminals from each other's territory. Other treaties are multilateral—between three or more states—and can involve such subjects as international commerce, patent and copyright regulations, regulation of mail and other communications, use of the oceans for fishing and exploration, treatment of prisoners of war, and development or deployment of various kinds of weapons. In the case of multilateral treaties, there is usually an activating or "triggering" provision in the agreement that stipulates the minimal number of ratifications that must be obtained before the treaty takes legal effect (is "in force"). For example, the Biodiversity Treaty that was drafted at the 1992 Earth Summit in Rio was to become law upon ratification by thirty countries, which occurred when Mongolia in December of 1993 became the thirtieth state to deposit its ratification with the United Nations. (To date, more than 180 states are parties to the treaty.)

Although the past century has witnessed much more multilateralism than previous eras—more than 4,000 new multilateral treaties were concluded between 1945 and 1995, an average of almost ninety per year—an overwhelming majority of treaties in force are bilateral.[27] It is estimated that multilateral treaties are "only 10% of all treaty activity in the world."[28] Multilateral agreements, though, are the ones of greatest relevance to international law, especially those multilateral treaties that deal with issues of broad importance and seek to involve as many members of the international community as possible, such as the UN Charter. The UN Charter and the Universal Postal Union Constitution come as close as any treaties to universality. A creative way in which the international system attempts to encourage maximum, worldwide treaty participation is to permit countries to become parties to a treaty by opting out of certain provisions they find distasteful through the use of "reservations," although not all treaties allow such selective compliance.

I have noted that there have been increased efforts to use treaties to codify traditional, customary rules of international law. For example, the Vienna Convention on Diplomatic Relations of 1961, ratified by almost every country, reiterated the longstanding, "sacred" rule of international law requiring that the immunity and inviolability of embassies and diplomats be respected. Iran, a party to the treaty, was in violation, then, of both customary law and treaty law when it seized the fifty-two Americans in the U.S. embassy in 1979.[29] Among the provisions of the treaty are the following: diplomatic agents and members of their families cannot be arrested and prosecuted by the host government for any crimes committed, even a blatant act of murder or a hit-and-run accident; diplomatic agents are immune not only from host state criminal jurisdiction but also from civil claims, which means that they cannot be punished for damaging someone's property or passing bad checks and cannot be evicted by landlords for failure to pay the rent. In New York City alone, where diplomats abound at UN headquarters, in some years an estimated 140,000 parking tickets worth $15 million have gone unpaid as diplomats continue to triple park, block major thoroughfares, and generally go about their business blissfully free from the restrictions that apply to most motorists.[30] However, what might seem to be a grossly unfair system of rules to the New York City cab driver or the person on the street is necessitated by the desire of national governments to ensure that their diplomats are not harassed in any fashion by the host country to which they are assigned. If a diplomat were to abuse such diplomatic immunity, by becoming a mass murderer or a notorious hotrodder and check bouncer, the remedy would be for the host state to request a waiver of immunity from the diplomat's government or to declare the diplomat *persona non grata* and expel that individual from the country.

Although some treaties simply transcribe customary law into written form, keeping the traditional rules intact, other treaties are designed to revise the customary law. For example, the 1982 UN Convention on the Law of the Sea, a 200-page document negotiated by 150 countries, incorporated some elements of the traditional law of the sea—such as the right of "innocent passage" enjoyed by all ships in the territorial waters of coastal states, the right of "hot pursuit" by coastal state vessels against foreign ships violating the laws of the coastal state, and absolute freedom of navigation for all ships on the "high seas" outside any state's boundaries—but also modified some existing rules, such as extending the width of the territorial seas from three to twelve miles.

In some instances, treaties have been used to develop rules in new areas of concern for which no law has existed or been necessary before. For example, the Outer Space Treaty of 1967, now ratified by some 100 states, requires the signatories to refrain from deploying weapons of mass destruction in outer space and to consider the moon and other celestial bodies beyond any state's sovereign control. As a party to the treaty, had the United States attempted to declare the moon its sovereign territory when it was the first to land there in 1969, the government would have been acting illegally in violation of the 1967 agreement.

It is evident that even in the absence of a world legislature, machinery exists to create written rules that are considered legally binding, with bilateral treaties drafted by the foreign ministries of individual countries and multilateral treaties drafted by the UN International Law Commission or bodies such as the Law of the Sea Conference, the specialized agencies, or other entities. There are literally thousands of treaties in effect around the world, and the number is growing not only as a function of the proliferation of states but, more importantly, as the increased volume and complexity of international interactions lead governments to seek more formalized arrangements in regulating intercourse between states. One estimate is that more than 40,000 international agreements have been concluded since 1900, most of them since 1945.[31] The growth of treaties in modern times is reflected in the fact that in 1892 the official compendium of treaties entered into by the United Kingdom numbered only 190 pages, whereas by 1960 it exceeded 2,500 pages.[32] For the international system as a whole, "treaties concluded between 1648 and 1919 fill 226 thick books, between 1920 and 1946 some 205 more volumes, and between 1946 and 1978, 1,115 more tomes."[33]

There is even a treaty on treaties—the Vienna Convention on the Law of Treaties of 1969 (not in force until 1980)—which codifies the customary rule of *pacta sunt servanda*. Only about one-third of the countries of the world are party to this instrument, but virtually all have acceded to many of its provisions that are merely restatements of customary law. This convention stipulates the circumstances whereby a state unilaterally can legally terminate its involvement in some treaty. A state can back out of a treaty commitment, for example, if the agreement has an "escape hatch" provision (say, a requirement to provide at least six months' advance notification of intent to withdraw). A state can also legally terminate its treaty obligations if it can demonstrate that it had been coerced into signing the treaty originally, that the treaty was founded on fraudulent grounds or signed by an unauthorized national representative, or that the present conditions are so radically different from those existing at the outset of the treaty as to render it impossible for that party to continue honoring the terms of the pact (the last condition is known as *rebus sic stantibus*). Despite the availability of these loopholes, states tend to use them only sparingly.

It is sometimes argued that there are a few rules of international law that states *cannot ever contract out of,* that is, cannot choose to circumvent whether a party to a treaty or not. This is the much debated concept of *jus cogens,* which is based on the "natural law" tradition that views law as deriving from higher principles of justice that have universal validity for all people; according to the naturalists, law is not "made" but "discovered," and, hence, is not consent-based. The Vienna Convention on State Treaties defines *jus cogens* as a "peremptory norm" of international law "from which no derogation is permitted and which can be modified only by a subsequent norm of general international law having the same character." The problem has been to get universal agreement on what, if any, such norms exist in international affairs. The closest the international system has come is the norm against aggression, embodied in Article 2 of the UN Charter, the implication being that two countries which enter into a pact to attack another country would be acting illegally. The concept of *jus cogens* is almost incompatible with the concept of state sovereignty, and therefore remains problematical.

Indeed, perhaps the biggest indictment of international law is its essentially voluntary nature. Individuals in the United States and other municipal legal systems do not have the prerogative of deciding whether to agree to be bound by some rule of law or to qualify acceptance with "reservations," or whether to terminate their acceptance of some rule. The consent basis of law is generally unheard of in such systems, including democracies, although obligation arises not out of "higher principles" but deliberate legislation (called "positive law"); once a rule of law is promulgated, everyone in the society is expected to abide by it regardless of whether everyone approves of it. As Michael Glennon says, "one can hardly decide that one will no longer be bound by the rule prohibiting bank robbery."[34] However, the effectiveness of a legal system, whether municipal or international in character, may consist not so much in how many members of the society have an obligation to obey the law as how many actually *do* obey the law. We next examine the extent to which international law is obeyed and enforced.

The Breaking of International Law: How Is the Law Enforced?

Another common indictment of international law is not the absence or ambiguity of the rules but the lack of enforcement—the complaint that international law is broken regularly with impunity because of the lack of a central policing agent. United Nations peacekeeping forces perhaps most closely approximate an international police body, but they are organized sporadically as temporary responses to various crisis situations and are designed to maintain peace, not necessarily to enforce law. (Like London "bobbies," they rarely are fully armed; unlike the London police, they do not have any badge of authority to assist them.) At least twice in its history, the United Nations helped to organize a military force to punish aggression, in the case of North Korea in 1950 and Iraq in 1991, but those were exceptional and not all would agree they were truly police actions mounted by the global community under the UN flag (as opposed to the U.S. flag).

Sanctions against violators of international law exist, but they are primarily based on the principle of *self-help*; if one state harms another state (for example, seizes its financial assets), it is usually left to the aggrieved state to take action to punish the offender through reprisals or retaliation of some kind (for example, reciprocal seizure of the offender's assets held by the aggrieved state's banks). Although self-help also operates to some extent in municipal legal systems—such as defending oneself against assault or making a citizen's arrest—it tends not to be the norm in those systems.

However, what is most striking about the international legal system is not how often the law is broken but how often it is obeyed, despite the lack of "traffic cops" to provide a central coercive threat of punishment against would-be offenders. To be sure, there are frequent violations of international law, most notably those serious breaches that are reported on the front pages of newspapers, such as the seizure of the U.S. embassy in Iran, the genocidal acts committed in Sudan and elsewhere in recent years, and various acts of violent aggression at odds with the UN Charter. True, international law tends to be weakest in the most "high-politics" situations and strongest in the most "low-politics" situations.[35] But, as Louis Henkin has stated, "international law does far better than its reputation."[36] As noted earlier, people tend to notice the conspicuous failures of international law, while neglecting to notice the ordinary workings of international law in the everyday life of the international system. The fact is, if one takes into account the plethora of treaties and customary rules of international law that exist today, it can be said that, using Professor Henkin's famous words, "almost all nations observe almost all principles of international law and almost all of their obligations almost all of the time."[37] In other words, international law gets "enforced" in its own way.

To understand why this is so, we need to consider the basic reasons why people obey laws in any society. The first is the threat of punishment for illegal behavior (the *coercive* motive), something that realists tend to dwell on. A second is the mutual interests that individuals have in seeing that laws are obeyed (the *utilitarian* motive), something that liberal institutionalists tend to stress. A third is the internalization of the rules by the members of the society, i.e., habits of compliance; people obey the law because that is what they have come to accept as the legitimate, right thing to do (the *identitive* motive), something that constructivist thinkers highlight. All of these elements can operate to produce obedience to the law.

Consider for a moment why most people bother to obey a stop sign at a busy intersection. One reason is the coercive element—the possibility that a police officer might be lurking around the corner and might stop you if you do not stop yourself. Another is the utilitarian motive—the possibility that another car might accidentally collide with your vehicle if you pass through the intersection without stopping. As powerful as these two motives are, the main driving force behind the inclination to stop at a stop sign is probably the simple habitual nature of the act, which has been inculcated as part of the "code of the road." (Even if one were driving through the middle of Death Valley in California, where no police cars or other vehicles were visible for several miles, there would be a tendency to stop if somehow one were to encounter a red stop sign sticking out of the desert sand!)

The point is that law and order can function to some extent even in the absence of police; indeed, any society that relies primarily on coercive threats as the basis for order is one that is terribly fragile. Although habits of compliance—the most solid basis for law—are not well-developed in the international system, the mutual interests of states in having a set of rules that prescribe as well as proscribe patterns of behavior provide a foundation for the international legal order. States are willing to tolerate certain constraints on their own behavior because it is widely recognized that international commerce, travel, and other forms of international activity would be exceedingly difficult otherwise. A state will be reluctant to violate a particular rule in a particular instance in order to achieve an expedient, short-term gain, if the effect is to weaken an area of law that it wishes to preserve in the long-term. Even "rogue states" have to get their mail, and hence have a stake in not undermining the international postal order.

But there are more weighty reasons why all states experience pressure to obey rules. One might ask: If treaties are merely pieces of paper, to be discarded at the whim of the signatories when it no longer suits their needs, then why do so many diplomats haggle over the fine print during the drafting stage, and why do so many states frequently resist intense lobbying from the international community to commit to an agreement? The answer is that states understand quite well the concept of *pacta sunt servanda,* that, with ratification, they incur legal obligations that can be ignored only at the risk of developing a reputation as a "cheater" and suffering the penalty of finding few takers willing to enter into agreements with such an unreliable partner the next time (what liberals call "the shadow of the future"). In addition to this logic of "reciprocity," additional pressures to abide by international law may come from subnational and transnational sources, such as domestic interest groups and NGOs operating in environmental, human rights, and other fields.

Abram Chayes and Antonia Chayes argue that, to the extent countries violate treaties, it is often due more to a lack of adequate technical, financial, and other resources ("state capacity") to carry out their obligations than to willful disobedience.[38]

Recalling the earlier mention of escalating demands and an overloaded global policy system, one should not be surprised that the adoption of global policy in the form of a treaty does not insure its full implementation. Less developed countries, in particular, face many strains in trying to comply with their international obligations, whether it is filing annual reports with the United Nations on efforts to combat terrorism or submitting records to the International Maritime Organization regarding the volume of pollutants dumped overboard from ships that sail under their flag. Witness the fact that, after Tajikistan became a sovereign state in 1993 upon the breakup of the Soviet Union, its resources were so scarce that its UN ambassador had to serve as a one-man diplomatic corps and had to cook his own state dinners.[39] Evidencing similar "lack of capacity," Guinea-Bissau in 1999 could not pay the rent on the Manhattan office housing its minister to the United Nations, causing the landlord to turn off the electricity and other utilities (in lieu of eviction) and reducing the ambassador to working in the dark at night equipped with nothing more than a flashlight and cell phone.[40] It remains to be seen how such states can be expected to participate meaningfully in the global policy-making process, including the formulation, adoption, and implementation of rules of international law.

It is curious that critics argue that international law is virtually nonexistent because it is frequently broken. If one were to apply the same test of effectiveness to municipal law that is generally demanded of international law—100 percent conformity to and enforcement of the law, or close to it—then one would have to conclude that there is no law anywhere in the world, not only between nation-states but also within them. Even in as highly developed a legal system as the United States, "the fact is that only about a third of all serious crimes [ranging from murder to auto theft] . . . are ever even reported to the police by the victims. Of all serious crimes reported, in only 19 percent of cases is a suspect ever arrested, although the figure can go as high as 78 percent for murder. Only about half of all suspects arrested are ever convicted. And only a quarter of those convicted actually ever 'do time' for their crime."[41] A violent crime of some sort is committed in the United States every 22 seconds, a murder every 32 minutes.[42]

If one adds the number of people who exceed the speed limit on America's highways, then the effectiveness of law enforcement in the United States becomes that much more dubious. It is worth noting, however, that law can have an impact in constraining behavior even when it is broken. Before the U.S. Congress (in response to the energy crisis) lowered the speed limit on most U.S. interstates in 1974 from 70 to 55 mph, motorists often went 75 or 80 mph, compared with a typical speed of 65 or 60 mph after the reduction. Some observers have argued that in the international system as well, international law can have a "braking" effect that curbs excessive behavior, in that many states will try to bend the law without breaking it or will try to limit the extent of their departure from the law so as to be able to claim they were acting at least within the spirit of the law. Abram Chayes has shown, for example, that even in as "high-politics" a situation as the Cuban missile crisis in 1962, American decision makers were sensitive to the requirements of international law and took it into account in mounting a naval blockade against Russian ships steaming toward Cuba; although the blockade was technically a violation of international law, it was not as blatant a violation nor as provocative an act as other options would have been.[43]

Indeed, one is hard pressed to find many examples where a state admitted that any of its actions were illegal, precisely because states recognize the value of being perceived as a law-abider. When was the last time you heard a head of state say, "Yes, we acted illegally, and we are proud of it"? In order to be positioned even to remotely make the claim of legality for their actions, national leaders have felt a need to try to operate within the rough

© Reprinted with permission of North American Syndicate.

"You see a car come by here traveling within the speed limit?"

Law enforcement in municipal law.

parameters of the law as much as possible, stretching it more often than brazenly, openly showing contempt for the law. In this way, through at least token bows to the rules more than through slavish devotion to them, states enable international law to subtly impact international politics.

I do not mean to minimize the problem of law enforcement in international law, only to suggest that unfair and unrealistic standards are sometimes applied in evaluating the effectiveness of international law relative to national law.

The Adjudicating of International Law: Who Are the Judges?

In municipal legal systems, courts are used to determine whether a particular law has been violated in a particular instance when one party accuses another party of an infraction. In the international system, judicial institutions also exist, such as the International Court of Justice (the ICJ, commonly referred to as the World Court), which can be used when one state accuses another of violating the law. However, such international institutions are extremely weak insofar as the disputants tend to judge for themselves whether an offense has occurred, or at least tend to reserve for themselves the decision whether to go to court. Whereas in municipal systems one disputant can normally compel the other party to appear in court, international tribunals such as the World Court generally lack compulsory jurisdiction. As in the *United States Diplomatic and Consular Staff in Tehran* case which the United States brought before the World Court in 1979, one party—in this instance, Iran—can simply refuse to acknowledge the jurisdiction of the Court and to participate in the judicial proceedings. The United States itself refused to accept the jurisdiction of the Court in the 1986 case in which Nicaragua filed suit criticizing the United States for mining Nicaraguan harbors and carrying on illegal intervention (*Case Concerning Military and Paramilitary Activities In and Against Nicaragua*).

The World Court consists of fifteen judges whose term of office is nine years. Elected by the UN membership, requiring the approval of both the UN Security Council and General Assembly, the judges are generally drawn from every major legal system in the world, with certain countries, such as the United States, each assured of one seat at all times; if the Court happens to be hearing a case involving a state that does not have a seat on the Court, that state may appoint one of its own nationals as an *ad hoc* judge for that particular case—despite the fact that judges on the Court are supposed to be impartial international magistrates and not representatives of their national governments.

Only states are eligible to appear as litigants before the Court in its normal proceedings, based on the traditional view that only states have rights and obligations under international law. If private individuals have a grievance against their own government, they are expected to resolve the matter in their own state's courts; if they have a grievance against a foreign government, they must ordinarily use that country's courts or persuade their own government to take the case before the World Court.[44] However, there has been a growing willingness of the Court to accord some nonstate actors at least limited standing before the Court and to issue "advisory opinions" in their favor, such as the 2004 *Legal Consequences of the Construction of a Wall in the Occupied Palestinian Territory* case which was brought by the UN General Assembly against Israel. (As far back as 1949, the ICJ had ruled, in the *Reparations for Injuries Suffered in the Service of the United Nations* case, that international organizations such as the United Nations had "legal personality" to bring claims before the Court; the ICJ ruled that the state of Israel owed the United Nations compensation for failing to exercise "due diligence" in protecting Count Bernadette, the UN mediator in Palestine who was assassinated while on a diplomatic mission there.)

The World Court sits in The Hague, Netherlands. Some wags might be tempted to note that all the Court seems to do for the most part is, indeed, sit. Despite the fact that 191 states are parties to the ICJ Statute that established the Court (all signatories to the UN Charter automatically accept the Statute), the Court has not had a busy docket. The ICJ has received a total of only 107 "contentious" cases ("non-advisory" in nature) between 1946 and 2003; in roughly one-third of these, it has not rendered a judgment. For much of the history of the Court, there was a declining caseload, with twenty-nine cases submitted during the 1950s, only six during the 1960s, seven during the 1970s, and five in the

1980s.[45] However, beginning in 1989, the Court experienced a modest revival, with one observer noting that

> we are seeing something new. Canada and the United States led the way by using the [special] Chambers procedure of the Court—a panel of judges from the Court plus one each from the opposing states—in the *Gulf of Maine* case. Mali and Burkina Faso followed suit. Then came El Salvador and Honduras in a case concerning the *Land Island and Maritime Frontier* dispute. More recently, the United States and Italy agreed to submit an investment dispute to the ICJ Chambers in a case concerning Electronic Sicula. . . . Not exactly a thundering herd, but a sign of something new leading perhaps to the more frequent and effective use of the Court.[46]

Between 1990 and 1998, the Court had an average of ten cases pending before it. In 2004, there were twenty cases pending, most of which dealt with Serbia bringing suit against NATO countries for bombing its territory during the 1999 Kosovo War (*Legality of the Use of Force Against the Former Yugoslavia*), but others dealing with boundary and other disputes, such as the altercation between Benin and Niger over ownership of the Niger River in Africa (*Frontier Dispute*).[47] The innovative use of the "chambers" procedure that permits cases to be heard more efficiently and cheaply by a subset of judges (usually five) may encourage greater ICJ use in the future. However, many observers question whether the Court's docket will be crowded anytime soon.[48]

The lack of business, again, has been largely a function of the lack of compulsory jurisdiction. As of 2004, only sixty-five countries—only about one-third of the international system—had signed the "Optional Clause" of the ICJ Statute, agreeing to give the Court compulsory jurisdiction in certain kinds of disputes. Moreover, even states that have signed have attached so many reservations to their acceptance of the Court's jurisdiction as to render the clause feeble. The United States, for example, before it formally withdrew its declaration of acceptance in 1986 over the Nicaraguan incident, had agreed to give the Court compulsory jurisdiction except for those "disputes . . . which are essentially within the domestic jurisdiction of the United States *as determined by the United States of America*" (known as the Connally Amendment). The compulsory jurisdiction problem has been partially overcome by the practice of parties to investment and other treaties writing mandatory jurisdiction clauses into the agreements, but much more has to be done before the Court resembles domestic counterparts.

Where the Court has reached a judgment in a case, its decision has usually been obeyed, even though the ICJ "has no bailiffs . . . to ensure compliance."[49] Some exceptions have already been noted, such as Iran refusing to comply with the court order in the Iranian hostage case and the United States refusing to accept the Court's decision in the Nicaraguan case. A few other acts of defiance by states can be cited as well, such as Albania refusing to pay the damages awarded by the Court to the United Kingdom for destruction of British ships in the *Corfu Channel* case in

1946, but the bulk of Court rulings have been honored. One should not be surprised by the ICJ's overall favorable compliance record, since "states do not, as a general rule, refer their more sensitive legal disputes to the ICJ."[50] The fundamental problem remains that, in disputes involving vital interests, states have generally been unwilling to entrust a third party with ultimate, binding decision-making competence; and in disputes over more trivial matters, states have not felt the need to use the Court because it is far simpler and more economical to settle "out of court."

In fairness to the Court, it might be said that most disputes that arise in domestic law are also settled out of court through a process of bargaining not unlike that found in the international system. At times, the very act of one state bringing suit against another state before the Court has put pressure on the parties to reach a settlement on their own, such as Nauru's 1989 ICJ filing against Australia asking it to pay for the rehabilitation of one-third of the island damaged by phosphate mining during the colonial era, which resulted in Australia paying $75 million in restitution in 1993 to avoid further litigation (*Case Concerning Certain Phosphate Lands in Nauru*). Still, even the most charitable apologist for the Court would have to admit that it has been an extremely ineffective, largely ignored international institution despite its representing the "highest legal aspiration of civilized man."[51]

Fortunately for the international legal system, the World Court is not the only adjudication vehicle. A variety of other courts exist, including several at the regional level, such as the European Court of Justice. More importantly, *national* courts play a key role in the application of international law in those instances in which international issues arise in domestic suits. The constitutions of most countries stipulate that treaties and other elements of international law are considered the supreme law of the land, at least coequal with the highest national statutes, and are to be given due respect in the deliberations of national courts; in this sense, national judges are agents of not only municipal law but also international law. It is true that if a conflict exists between some rule of municipal law (say, an act of Parliament in the British system) and a rule of international law (say, a treaty entered into by the United Kingdom), national judges are inclined to favor municipal law. However, these problems do not arise as often as one might think and are not always resolved in favor of the national law. In the United States, for instance, when there is a conflict between an act of Congress and a treaty entered into by the United States, the one that was enacted later takes precedence; treaties take precedence over any state or local statutes in the United States regardless of the timing element.

An unusually strong statement of the priority that might be given in the future to international law over national law recently came from U.S. Supreme Court Justice Sandra Day O'Connor: "I suspect that over time we will rely increasingly—or take notice, at least—on international and foreign courts in examining domestic issues [such as capital punishment]."[52] Not all observers shared Justice O'Connor's enthusiasm for international law trumping national law, and the jury is still out on how the relationship between international courts and national courts will evolve.

Adjudication, then, like lawmaking and law enforcement, tends to occur in a more convoluted fashion in the international system than in national systems

The Verdict on International Law

Clearly, international law is an imperfect, flawed legal system. It is qualitatively different from municipal legal systems in many respects, but nonetheless it can claim the status of "law." It is odd when realist critics dismiss international law with the argument that it "favors powerful over weak states."[53] Can one identify any legal system that is truly power-neutral, granted some are less arbitrary in the application of law than others? In the international system, as in national societies, law is essentially based on politics. That is, the legal rules developed by a society—although they might have some utilitarian value for all members—tend to reflect especially the interests of those members of society who have the most resources with which to influence the rule-making process. Although the law in some societies might be based on a wider, more just set of values and interests than in other societies, underlying political realities invariably shape the law. Much of the current body of international law, for example, evolved from the international politics of the nineteenth and early twentieth centuries, when Western states dominated the international system. The traditional rules that were created to promote freedom of the sea, protection of foreign investment, and many other international activities tended to reflect the needs and interests of these powers.

However, lest one come away completely cynical about international law, it bears repeating that, once rules of international law have become established, they tend to take on a life of their own, inhibiting to some extent what not only weak powers can do but also great powers, given the "reciprocity" pressures alluded to in this chapter. At the same time, when political realities change along with technological conditions and other factors, pressures mount to alter the law so that it better reflects the new environment. The contemporary international system can be thought of as a society in ferment, with weapons of mass destruction, globalization and the growth of multinational corporations, and revolutionary advances in travel and communications threatening to make many of the existing rules obsolete. An equally important impetus for change in the legal order is provided by the shifting power equation in world politics, as traditional powers find it difficult to impose their will on former colonies clamoring for a rewriting of the rules more compatible with their interests, and all states are having to cope with challenges posed by nonstate actors. Then, too, as constructivists argue, sometimes the law changes in response not to material conditions but to ideational factors, namely normative progress.

In the next part of the book, I attempt to flesh out in specific issue-areas the workings of international law and the complicated contemporary forces that are presenting new problems and opportunities for the further development of international law. The journal *Global Governance* suggests the menu of concerns that deserve our attention when it invites discussion of "the contribution of international institutions and multilateral processes to economic development, the maintenance of peace and security, human rights, and the preservation of the environment."[54] Chapters 4–8 will focus on these and other areas. Each chapter starts with a vignette that calls attention to real-world issues that bring international law into play, with the bulk of the chapter then devoted to discussing the application of the law—describing the major substantive legal-formal rules that operate in that field and, just as importantly, analyzing how the rules are shaped by politics and in turn shape politics. We want to see how nation-states in the twenty-first century are both "shooting pool" (to use the realist "billiard ball" metaphor) and "pooling sovereignty" (to borrow the idealist metaphor).

II

International Law at Work

Shooting Pool and Pooling Sovereignty

On intervention and war:

> The protection of the nation against destruction from
> without and disruption from within is the overriding
> concern. . . . Nothing can be tolerated that might
> threaten the coherence of the nation.
>
> —*Hans Morgenthau*, Politics Among Nations, *1967*

> If somebody comes after innocent civilians and tries to
> kill them en masse because of their race, ethnic
> background, or religion, and it's within our power to
> stop it, we will stop it.
>
> —*The so-called Clinton Doctrine on humanitarian intervention*

> Nothing like D-Day [during World War II] will happen
> again not because human nature has improved, but
> because weaponry has. Making war on that grand scale
> is obsolete.
>
> —*Herman Wouk, in a 1994* Washington Post
> *column "Never Again"*

On economics:

In the Cold War, the most frequently asked question was: "How big is your missile?" In globalization, the most frequently asked question is: "How fast is your modem?"

—*Thomas Friedman,* The Lexus and the Olive Tree, *1999*

Welfare, not warfare, will shape the rules [and] . . . dictate the agenda.

—*Josef Joffe, in a 1992 essay*

On ecology:

There are no . . . limits to the carrying capacity of the Earth that are likely to bind any time in the foreseeable future.

—*Lawrence Summers, U.S. deputy secretary of the treasury, 1994*

We are fast approaching many of the earth's limits.

—*World Scientists' Warning to Humanity, signed by over 1,600 of the leading scientists from seventy-one countries, including a majority of Nobel Prize winners in the sciences, issued in 1992, at the time of the Earth Summit*

Good planets are hard to find.

—*Graffiti found on a bridge in Rock Creek Park in Washington, D.C. (cited in Lester Brown et al.,* State of the World, *1989)*

4

Human Rights:
What Happened to Sovereignty?

> *Some years ago, the* New York Times *ran a story entitled "Motorists in Nigeria Again Face the Whip," reporting that "traffic authorities here [in Lagos] are reintroducing roadside whippings for traffic offenders. . . . A large number of the springy whips have been ordered and soldiers will be assigned to administer beatings. [The chairman of the traffic committee] warned . . . that violators would be dealt with severely for using unroadworthy vehicles or for parking on highways."*[1]
>
> *What, if anything, does international law have to say about such seemingly barbaric behavior? Does international law in any way protect Nigerians from the excesses of their own government, whether it be torturing the owner of a jalopy or engaging in far more extreme behavior, such as genocide? What about if I, as an American, were to find myself the object of police brutality in Nigeria—would I enjoy any more protection under international law than my unfortunate Nigerian brethren? And, to the extent that any rules of international law exist which cover such contingencies, how have they arisen and how are they applied?*

IN CHAPTER 2, I NOTED that most observers would agree that "the starting point of international relations is the existence of states, of independent political communities." Until fairly recently, this also seemed to be the ending point as well, insofar as nonstate actors were given relatively little attention in the study of international politics generally and international law in particular. The 1933 Montevideo Convention on the Rights and Duties of States, which offers the classic legal definition of statehood, made no mention of other entities. Article 1 of the convention specifies: "The state as a person of international law should possess the following qualifications: (a) a permanent population; (b) a defined territory; (c) a government; and (d) capacity to enter into relations with other states."[2]

However, as noted in chapter 3, nonstate actors (international organizations, multinational corporations, and individuals) have been gradually and grudgingly acquiring the status of "international legal persons" alongside sovereign nation-states, even if the latter remain the main subjects that enjoy rights and incur obligations under international law. Although neither you nor I, or Greenpeace or the World Wildlife Fund, or Toyota or Shell Oil can enter into a treaty or appear before the World Court, international law is increasingly according such actors a degree of recognition as autonomous entities with legal capacity.[3]

We focus in this chapter on *individuals* and the field of "human rights." Anne-Marie Slaughter has argued that "international law is undergoing profound changes that will make it far more effective than it has been in the past. By definition, international law is a body of rules that regulates relations among states, not individuals. Yet over the course of the 21st century, it will increasingly confer rights and responsibilities directly on individuals."[4] Realists might question whether this is an empirical statement of what is likely to ensue, or a normative statement of what a desirable future might look like. Yet, idealists can point to some historical trends that support Slaughter's prediction.

One should not underestimate the challenges that human rights advocates face. There is a clear, fundamental tension between the concept of sovereignty and the concept of human rights, since, on the one hand, sovereignty implies the existence of a government that claims complete authority to regulate everything and everybody within its borders while, on the other hand, human rights implies the existence of rights that all human beings possess which even one's own government cannot infringe upon and deny and which can be protected by external elements, namely the international community, as through the United Nations.[5] Sovereignty remains a core legal precept in the international system, despite pressures to pool sovereignty. Indeed, if one were to survey the leaders of every country in the world, perhaps the one value there would be universal agreement on is that all would insist their government presides over a sovereign state. How, then, does one reconcile the fact of sovereignty with the existence of human rights? How, for example, can one explain headlines like the one cited earlier, "UN Investigator Faults Sudan for Atrocities," referring to the complicity of the Khartoum government in committing genocidal acts against Sudanese citizens and the presumption that the United Nations has any say in Sudanese internal affairs? Although human rights is one of the weaker areas of international law in terms of compliance, we will explore here how these contradictions get resolved and how there has been at least some progress in this field.

Before we examine how governments treat their own people, we need to examine what international law has to say about how governments are expected to treat foreigners.

Treatment of Aliens

One must first understand the distinction between "aliens" and "nationals." Any given country is composed of a multitude of individual persons, most of whom are citizens, or *nationals,* of that state. However, also traveling or residing within each state are *aliens,* persons who are nationals of another state or may even be stateless (if their citizenship has been lost for some reason). In general, a national refers to

a person owing permanent allegiance to a particular state, and it is a status acquired either through birth or through naturalization. Regarding birth, some
countries, such as the continental European states, stress the *jus sanguinis* (blood)
principle, whereby a child automatically acquires the nationality of the parents regardless of where the child is born. Other states, such as the United States, use not
only the *jus sanguinis* principle but also the *jus soli* (territorial) principle, whereby
any child (with a few minor exceptions) who is born on their soil is eligible for citizenship regardless of the nationality of the parents. Hence, a child born to Belgian
parents in the United States would be eligible for both American and Belgian citizenship. Nationality can also be gained through *naturalization,* the process
whereby a foreigner attains citizenship after complying with the application procedures stipulated by the state. Since there is no global treaty or other uniform international law governing the determination of citizenship, each state is essentially
free to decide for itself who it will call a "citizen" (for an exception to this, see the
Nottebohm case).

With the increased volume of transnational business-related and tourist travel,
countries are finding more aliens visiting or residing within their borders. (This
does not take into account the waves of uprooted refugees seeking temporary
refuge in a neighboring country or the waves of immigrants, legal or illegal,
seeking to relocate long-term.) The basic maxim that has always applied to foreigners is "when in Rome, do as the Romans do." That is, foreigners are expected
to obey host country laws and (with the exception of foreign diplomatic personnel
covered by the Vienna Convention or foreign military personnel stationed there
who are covered by "status of forces agreements") can be prosecuted by the latter's
courts for committing crimes of murder or theft, or engaging in any other activities proscribed by the state. However, under the body of international law known
as "state responsibility for injury to aliens," which is mostly based on custom,
there has been a long tradition stipulating that, in certain respects, aliens are entitled to special treatment different from the manner in which the host government
deals with its own nationals. In particular, just because a host government might
be a dictatorship that denies any semblance of due process of law and the right to
a fair trial, this does not mean that an alien accused of committing a crime in that
country must necessarily settle for the same level of justice reserved for nationals
of that state. Governments can invoke a legal right to have their citizens accorded
a *minimum international standard of justice* by any host state in which their citizens
happen to be while abroad, no matter what the standard of justice is in the host
country; technically, the right belongs to the government more so than its individual citizens. If the minimum standard is not observed, injured parties can request their own government to seek redress from the host state.[6]

These are not mere academic issues, since they can critically affect individual
lives—for example, if you happened to have been an American or other foreigner
attending the World Festival of Black and African Arts and Culture in Nigeria
around the time that the aforementioned roadside whippings of motorists were occurring. So, also, if you are an American accused and convicted of theft in Saudi

Arabia, where the penalty meted out in such cases can be the amputation of a hand, or, as two Australians found out in a celebrated 1986 case, if you are caught possessing half an ounce of a hard drug (or more than seven ounces of marijuana) in Malaysia, where the automatic penalty is death by hanging. Singapore also hangs drug offenders, and deals harshly with lesser crimes as well; in the highly regimented society where chewing gum is illegal, an American was ordered "caned" (whipped) in 1994 for prankishly spray-painting automobiles.

Many governments, notably in the developing world, have voiced opposition to the customary notion of a minimum *international* standard, viewing it as an artifact of the old colonial era when the United States and other Western states tended to dictate legal norms. Instead, several states today claim that they are free to discriminate against foreigners (in regard to enforcement of contracts and other matters) or that, at best, their only obligation to foreigners is to ensure that the latter obtain equal treatment with their own citizens in accordance with the established *national* standard. Even for those states that accept the idea of an international standard, differences obviously arise as to what constitutes a minimum degree of justice. Indeed, many legal authorities in Europe and elsewhere, where capital punishment has been outlawed as "inhumane," have questioned whether the continued use of the death penalty in the United States meets international standards. Hence, this is an area in which international law is in flux, with efforts being made to codify rules in order to give the law greater precision and certainty. A Draft Convention on the International Responsibility of States for Injury to Aliens was published in 1961, but has yet to be adopted. Other codification projects have been undertaken as well, with no major multilateral treaty yet in force that defines what constitutes "denial of justice" or other failure of state responsibility.

Despite tensions between states over these issues, most states, in practice, are usually quite sensitive to not offending other states in the treatment of the latter's citizens. Even in the case of the Nigerian roadside whippings, the government was careful to suspend the practice temporarily during the World Festival it was hosting at the time, not wanting to alienate potential tourists and not wanting to show a face of Nigeria that could have been embarrassing to the outside world. The realities of politics often override official governmental positions that foreigners do not merit special treatment and must settle for local justice. For example, in countries such as Saudi Arabia, Pakistan, and Iran, whose legal systems are based on *sharia* (Islamic law), in addition to amputating a hand as the official state sanction for robbery, the punishment meted out for alcoholic drunkenness is public flogging, while the punishment for adultery is death by stoning; Saudi Arabia in recent years has averaged two public beheadings every week, for murder and other crimes, in a Riyadh plaza known as "Chop-Chop Square."[7] Generally speaking, however, only rarely are these penalties inflicted on foreigners, particularly non-Muslim foreigners (although this did not stop Iran from administering eighty lashes in a Tehran public square to a Texas woman in 1994 who had been found guilty of drunkenness and prostitution, nor did it prevent the hanging of a

Westerner by Malaysian authorities despite pleas from the Queen of England that the punishment be waived).[8]

It should be noted that, if a foreigner is arrested by the local authorities and subjected to criminal proceedings, the first line of defense is to contact one's consular officials, who, under the 1963 Vienna Convention on Consular Relations (ratified by over 160 countries, including the United States), are entitled "without delay" to be notified of the arrest and to be provided access to any incarcerated nationals. This assumes the accused is read his or her rights, under the treaty, to be allowed communication with home embassy personnel. Interestingly, the United States recently has been charged by the World Court with violations of the Vienna Convention.[9] One notable case (*Case Concerning the Vienna Convention on Consular Relations*) was brought by Paraguay against the United States in 1998, and involved a Paraguayan citizen, Angel Francisco Breard, who had confessed to murdering a woman in Virginia, had been ordered executed by the state of Virginia, but had never been informed by the local authorities about his Vienna Convention right to seek consular help. Breard had been arrested in 1992, but his government did not learn of his imprisonment until four years later. Paraguay filed suit in U.S. federal court to stay the execution, but could not convince the federal judiciary or the Clinton administration to intervene to override the state court verdict. Despite an eleventh-hour appeal by Paraguay to the International Court of Justice (ICJ), which issued a decision on April 9, 1998, ordering the United States to postpone the execution until the full case could be heard by the World Court, the execution was carried out on April 14, 1998. The United States candidly admitted it had violated international law, although it argued the violation was not deliberate but rather was an oversight by the Virginia police, and apologized to Paraguay, along with insuring that it was taking "steps to ensure future compliance with the Vienna Convention at both the federal and state level (including providing pocket-sized reference cards to law enforcement officers [similar to 'Miranda card warnings' American police carry to warn detainees of the right to an attorney])."[10]

The apology and assurances did not help Angel Breard, but it was at least a partial victory for international law, causing a powerful state to admit the wrong done to a weaker state and to take action to minimize future breaches of the law, in recognition of American self-interest that was at stake in upholding the Vienna Convention. As the U.S. judge on the World Court said, explaining his decision to join all the other judges in voting against the United States, "The citizens of no state have a higher interest in the observance of [Vienna Convention] obligations than the peripatetic citizens of the United States."[11]

Treatment of Citizens

States tend to be more worried about provoking international incidents and outrage over treatment of foreigners than over treatment of their own people. However, as the latter has come under greater scrutiny in the world media in recent years, states are having to pay more attention to possible fallout from well-publicized human rights abuses within their own political systems. There has been a gradual movement to require national governments to observe a minimum international standard of justice not only with regard to aliens within their borders but also with regard to their very own *citizens,* on the assumption that there are certain "rights one has simply because one is a human being."[12] Whether those rights include protection from roadside whippings for defective automobiles is open to question; to the extent that Nigerian nationals might be protected by international law against such punishment, it would have to fall under the 1984 Convention Against Torture and Other Cruel, Inhuman, or Degrading Treatment or Punishment (not ratified by Nigeria until 2001) or some other human rights treaties to which Nigeria is a party. This section offers a brief history of the development of human rights regimes, both the politics that have driven the emergence of international law in this area as well as the impacts this body of law has had on national and international politics.

The Politics of Human Rights Law

As Stephen Krasner states,

> The struggle to establish international rules that compel leaders to treat their subjects in a certain way has been going on for a long time. Over the centuries the emphasis has shifted from religious toleration, to minority rights (often focusing on specific ethnic groups in specific countries), to human rights (emphasizing rights enjoyed by all or broad classes of individuals). In a few instances states have voluntarily embraced international supervision, but generally the weak have acceded to the preferences of the strong. . . . [For example], all of the successor states of the Ottoman Empire, beginning with Greece in 1832 and ending with Albania in 1913, had to accept provisions for civic and political equality for religious minorities [Christians] as a condition for international recognition. The peace settlements following World War I included extensive provisions for the protection of minorities. Poland, for instance, agreed to refrain from holding elections on Saturday because such balloting would have violated the Jewish Sabbath.[13]

Professor Krasner offers a useful historical perspective on the human rights movement. Certainly, power relationships have played an important role in the movement, as realists would predict. Power continues to be a key variable, reflected in the fact that when Yugoslavia disintegrated in the 1990s into several new states (Croatia, Slovenia and others), international recognition of these Yugoslav "successor states" was contingent upon their willingness to accept externally-imposed minority rights. These states were not as well-positioned to resist humanitarian demands from the international community as was a powerful actor like Russia (in the case of Moscow's treatment of its Chechnyan population) or China (in the case of Beijing's handling of Tibet). However, power is not the lone variable at work here. The abolition of the slave trade, and then slavery altogether, in the nineteenth century owed not only to the lead role played by Great Britain but also to "transnational advocacy networks"[14] of religious and other groups (as liberal

National Archives (111-SC-215895)

The photo, taken on November 20, 1945, shows the Nuremberg Trials of former Nazi leaders in progress in the courtroom at the Palace of Justice in Nuremberg, Germany, before the International Military Tribunal. The prosecution staff is seated at tables to the left; the defendants are seated in two rows on the right with their counsels at tables in front of them. American military police stand guard to the rear. The question remains: Was this a triumph of human rights, or victor's justice?

thinkers would note) as well as changed norms about the acceptability of human bondage (as constructivists would stress). Likewise, the growth of universal human rights after World War II was not solely a function of the pressure applied by the United States as a global superpower; indeed, some human rights instruments have been produced with only lukewarm or no support from the United States. Moreover, Krasner, in suggesting the more things change the more they stay the same, may underestimate the extent to which the inherent tension between sovereignty and human rights has become more problematical over time.[15]

World War II marks a pivotal moment in the historical effort to extend human rights protection under international law to *all* individuals on the globe. As David Bederman puts it, "the Second World War marked the ultimate transition of international law from a system dedicated to State sovereignty to one also devoted to the protection of human dignity."[16] Most notably, at the Nuremberg Trials immediately following World War II (1945–1949), leaders of Nazi Germany were charged with having committed, along with other crimes, crimes against humanity. German officials were convicted of having violated the rights of the indigenous Jewish population in Germany and neighboring states by engaging in genocide, killing an estimated 6 million Jews; as a result, several German leaders were sentenced to life imprisonment or execution. Nuremberg, therefore, was a landmark event in setting an important precedent supporting the proposition that individuals have rights (and, also, obligations) under international law (*Nuremberg Trials*).[7]

Critics of the Nuremberg Trials have argued that they did not reflect the evolution of international law but simply amounted to "victors' justice," where the winners of the war arbitrarily asserted the existence of certain rules that were used as a pretext to punish the leaders of a vanquished state. These critics point out that the United States, which supported such strong penalties against German leaders at Nuremberg, resisted any calls for international tribunals to hold American officials accountable for atrocities allegedly committed by American forces during World War II (and later in Vietnam) in the form of strategic bombing of population centers. Although the United States was not guilty of atrocities on the scale of the Germans, certainly not toward its own people (notwithstanding the internment of Japanese-Americans on the West Coast after Pearl Harbor), Washington invited charges of hypocrisy in refusing to permit any scrutiny of its own behavior by an international body. These issues surfaced again in the 1990s, when the United States joined other countries under the auspices of the United Nations to organize special tribunals (the first since Nuremberg) to consider alleged acts of genocide and war crimes committed by the leadership in the former Yugoslavia and Rwanda, yet refused to endorse the establishment of the new International Criminal Court, designed as a permanent Nuremberg-type institution, lest its sovereignty be compromised.

Despite the uneven application of the Nuremberg principles, the significance of Nuremberg nonetheless was that it clearly challenged the traditional notion that only states were subjects of international law. The UN Charter, drafted in 1945, had included only a vague reference to human rights, stating in Article 55 that the United Nations "shall promote . . . universal respect for, and observance of, human rights and fundamental freedoms for all without distinction as to race, sex, language, or religion." Although Article 56 went on to say that "all Members pledge themselves to take joint and separate actions" in support of human rights, Article 2 (7) limited the enforcement of human rights by stipulating that "nothing contained in the present Charter shall authorize the United Nations to intervene in matters which are essentially within the domestic jurisdiction of any state." As a treaty, then, the Charter's provisions on human rights were lacking in both concreteness as well as teeth. On the heels of Nuremberg, efforts were made to rectify both problems.

The Universal Declaration of Human Rights, a resolution passed by the UN General Assembly on December 10, 1948, attempted to specify the content of human rights. The resolution was adopted by a vote of 48–0, with 8 abstentions that included the Soviet Union, Saudi Arabia, and South Africa. The declaration called upon governments to promote a variety of rights, both civil and political (for example, the right to a fair trial, protection from cruel and inhumane punishment, freedom of expression and religion) as well as economic and social (for example, the right to an adequate standard of living, the right to work, the right to an education). However, as a General Assembly resolution, the declaration was, at best, "soft law"—a moral pronouncement more than a legally binding document.

Hence, there was still a need to develop instruments that more clearly articulated member obligations and could be made binding on those states choosing to ratify them. Over the next several decades, more than a dozen multilateral treaties were produced, usually opened for signature and ratification only after approval by a majority vote in the UN General Assembly, including separate conventions dealing with genocide, racial discrimination, discrimination against women, political and civil rights, and economic and social rights.[18] The latter two conventions, along with the Universal Declaration, are often referred to as the "International Bill of Human Rights." The move to translate the Universal Declaration's hortatory statement of principles into treaty form is an example of the tendency for soft law to morph into hard law over time. That this was achieved through the drafting of several different treaties, as opposed to a single comprehensive convention, owed to the political reality that some countries (authoritarian states, particularly in the communist bloc) were somewhat resistant to granting "individualistic" political rights, while other countries (capitalist states, notably the United States) were resistant to granting "collectivist" economic and social rights.

The following is a summary of the key provisions and current status of major human rights treaties (with the number of state parties, as of 2005, indicated in parentheses).

- The first important human rights treaty after World War II was the 1948 Genocide Convention (ratified by 135 parties); approved the day before the Universal Declaration, the treaty bans killing and other acts that intend to "destroy a national, ethnic, racial or religious group."

- The 1965 International Convention on the Elimination of All Forms of Racial Discrimination (169 states) requires each member country to "review governmental, national, and local policies, and to . . . nullify any laws and regulations which have the effect of creating or perpetuating racial discrimination" and to "prohibit . . . racial discrimination by any persons, group or organization."

- The 1966 Covenant on Civil and Political Rights (152 states) and the 1966 Covenant on Economic, Social, and Cultural Rights (149 states) reiterate many of the rights enunciated in the Universal Declaration.

- The 1979 Convention on Elimination of All Forms of Discrimination Against Women (177 states) followed earlier women's rights treaties that had dealt with political participation, marriage, and other issues.

- The 1984 Convention Against Torture (136 states) attempts to define torture, bans torture under any circumstances, and requires states to ensure that "the victim of an act of torture obtains redress."

- The 1989 Convention on the Rights of the Child (192 states) stipulates "inalienable" rights enjoyed by children, including the establishment of a minimum age (18) under which minors cannot be recruited for military service and sent into combat.

In addition to the fact that many states have not ratified several of these conventions, many that are parties have interpreted the requirements loosely.[19] The laborious global policy process of developing rules in the human rights field, and the gaps that persist, can be seen in the case of the Covenant on Civil and Political Rights and the Covenant on Economic, Social, and Cultural Rights. First discussed by the UN General Assembly in 1954, they were not adopted and opened for signature until 1966, and did not come into force until 1976 (when the required 35th ratification occurred). Even the United States, an early catalyst behind the Universal Declaration (led by Eleanor Roosevelt), did not ratify the Covenant on Civil and Political Rights until 1992; President Carter had signed it in 1977, but fifteen years elapsed before it was finally ratified, only after the U.S. Senate was satisfied with various "understandings," "declarations," and "reservations" that the United States attached which addressed Washington's concerns about provisions of the treaty limiting capital punishment, infringing upon First Amendment rights through imposition of speech codes, and otherwise conflicting with U.S. law. The United States has never acceded to the Covenant on Economic, Social, and Cultural Rights, also signed by Carter in 1977, because it is viewed by conservative members of the U.S. Senate as promoting excessive governmental regulation, for example by guaranteeing paid leave for women before and after childbirth, and posing conflicts with domestic law relating to "right to work" and other issues.

Similarly, the United States has not yet ratified the Convention on Discrimination Against Women, since it contains language considered stronger than that contained in the Equal Rights Amendment, which failed to gain the necessary support to be added to the U.S. Constitution in the 1980s. Indeed, the United States did not become a party to the Genocide Convention until 1988, forty years after its inception, when it decided that the anti-capital punishment provisions did not violate states rights under U.S. domestic law; and the United States has remained, with Somalia, as the only non-party to the Convention on the Rights of the Child, a main sticking point being the treaty language thought to interfere with the rights of parents to discipline their kids and the rights of states to execute juvenile offenders. (Once it was assured that it could meet its volunteer army's numerical recruitment goals, the United States did belatedly agree to raise its military combat age requirement from 17 to 18, by ratifying a 2002 protocol on child soldiers, but still remains outside the parent treaty.) Commenting on the spotty American commitment to human rights treaties, Michael Ignatieff has characterized the United

States as "a nation with a great rights tradition that leads the world in denouncing human rights violations but which behaves like a rogue state in relation to international legal conventions."[20]

In fairness to the United States, one could argue that its reluctance to join as many human rights treaties as some other countries reflects not so much contempt for international law as respect for the *pacta sunt servanda* principle, that is, Washington's belief that it could not honor treaty provisions at odds with U.S. municipal law and norms, and hence its aversion to becoming an outlaw state even if, as a result, it risked being viewed as a pariah outside the mainstream of human rights thought. Contrast Washington's behavior with that of many parties to the Convention on the Rights of the Child, who have employed more than 300,000 child soldiers (as young as eight years of age) in armed conflict; in 2002, UN Secretary General Kofi Annan reported that twenty-three parties, including Liberia, Burundi, and the Congo, were guilty of treaty violations.[21] Contrast U.S. behavior, also, with many Asian, African, and Middle East countries that, unlike the United States, are parties to the Convention on Discrimination Against Women; although there is still considerable sexism in American society, the United States record of sexual equality is far superior to the likes of Chad, Ghana, Kenya, Nigeria, China, Japan, Malaysia, Myanmar, Kuwait, and Saudi Arabia (where, under strict Islamic tenets, women are not even permitted to drive a car much less vote). Saudi Arabia is one of the 136 states that have acceded to the 1984 Convention Against Torture (as is the United States), yet this has not ended the weekly floggings, stonings, and beheadings in "Chop-Chop Square." Then, too, there is the example of Russia and Iraq as original members of the Covenant on Civil and Political Rights, having joined in 1976 (long before American ratification), despite never permitting even the semblance of a free press.

The UN General Assembly exercises general oversight of human rights regimes. Criticism of human rights abuses throughout much of the cold war era tended to be highly selective, as the majoritarian voting power of an anti-Western bloc of states resulted mainly in resolutions condemning pro-American governments—for example, in Chile (over the excesses of the Pinochet government), South Africa (over apartheid), and Israel (over treatment of Palestinians in the occupied territories captured in the 1967 Six Day War)—while generally sparing communist, Arab, and third world governments from censure. President Jimmy Carter's human rights campaign in the 1970s, which promised more even-handed behavior by the United States in criticizing both right-wing dictatorships (its friends) and left-wing dictatorships (its enemies) in return for reciprocal behavior in the UN General Assembly, fell on deaf ears as assembly actions remained grounded in East-West politics and skewed against governments supportive of Washington, leaving Carter saddled with the label of "idealist." Only toward the end of the cold war did the assembly bias begin to recede. The countries which have been the subject of human rights investigations in the post–cold war era include Afghanistan, Cuba, China, Equatorial Guinea, Myanmar, and the Sudan.

The Impact of Human Rights Law on Politics

Obviously, there are grounds for much cynicism toward human rights law. Oona Hathaway has researched the efficacy of human rights treaties, addressing the question, "Do human rights treaties make a difference?" by examining a database of 166 countries over a nearly forty-year period to determine whether ratification of such treaties improves a state's human rights record; she found that ratifiers do not differ significantly in their behavior from non-ratifiers, and that some of the countries that have joined human rights treaties have worse records than those that have not joined. [22] There remains a gap between the rhetoric used by governments in support of human rights and their actual observance of human rights treaties. Respect for even basic rights, such as free speech, is still very weak in many countries, although the recent democratization movements in Eastern Europe, Latin America, and elsewhere have improved the overall picture considerably. Following the fall of the Berlin Wall, Freedom House reported in the early 1990s that the "world stands at the high water mark of freedom in history," with almost 70 percent of the world's people living in countries that are rated as either "free" (25 percent) or "partly free" (44 percent).[23] Freedom House's latest annual survey shows continued progress, with 88 countries "free" (representing 44 percent of the world's population) and 55 "partly free" (21 percent), compared to 49 "not free" (35 percent).[24] Yet not only does that leave one-third of humanity living in "not free" countries, where imprisonment for "political" crimes occurs regularly, but even in many democracies "human rights violations occur everyday." [25]

In highly repressive societies, data on such abuses are difficult to obtain because of government secrecy and distortion, but various nongovernmental organizations (NGOs) have managed to improve the monitoring of governmental human rights records worldwide; these include Freedom House, Amnesty International, Human Rights Watch, and the International Commission of Jurists. IGO involvement through the UN Human Rights Commission (a subsidiary body of the Economic and Social Council) and the Office of the UN High Commissioner for Human Rights has also been a core element of human rights regime enforcement. The UN Human Rights Commission first received authorization in 1970 to investigate complaints regarding "a consistent pattern of gross and reliably attested violations of human rights and fundamental freedoms." The Commission conducts much of its business under confidentiality rules (so-called 1503 procedures) but publicizes an annual "black list" of countries being scrutinized, attempting to use "mobilization of shame" as a tactic for promoting compliance with international conventions and norms. There is also a Human Rights Committee charged with monitoring compliance with the Covenant on Civil and Political Rights, as well as separate committees, working groups, and special rapporteurs appointed to monitor the specific conventions on race, gender, and torture—fielding and investigating complaints from individuals and groups.[26]

The UN monitoring system is heavily dependent on the good faith of governments to submit annual reports on their treaty compliance, which not only invites "recalcitrant states to violate human rights with impunity" but also poses problems for a state that "lacks the skills or the resources required for a conscientious review of its practices" even "if the government is well intentioned." [27] The growth of UN human rights treaties and machinery has not prevented such outrages over the past decade as genocidal violence in Rwanda and Sudan, as well as the continuation of tribal practices of "giraffe women" in Myanmar (where six-year old girls are made to wear 5-pound coils of brass rings around their necks), female genitalia mutilation in Kenya, Sierra Leone, and other African societies, and gang rapes or murders of women in Pakistan and other Islamic societies in order to avenge adultery or other dishonorable conduct by them or their relatives. [28] To many observers, an especially sad commentary on respect for human rights was the election of Libya, long under the dictatorial yoke of Muammar Gaddafi, to chair the UN Human Rights Commission in 2003. UN custom calls for the commission chairmanship to rotate between the United Nations' five geographical groupings; it was Africa's "turn," and the African states nominated Libya (at least partially as a reward for recent Libyan foreign aid dispensed to many countries on the continent), with Libya then able to gain majority support from the 53-member body that included the likes of Saudi Arabia, Sudan, Cuba, and Zimbabwe. Multilateralism has its benefits but also its frustrations.

Still, even though enforcement machinery remains weak, the increased attention of NGOs and other watchdog groups, tied to increased concern about image-building in many capitals in the media age, has given human rights issues more importance on the global agenda than many realists might have predicted. At UN conferences in recent years, NGOs have had a twofold presence—first, a limited number have been accredited to participate directly in the official deliberations of governments, and, second, a larger number have participated informally in separate NGO Forums, with the latter often making news headlines that attract world interest. The growing role of NGOs in agenda-setting as well as global policy formulation and adoption in the human rights field is described by Margaret Karns and Karen Mingst in their discussion of global efforts to curb violence against women:

> The 1993 World Conference on Human Rights [organized by the UN] . . . put the issue of violence against women on the agenda. The success of the Vienna conference in marrying human rights and women's rights can be attributed to the ninety or so human rights and women's NGOs that organized the Global Campaign for Women's Human Rights. A key element in that campaign was the focus on gender-based violence. At the NGO forum, the Global Campaign organized [a tribunal] . . . presided over by four international judges. It heard testimony of women from twenty-five countries who . . . put a human face on domestic violence . . . and other problems. [Their efforts helped] produce Article 18 of the Vienna Declaration and Programme of Action that declared: "The human rights of women and of the girl-child are an alienable . . . part of universal human rights. [29]

AP Photo/John McConnico

The photo depicts Burqa-clad women in Afghanistan, on September 15, 2001, prior to the U.S. attack on the Taliban government as retaliation for the Taliban role in protecting al Qaeda perpetrators of the September 11 attacks. Under Taliban rule, women were forced to cover themselves from head to toe in Afghanistan. Strict dress codes are still enforced in many Islamic countries.

These same themes were reiterated at the 1995 UN World Conference on Women, held in Beijing, as a follow-up to the first three UN women's conferences held in 1975 in Mexico City, 1980 in Copenhagen, and 1985 in Nairobi. Since Mexico City, "the number of NGOs [had] increased exponentially and shifted perceptibly from women in the North to women in the South," with the number of women NGO Forum participants jumping from over 6,000 in 1975 to an estimated 25,000 in 1995.[30] One should not exaggerate either the power of NGOs or the significance of the somewhat platitudinous wording of the assorted declarations, action plans, and other outputs often emanating from UN conferences, but nor should they be dismissed as irrelevant.

As Louis Henkin and his colleagues have noted, "International human rights principles and obligations influence how governments behave in ways different from the influence of other international law and institutions. 'Horizontal enforcement' of international norms—compliance induced by fear of retaliation—does not operate effectively in the law of human rights. But respect for human rights obligations is enhanced by international monitoring and international criticism . . . as well as by criticism at home invoking international standards. International human rights norms . . . promote change." [31] As the Freedom House democratization statistics show, there in fact has been some progress, even if daunting problems remain. Certainly, the world is better off as a result of the human rights movement since World War II. Henkin and his colleagues put things in perspective:

> International human rights suggest that the relation between the individual and society can, and have, become a subject of international politics and international law. By that development, the international system abandoned the traditional view that how a society treats its own inhabitants is no one else's business. But the idea dies hard, and the end of the Twentieth Century continues to witness recurrent challenge to international human rights, flying banners of "state sovereignty." [32]

Human Rights Challenges in the Twenty-First Century

The post–cold war era presents numerous obstacles to the future development of human rights, but also new opportunities. The end of the cold war in 1989, with the demise of the Soviet bloc, held out the promise of forging a global consensus on human rights built around Western, liberal-democratic principles. Whereas most international law textbooks during the cold war had referred to disparate Western, marxist, and third world views of international law, few marxist governments remained by the end of the 1990s, and even the third world nomenclature—owing its origins to the notion of a "third pole" of less developed countries situated between the first and second worlds in the East-West conflict—seemed an anachronism. [33] Some observers took to dividing the world into the "first world"— the Western industrialized democracies—and the "two-thirds world," or "Global South"—the motley collection of former communist states, third world, "fourth world" (super-poor), or middle-income developing countries as well as newly industrializing countries (NICs) and next NICs, all seemingly trying to emulate the success of the "first world." [34] Globalization (the "coca-colonization" of the planet) seemed to augur a growing homogenization of values. The following statement by Gideon Gottlieb captured the prevailing rosy mood in the 1990s:

> For the first time [since the Concert of Europe immediately following the Napoleonic wars, when conservative viewpoints dominated among the major actors] . . . the world is united on what constitutes legitimate rule. This, in itself, is a momentous political development. Liberal democracy is the unchallenged standard of legitimacy almost everywhere on earth. . . . Francis Fukuyma [whose 1989 article proclaiming "the end of history" was cited in chapter 1] has observed that "as mankind approaches the end of the

millennium, the twin crises of authoritarianism and socialist central planning have left only one competitor standing in the ring as an ideology of potentially universal validity: liberal democracy."[35]

Others, however, questioned this optimism. In particular, Samuel Huntington at the same moment warned of a "clash of civilizations" based on competing cultural values, arguing that "the paramount axis of world politics will be the relations between 'the West and the Rest' . . . ; a central focus of conflict for the immediate future will be between the West and several Islamic-Confucian states."[36] Another commentator elaborated on how "Asian democracy," with its greater reverence for authority and its exaltation of the group over the individual, differed from the Western model:

> Efforts to promote human rights in Asia must . . . reckon with the altered distribution of power in the post–Cold War world. . . . Western leverage over East and Southeast Asia has been greatly reduced. . . . For the first time since the Universal Declaration was adopted in 1948, countries not steeped in the Judeo-Christian and natural law traditions are in the first rank. That unprecedented situation will define the new international politics of human rights. It will also multiply the occasions for conflict. . . . The self-congratulatory, simplistic, and sanctimonious tone of much Western commentary at the end of the Cold War and the current triumphalism of Western values grate on East and Southeast Asians.[37]

It also grated on adherents of Islam in the Middle East and elsewhere, whose political systems had a strong theocratic bent that prevented the elevation of secular legal precepts above religious law, especially over matters such as the status of women and privacy rights. In addition, there remained disagreement surrounding the concept of economic and social rights ("second-generation" human rights), with even West-West conflict increasingly apparent between the United States and many Western European countries over the relative importance of civil liberties, property rights, and free markets versus welfare-state entitlements (such as the "right to shelter").

A mix of domestic politics, rational calculation of national interests, and deeply held values were at work here, although constructivists could argue that conflict seemed rooted more in ideas than material factors. All of these divergent viewpoints about humanitarian norms were expressed at the aforementioned 1993 UN World Conference on Human Rights in Vienna, where national delegations debated everything from "the rights of the disabled" and "the rights of gays and lesbians" to "the right to development" and "the right to a clean environment" ("third generation" human rights). According to one commentator, the conference "appeared to take a step backward in terms of *globally* defining human rights. China and Indonesia were the front-runners in the final conference statement. It [contended] that Western-derived human rights standards should now be tempered by 'regional peculiarities and various historical, cultural and religious backgrounds.' " [38] The meeting ultimately produced a declaration embodying a fragile, uneasy consensus. The Vienna Declaration's affirmation of human rights as "universal, indivisible and interdependent" papered over, on the one hand, the charges of cultural imperialism leveled against the West by "the Rest" and, on the other hand, the criticisms leveled against the developing world for spinning off yet another generation of new "rights" before earlier ones had been consolidated.

By January of 2001, Thomas Franck and other veteran human rights watchers were having to ask, "Are Human Rights Universal?" [39] By September of that year, following the attack on the World Trade Center in New York City by Islamic fundamentalists, larger questions loomed. Michael Ignatieff went so far as to suggest that "the question after Sept. 11 is whether the era of human rights has come and gone," [40] referring to the fact that the need for the United States and other countries to fight the war on terrorism gave China, Russia, and other authoritarian regimes excuses to crack down on political dissidents and separatist movements, made it less likely that Washington would pressure these governments to liberalize their political systems, and raised concerns about undermining of civil liberties even in Western democracies (for example, the Patriot Act's possible threat to privacy and due process in the United States).

Where, then, does this leave human rights in the twenty-first century? Despite Ignatieff's lament, there remain some hopeful signs. First, certain human rights gains seem irreversible, as "divine right of kings" hardly figures to make a comeback as a basis for exercising authority—even in Saudi Arabia, there are growing pressures for the royal family to begin to open up the political system to electoral politics. Second, even if human rights globally have been lagging lately, there are regional human rights regimes worth noting, particularly in Europe. The Council of Europe is an IGO composed of over forty nation-states, whose European Court of Human Rights not only hears inter-state complaints but also allows individual citizens to sue their own government for violation of the European Convention on Human Rights. Among the recent rulings have been decisions ordering Britain to rescind its ban on homosexuals serving in the military and admonishing Britain, also, for failing to protect a 9-year-old boy from severe corporal punishment by his parents. [41] "Remarkably, sovereign states have respected the adverse judgments of the Court . . . [and] have reformed or abandoned police procedures, penal institutions, child welfare practices . . . and many other important public matters." [42] A further assault on sovereignty is being mounted by the European Court of Justice (ECJ) in the twenty-five-member European Union, where the proliferation of suits ranging from sexual discrimination grievances to hazardous waste dumping complaints is causing the ECJ's caseload to grow by more than 10 percent a year. Moreover, the EU has improved the human rights situation in Cyprus, Romania, and Eastern European states that were required to meet EU rights standards prior to their admission into the Union in 2004, and is applying pressure on Turkey to reform as well before its application for membership will be considered. [43]

Third, there has been a growing worldwide movement to institutionalize punishment for the worst atrocities through the establishment of an International

Criminal Court (ICC) that is intended to be a permanent "Nuremberg Trial" judiciary. The trials that had been organized by the United Nations in the 1990s to prosecute the leadership of the former Yugoslavia and Rwanda—Serb President Slobodan Milosevic was charged with war crimes and crimes against humanity, notably ethnic cleansing of Bosnian civilians in Bosnia-Herzegovina and Albanian civilians in Kosovo, while Rwandan Prime Minister Jean Kambanda was charged with genocide against ethnic Tutsis—were *ad hoc* tribunals established solely to hear those two cases. (Kambanda was sentenced to life in prison. The Milosevic trial had not yet concluded as of late 2005, although lower-level officials were sentenced to several years in jail. Capital punishment was ruled out as a penalty. See *Case Concerning Application of the Convention on the Prevention and Punishment of the Crime of Genocide.*) Meanwhile, there have been other dictators who escaped punishment for human rights abuses, such as General Augusto Pinochet, the former president of Chile, who a Spanish court attempted in 1998 to prosecute for torture and other human rights violations committed during his tenure in the 1970s and 1980s. Spain had requested his arrest and extradition from the United Kingdom, where he was receiving medical treatment at the time. Pinochet asserted the traditional legal principle of "head of state immunity" from prosecution in the national courts of another country, which the British authorities rejected, although they ultimately denied the Spanish request, citing Pinochet's ailing health that prevented travel (*R. v. Bow Street Magistrate, Ex Parte Pinochet Ugarte*).[44] Along with Spain, Belgium and some other countries in the 1990s invoked "universal jurisdiction" over "crimes against humanity" as a basis for asserting their right to try foreign heads of state in their courts for human rights violations.[45] However, many observers were uneasy with municipal courts performing this function, since an international court figured to be better able to assure impartiality and speak for the international community.[46]

Hence, many states worked hard to create the ICC as just such a forum, as a Nuremberg-style sitting court that hopefully would serve to deter future atrocities and, if deterrence failed, to punish those individuals responsible. Among the leaders were middle-power states such as Australia, Canada, Netherlands, and Sweden. These efforts culminated in a gathering of almost 150 states in 1998 to finalize the drafting of the Rome Statute establishing the Court in The Hague, Netherlands. A total of 120 countries voted in favor, twenty abstained, and seven opposed, including the United States, Israel, China, Iraq, and Libya. The ICC officially came into existence in 2002, with the sixtieth ratification of the Rome Statute; as of 2005, roughly 100 countries were parties. The Statute authorizes prosecution of any individuals (private citizens, military personnel, and former or current public officials—from member or nonmember states) who are accused of any of the following crimes: war crimes (either in a civil or interstate conflict), genocide, or crimes against humanity. In addition to cases that may be referred by the UN Security Council, proceedings may be initiated by any ICC member state on whose territory the alleged crime occurred or by the state of the nationality of the accused; the state whose national has been charged with a crime is given the first opportunity to try that individual, but must defer to the ICC if it is unwilling or unable to take action.[47]

Although President Clinton was an early ICC supporter, he and others in Washington had misgivings about some final provisions of the Statute, based both on national security considerations and concerns about how the treaty would "play in Peoria" and elsewhere in domestic American politics. Clinton reluctantly signed the Statute just before leaving office, declaring it "flawed" but arguing that he felt compelled to do so since only those states willing to sign by December, 2000 would be permitted to participate in the future development of the Court's procedures. The United States has not yet ratified the treaty, despite the fact that most European nations and U.S. allies have. The main American objections are: (1) the Statute undermines the primacy of the UN Security Council, and hence the American veto power, by permitting cases to be initiated by any member state or by the ICC prosecutor; (2) American leaders or American soldiers might well be prime targets of an ICC investigation, given the relatively heavy involvement of U.S. armed forces in peacekeeping, humanitarian intervention or other overseas military operations (for example, George W. Bush might conceivably be apprehended while traveling abroad and indicted over alleged Iraq War transgressions); and (3) ICC procedures under the Rome Statute are to be determined by a majority of states party to the treaty, so that, assuming the ultimate goal is to make the treaty universal, the majority of the world's countries that are "not free" or "partly free" might be positioned to dominate the Court over the will of its democratic members.[48]

Two dozen African and Latin American states with questionable human rights records are already parties, prompting questions about whether the recent genocidal acts of officials in the Sudan will be given as much attention by the ICC as the treatment of the Palestinians at the hands of democratic Israel. How realistic is it to think that law will be completely divorced from politics here any more than it is in other aspects of international relations? Also open to question is how such a body can function while a major actor such as the United States remains outside its purview.

Conclusion

At times it seems that nonhuman rights are taken more seriously than human rights, as animals increasingly are being accorded protection as "international legal persons" under such instruments as the Universal Declaration of the Rights of Animals (the Animal Charter) adopted by the UN Educational, Scientific and Cultural Organization.[49] However, human rights advocates have managed to make significant strides in tempering the law of the jungle, getting states to accept some constraints on their behavior toward foreigners as well as their own citizens. If the post–World War II human rights movement "turned traditional conceptions of sovereignty almost inside out,"[50] the post–cold war extension of this movement, in the form of "humanitarian intervention," has rendered sovereignty "no longer sacrosanct"[51] altogether. As Anne-Marie Slaughter has commented, "a distin-guished commission appointed by the Canadian government at the suggestion of the UN secretary general released a report at the end of 2001 that defined a state's membership in the United Nations as including a responsibility to protect the lives and basic liberties of its people—and noting that if a member state failed in that responsibility, the international community had a right to intervene."[52] Still, such norms are not fully established and are being contested by many states, big and small. In the next chapter, we examine the rules governing humanitarian inter-vention and the use of armed force in general, as we focus on the body of law known as *ius ad bellum* (relating to the prohibition of war) and *ius in bello* (relating to the conduct of war) and how it has been evolving in response to a changing po-litical scene.

5

War and Peace:
Do We Need New Rules for an Old Problem?

On September 11, 2001, between 9:00 a.m. and 11:00 a.m., as many as 3,000 people—mostly Americans but also foreign nationals from dozens of other countries—perished when the twin towers of the World Trade Center in New York City collapsed after being struck by two airplanes; the Pentagon Building in the nation's capital was hit by a third plane, also resulting in substantial loss of life; a fourth plane crashed in rural Pennsylvania before it could reach its intended destination. The attack had been perpetrated by al Qaeda, a terrorist group based in Afghanistan, whose Taliban government had harbored Osama bin Laden and his Islamic fundamentalist followers and who refused to surrender them to U.S. authorities when the Bush administration requested their capture and extradition following the 9/11 incident. Immediately after 9/11, the UN Security Council passed Resolution 1368, recognizing the United States' "inherent right of self-defense" and expressing the council's "readiness to take all necessary steps to respond to the terrorist attacks of 11 September 2001, and to combat all forms of terrorism." The United States subsequently, within one month of the attack, launched air and ground strikes against the Taliban and al Qaeda, eliminating the Taliban and dispersing the al Qaeda network. A new Afghan government under Hamid Karzai was elected by a tribal council in June of 2002.

By the summer of 2002, the Bush administration was also considering the need for "regime change" in Iraq as well, not because of any attack by the Iraqi leader Saddam Hussein on the United States, but because of the failure of Iraq to comply with UN Security Council Resolution 687, passed in 1991, at the end of the first Gulf War. Iraq had invaded Kuwait in 1990 and had attempted to annex that country, the first time any UN member had sought to eliminate another member of the international community, which triggered a UN-authorized, U.S.-led coalition ("Desert Storm") that forced Iraq's retreat and surrender. Saddam agreed to the terms of Resolution 687, which required him to renounce any biological, chemical, or nuclear weapons (WMD) programs and to permit UN inspectors into the country to monitor

AP Photo/Carmen Taylor

On September 11, 2001, the World Trade Center in New York City was attacked by terrorists who had skyjacked two airplanes and flew them into the twin towers. This photo shows the south tower on fire and the north tower about to be hit. Some 3,000 people were killed.

disarmament. Over the next decade, however, Iraq frustrated the UN weapons search, forced the inspectors to leave in 1998, and refused to account for its weapons stocks, including chemical weapons Saddam was known to have used against Iran in the 1980s and against his own people, the Kurds, in 1988. Following 9/11, the Bush administration became increasingly concerned about Iraq's suspected WMD capabilities and links to terrorist groups in the Middle East. In November 2002, Washington was able to get the UN Security Council to pass Resolution 1441, giving Saddam "a final opportunity" to allow the inspectors back in to do their job and also demanding a "full disclosure" report of his weapons programs by January, warning "serious consequences" if he did not comply. When Saddam continued to obstruct full cooperation and compliance, the United States attempted to get another Security Council resolution passed explicitly authorizing the use of armed force against Iraq, but failed to get the necessary support from council members France, Russia, and China, who all threatened to veto the proposal. Finally, on March 19, 2003, the United States launched a military invasion dubbed "Operation Iraqi Freedom," supported by the British and a few other countries constituting a "coalition of the willing." The Saddam Hussein government was toppled in twenty-six days, but the postwar reconstruction of Iraq and establishment of a viable government proved more daunting, hindered by insurgent suicide bombings and other internal warfare waged against the occupation forces and the interim Iraqi authority

Both the Afghan and Iraq invasions posed interesting international legal questions. In the case of the Afghan attack after 9/11, the United States invoked the traditional right of self-defense and, in addition, obtained the blessing of the UN Security Council, which had demanded the Taliban turn over bin Laden to Washington and had come close to authorizing a global "war on terrorism." Even so, many international lawyers questioned whether the American invasion was legal, arguing that it amounted to retaliation more than self-defense and that, since the 9/11 attack had been committed by a nonstate actor rather than by the Taliban government itself, the United States had no right to bomb Afghanistan and remove the government. Far more questions were raised about the legality of the U.S. action in Iraq. The United States had invoked a variety of legal rationales to justify its behavior, including "collective security" (the claim that the United States was simply enforcing Resolutions 687 and 1441 as well as other Security Council resolutions that Saddam had ignored in violation of the UN Charter); the right of "preemptive self-defense" against a country that was thought to have WMD capabilities and terrorist connections and might possibly threaten American security in the future (what became known as the Bush Doctrine); and the right of "humanitarian intervention" (the right to intervene to protect a people from its own government and to unseat that government if it had engaged in genocide and crimes against humanity, such as Saddam's gassing of its Kurdish population and the torture and killing of over 300,000 Iraqi citizens). Most observers dismissed these arguments and concluded that the American attack was nothing more than an illegal aggression.[1]

The complex issues raised by the Afghanistan War and Iraq War cases were symptomatic of the growing murkiness of both the political and legal landscape relating to the use of armed force in world affairs. Although in many respects both conflicts were examples of old-fashioned interstate war, they also involved the ingredients of civil strife, humanitarian intervention, terrorism, and other complicating elements. To what extent is national regime change—the overthrow of the government of a sovereign state—permitted by international legal regimes governing the use of force, even when done in the name of "humanitarian intervention"? What does international law have to say, as well, about the circumstances under which one state can punish another state for warlike actions committed by nonstate actors based in the latter's territory, such as Afghanistan? Are captured terrorists entitled to the same prisoner of war protections normally granted to soldiers? What military or other sanctions are permissible when a state, such as Iraq, violates

> *chemical, biological, or nuclear arms control agreements? And, in an age of WMDs, must a state, say the United States, wait and absorb the first shot—which could be a radioactive bomb or anthrax or nerve gas attack on New York City or Washington, D.C.—before it can legally respond in "self-defense"? These and other questions will be considered in this chapter as we examine the "laws of war" (and peace) and how, if at all, they constrain nation-state behavior.*

WE START WITH THE OBSERVATION that law itself can serve as a surrogate for war, in that states often are content to wage conflict—bargain—over a disputed matter by exchanging legal broadsides (trading various legal claims) rather than exchanging bullets. In other words, international law provides a vehicle for communication and sublimation of hostility, performing a function similar to how Winston Churchill once characterized the "talk-shop" role of the United Nations: "jaw-jaw is better than war-war." As one commentator remarks, "international law provides a language for diplomacy. . . . When international actors speak [when they try to resolve international issues], they use the idiom of international law."[2] Another commentator notes, "international law functions as an alternative to violence in contemporary conflict situations . . . by providing a medium through which the intentions of states can be set forth without the application of force. . . . Since the threat or use of force has also [often] been a communicating device in the international bargaining process, law can serve . . . as a substitute in that process."[3] Of course, when diplomacy fails, war at times is resorted to as the final arbiter in a dispute. War, to use the famous definition of the nineteenth-century Prussian strategist Klaus von Clausewitz, is "the continuation of policy by other means."[4] However, even when war is employed as an instrument of statecraft and the threshold is crossed from diplomacy to force, international law usually operates to some extent, not only because states invariably invoke international law to justify their resort to force but also because international law places limits on how a war may be conducted.

International law aside, there is some question as to whether Clausewitz's cavalier notion of war still applies today. The twentieth century, after all, saw new realities in warfare. The first Nobel Peace Prize was awarded in 1901 to Henri Dunant, the founder of the International Committee of the Red Cross. Alfred Nobel, the Swedish inventor of dynamite, had hoped that nitroglycerin's sheer destructive power would ironically be a force for peace insofar as it would make war unfightable and unwinnable and, therefore, unthinkable. Many others also have harbored the dream that, where international organization and law had failed, the growing destructiveness of modern weaponry itself would so fundamentally alter warfare as to render war a relic of the past. The fact that the twentieth century witnessed the greatest carnage in human history—over 100 million war-related deaths, four-fifths of which were civilians (as noted by Charles Tilly)[5]—may yet provide the necessary impetus for humanity's rethinking war as a tool of policy, at the same time that it stands as testimony to the difficulty of eradicating organized violence however irrational such violence may seem.

As realists stress, war—whether war preparation, war avoidance, war fighting, or war termination—has always constituted the "highest" form of politics among nation-states. Few "games" nation-states have played over time have involved higher potential stakes than those having to do with arms races and arms control. It is hard to dispute Hans Morgenthau's statement[6] that concern over protecting a nation's physical security and territorial integrity has typically been at the top of every country's agenda. In the American case, for example, "national security was the realm of foreign policy that most concerned the Founding Fathers. We are and have always been a nation preoccupied with security."[7] Even if, as liberals note, economic and other issues compete for foreign policy makers' attention, protection from military attack is still considered the foremost responsibility of a national government toward its citizens. Indeed, the twentieth century saw the expansion of the "national security state" just as it saw the proliferation of ever more deadly conventional weapons as well as weapons of mass destruction. The twenty-first century began much like the twentieth century ended, with global military expenditures continuing to hover around $1 trillion (roughly half of which was accounted for by the United States).[8] It is little consolation that, since World War II, national armies and armaments have been housed in what are called defense departments rather than war departments.

Hence, war is obviously not a relic but remains a very real part of the fabric of world politics. Still, the nature of warfare has been changing, and with it the nature of the threats nation-states confront. In the following pages, I examine the changing face of global violence and the special problems the contemporary international system poses for global governance in this issue-area, as humanity continues its ongoing effort to develop rules regulating the outbreak and conduct of war.

The Changing Nature of Global Violence

Much of the history of international relations since the Peace of Westphalia has revolved around interstate war, most notably war between great powers, especially fought over real estate. Some of these conflicts have been systemic, involving much of the international system, such as the Napoleonic Wars, World War I and World War II, and some have been more confined, such as the Franco-Prussian War of 1870–71 and the Russo-Japanese War of 1904–05. As suggested by Clausewitz, throughout the centuries war was understood to be a legitimate, if lamentable, vehicle for expanding national power, which tended to be equated with *territorial expansion*. One of the most profound changes in world politics has been the recent movement away from this historical pattern.

This thinking began to shift after World War I, but it took World War II for it to congeal. State behavior changed after 1945 due to a variety of factors, including, first, the development of weapons of mass destruction that made great powers gun-shy in using armed force vis-à-vis each other and, second, the development of democratic, anti-colonial norms that made the imposition of foreign rule less acceptable and hence constrained great-power use of armed force vis-à-vis weaker states. The decolonialization process led to a tripling of the number of sovereign nation-states between 1945 and 1990, most of which were quite weak. While both the United States and the Soviet Union during the cold war sought to recruit the new nations into their respective blocs, their efforts were only mildly successful, not only because the two giants tended to neutralize each other in many areas but also because the new third world nationalism placed limits on what superpowers could do to cajole or coerce even tiny states into line. In particular, because of the widespread aversion to foreign rule, along with the mutual fear of conflict escalation, the two superpowers—more than great powers in the past—were inhibited from expanding their influence through direct territorial annexation or occupation. Although territorial concerns continued to play a role in world politics among lesser powers—for example, disputes between Morocco and Algeria over the Spanish Sahara and between Israel and various Arab states over lands controlled by Israel following its achieving statehood—they were not the essence of superpower competition. Soviet territorial annexation ceased with the absorption of Estonia, Latvia, and Lithuania at the very end of World War II, while the United States had long since ended its own record of territorial aggrandizement. Instead of acquiring land, the object of superpower competition was to gain influence over the foreign policies of individual third world states through overt or covert intervention, frequently propping up governments one side favored or destabilizing governments one side opposed. The time-honored balance of power game continued to be played but in a somewhat different manner than in the past. If the world map had previously resembled a gigantic "Monopoly" board on which the players competed for property, the map in the post–World War II era looked more like a "chessboard" in which two players attempted to manipulate a set of pawns for maximum advantage.

Although cynics might say that the superpower attempts to substitute subtle forms of control—manipulation of puppet, satellite regimes from the outside, or neocolonialist economic penetration and domination from within—in lieu of more blatant territorial incorporation and ownership amounted to a distinction without a difference, such a view fails to recognize just how much business as usual had changed. Robert Jackson describes the fundamental alteration in interstate relations that had taken place:

> Until as recently as the end of the First World War the birth and death of sovereign entities and the transfer of territorial jurisdictions from one State to another was a predictable and legitimate consequence of war and peace. Today, however, it is increasingly unimaginable owing not least to the norm of territorial legitimacy which has spread around the world and has preserved thoroughly disintegrated states, such as Chad, Sudan, Uganda, Ethiopia, and even totally anarchic Lebanon and Somalia. . . . The existing territorial pattern of sovereign statehood in all of the major regions of the world seems to have acquired a sanctity which few if any powers are pre-

pared to violate or even dispute, presumably because they desire to avoid not only the universal condemnation but also the threat to international order which such an action would provoke. Since 1945 there have been very few significant territorial grabs anywhere in the world. . . . The survival of even the tiniest countries is internationally guaranteed today. State survival nowadays is seen as a matter of right rather than power.[9]

One reason the United States was able to mobilize virtually the entire United Nations membership to counter Iraqi aggression against Kuwait in 1991 was because, in seeking to incorporate all of Kuwait within Iraq's boundaries, Saddam Hussein was seen as violating what had become an "iron law" of international relations, that is, since 1945 no state, big or small, had dared walk into the UN General Assembly and through armed force remove the seat of another recognized member of the international community. Perhaps Saddam might have succeeded had he opted to install a puppet government in Kuwait or had been willing to settle for a smaller sliver of real estate, but his ambition exceeded the parameters of acceptable international behavior.

The point here is that well before the end of the cold war the rules of the game had shifted toward what Mark Zacher calls "the territorial integrity" norm, and that the post–cold war era has only accentuated this trend; Zacher notes that the last successful use of armed force for purposes of territorial annexation was Morocco's seizure of the Spanish Sahara in 1976.[10] So the central problem that has preoccupied students and practitioners of international relations throughout the ages—interstate war, particularly great-power war, fought over territory—has become a relatively peripheral concern. Interstate wars have become remarkably infrequent (especially taking into account the tripling of the number of states in the international system which potentially could be candidates for war), while great-power war has become nonexistent. However, this is offset by the fact that the threatened and actual use of violence is still prevalent on the planet, and that it tends to take a more complex form which in some respects can be harder to get a handle on, both conceptually and legally, than in the past. How so?

First, to the extent that violence occurs *between* states, it tends to be not so much in the form of what we commonly think of as war (large-scale, all-out, sustained armed combat between organized national armies), but rather "force without war" (intermittent, limited hostilities, with ill-defined beginnings and endings). Second, the main mode of violence today is not interstate but rather intrastate, that is, civil wars *within* states, several of which can become internationalized as external actors are drawn into the fray, making such conflicts hybrid mixes of internal and cross-border conflagrations. Third, there is a growing concern over "extrastate" violence, that is, unconventional security threats posed by nonstate actors, including transnational terrorist and criminal organizations, which can potentially disrupt national order and world order through skyjackings, drug trafficking, cyberspace interference, and other means. Force without war, civil war (purely internal or internationalized), and terrorism are hardly novel elements of world politics, but what is novel is that they have seemingly displaced interstate war as the focus of high politics in the Westphalian state system.[11] Let us briefly examine each of these three areas of concern.

Force without War

A 1998 study reported that, as the twentieth century was drawing to a close, "the world had fewer active conflicts than at any time since World War II,"[12] the authors counting less than thirty ongoing conflicts in which there were over 1,000 casualties. The same authors five years later counted roughly the same number of conflicts, noting that "most of these, as has been the case for years, [were] intrastate," that there was a continued absence of great-power conflict (the so-called long peace), and that the violence was confined largely to the less developed world.[13] Other studies confirmed that in the post–cold war era, "violent conflicts continue to decline."[14]

Admittedly, counting the number of wars occurring at any given moment is a trickier proposition than it used to be. Distinctions between war and other forms of international violence used to be more clear-cut, because wars in the past were definable in legal terms and had fairly clear initiation and termination dates. A war usually was said to start when one state issued a formal declaration of war against another state, as in World War II; it normally ended with a formal treaty of peace between the warring parties.[15] Since World War II, however, states have tended not to issue declarations of war prior to initiating hostilities, perhaps because armed aggression is illegal under the United Nations Charter. The hostilities that do occur between two or more states can be isolated one-shot affairs or can go on for days, months, and in some cases years, often interrupted by periods of peace, only rarely concluding with a formal peace treaty.

Barry Blechman and Stephen Kaplan have labeled such a phenomenon "force without war." They identified more than 200 different incidents during the cold war in which the United States used armed force in some fashion short of war, and 190 such incidents in the case of the Soviet Union.[16] It is important to reiterate that the two superpowers did not exchange fire with each other and that, even when they resorted to armed force against others, it tended to be in a somewhat restrained fashion, typified by the hour-long strafing of Muammar Gaddafi's tent headquarters by U.S. jets in 1986, to send a warning to the Libyan leader to cease sponsoring terrorism against American targets. Even when hostilities occurred that were more extensive and had all the earmarks of war, such as the Korean War during the 1950s and the Vietnam War during the 1960s, each of which cost roughly 50,000 American lives and thousands of other Asian casualties, or the Afghanistan War at the end of the 1970s, which likewise resulted in enormous casualties for the Soviet Red Army and their adversaries, in the end only a small fraction of the available arsenals were utilized by the losing side in these undeclared actions.

Many cases of force without war can be found in the post–cold war era. Note, for example, the border clashes between Peru and Ecuador in 1995 (over a boundary dispute dating back more than fifty years), the periodic skirmishes between India and Pakistan along the Kashmir cease-fire lines (dating back to the partition of the Indian subcontinent in 1947), the occasional sorties flown by U.S. planes over Iraq following the first Gulf War, and China's 1996 conduct of missile "tests" in waters within thirty miles of Taiwan's major ports (aimed at intimidating Taiwan into refraining from declaring its independence from the mainland).[17] Hence, in contrast to the "total wars" of the past, such as World Wars I and II, we see references today to "limited wars," "low-intensity conflicts," and even such euphemisms as "peaceful engagement." (The latter was the name the Pentagon gave to the American military intervention in Panama in 1989, aimed at removing Manuel Noriega from power after the dictator was linked to drug trafficking in the United States and after economic and other pressures had failed to dislodge him.)

There have been a number of explanations that have been offered to account for the growing reluctance on the part of highly developed societies—those with the most to lose in an escalating conflict—to engage in all-out war. The increasing destructiveness of weaponry is the most obvious inhibiting factor. Still, skeptics point out that humanity has shown a capacity for mindless violence on a mass scale throughout history. Rome's complete destruction of Carthage in the Third Punic War arguably was the equivalent of "nuking" that society. More lives were lost in the conventional air bombing of Hamburg, Dresden, and Tokyo during World War II than were lost through the dropping of the atomic bomb on Hiroshima and Nagasaki. Evan Luard has said: "There is little evidence in history that the existence of supremely destructive weapons alone is capable of deterring war. If the development of bacteriological weapons, poison gas, nerve gases, and other chemical armaments did not deter war before 1939, it is not easy to see why nuclear weapons should do so now."[18] However, James Lee Ray has posited an interesting constructivist argument that it is not the mere existence of weapons of mass destruction which accounts for the "long peace" among great powers since 1945, but "moral progress"—the internalization of a new understanding that major war no longer makes sense in terms of any cost-benefit calculus.[19]

It has been said that war determines not who is right but who is left. In the event of a major war between highly developed, well-armed societies in the twenty-first century, there may be no one left in the aftermath. Ray hints that, as happened with the once entrenched institutions of slavery and colonialism, war may be on its last leg; he speaks of "the end of international war," just as others speak of "the obsolescence of major war."[20] Although it seems quite premature to reach such a conclusion, two other factors in addition to changing weapons technology are thought to be promoting a "zone of peace,"[21] at least in the Northern, developed half of the globe, a sector that might extend gradually to other regions. One is the trend toward greater democratization, which, if it were to continue worldwide, would likely have an inhibiting effect, since democracies virtually never go to war against each other (a phenomenon called "the democratic peace")[22] and since democracies allow a free press that, particularly through electronic media, supposedly dampens the appetite for war by bringing home the reality of battle with unprecedented immediacy ("the CNN effect").[23] The other is the trend toward greater economic interdependence, since, as the economies of states become increasingly intertwined, war becomes all the less attractive.[24] Thomas Friedman has advanced a "golden arches theory of conflict prevention," arguing that no two countries which have had a McDonalds restaurant (symbolizing societies that have become mass consumption-oriented) have ever fought a war against each other.[25]

Clearly, humanity, including the North, has not yet altogether lost its stomach for war-fighting, as evidenced by the 1999 Kosovo War and the 2003 Iraq War, which have been called the prototypical wars of the future and, hence, deserve special attention here. I dwell on these two cases, also, because the war-fighting techniques (the "rules of engagement") they displayed have implications for the evolution of international law governing the targeting of population centers and other aspects of warfare.

The Kosovo War started when Serbia (the former Yugoslavia) stepped up its campaign of oppression against Kosovo, an enclave within Serb borders comprised predominantly of ethnic Albanians. As genocidal "ethnic cleansing" of the Kosovars mounted, the United States and its NATO allies were pressured to enter the conflict in the name of "humanitarian intervention," partly to reverse the expulsion of more than a million refugees from their homes and partly to prevent a widening of the war in the Balkans that could damage Western interests. NATO had attempted to get prior UN Security Council authorization to use force, but ultimately had to proceed without approval due to a Russian veto. For 78 days, NATO warplanes, mostly American, bombed Serb military and industrial targets in an effort to pressure Slobodan Milosevic, the Serb leader, to surrender to Western demands for greater autonomy for Kosovo. There was a notable reluctance on the part of NATO countries to put ground troops into the conflict, for fear of excessive casualties that might decrease support for the war at home. Instead, the war was fought totally from the air, using push-button precision munitions fired from long distances, out of range from Serb anti-aircraft batteries. In almost 10,000 bombing runs, no allied airmen were killed and only two planes were lost. In the end, in response to considerable destruction of bridges, power plants, and other infrastructure, Milosevic agreed to come to the bargaining table and allow a United Nations presence in Kosovo, where a fragile peace still holds; he was eventually tried in The Hague for crimes against humanity. (Friedman acknowledged that Yugoslavia and all the NATO allies had "Big Mac" consumer cultures, but explained away the Kosovo War as an exception that proved the rule, insofar as the West was unwilling to shed its blood for the cause, and the Serbs themselves "wanted McDonalds re-opened [that is, wanted to return to normalcy] much more than they wanted Kosovo re-occupied."[26])

Most observers at the time argued that the United States and its NATO allies were fortunate to have achieved victory so cheaply in Kosovo, that ground forces might be necessary in future conflicts, and the willingness of the United States and Western societies to endure casualties would be more severely tested at a

AP Photo/Khalid Mohammed

U.S. troops and Iraqi police gather around a crater left in the yard of a police station in Baghdad after insurgents detonated several car bombs that killed eight policemen and a baby. Such scenes raise the question of whether conflicts such as the Iraq War, where military fronts are often blurred, require new "rules of engagement."

later date.[27] After all, it only took the death of eighteen U.S. Army Rangers in Somalia in 1993 to prompt an American withdrawal from what had also been a "humanitarian intervention" mission (to provide food and other aid to the people living in a society torn by rival clans and warlords), with the pullout traced particularly to a widely televised image of an American soldier's body being dragged through the sand. The Iraq War a decade later would pose a much stiffer challenge in terms of American leaders selling personal sacrifice to the American public.

The U.S. decision to invade Iraq in March of 2003, in response to Saddam Hussein's defiance of UN resolutions but without explicit UN authorization of the attack, was discussed at the outset of this chapter. Like the Kosovo War, the military campaign was quick and relatively inexpensive, lasting less than one month and resulting in fewer than 100 American combat fatalities. The "shock and awe" bombing raids on Iraqi cities, relying on precision-guided weapons to wreak devastation on Saddam's palaces and various strategic targets throughout the country, were supplemented by ground forces that met little resistance. As in Kosovo, "regime change" was followed by efforts by the occupation forces to reconstruct the country politically and economically. However, unlike Kosovo, the postwar reconstruction was accompanied by serious renewed violence perpetrated by rebels belonging to various ethnic and religious factions hoping to drive the United States out of Iraq and frustrate American efforts to implant a democratic government in Baghdad. By late 2005, American military deaths had climbed to over 2,000, inviting comparisons with the "quagmire" experience in Vietnam. Although the Iraq conflict differed from Vietnam in several respects, it (along with Kosovo) shared some similar features, notably the blurring of internal war and external war. The international legal issues surrounding such conflicts will be treated later in the chapter, but first we need to examine the other categories of contemporary global violence.

Civil Wars

Civil wars clearly are not a new phenomenon. As long as there have been nation-states, there have been conflicts within states that have led to internecine fighting between rival groups. Although civil strife is not new, it has been an especially visible feature of world politics since 1945, and it has come increasingly to preoccupy the international community in the post–cold war period. The decolonialization process after World War II produced new states often having highly unstable political systems prone to internal unrest. Civil wars have also taken place in long established states, in Latin America and elsewhere. K. J. Holsti estimates that "more than two-thirds of all armed conflict in the world since 1945 has taken the form of civil wars." [28] Another study reports that between 1989 and 1997, "the vast majority [of conflicts]—97 of the 103—took place exclusively within the boundaries of a single country. The remaining 6 involved wars between opposing states [most of which had dissipated by 1997]." [29] The International Commission on Intervention and State Sovereignty notes: "The most marked security phenomenon since the end of the Cold War has been the proliferation of armed conflicts within states." [30]

As one writer comments, "today's typical war is civil, started by rebels who want to change their country's constitution, alter the balance of power between races, or secede." [31] Of special consequence for international politics has been the increasing tendency over time for civil wars to become *internationalized* (to involve foreign military forces). One study found that "the percent of civil wars internationalized" rose from 18 percent in the 1919–1939 period to 27 percent in the 1946–1965 period to 36 percent in the 1966–1977 period. [32] During the cold war, much of the internationalization was driven by the East-West geopolitical competition, with the aforementioned interventions by Washington or Moscow seeking to bolster one side or the other in places such as Vietnam, Afghanistan, Ethiopia, and the Dominican Republic. The Soviet Union and proxy states often assisted in "wars of national liberation," in which revolutionary groups trying to overthrow colonial rule (for example, in Angola and Mozambique) resorted to guerrilla warfare *insurgency* tactics to overcome the stronger conventional military forces of the established authorities, which in turn were trained by the United States or its regional allies in *counterinsurgency* tactics to resist the guerrillas. As the Somalia and Kosovo cases show, internationalization of civil wars has continued into the post–cold war era.

However, there is an important difference between the pattern seen during the cold war and the pattern evidenced since. First, civil wars in the post–cold war era tend to be rooted far more in ethnic differences than ideological differences, represented by recent ethnopolitical conflicts in Rwanda (between Hutus and Tutsis), Sudan (between blacks and Arabs), and the former Yugoslavia (between Bosnians and Kosovars and their Serb rulers).[33] Second, interventionism in the post–cold war era has tended to be multilateral in character, often sponsored by regional or global organizations claiming a right of "humanitarian intervention" in chaotic, failed states to relieve mass starvation, stop atrocities, or otherwise provide humanitarian help, as in Somalia, Haiti, Sierra Leone, and Liberia.[34] Intrastate conflict particularly has the potential to become internationalized as refugees flee to neighboring countries to seek sanctuary, as foreign states send arms or supplies to favored factions, and as multilateral efforts are mounted to bring an end to the fighting. In such circumstances, the "sanctity" of borders that Robert Jackson referred to can become meaningless, and the applicable laws of war more ambiguous.

Terrorism

Although terrorism has attracted special attention of late in the United States, in the wake of the 9/11 attacks, the phenomenon has a long history in other parts of the world. The term itself can be traced back at least some 900 years to Persia where a violent group arose that gave us the word for "assassin."[35] Among scholars, lawyers, and policy makers, there is no general agreement on a clear definition of terrorism. One study notes that the term had at least 109 different definitions between 1936 and 1981, and many others have appeared since.[36] The search for an authoritative definition has been likened to "the Quest for the Holy Grail."[37] It has been said that one person's terrorist is another's freedom fighter. However, if one accepts this view, then any act of violence can be excused and legitimized, however barbarous, as long as someone invents a justification.

One simple, helpful definition considers terrorism "premeditated, politically motivated violence perpetrated against noncombatant targets by subnational groups or clandestine agents, usually intended to influence an audience."[38] This definition suggests that terrorism entails a combination of at least three elements. First, terrorism ordinarily involves the threat or use of *unconventional violence*—violence that is spectacular, violates accepted social mores, and is designed to *shock* so as to gain publicity and instill fear in the hope of extorting concessions. Terrorists generally observe no "rules" of combat whatsoever. Their tactics can include bombings, hijackings, kidnappings, assassinations, and other acts.

Second, terrorism is characterized by violence that is *politically* motivated. The political context of terrorism distinguishes it from mere criminal behavior such as armed robbery or gangland slayings, which may be every bit as spectacular but are driven primarily by nonpolitical motives. One would not ordinarily call the Mafia, for example, a terrorist organization, even though it is heavily involved in international drug trafficking and other criminal activities, at times in league with terrorist groups, prompting references to "narcoterrorism." Most terrorist groups are more clearly motivated by political goals, ranging from the creation of a national homeland to the elimination of foreign cultural influence in a region to the total political and economic transformation of society.

A third key distinguishing characteristic of terrorism, following from the first two, is the almost incidental nature of the *targets* against whom violence is committed. That is, the immediate targets of terrorism—whether persons or property, civilian or military—usually bear only an indirect relation to the larger aims impelling the terrorist but are exploited for their shock potential. Sometimes the targets are carefully chosen individuals (prominent business leaders or government officials), while on other occasions the targets are faceless, nondescript masses (ordinary men, women, and children randomly slaughtered in airports, department stores, and other public places).

There is a fourth ingredient of terrorism one might add, having to do with the nature of the *perpetrators* of such violence. It can be argued, with some qualifications, that organized terrorism tends to be the work of nonstate actors, that is, it is mainly the tactic of "outgroups"—the politically weak and frustrated (such as al Qaeda and other Islamic fundamentalists throughout the Middle East and South Asia, the Irish Republican Army in Northern Ireland, Shining Path in Peru, or Basque separatists in Spain)—who see terror as the best tool for contesting the sizable armies and police forces of the governments of nation-states. Although certain excessive forms of violence used by government authorities themselves are sometimes referred to as "state terrorism"—in particular the systematic torture and repression a government inflicts on dissidents within its own society, or assassinations and "dirty tricks" committed by secret state agencies abroad—the terrorism label normally does not apply to actions taken by official government bodies. Unlike the latter, terrorists generally do not wear uniforms, although many in the past have been at least indirectly supported and sponsored by governments.[39]

Although, based on statistics provided by the U.S. State Department, there has been a long-term decline in the number of incidents of international terrorism since 1980, there has been a rise in the number of casualties.[40] Among the most high-profile terrorist incidents recently, in addition to the 9/11 attacks, were the nerve gas attack in a crowded Tokyo subway in 1995 (when the Japanese Aum Shinrikyo cult succeeded in killing twelve persons and injuring 5,500 others); the bombing of four trains in Madrid, Spain, in 2004 that took the lives of some 200 commuters and wounded 1,400 others (thought to be the work of either Basques separatists or al Qaeda); the 2004 killing of 331 people, including 150 children, in a schoolhouse in Beslan, Russia (by militants supporting Chechnyan independence); and the murder of over fifty subway and bus passengers in the middle of London in 2005 (attributed to Islamic radicals). Modern industrial society is especially susceptible to nightmarish scenarios, given such inviting targets as not only jumbo jets but giant skyscrapers, nuclear power stations, electronic grids, and computer networks. The existence of modern communications technology en ables terrorists to receive instant publicity through the world's mass media and can contribute to an epidemic effect worldwide, in addition to enabling terrorists to coordinate their efforts across regions. What is most worrisome is the rise in the number of religious-based terrorist groups, who appear to prefer a lot of people "dead" to a lot "watching" and who might acquire access to weapons of mass destruction through smuggling of "loose nukes" from the former Soviet Union, where many nuclear facilities lack adequate security, or through other avenues.[41]

Of course, "the best way to keep weapons and weapons-material out of the hands of nongovernmental entities is to keep them out of the hands of national governments."[42] In 1998, U.S. Secretary of State Madeleine Albright, "citing the increasing threat to civil aviation posed by shoulder-fired surface-to-air missiles," issued a call for "an international agreement to place tighter controls on the export of such portable, easily concealed weapons."[43] Of even greater concern are concealed weapons in the form of bags of plutonium, vials of anthrax and Ebola virus, canisters of nerve gas, and the like. In engaging in arms control efforts covering everything from small arms and shoulder-fired surface-to-air missiles to nuclear-tipped ICBMs, the international community today is continuing a long tradition in the Westphalian state system, that is, pursuing humanity's quest to fulfill the biblical prophecy that nations "shall beat their swords into plowshares, and their spears into pruning hooks . . . and neither shall they learn war anymore" (Isaiah 2:4). The strengthening of arms control regimes is part of a larger governance project facing the contemporary international system in the military security issue-area. As "war and peace" have become "messier,"[44] international law has been somewhat in flux in regulating such matters, with some traditional rules still applying while newer ones are emerging as well. It is that subject we take up next.

War and the Evolution of International Law

Although the great body of international law consists of rules governing interaction among nations during peacetime, there also exists an important corpus of law having to do with war. Some of these rules pertain to the *commencement* of war, that is, the circumstances under which it is legal for a state to resort to the use of armed force against another state. Other rules pertain to the *conduct* of war, that is, the kinds of behavior that are permissible by governments once a war is underway, regardless of how it started (often referred to as "the laws of war"). If the former rules were fully effective, there would be little need for the latter.

Efforts to Regulate the Outbreak of War

Throughout history there have been attempts to regulate the outbreak of war, going back to the "just war" position advanced by St. Augustine in the fourth century A.D. and later Grotius in the seventeenth century; this position held that the use of violence was legitimate and perfectly legal as long as the purpose was not self-aggrandizement or petty revenge but rather correction of some major wrong-doing (and as long as the means used were proportionate to the provocation).[45] In the eighteenth and nineteenth centuries, legal efforts were devoted more to making war a more civilized affair than actually banishing or restricting its occurrence. Not until the twentieth century, with the League of Nations Covenant and the Kellogg-Briand Pact following the ravages of World War I, were efforts made to explicitly *outlaw* war.[46] The 1919 Covenant, eventually ratified by seventy-three countries (representing most of the international system at the time), contained a modest prohibition on war, stating (in Article 12) that the only obligation of states to refrain from the use of armed force was that they at least first exhaust all peaceful settlement procedures and "in no case resort to war until three months after the award by the arbitrators or the judicial decision or the report of the Council." Member states that did not observe this requirement were to be subject to collective sanctions by the League, a threat that failed to deter or punish acts of aggression in the interwar period, such as Italy's attack on Ethiopia in 1935, which was met with only half-hearted economic penalties ("a brief boycott of Italian-made shoes").[47] The 1928 Kellogg-Briand treaty, also ratified by almost every nation, was a more ambitious denunciation of war but one with even less teeth; it declared that "the settlement of all disputes . . . shall never be sought except by pacific means." World War II demonstrated the hollowness of such pious condemnations of violence.

The United Nations Charter, drafted at the San Francisco Conference in 1945, sought to specify more clearly the proscription against the use of armed force in international relations, and to provide stronger enforcement machinery should the norm be violated.[48] Chapter 1, in Article 1 (1), plainly notes that the primary purpose of the organization is "to maintain peace and security" and "to take effective collective measures" toward that end. Under Article 2 (4), all member states are obligated to "refrain . . . from the threat or use of force against the territorial integrity or political independence of any state." In other words, *any first use of armed force* by one state against another state—no matter how limited—constitutes aggression and is *illegal*.

In lieu of armed force, Chapter VI of the Charter urges "pacific settlement of disputes" through such mechanisms as mediation, arbitration, and adjudication (Article 33). Force may be used legally only under the following conditions: (1) in self-defense by an individual state or alliance of states (e.g., NATO) against the armed attack of another state; (2) in the service of the United Nations as part of a "collective security" operation or other operation approved by the UN Security Council in response to a "threat to the peace"; or (3) in the service of a regional security organization (e.g., the Arab League or Organization of American States) as long as it is approved by the UN Security Council. Chapter VII gives expression to the "collective security" concept that was inherited from the League of Nations Covenant, but contains more elaborate language and more detailed implementation procedures. Article 39 states that "the Security Council shall determine the existence of any threat to the peace, breach of the peace, or act of aggression and shall . . . decide what measures shall be taken in accordance with Articles 41 and 42." The latter articles refer to the possible use of economic and military sanctions against violators of the Charter, and are followed by further articles providing for a Military Staff Committee and other machinery.

The creation of the United Nations, particularly the Chapter VII provisions of the Charter, owed to a confluence of several factors that realists, liberals, and constructivists might all point to. Certainly, the *realpolitik* convergence of power and self-interest was at work. The main architects of the Charter were the major winners of World War II, who were led by the United States and included Britain, France, the Soviet Union, and China (the latter initially represented by the prowestern Nationalist regime in Taiwan rather than by the communist regime in Beijing). In calling for an end to war, they were reflecting their joint stake in maintaining the status quo, to be managed through a "concert of great powers" approach to world order based on the special privileges and responsibilities "the Big Five" were given on the Security Council as the self-appointed chief guardians of the peace. They alone were allocated permanent seats on the council and the power to veto any decisions of importance.

However, there was more to the United Nations than can be explained solely by realist theory. As Senator Tom Connally, a member of the American delegation to the San Francisco Conference, put it at the time in response to "little countries bellyaching" about perceived American bullying over the writing of the Charter, "We're doing all this for them. We could make an alliance with Great Britain and Russia and be done with it."[49] Disingenuous as Connally's words sounded, they represented a genuine shift in the American worldview. Whereas after World War I the United States Senate had failed to ratify the League of Nations Covenant despite President Woodrow Wilson's strong backing, rejecting American membership in the world's first comprehensive global organization because it "feared a diminution of U.S. sovereignty,"[50] after World War II Washington opted for at least some degree of "pooling of sovereignty" out of mutual interests with other capitals in avoiding World War III. It would have been simpler to rely entirely on traditional alliances than to invest the diplomatic and financial effort needed to create another global organization, but it was deemed important to clothe American power and interests in the kind of legitimacy that the United Nations could provide, even if some restrictions on American freedom of action might result.

John Ruggie has argued that the establishment of global organizations such as the League and the United Nations in the twentieth century had less to do with "instrumental rationality" than ideational factors relating to American idealist impulses. Ruggie comments that "while numerous descriptions of this 'move to institutions' exist, I know of no good explanation . . . of why states should have wanted to complicate their lives in this manner." He believes it was not "American *hegemony*" that led to the creation of the United Nations, but "*American* hegemony," that is, a distinctive American mindset not historically associated with great powers.[51] It also may be the case, as Inis Claude has said, that the "idea" and "habit" of international organization had "taken hold" in the international community as a whole.[52]

States do not have to join the United Nations. In their sovereign capacity, they can opt to remain outside the organization. Switzerland, for example, refused to join until 2002. However, once a state joins—by ratifying the UN Charter, a treaty—it is then expected to meet its obligations, in keeping with the *pacta sunt servanda* rule.

Unfortunately, the UN Charter frequently has been violated, particularly the provisions having to do with collective security. Collective security hypothetically obligates the entire UN membership, which by 2005 had come to total 191 states, to coalesce in a grand coalition against any aggressor state should the UN Security Council authorize action under Chapter VII; few decisions taken by UN organs are binding on the entire membership, and thereby contravene the sovereignty principle, but Chapter VII decisions are in that category. From the start, collective security suffered from the questionable assumptions that

(1) peace would be considered indivisible

(2) it would be easy to define aggression and assign culpability

(3) alignments would remain sufficiently flexible and alliance commitments unencumbered to permit the mobilization of grand coalitions against aggressors

(4) a grand coalition could be formed that would invariably be superior to any aggressors' forces, thus successfully deterring the illegal use of force or punishing it when it occurs.

Not only did the cold war shatter any chance of Big Five unity in support of collective security, but the Big Five veto privilege invited resentment and charges of double standards; since the veto power meant that Chapter VII could never be invoked against any of the permanent members of the Security Council, the other countries were left to wonder who would police the policemen.[53]

Between 1945 and 1990, in only a handful of cases did the promise of collective security come close to being fulfilled, most notably in the Korean War in 1950 (when the United Nations responded to North Korea's aggression against South Korea) and the Gulf War in 1990 (when the United Nations responded to Iraq's aggression against Kuwait). Those cases were unusual, however—made possible in the first instance by the Soviet Union's absence from council proceedings (due to Moscow's protesting the seating of the Nationalist Chinese in place of the Communist Chinese, rendering it unable to veto a resolution calling for UN action) and in the second instance by Iraq's extraordinarily brazen, unprecedented attempt to eliminate another UN member, coupled with the momentary unity of the Big Five in the immediate post–cold war era (with China agreeing to abstain rather than veto UN authorization of force). Even these two cases did not constitute collective security in the full sense. In the Korean case, the council (through Resolutions 83 and 84) technically only recommended that members provide military or other assistance to a unified command, which was permitted to use the UN flag and whose commander was to be selected by the United States. In the Kuwait case, the council (through Resolution 678) merely authorized member states to "use all necessary means" to "restore international peace and security in the area," essentially contracting out to the United States and any other willing partners the job of repelling Iraqi aggression, and leaving vague how much coordination was to occur through the United Nations itself. In addition to these two cases, mandatory economic sanctions were authorized under Chapter VII on two occasions during the cold war—against Rhodesia in 1966 and against South Africa in 1977, both involving white minority regimes thought to pose a "threat to the peace."

It was precisely the failure of Chapter VII that resulted in the increasing use of a creative alternative that came to be known as "peacekeeping." Peacekeeping (which is not mentioned in the Charter and is sometimes referred to as Chapter VI½) was first used in 1956, when 6,000 blue-helmeted UN troops (UNEF) were sent to the Middle East during the crisis that ensued over control of the Suez Canal, serving as a buffer force to maintain a ceasefire between the Egyptian and Israeli armies.[54] The peacekeeping role differed from collective security in that UN contingents were dispatched to provide a neutral military presence rather than punish an aggressor, they could not operate without the consent of the warring parties, and they could be ordered out at any time the host countries desired (as happened when Egypt ordered UNEF's withdrawal in 1967, leading to renewal of hostilities with Israel in the Six-Day War, followed later by the Yom Kippur War of 1973). A total of thirteen peacekeeping operations were authorized by the Security Council prior to 1988, including major deployments in Kashmir on the India-Pakistan border, in the Golan Heights between Israel and Syria, and in Lebanon, Cyprus, and the Congo.[55] However, by the 1980s, even peacekeeping had fallen into disuse and the organization was being written off by some as moribund.[56]

With the winding down of the cold war in the late eighties, there was suddenly a renewed burst of UN energy in the peace and security field. More peacekeeping missions were authorized between 1988 and 1992 than in the entire previous history of the organization, with the UN *inter alia* called upon to oversee the withdrawal of Soviet troops from Afghanistan and the removal of Cuban and South African troops from Angola and Namibia, to arrange an armistice between Iran and Iraq in their decade-long war, to provide observers to monitor elections ending the Nicaraguan civil war, and to rebuild Cambodia (Kampuchea) following the end of Vietnamese occupation (repairing bridges and other infrastructure, demining the countryside, repatriating refugees, and facilitating free elections), as well as put out fires in other hotspots.[57] As the post–cold war period wore on, "peacekeeping" took on a more expansive meaning, becoming almost indistinguishable from "peacemaking," "peacebuilding," "peace enforcement," and other functions, few of which had any explicit legal basis in the UN Charter.[58] ("Peace enforcement" was labeled by some as Chapter VI¾, since it referred to the use of armed force by UN military personnel who, as in Somalia, may have arrived on the scene as neutral peacekeepers but, having been fired upon by governmental or rebel groups and prevented from carrying out their mission, were then cast in what amounted to a collective security role of punishing violators of the UN Charter.)

In the post–cold war period, "Chapter VII has been invoked on many occasions to authorize the use of force or various types of sanctions. In Bosnia, Haiti, Northern Iraq, East Timor, and Sierra Leone, the Security Council authorized the use of force either by a regional organization such as NATO (Bosnia) or by a 'coalition of the willing' led by a country willing to commit military forces to the effort such as the United States (Haiti), Australia (East Timor), France (Rwanda), and Great Britain (Sierra Leone)."[59] Chapter VII sanctions also have included import-export restrictions (for example, a ban on trade in "conflict" diamonds from Liberia, whose civil war was fueled by weaponry purchased through revenue from diamond sales), restrictions on air travel of government officials (for example, in the case of Libya, over its sponsorship of terrorism), and other measures designed to change state behavior deemed undesirable by the international community.[60]

What does one make of all this—of the UN Charter's impact on states in restraining their use of armed force in international relations? The United Nations has compiled a mixed record, scoring successes in some cases (such as Namibia and East Timor) but failing more often than not.[61] Looking beyond the United Nations' contribution to peace in specific cases, and evaluating overall compliance with the Charter, the picture is more complicated. Michael Glennon has argued that state practice—in effect, customary law—has superceded the UN Charter, that states may mouth support for Article 2 (4) but in fact regularly ignore it in their actual behavior, and that the proscription against the first use of armed force has "collapsed" as "the rules of the Charter do not today constitute binding restraints on intervention by states."[62] A contrary view has been voiced by Louis Henkin. Henkin, echoing Mark Zacher's views about the "territorial integrity" norm, contends that, even though the resort to armed force continues to be a feature of contemporary world politics, "the norm against the unilateral national use of force has survived. Indeed . . . the norm has been largely observed . . . and the kinds of international wars which it sought to prevent and deter [wars between states] have been infrequent."[63]

However—and this is the rub—the norm against unilateral force has been less effective in the grayish areas discussed earlier in this chapter, such as "force without war," and is especially problematical in dealing with the most common forms of planetary violence today, namely intrastate and extrastate hostilities. As Joseph Nye comments, "the doctrine of collective security enshrined in the UN Charter is state-centric, applicable when borders are crossed but not when force is used against peoples within a state."[64] Anthony Clark Arend and Robert Beck, among others, have examined "the challenges to the Charter paradigm" and have called for a "post-Charter paradigm."[65]

What rules apply to civil wars? The rules governing the outbreak of hostilities have been inadequate to cope with internal wars and mixed internal/external conflicts (internal wars involving outside intervention).[66] During the cold war, to the extent that the United Nations became involved in such conflicts, the organization usually relied on the vague "threat to the peace" reference in Article 39 as legal justification for taking action. It was always hard, and still is difficult, to sort out the obligations that international actors have in situations of civil strife, partly because much international law in this area is based on customary rules open to varying interpretations and partly because of the inherent complexities of these situations.[67] In these conflicts, it is often the case that, rather than one state engaging in an armed attack on another state, there is a government seeking foreign support to quell a rebellion or a rebel group seeking foreign support to overthrow a government. The rules governing the right of a state to intervene militarily in an internal conflict in another state are fairly straightforward: the former can intervene as long as it has the permission of the latter's government, but otherwise cannot. The intrusion of foreign troops or clandestine agents into a domestic conflict on the side of the rebels to subvert an established government constitutes aggression and is a violation of the UN Charter. However, neither can foreign military assistance be provided to a government on the brink of collapse, since a government has a legal right to invite such assistance only if it can claim to exercise effective control and authority over its own population. The problem, of course, is this is the very condition that is often in dispute during a civil war. The rules failed to regulate the insurgency/counter-insurgency dance played by the United States and the Soviet Union during the cold war. They continue to be plagued by difficulties in the post–cold war period.[68]

What rules apply to humanitarian intervention and regime change? It has been noted that foreign involvement in civil wars in the post–cold war era frequently has taken the form of "humanitarian intervention." The so-called Clinton Doctrine stated that "if somebody comes after innocent civilians and tries to kill them *en masse* because of their race, ethnic background, or religion, and it's within our power to stop it, we will stop it."[69] UN Secretary General Kofi Annan seemed to endorse this same principle when he said that the protection of human rights must "take precedence over concerns of state sovereignty," that sovereignty cannot provide "excuses for the inexcusable," and that the UN Charter "was issued in the name of 'the peoples,' not the governments, of the United Nations."[70] The traditionalist view is that international law grants "no general right unilaterally to charge into another country to save its people from their own leaders."[71] But what about *multilateral intervention,* that is, an action taken by the international community at large, triggered by either ethnic cleansing or other atrocities committed by a dictatorial regime (as in the case of the 1992 UN-authorized intervention to protect Bosnians in the former Yugoslavia) or the collapse of civil order and the spread of starvation and suffering in failed states (as in the case of the UN-authorized intervention in Somalia that same year)? If the international community waits for an invitation before acting in these situations, a humanitarian response may be impossible, because no repressive regime would welcome external oversight in the first case, and there would be no functioning regime able to issue the invitation in the second case. There is a widely held view that "humanitarian military intervention now must be multilateral to be legitimate,"[72] yet international law is not entirely clear on this point. As William Slomanson observes, "The permissible contours of humanitarian intervention have not been defined in a way that represents a meaningful State consensus. An essential reason is that . . . neither word has been precisely defined."[73]

One author remarks that "the UN can help states to pool the costs and risks of humanitarian intervention and can provide a forum through which international suffering is made more salient."[74] However, realists and other critics have raised concerns that humanitarian intervention threatens Westphalian ordering arrangements and is at odds with the UN Charter, insofar as it contradicts Article 2 (7), which stipulates that "nothing contained in the Charter shall authorize the United Nations to intervene in matters which are essentially within the domestic jurisdiction of any state." Although Article 2 (7) adds that "this principle shall not prejudice the application of enforcement measures under Chapter VII," many UN members have expressed fears that such language—which was relied on to establish the ad hoc international criminal tribunals used to try the leaders of the former Yugoslavia and Rwanda—is an invitation for Security Council members to interfere in the domestic affairs of smaller, weaker states.[75] Of greatest concern is a state or group of states using the "humanitarian intervention" norm as a pretext to bring about regime change without any UN approval, as happened with the NATO bombing of Kosovo in 1999 that ended the reign of Slobodan Milosevic.[76] The 114 members of the Non-Aligned Movement, representing the developing nations, have condemned such intervention, declaring it has "no legal basis under the Charter."[77] The theory and practice of humanitarian intervention remain mired in controversy.[78]

What rules apply to "self-defense" against states and nonstate actors? The two cases cited at the outset of the chapter—the 2001 U.S. attack on Afghanistan and the 2003 U.S. attack on Iraq—also involved regime change, with Washington paying lip service to "humanitarian intervention" as one justification for the use of armed force in both instances, but the main legal rationale related more to "collective security" and, even more so, "self-defense." Washington found it easier to claim international law was on its side in the Afghanistan War than the Iraq War, although both presented a thicket of legal questions.

Regarding Afghanistan, the United States clearly was attacked on September 11, 2001, when airplanes struck the World Trade Center and the Pentagon. However, the attack was perpetrated not by another state but by a nonstate actor, al Qaeda. What rules of international law apply here? Although not binding, UN General Assembly resolutions can be taken as evidence of customary law. Relevant, then, is the fact that, in 1985, for the first time, the United Nations formally went on record as condemning terrorism; the UN General Assembly unanimously approved Resolution 40/61, which unequivocally "condemns, as criminal, all acts . . . of terrorism wherever and by whoever committed" and "calls upon states to fulfill their obligations under international law to refrain from organizing, instigating, assisting, or participating in terrorist acts in other States, or acquiescing in activities within their territory directed toward the commission of such acts." As with human rights, there is no general convention on terrorism. Instead, there are several conventions focusing on various aspects of terrorism, including three aviation-related treaties that obligate signatories to effect the safe release of skyjacked passengers and to prosecute or extradite skyjackers or aircraft saboteurs in their custody (the 1963 Tokyo Convention, the 1970 Hague Convention, and the 1971 Montreal Convention). Although the development of these norms and treaties contributed to a substantial decline in skyjackings over time,[79] they did not eliminate the phenomenon completely, as seen on 9/11.

None of the above addressed the following question: To what extent can State A (say, the United States) enter the territory of State B (say, Afghanistan) to apprehend or kill actors (such as Osama bin Laden and his associates) thought to have been responsible for a terrorist attack on State A? International law does not condone a state trespassing into another state to abduct alleged criminals or terrorists; states are supposed to rely on bilateral extradition treaties as a basis for requesting the arrest and transfer of wanted fugitives. When, in 1960, Israeli commandos captured former Nazi officer and Holocaust executioner Adolph Eichmann in Argentina and returned him to Israel to stand trial for crimes against humanity, Israel later acknowledged that it had acted illegally in trespassing onto Argentine territory, and offered an apology (*Attorney-General of Israel v. Eichmann*); similar abductions have occurred elsewhere and generally have been considered violations of international law.[80] Since the mid-1960s, Israel periodically has launched military raids into Lebanon and other neighboring Arab countries to strike at alleged "terrorist" bases following attacks by PLO and other groups on Israeli settlements; these actions, though targeted at terrorist operations and not at the states themselves, have been criticized by many UN members as acts of aggression rather than legal acts of self-defense, since—aside from the fact that many members have viewed the Palestinians as freedom fighters—in the eyes of the international community Israel has failed to establish a clear link between the militants and the host government. (Israeli incursions into Arab states to apprehend or punish terrorists are to be distinguished from the Israeli-Arab interstate wars fought in 1956, 1967, and 1973, since they pose different legal issues from traditional aggression by one state against another). Although state practice has been inconsistent, the general rule is that, if State B is not clearly sponsoring or harboring the terrorists but merely finds itself used as a refuge, State A cannot intrude upon the latter's sovereignty by engaging in military activity on its soil without its permission. On the other hand, if State B can be shown to be an active sponsor or close collaborator giving succor to the terrorists, and has not taken adequate steps to prevent terrorism, then State A is on stronger legal footing in taking military action.[81]

In bombing Afghanistan and removing the Taliban government that had refused to surrender bin Laden, the United States invoked the customary right of self-defense codified in Article 51 of the Charter, and was backed by UN Security Council resolutions that not only affirmed that right but, under Chapter VII, went even further in calling for a strengthened global anti-terrorism regime to facilitate a "war on terror" worldwide.[82] It helped the American legal cause that citizens of several dozen states had been victims of the 9/11 attacks, that only three UN members had ever recognized the Taliban government as the legitimate leadership of Afghanistan (the United Arab Emirates, Pakistan, and Saudi Arabia, all friendly to the United States), and that few UN members were willing to incur the wrath of the United States by contesting the legitimacy of its actions under the circumstances.

In the case of the American invasion of Iraq in 2003, Secretary General Annan said it was illegal since the United States could not invoke the right of "self-defense" (the United States had not been attacked by Iraq) and could not invoke the "collective security" chapter of the UN Charter (Washington had never received specific authorization from the Security Council to mete out military sanctions against Saddam Hussein's government despite Saddam's repeated violation of Security Council resolutions, due to opposition to war on the part of France, Russia, and China).[83]

The most interesting legal argument advanced by Washington was the right of *anticipatory* or *preemptive* self-defense. Seemingly in violation of the UN Charter's ban on the first use of armed force, such a justification had been relied on by Israel in 1967 when its troops crossed the border and attacked Egyptian forces thought to be massing for an impending invasion of Israel, and in 1981, when its planes destroyed an Iraqi nuclear reactor thought to be a threat to Israeli security. There is a long "just war" tradition that provides some support for this position,[84] although the onus is put on the attacker to demonstrate that the resort to force is necessary. As Hugo Grotius put it, "Fear with respect to a neighboring power is not a sufficient cause. For . . . self-defense to be lawful it must be necessary; and it is not necessary unless we are certain, not only regarding the power of our neighbor, but also regarding his intention."[85] To the extent there exists a customary right of anticipatory self-defense, the *Caroline Case* is often cited as providing the standard definition. In 1837, the *Caroline,* a ship owned by U.S. nationals and docked on the American side of the Niagara River, was attacked by the British navy and sent over Niagara Falls because the British feared that the vessel would be used to support an insurrection by Canadian rebels; U.S. Secretary of State Daniel Webster, in protesting the action, stated that, for such action to be legal, it would have to be demonstrated that "the necessity of that self-defense is instant, overwhelming, and leaving no choice of means, and no moment of deliberation."[86]

In justifying its invasion of Iraq, the Bush administration claimed that there was reason to believe that Saddam had weapons of mass destruction (based on his use of chemical weapons in the 1980s against Iran and the Kurds), that he was a serial aggressor as well as a state sponsor of terror, and that he posed a threat to U.S. security which could not be ignored in the post–9/11 era. Bush went so far as to enunciate the so-called Bush Doctrine, which gave the United States the right to engage in the preemptive use of armed force against any country thought to *possibly* pose a threat to U.S. security.[87] However, critics of the American attack argued that it did not meet the *Caroline* test, that it appeared to represent a "preventive war" rather than a "preemptive war," that is, a war Washington wanted to fight rather than one it needed to fight. They pointed out that no attack by Iraq was imminent, there was no clear evidence it still possessed WMDs, and there was no clear connection between Iraq and the 9/11 terrorists. Moreover, critics worried that the Bush Doctrine was a dangerous deviation from the UN Charter that could invite and legitimize all kinds of first strikes, including, hypothetically, an attack by Pakistan against nuclear-armed India, or India against nuclear-armed Pakistan.

On the one hand, it perhaps was reasonable for the Bush administration to take the position that, after 9/11, the United States could not afford to be a "sitting duck" waiting for a state or nonstate actor to initiate a WMD attack on New York City or another American target before retaliating. Yet, on the other hand, the relatively loose definition of "self-defense" implied in the Bush Doctrine threatened to unravel the entire Charter regime that had been developed to control the outbreak of war. In 2004, the UN Secretary General's High-Level Panel on Threats, Challenges and Change attempted to address the problem by calling for legalizing the use of armed force in a "preventive" manner to eliminate the potential for horrific terrorist attacks as long as such use of force against terrorist sanctuaries is authorized by the UN Security Council.

The "war on terror" itself had no apparent ending in sight, seeming to become a permanent part of the human condition. Also unclear was the question of which "laws of war" should apply in conducting the war, in terms of the scope of the battlefield, the treatment of captured prisoners, and other issues. The *Caroline* case had suggested standards governing not only the "necessity" to use force but also the "proportionality" of force, recognizing the long-standing "just war" prescription that, no matter how a war begins, there is an obligation to refrain from using force in a manner that is excessive or inhumane. The changing nature of global violence today is making the rules governing the *conduct* of war no less of a legal minefield than those governing the onset of war.

Efforts to Regulate the Conduct of War

Over the centuries, humanity, failing to ban war altogether, has attempted to make it at least more "humane" by regulating its conduct through agreed upon rules of engagement. Some of the efforts to inject a dose of civility into warfare have seemed paradoxical and almost comical, such as the prohibition (embodied in the Hague Convention of 1907) against the use of "dum-dum" expanding bullets and the use of "deceit" in the form of misrepresenting a flag of truce or wearing Red Cross uniforms as a disguise—especially at a time when poisonous gas and other atrocities were legally permissible. However, absurd as they might appear and as erratic as their observance has been, the laws governing the conduct of war have often succeeded in limiting the savage nature of war to some extent.[88]

One of the main traits that distinguishes nation-state armies from terrorist cells is that the former are held to a higher standard of conduct based on customary and treaty law dating back at least to the mid-nineteenth century. The first major multilateral instrument that attempted to regulate modern warfare was the Declaration of Paris in 1856, which placed restrictions on sea warfare, prohibiting privateering, circumscribing contraband goods subject to seizure, and delimiting the conditions for implementing naval blockades against enemy coastlines. Other treaties followed that reflected (1) the mutual interests states shared in managing hostilities; (2) the agendas of various national leaders concerned about other states gaining military advantage through newly emerging weapons technology; and (3) new norms and sensibilities. Important milestones included the Geneva Convention of 1864 (revised in 1906) that codified rules for treatment of the wounded in the field, the Hague Conventions of 1899 and 1907 that codified acceptable practices of land warfare and specified the rights and duties of belligerents and neutrals, and the Geneva Conventions of 1929 and 1949 that developed guidelines for humane treatment of prisoners of war (POWs). The four 1949 Geneva Conventions restated the POW rules (for example, limiting the amount of information that could be coercively extracted from prisoners) and added new rules for protecting civilians from indiscriminate violence, after World War II saw widespread abuses of captured soldiers as well as widespread killing of innocent civilians through strategic bombing of population centers. The Geneva Conventions were supplemented in 1977 by Protocol I on "The Protection of Victims of International Armed Conflict" and Protocol II on "Protection of Victims of Non-International Conflicts." The 1949 Geneva Conventions have been universally accepted, with 192 states having ratified them, while the two Protocols each have over 150 parties.

As military technology and strategy has evolved—with ever more lethal weaponry and with whole societies and economies involved in war efforts and considered legitimate targets—it has became harder to maintain the distinction between combatants and noncombatants. In World War I, which witnessed indiscriminate sinking of ships by submarines, almost as many civilians were killed as soldiers. In World War II, which witnessed aerial bombardment of German and Japanese cities, more civilians died than soldiers. I noted earlier how contemporary warfare, as seen in Kosovo and Iraq, increasingly produces pressures for countries such as the United States to avoid ground combat operations that could result in heavy military casualties and to rely instead on "shock and awe" air campaigns which, however surgically aimed at targets of "military necessity," inevitably result in substantial collateral damage of civilian areas. Intrastate and extrastate conflicts exacerbate these problems, since rival factions in civil wars often sack towns and villages, brutalizing the sympathizers of each side, and since terrorists tend to designate randomly selected noncombatants as their prime targets.

What rules apply to the protection of civilians and POWs in warfare? Intrastate and extrastate conflicts pose special problems today for implementation of POW conventions and other rules governing treatment of combatants. In guerrilla warfare, armies do not normally confront each other across well-defined fronts, and soldiers do not even always wear uniforms. Not only are customary distinctions between civilians and combatants blurred, but so, too, distinctions between soldiers and common criminals. A national government experiencing rebellion is understandably reluctant to extend to rebels the same status normally reserved for enemy soldiers, preferring to dismiss them as "rioters" or "thugs" rather than legitimizing them as "freedom fighters." There is even greater reluctance to accord POW status to terrorists, who observe no Geneva Convention rules regarding the wearing of proper insignia, or functioning through a regular chain of command, or honoring humanitarian law in their use of force. The United States, upon capturing al Qaeda and Taliban fighters in Afghanistan after 9/11, branded most of the prisoners as "enemy combatants" not entitled to POW protection, jailed them at the U.S. naval base at Guantanamo Bay, Cuba, and in some cases subjected them to tough interrogation methods that included torture. Human rights watchers were critical of American behavior, not only at Guantanamo but also at the Abu Ghraib prison in Iraq, where American military personnel abused and humiliated Iraqi prisoners captured in the 2003 Iraq War.[89]

As questionable as American behavior was in what was called the second Gulf War, it paled by comparison with Iraq's behavior during the first Gulf War in 1990–1991. As David Scheffer comments, "the Gulf War was the most significant test of the laws of war since World War II. . . . The record of Iraqi compliance with the laws of war . . . was dismal. Examples of Iraq's conduct include the following: the detention of foreign hostages in Iraq as 'human shields' . . . the placement of military targets within civilian areas . . . the torture of Kuwaiti citizens . . . [and] the mistreatment of prisoners of war from the coalition forces, including televised interrogations."[90] All of these were violations of the 1949 Geneva Conventions. In addition, Iraqi armies burned 700 oil wells in Kuwait, causing massive atmospheric pollution, in violation of the 1977 Protocol I's proscription against employing "means of warfare which may be expected to cause widespread, long-term and severe damage to the natural environment."[91]

As with other bodies of international law, the laws of war suffer from lapses in compliance, and at times gross violations, that might lead one to dismiss the rules as irrelevant. However, the Geneva Conventions and other rules at least provide a baseline of expectations against which state behavior can be measured. Moreover, it is probably the case that most states observe most rules during warfare and, at the very least, are sensitive to being accused of committing war crimes. For example, even in the case of the American "shock and awe" air campaign over Iraq in 2003, the *New York Times* reported that the American commanders took "extraordinary steps to limit collateral damage. The Army's Third Infantry Division [had] a team of lawyers to advise on whether targets are legitimate under international conventions—and a vast database of some 10,000 targets to be avoided, such as hospitals, mosques, and cultural or archaeological treasures."[92]

What weapons may be used in warfare, and how have armaments been controlled? A more salient example of the impact of the laws of war is the fact that chemical weapons (mustard gas, hydrogen cyanide, and other agents) were used extensively during World War I, causing horrible effects, but—after the signing of the 1925 Geneva Protocol that banned the first use of lethal chemical weapons—were not employed at all during World War II. Whether due to new norms or the mutual fears associated with unpredictable chemical arsenals, or both, the ban has held (other than Saddam's usage in the 1980s).[93]

The 1925 Geneva Protocol is just one of numerous international regimes that impose restrictions on the testing, production, stockpiling, transfer, deployment, and use of various kinds of weapons, including both conventional weapons and weapons of mass destruction. Arms control has a long lineage—the first known international agreement to limit chemical weapons dates back to 1675, shortly after the Peace of Westphalia, when the French and Germans signed a pact in Strassenbourg not to use poison bullets in warfare; and long before that, in 1139, the Lateran Council attempted to outlaw the use of crossbows between Christian armies. Arms control regimes have proliferated since World War II, with negotiations occurring in a variety of settings, including the Geneva-based Conference on Disarmament and special sessions of the UN General Assembly. These regimes represent progress but are imperfect, with several states refusing to ratify treaties, compliance spotty even among the legally-bound parties in some cases, and many issues not covered by any agreements.

For instance, one can point to the 1980 Convention on Prohibitions or Restrictions on the Use of Certain Conventional Weapons Which May Be Deemed to Be Excessively Injurious and to Have Indiscriminate Effects, which placed limits on the use of napalm, booby traps, and other devices. Only 100 countries had ratified the treaty as of 2005. The 1998 Anti-Personnel Landmine Treaty (Ottawa Treaty) specifically sought to outlaw the use of landmines in warfare. At the time the treaty was opened for signature, it was estimated that in over 60 countries there were some 100 million landmines buried in the ground, left over from various conflicts. Landmines tend to claim innocent civilians, often children, as their main victims as the latter accidentally trigger the devices. They have been called the "Saturday night special of civil wars," and Cambodia (Kampuchea)—one of the most landmine-littered landscapes in the world—has been called a "nation of amputees" as a result of its brutal internal conflict during the 1970s and 1980s.[94] As of 2005, 143 states had ratified the Ottawa Treaty, with the United States, Russia, and China among the more conspicuous absentees (Washington claiming it needed to continue to rely on mines to prevent a potential attack by waves of North Korean soldiers against South Korea). The United States does participate in the 33-member Wassenaar Arrangement, aimed at controlling illicit trafficking in small arms and other conventional weaponry.

What about "big" arms, particularly WMDs? The aforementioned Geneva Protocol of 1925 banned the first use of chemical weapons by any state, but was interpreted to permit the production, stockpiling, and use of chemical weapons in retaliation for another state's prior use. In an effort to outlaw chemical weapons altogether, the 1993 Chemical Weapons Convention (CWC) obligated all states party to the treaty "never under any circumstances to develop, produce, otherwise acquire, stockpile or retain chemical weapons, or transfer, directly or indirectly, chemical weapons to anyone" or "to use chemical weapons." Any parties that already had chemical weapons were obligated to destroy those arsenals within ten years following the treaty entering into force. A verification system was established in the form of a new IGO headquartered in The Hague, called the Organization for the Prohibition of Chemical Weapons (OPCW), which, upon the "challenge" of any member state, was allowed to do on-site inspection in any state suspected of violating the treaty. The treaty took effect in April 1997, six months after the sixty-fifth ratification, and by 2005 had over 160 parties. The CWC is considered a landmark agreement since it is "the first comprehensively verifiable multilateral treaty that completely bans an entire class of weapons, and firmly limits activities that may contribute to the production of those weapons."[95]

However, there are problems surrounding the CWC. Three-fourths of the two dozen states thought to have chemical weapons capabilities have joined the treaty, led by the two with the largest arsenals, the United States and Russia (the former having 30,000 metric tons and the latter 40,000 metric tons). Although both have acknowledged the existence of these stockpiles and have committed themselves to destroying these by the end of the current decade, environmental and financial problems have hampered the dismantling efforts.[96] Moreover, in addition to those countries thought to possess chemical weapons that have not yet ratified the CWC, such as Egypt, Syria, Israel, and North Korea, there are some parties to the treaty that are assumed to be in possession of chemical weapons which have not formally "declared" them, such as China and Iran.[97] Given the ease with which one can conceal chemical weapons—it is easy to make and store these in a basement or garage, or to hide them in "dual-use" facilities such as paint factories—concerns have been raised about the "transparency" of the verification regime and whether cheating can be detected.

Similar problems have plagued the 1972 Biological Weapons Convention. Now ratified by over 150 states, including the United States and Russia, the treaty prohibits any development, production, and stockpiling of toxins and other bacteriological weapons for use in germ warfare. The United States and Russia claim to have terminated their biological weapons programs in the 1970s, although there is still some question whether they and a few other states (the same ones suspected of developing chemical weapons) continue to possess some stockpiles.[98] A major weakness of the treaty is the absence of any verification procedures, so that it is exceedingly difficult to judge how much compliance has actually occurred. An effort in 2001 to produce a Biological Weapons Protocol that would have created a counterpart to the OPCW failed, largely due to U.S. lack of trust in the detection apparatus. Nonetheless, the regime can be considered a success in that states have refrained from using biological weapons against other states.[99]

The photo shows the second atomic bomb test at Bikini Atoll in the Pacific, July 24, 1946. The birth of the atomic age led to the Nuclear Non-Proliferation Treaty, which attempted to limit the members of the "nuclear club" and which is now on the brink of collapse in the wake of recent suspected violations by North Korea and Iran.

The centerpiece of the nuclear arms control regime is the 1968 Nuclear Non-Proliferation Treaty (NPT). The treaty has been endorsed by almost the entire UN membership, the only remaining holdouts being India, Pakistan, and Israel. The NPT has been one of the most remarkably successful arms control treaties in history, insofar as much of the international system has defied "realist" expectations in agreeing to deny themselves the ultimate badge of national power and prestige. The NPT obligates states that do not have nuclear weapons to refrain from developing them, and obligates existing nuclear weapons states to refrain from transferring such weaponry to the nuclear have-nots. A tremendous accomplishment was the agreement, in 1995 (as the NPT was about to expire), to renew the NPT in perpetuity. The nuclear powers had to overcome objections by many states that contended that the United States and other members of the nuclear club had not done enough to build down their own nuclear arsenals and to adopt a comprehensive ban on any future nuclear testing.[100]

Seven countries currently are official members of the "nuclear club," whose membership includes only those states which have openly detonated a nuclear explosive. The club includes the United States, Russia, Britain, France, and China (all of which were nuclear "haves" by 1968), along with India and Pakistan (NPT non-signatories which officially joined the club in 1998). Israel (the only other non-signatory) is presumed to have nuclear capabilities. Brazil, Argentina, and South Africa had active programs in the 1980s, but have since renounced any intention to build nuclear weapons, as have states such as Japan and Germany, which clearly have the technological base and resources to go nuclear if they chose to but have thus far "abstained." Three former Soviet republics—Belarus, Ukraine, and Kazakhstan—have transferred leftover nuclear weapons on their soil to Russia.[101] Total stockpiles are down from the almost 50,000 nuclear weapons that existed during the cold war, thanks to deep cuts in superpower arsenals negotiated by the United States and Russia. However, the world still has over 28,000 nuclear warheads, containing the explosive power of roughly 200,000 Hiroshima bombs, with the United States and Russia accounting for over 90 percent of the total.[102] Further progress depends not only on actions taken by Washington and Moscow but decisions taken in other national capitals. In question is whether the existing nuclear nonproliferation regime is still effective in constraining state behavior or whether the entire edifice is at risk of collapsing.

In particular, alarm bells have been sounded recently over the fact that two parties to the NPT, North Korea and Iran—in violation of their treaty commitments—took steps in the 1990s to establish active nuclear weapons programs and may be close to developing at least a limited capability. Under the NPT, states are permitted to pursue peaceful nuclear energy programs, including engaging in either uranium enrichment or plutonium production from reprocessing spent fuel (both potential bomb-making materials), as long as they report their activities and submit to inspections by the International Atomic Energy Agency, the UN agency charged with monitoring NPT compliance. In 1993, North Korea was found to be in breach of its obligations, due to its engaging in reprocessing without notifying the IAEA. When it tried to take advantage of a NPT loophole to withdraw from the treaty, Pyongyang was persuaded to remain in the NPT and was promised economic inducements to end its weapons program, although there is no evidence it has terminated its nuclear aspirations. The fact that North Korea was promised economic benefits for its NPT violation, rather than being subjected to economic or other sanctions, seemed to send a signal to other states, such as Iran, that "crime pays." By 2000, Iran was also suspected of violating its NPT obligations under the guise of "peaceful nuclear energy" development, with the international community equally ambivalent over how to deal with the threat and the future of arms control uncertain.

Interestingly, unlike in the case of chemical and biological weapons, there is no explicit rule of international law banning the first use of nuclear weapons in warfare. If one country were to initiate a conventional, non-nuclear attack against another country, the right of self-defense the UN Charter permits the second country includes the right to retaliate with nuclear strikes if the latter is one of the nuclear "haves." At least that is the position the United States took throughout the cold war, when Washington was concerned that, without the threatened nuclear deterrent, the Soviet Union might be tempted to take advantage of its superiority in tanks and conventional forces in Eastern Europe to invade Western Europe. A 1961 UN General Assembly resolution outlawing the use of nuclear weapons had no legal effect. In 1994, the UN General Assembly voted to ask the World Court in The Hague for an advisory opinion on the question: "Is the threat or use of nuclear weapons in any circumstances permitted under international law?" The General Assembly request followed a similar request made earlier by the World Health Organization, which was concerned about the health and environmental effects of using such weapons. The World Court ended up equivocating on this issue, although many commentators have argued that nuclear weapons are covered under the body of customary and treaty law prohibiting the use of weapons that inflict indiscriminate violence on civilians (*Legality of the Threat or Use of Nuclear Weapons*).[103]

Conclusion

If one looks at the global policy process—from agenda-setting to implementation—that has produced international regimes in the security issue-area, one can plainly see state-centric, "billiard ball" politics at work, with national governments, especially those presiding over the most powerful nations, taking the lead role in pushing for regimes that serve their national interests. Suffice it to say the main reason Washington and Moscow worked together to promote the NPT was their mutual interests in legalizing their virtual monopoly possession of nuclear weapons; similarly, it was in their interests to promote the biological and chemical weapons conventions, since "the poor person's nuclear bomb" was superfluous to the nuclear-armed states yet potentially menacing in the hands of others. Still, the behavior of other states—the acts of self-abnegation that a majority of countries in the international system have undertaken in foregoing ABC weapons—perhaps speaks to other, more idealistic impulses at work in world politics.

It should be noted that some "cobweb" elements can be discerned as well in the development and operation of security regimes. Aside from the important role played by the United Nations and other IGOs as forums for regime negotiation and instruments of regime implementation, such as the involvement of the International Civil Aviation Organization in formulating and administering the anti-skyjacking conventions, other kinds of nonstate actors have contributed to the growth of international law in the war-peace area. To cite just two examples: The International Campaign to Ban Landmines, a coalition of over 1,400 NGOs in ninety countries, is widely credited with using the Internet and the mass media to put the landmine issue on the global agenda and, along with Canada and other like-minded countries, persuading national governments to sign the 1998 Ottawa

Treaty. The International Red Cross was given responsibility for drafting the 1977 Geneva Protocols that added to the protection of civilians in interstate and intrastate wars and, alongside *Medecins Sans Frontiers* (Doctors Without Borders) and other relief agencies, has been deeply involved in the application of humanitarian law.

In addition to national and transnational actors, we should also keep in mind the subnational politics that shapes global policy in all issue-areas. Focusing on American bureaucratic politics, Abram and Antonia Chayes describe the arms control process as one that involves the interaction of internal and international politics, along the lines of Putnam's two-level games:

> The [treaty-making] process goes on both within each state and at the international level. . . . [The] list of the U.S. groups normally involved in arms control negotiations includes the national security staff, the Departments of State and Defense, the Arms control and Disarmament Agency, the Joint Chiefs of Staff, the Central Intelligence Agency, and sometimes the Department of Energy. . . . These groups themselves are not unitary actors. . . . Much of the extensive literature on U.S.-Soviet arms control negotiations is devoted to analysis of the almost byzantine complexity of these internal interactions. [104]

Interest groups also are part of the equation. For example, the Chemical Manufacturers Association (CMA), the trade association that represents Dow, Dupont, and other major American chemical companies, was invited by the U.S. delegation to participate in the internal U.S. policy deliberations during the Chemical Weapons Convention talks; chemical plants manufacture insecticides, dyes, and other products containing agents that can readily be precursors to weapons, and Washington wanted to be careful not to take decisions on restricting the production and export of chemicals that could adversely affect American firms. Initially, the chemical industry was lukewarm to the negotiations, wary of costly governmental regulations and intrusive on-site inspections that might encourage industrial espionage. However, once it became resigned to the need for a treaty, it worked to protect its interests as best it could, urging a uniform industry-wide set of rules and ultimately endorsing an even more far-reaching international inspection regime than the U.S. Defense Department was willing to permit; CMA was especially fearful that, should the U.S. fail to become a party to the treaty, American chemical companies could stand to lose $600 million in annual export sales under the proposed sanctions for noncompliance. Commenting on how the CMA eventually came "on board," a U.S. congressman said that "had it not been for CMA, there would not have been a Chemical Weapons Convention."[105] No doubt similar dynamics were at work on other country delegations at the series of meetings that culminated in the signing of the 1993 Chemical Weapons Convention.

The above anecdote reinforces the point that international law is the creature of complex forces. As the "national security" issue-area continues to grow in complexity, and as warfare issues blend with welfare concerns, we are likely to see an increase in cobweb politics in the shaping of international regimes. The decline of interstate war as a pervasive constant in international relations has opened up space for non-war-peace issues to rise on the agenda of nations. Playing on Clause-witz's famous line, economics is now being called by some "the continuation of war by other means."[106] In the next chapter, we examine global governance in the economic arena and how humanity is attempting to manage the tensions between the welfare state and globalization.

6

International Economic Relations and International Law: Regulating States and Markets

Increasingly, Americans are eating foods imported from abroad, especially fruits and vegetables. It is estimated that some 40 percent of the fruit consumed by Americans is now imported, along with 15 percent of the vegetables, and that these numbers are likely to increase as people demand access to fresh produce year-round. In October 1997, because of growing concern about food safety in the wake of recent outbreaks of diseases tied to Guatemalan raspberries, Mexican cantaloupes, and Thai coconut milk, President Clinton announced that he would ask Congress to require the U.S. Food and Drug Administration "to ban imports of fruit and vegetables from countries that did not meet American food safety standards." [1] Meat and poultry imports had long been subject to inspection by federal regulators, and the new policy sought to extend national safeguards to foreign produce as well. As President Clinton put it, "Our food safety system is the strongest in the world, and that's how it's going to stay." [2]

At first glance, the president's announcement seemed a reasonable assertion of a national government's right to protect the public health of its citizens. After all, the twentieth century had seen the expansion of the "welfare state"—the growing regulatory role of government in managing the economic and other sectors of society in support of full employment, increased life expectancy, and other national goals. However, questions immediately arose over whether increased national regulation of food imports by the United States might be at odds with international regulation of trade under the newly developed rules of the World Trade Organization (WTO), an IGO headquartered in Geneva that had been created to promote "free trade." The Marrakesh Agreement, over 26,000 pages long, had been signed by 117 states on April 15, 1994. Within six months, eighty-one countries accounting for more than 90 percent of world trade—all the major industrialized countries, including the United States, as well as most major developing countries—had ratified the treaty, enabling the WTO to be born on January 1, 1995. The preamble to the WTO treaty reflected the growing movement away from government control toward free-market economics: WTO members agreed to promote "reciprocal and mutually advantageous arrangements directed to the substantial reduction of tariffs and other barriers to trade and to the elimination of discriminatory treatment in international trade relations."

Individual states could still impose restrictions on imported food-stuffs, but any WTO member adopting such regulations—particularly if they exceeded the minimal safety requirements mandated by the Codex Alimentarious (Latin for "food law")—had to provide clear evidence that the imports posed health or other hazards as opposed to merely harming the profits of domestic producers and jobs of domestic farm workers. Established in 1963 by the UN Food and Agriculture Organization and the World Health Organization "to facilitate the world trade in foods [through] internationally accepted standards," the Codex was relied on by the WTO as the basis for determining the reasonableness of national food standards, even though critics maintained its relatively lax guidelines allowed "trade to trump public health." [3] Under the WTO treaty, any state accusing another state of violating the free trade provisions of the pact could file a complaint before a special trade tribunal, which, if it found in favor of the plaintiff, could order the defendant to change its policies or face economic sanctions. The United States itself, in May 1997, had used the new WTO rules to force European countries to lift their ban on beef from cattle treated with growth hormones, arguing that the ban was an artificial barrier to trade aimed at keeping out American meat products rather than preventing mad cow disease or other ailments. The United States also attempted to use the WTO procedures to challenge the European ban on the import of genetically modified crops that American agribusinesses were anxious to sell overseas; based on the "precautionary principle," Europeans argued that there was sufficient scientific uncertainty associated with biotechnology to support the ban, while the United States contended the onus was on the Europeans to provide firmer scientific evidence about the adverse effects of genetically modified organisms in order to justify trade restraints that had the look of economic protectionism.

It remained to be seen whether Europeans and others would in turn protest President Clinton's claim that Washington had a right to impose its food inspection standards on the rest of the world. A typical reaction came from a Mexican official, who said, "It is very clear to us that behind all this are economic interests which want to prevent Mexican vegetables from entering the U.S." [4] Given the fact that the United States sold twice as much food abroad as it imported, and long had been a leading champion of trade liberalization in agricultural commodities, Washington had to be careful not to adopt policies that might invite accusations of a double standard and retaliation by its trade partners. Al-

though many observers complained about American hegemony over the world economy, the United States was at least partly constricted by the very rules on expanding market access it had had a hand in creating at Marrakesh, Morocco.

At issue here is, first, the extent to which food markets should be regulated and, second, which level of governance—national or international—should take precedence. Such concerns may not be as "high politics" in character as the concerns discussed in the previous chapter, but food fights and other trade wars can arouse considerable passions nonetheless. Witness the much-publicized case of Jose Bove, the Frenchman who in 1999—apparently oblivious to Thomas Friedman's "golden arches theory of conflict prevention"—led a group of fellow farmers in bulldozing a McDonalds restaurant in the small town of Millau, as a symbolic protest against the threat to French agriculture posed by American-led globalization that, through the WTO and other global organizations, seemed to be advancing a world-without-borders capitalist ethos in place of welfare state nationalism.

The issues raised here extend well beyond trade in foodstuffs and other goods, and well beyond the WTO. A large body of international law and set of international institutions have been established to help manage international economic relations in trade, investment, and monetary affairs, as well as regimes that facilitate the growth of international commerce by routinizing the flow of mail, telecommunications, and other transactions across national boundaries. Indeed, it is hard to imagine how international economic exchanges could occur in the absence of a web of such rules and institutions that confer a degree of order and predictability upon which economic actors can rely. Still, to Bove and other anti-globalization activists, the increased pooling of sovereignty that has accompanied globalization in the post–cold war era has amounted to a surrender of sovereignty, as many key decisions about economic policy are being made in multilateral forums, such as three-judge WTO dispute-resolution panels in Geneva, rather than in national capitals. The anti-globalization camp argues that these new arrangements favor multinational corporations (MNCs) and other powerful actors at the expense of smaller, poorer ones, while the other side argues that "a rising tide lifts all boats" no matter what flag they fly.

As in other issue-areas, international law in the economic sphere is still subject to the vagaries of politics, but it is increasingly informing politics as well, providing a framework overhanging what international relations scholars call "international political economy." Just as the face of global violence and the nature of the challenges to the national security state have changed over time, particularly of late, so too have the workings of the world economy and the nature of the challenges to national control over economic activity been undergoing

The photo captures the politics of food regulation, as it shows South Koreans protesting against U.S. beef imports allowed into South Korea despite concern that they might be tainted with mad cow disease.

major transformation. In this chapter, we want to explore how international economic law has evolved in response to developments in the international system and has itself been an engine of change—what rules have been instituted, by whom and for whom, with what impacts on wealth and poverty? We will also consider what obstacles and opportunities exist that might impede or enhance the future growth of law in this area.

TODAY, WE CAN SPEAK OF A WORLD ECONOMY even if there is no world government. True, national boundaries still matter (for example, the volume of trade between Toronto and Vancouver, two Canadian cities, is far greater than that between Toronto and Seattle, just across the border from Vancouver), but they seem to be receding in importance. The author Thomas Wolfe said, "You can't go home again." But Thomas Friedman has observed that "in the world of globalization, you won't be able to leave home again,"[5] given the emergence of a single, homogeneous marketplace one increasingly encounters wherever one roams in the world, whether it is in former communist states once insulated behind the Iron Curtain or in Middle East states still governing behind the veil of Islam, or in other regions seeking to preserve traditional culture. This global marketplace is sustained not only by transnational trade flows but also transnational capital flows, as firms in one country increasingly operate subsidiaries in other countries. McDonalds does business in 119 countries, serving 97 million customers daily, over half of them non-American; every day, five new McDonalds restaurants are opened, four of which are located outside the United States, with Japan alone having over 2,500 franchises and with the largest McDonalds on the planet now found in Beijing, China (among 80 others in that city). Coca-Cola is served 601 million times a day in virtually every country on earth, 70 percent of its income derived from overseas bottlers. MTV spans five continents, is beamed into over 100 countries, and attracts 80 percent of its viewership from abroad, while the "New World Order" (NWO) has taken on new meaning as a World Championship Wrestling tag-team whose matches are broadcast to 120 countries.[6]

Globalization is not to be equated simply with Americanization. Hardees, Burger King, Dr. Pepper, Ben and Jerry's ice cream, and countless other brand names found in American supermarkets and shopping malls are owned by companies that have their headquarters abroad. Although the United States is still the base of operations for the largest number of MNCs in the world, with General Motors, Microsoft and other U.S. firms continuing to expand their reach into overseas markets, its lead as a headquarters country is shrinking as American businesses themselves are increasingly falling prey to corporate buyouts by foreign interests, most recently seen in Chrysler's takeover by DaimlerBenz (the corporate board room moving from Detroit to Stuttgart, Germany), AMOCO's takeover by British Petroleum (the headquarters shifting from Chicago to London), and Ralston-Purina's purchase by Nestle (Checkerboard Square relocating from St. Louis to Lake Geneva, Switzerland).

It is somewhat ironic that, at a time when the "territorial integrity" norm has become sacrosanct in regard to international security, borders in the international economy are becoming ever more porous and blurred, to the point where some observers go so far as to talk about "the end of geography."[7] As far back as the 1970s, Charles Kindleberger at MIT opined that "the state is about through as an economic unit," referring to the burgeoning multinational corporation phenomenon.[8] Around the same time, Raymond Vernon of the Harvard Business School wrote *Sovereignty at Bay,* suggesting that MNCs might be the "new sovereigns," having outgrown the nation-state and wielding more power than many of them.[9] George Ball, U.S. undersecretary of state in the Johnson administration, confessed "the nation-state is a very old-fashioned idea and badly adapted to serve the needs of our present complex world,"[10] acknowledging that the nation-state seemed a

The photo, showing a Chinese boy with the familiar Coke can in the shadows of the Great Wall, symbolizes globalization and the "coca-colonization" of the world.

dysfunctional mode of organization given the litany of issues, economic and otherwise, that seemed to transcend national boundaries. Even the scholar most associated with the realist school, Hans Morgenthau, toward the end of his life in 1974, had some second thoughts, concluding that "the technological revolutions of our age have rendered the nation-state's principle of political organization as obsolete as the first modern industrial revolution of the steam engine did feudalism." [11] By the 1990s, when the term "globalization" was first coined, Walter Wriston, the former head of Citicorp, the largest U.S.-based bank, was writing about "the twilight of sovereignty," just as Robert Reich, Bill Clinton's soon-to-be secretary of labor, was asking "Who is 'US'?" [12]—both noting the growing penetration of national economies by external forces that were rendering the national identity of products and producers ever more indeterminate.

Despite globalization trends, the Westphalian logic that continues to dominate our view of the world still leads us, when we think of economics, to think in terms of the economic size and health of *countries*. Hence, the importance attached to such statistics as gross *national* product (GNP) or gross *domestic* product (GDP) of states. Based on the understanding that it is not so much countries that are rich or poor, but individual human beings, analysts also look at GNP or GDP *per capita*, as a measure of a country's standard of living. Obviously, a country can have a relatively high GNP but have a relatively low GNP per capita, such as India, while the converse is true as well, such as Norway. In recent years, there has been growing attention paid not only to the per capita income of countries but also to other indicators of national well-being. The UN Development Program (UNDP) has created a "Human Development Index" (HDI) that it has used annually to rank every country in the world on an aggregate measure that includes per capita income, average life expectancy, and percentage of the literate adult population. Not surprisingly, the countries that rank the highest on the HDI are found in the industrialized North (the top ten in 2005 were Norway, Iceland, Australia, Luxembourg, Canada, Sweden, Switzerland, Ireland, Belgium, and the United States), while those that rank the lowest are found in the less developed South, particularly in sub-Saharan Africa (the bottom ten in 2005 were Mozambique, Burundi, Ethiopia, Central African Republic, Guinea-Bissau, Chad, Mali, Burkina Faso, Sierra Leone, and Niger).[13]

Rich-poor gaps can exist not only between countries but also within countries. In addition to publishing HDI rankings of states, UNDP has collected data on per capita income, life expectancy, and literacy rates for different geographical regions, ethnic groups, or other categorical subgroups within a given state. For example, a recent *Human Development Report* asks, "Why in Nepal do Muslims have less than half the level of human development of Newars? Why in China is the HDI in the province of Qinghai barely half that of Shanghai?"[14] Commenting on another recent *Human Development Report*, the *New York Times* points out that in South Africa, "the white and black sections of the population are not just two different peoples but 'almost two different worlds.' If white South Africa were a separate country it would rank 24th in the world in terms of human development, while black South Africa would be in 123rd place, just above Congo. . . . In Brazil, the report highlights the discrepancy in living standards between the more prosperous south and the impoverished northeast, where life expectancy is 17 years shorter, adult literacy 33 percent lower, and average incomes 40 percent lower."[15] In Brazil, the richest 20 percent of the population account for roughly 65 percent of the national income, compared to 45 percent in the United States, where the income distribution pattern tends to be more egalitarian than that found in many developing countries but somewhat less egalitarian than that of many developed states.

Globalization has brought uneven benefits, as some countries and some people clearly are doing better than others. In country terms, "the year 2004 was a milestone for the world economy, which grew by 5.1 percent—the fastest in nearly three decades. Among the leaders were China, expanding at 9.5 percent, Argentina at 9 percent, and India at 7.3 percent. World output of goods and services increased from $7 trillion in 1950 to $56 trillion in 2004, while annual income per person grew from $2,835 to $8,753 during this time."[16] In human terms, the picture is less rosy. There have always been rich-poor gaps, but there is some concern that these gaps may be widening in the post–cold war era. In the world as a whole, the number of people living on less than one dollar a day appears to be rising and is nearing 1.5 billion. At the same time, the number of billionaires in the world has been multiplying rapidly (for example, during the 1990s, the number in Mexico increased from 1 to 24, and in the United States from 13 to 170).[17] All told, "828 million go to bed hungry, 114 million children of primary school age are not in school, [and] 11 million children die each year of preventable causes."[18] Although, according to the 2005 UN Millennium Project report, "economic development lifted millions of people out of poverty in the last decade," "some regions have made little progress or even experienced reversals."[19]

In chapter 1, I noted that order is not the only value served by law, that justice is widely considered an important byproduct as well. There are profound normative questions surrounding economic justice and governance of the international economy. In particular, what obligations do governments have toward their own citizens and toward foreigners in terms of improving material well-being, and how much coordination of the world economy through international institutions is possible and desirable? These are not new questions—they have long preoccupied writers and practitioners—but there are new complexities surrounding them.

The Changing Nature of International Political Economy: The Contest between Economic Nationalism (States) and Liberal Internationalism (Markets)

There are only two basic ways to organize an economy—around the *state* (government) or the free *market* (the private sector). There has been an ongoing historical drama pitting these two organizing principles against each other, with much economic thought over the years revolving around the search for the proper balance. Virtually all states today adopt a mixed form in practice, although some lean more heavily toward the statist end of the spectrum (notably communist states such as Cuba and China) while others tilt more heavily toward markets (notably states with a strong capitalist tradition such as the United States). This drama has played out not only within states but on the international plane as well, where it has shaped the evolution of international economic law. In order to understand the recent controversies swirling around the World Trade Organization and other aspects of the contemporary global economy, it is helpful to retrace some of this history.

From 1648 to 1945

The first nation-states in the early life of the Westphalian system during the seventeenth and eighteenth centuries were "mercantilist" in character. As Robert Gilpin has written, *mercantilism,* or "economic nationalism," took as "its central idea . . . that economic activities are and should be subordinate to the goal of state building and the interests of the state."[20] Mercantilism was consistent with realist thinking. The mercantilist state was interested in economic matters mainly as they related to using government levers, particularly tariffs and other trade policies, in support of military power and conquest. Exports were to be promoted as a way to generate gold bullion and other currency to pay for an army, while imports were to be discouraged in order to deny potential adversaries such financial resources. According to Jacob Viner, all mercantilists subscribed to the following proposition: "(1) wealth is an absolutely essential means to power, whether for security or aggression; (2) power is essential or valuable as a means to the acquisition or retention of wealth; (3) wealth and power are each proper ultimate ends of national policy."[21] Epitomized by France, the mercantilist state was far less concerned about the general welfare of the nation and citizenry at large. To be sure, monarchs had to be at least mildly attentive to their subjects' material well-being insofar as there was always the threat of domestic unrest and revolt, but Marie Antoinette's "let them eat cake" utterance reflected the prevailing mindset. The welfare state had not yet been born, as only the privileged few were thought to be entitled to enjoy the fruits of the nation's economic growth. Louis XIV and other rulers could hardly conceive of such notions as a "human development index" for their own people, much less for people living abroad.

The mercantilist model, which stressed the role of the state as a mode of organizing economic activity within and across national boundaries, was challenged by a competing model in 1776, when Adam Smith wrote *The Wealth of Nations,* which stressed free market, laissez-faire principles as an alternative basis for economic relations. Smith became known as the father of "free trade," and his model became known as *liberal internationalism.* The liberal internationalist school, grounded more in the idealist than realist paradigm, held that there were benefits to be derived from cooperation between national governments, that states shared certain mutual interests in collaborating to open up trade and investment opportunities for each other to maximize the special economic advantages of each country. Some countries might have particularly low labor costs, others abundant raw materials, and so forth. Ultimately, producers as well as consumers in all nations could expect to benefit from an international economy based on the most efficient use of resources. To this end, Smith called on governments to reduce tariffs and other "artificial" barriers to international economic activity and to allow goods and services to flow as freely as possible according to "natural" laws of supply and demand, so that the boundary between, say, Britain and France, would be no more an impediment to commerce than the boundary separating Paris and Marseilles.

Smith's ideas initially met with much resistance. In the United States, Alexander Hamilton was the leading early proponent of mercantilism. In his *Report on the Subject of Manufacturers,* presented to the U.S. House of Representatives in 1791, Hamilton urged that the federal government play a lead role in promoting America's industrialization and protecting domestic "infant industries" from cheap foreign producers so as to maximize national self-sufficiency; Hamilton stated, "Every nation . . . ought to endeavor to possess within itself, all the essentials of national supply. These comprise the means of subsistence, habitation, clothing, and defense."[22] In Germany, Friedrich List's *National System of Political Economy,* published in 1841, echoed Hamilton's economic nationalism. At a time when Great Britain had become the champion of free trade, List argued that London's liberal internationalism masked self-serving national interests; in the words of Gilpin, List contended that the British

> had actually used the power of the state to protect their own infant indus-tries against foreign competition . . . and they only became champions of free trade after having achieved technological and industrial supremacy over their rivals. . . . List believed that the British were merely seeking to advance their own national economic interests by gaining unimpeded access to for-eign markets through free trade. He . . . advocated erection of high tariff bar-riers to foster economic unification [of Germany], protect the development of German industry, and thus create a powerful German state.[23]

Although it may well be that British support for liberal internationalism hap-pened to square with British national interests, it was a position arrived at in London only after much internal, domestic conflict that pitted various economic groups in Britain against each other. The free trade doctrine was particularly ap-pealing to manufacturing interests, who welcomed lower tariffs on imported raw materials, as well as the emergent merchant class of capitalist entrepreneurs who saw vast opportunities for economic gain once they were freed of government-im-posed restrictions. However, entrenched economic interests who had benefited from the old mercantilist policies, notably aristocratic elites whose fortunes were tied to their land holdings and agricultural production, continued to seek govern-ment protection from foreign competition. With the repeal of the highly protec-tionist Corn Laws in 1846, the internationalists won out as Britain launched an era of free trade that was to flourish over the next several decades and result in a tremendous expansion of worldwide commercial activity.

Although throughout the nineteenth century, in Britain and elsewhere, liberal internationalism continued to be contested by economic nationalism, Adam Smith's dream seemed to be moving ever closer to reality. The laying of the first transatlantic telegraph cable in 1866 allowed the movement of money from London to New York and back in a matter of minutes, and presaged the $1 trillion a day computerized transactions that were to fuel global financial markets much later. Between 1870 and 1910, the British invested roughly a quarter of their sav-ings overseas, in railroads, mines, and other enterprises in their colonies and in the United States. Economic ties between the major powers of Europe had become so expansive by the early 1900s that these states on the eve of World War I recorded unprecedented high levels of exports and imports as a percentage of gross national products. Some analysts went so far as to call the late nineteenth and early twen-tieth centuries "the belle epoque [beautiful epoch] of interdependence,"[24] while others at the time recognized interdependence as a mixed blessing, observing that "the world is, more than ever before, one great unit in which everything interacts and affects everything else, but in which also everything collides and clashes."[25]

In the first half of the twentieth century, between 1914 and 1945, a series of major "collisions and clashes" occurred that produced a revival of economic nationalism and arrested the nascent globalization trends that had been building previously.

Erstwhile trading partners were trading bullets in World War I and World War II, and were trading relatively little of anything during the Great Depression in the in terwar period. The combination of World War I, the Great Depression, and World War II took the Westphalian state to a new level of development, as the two world wars resulted in ever bigger military establishments (national security states) while the worldwide depression contributed to ever bigger economic establishments (national welfare states).

The notion that national governments were obligated to concern themselves with job creation, social security, minimum wages, food safety, and other such matters was rooted in the acceleration of the Industrial Revolution, the growth of the middle class, and the advent of mass democracy in nineteenth century Europe and America, all of which produced growing demands on government for benefits and services. However, it was not until the Great Depression in the twentieth century, when unemployment in the United States and other countries exceeded 25 percent, that the concept of "the welfare state" firmly took hold, associated foremost with another Englishman, John Maynard Keynes. Keynes argued that governments everywhere should actively intervene in their national economy and engage in "fine-tuning," tweaking monetary and fiscal policy in response to whatever economic problems the country was experiencing, in particular stimulating the economy at a time of recession (as in the 1930s) through heavy public spending and tax and interest rate cuts and cooling the economy off at a time of inflation through the opposite measures. Franklin Delano Roosevelt's New Deal, which featured government jobs programs and other policies that eventually led to economic recovery, became the embodiment of Keynesian welfare state thinking and government intervention in the economy, although in Western Europe, even more so, efforts were made to develop "national industrial policy" around collaborative links between management, labor, and government. The "mixed economy" became the main model for industrial democracies, which remained committed to market-oriented capitalism but permitted a growing role for the state in socioeconomic planning and problem-solving as an alternative to the more extreme ideology of state ownership that the Soviet Union and some other states had adopted based on the earlier writings of Karl Marx. Marxism itself offered a third perspective on international political economy, one that viewed the global economy as revolving not so much around states and their national interests (mercantilism, or realism) or around the invisible, neutral hand of the market (liberal internationalism, or idealism) but around an inherently exploitative set of relationships between capitalist classes and working classes worldwide.[26]

There remained the question of how compatible the welfare state and national industrial policy were with free trade and a liberal international economic order of the type that Adam Smith had envisioned and that had been evolving up until it was interrupted by twentieth century war and depression. One form that government economic intervention took during the Great Depression in the interwar period was neomercantilist trade protectionism designed to shield one's own industries from foreign competition, symbolized by the Smoot-Hawley Tariff Act passed by the U.S. Congress in 1930, which imposed extremely high tariff duties on agricultural and manufactured imports to the United States. Ultimately this measure proved counterproductive insofar as it sparked retaliatory tariffs by other countries and led to a general contraction of world trade and a deepening of global recession, contributing in turn to the outbreak of World War II.

From 1945 to the Present

The second half of the twentieth century proved more conducive to Adam Smith's ideas than the first half. After World War II, there was a new determination to lower trade and other economic barriers so that the "beggar thy neighbor" mistakes of the interwar period would not be repeated. Given the "acute collective consciousness of the economic disaster of the Great Depression,"[27] free trade became internalized as a core norm in international economics.[28] Some observers noted, however, that standard realist explanations for the postwar revival of free trade were at least as cogent as liberal or constructivist explanations; "hegemonic stability" theorists pointed out that the experiences of the interwar period, when there was no clear economic hegemon, showed that hegemony was a necessary underpinning for a free trade system.[29] Just as Britain as the lead economy had been the champion of free trade in the nineteenth century, the United States as the dominant economy, with an interest in maximizing global market access, became the chief supporter of open borders in the postwar period. Whether due to U.S. hegemony or simply the power of the idea of free trade and the calculus of mutual interests, world trade did in fact increase more than twenty-fold between 1945 and 1990.

Although the second half of the twentieth century saw a growing web of economic interdependence, it was unevenly concentrated among the industrialized democracies, which accounted for the bulk of world trade and investment. Through much of the post–World War II period, the world economy reflected first, second, and third world divisions associated with the cold war, as various barriers persisted between the Western bloc countries (principally the United States, Western European states, and Japan), the Eastern bloc countries (the Soviet Union and its Eastern European satellites along with other marxist states), and the developing countries. The East-West geopolitical struggle between communist and noncommunist states limited economic intercourse between them, while the North-South divide between rich and poor states limited economic exchange between those countries. Hence, trade and investment flows predominantly followed a West-West pattern.[30] As one writer put it, "North America, Japan, and Europe [dominated] as originators and destinations of most international [trade] and investments."[31] East-West and North-South economic relations did expand over time, but remained on the margins of the world economy.

In pushing for an open world economy, the United States along with other Western countries had to confront the legacy of the Keynesian welfare state and the right of national governments to adopt policies that in some instances might restrict trade and foreign investment in the name of protecting jobs, the environment, or some other values demanded by their citizenry. In an effort to reconcile the seemingly contradictory requirements of a liberal international economic order on the one hand and what amounted to welfare state nationalism on the other hand, states entered into what John Ruggie has called the "compromise of embedded liberalism."[32] That is, states agreed that they would work together to maximize free trade and open borders as much as possible, recognizing, however, that each state retained the right to pursue protectionist policies whenever conditions warranted. The idea of free trade was refined to accommodate the idea of the welfare state. Driving much of this bargain was the attempt by states such as the United States to satisfy two competing sets of domestic interests—high-tech and other export-oriented industries that had a stake in opening up foreign markets, juxtaposed against steel, textiles and other older industries seeking to protect their predominately domestic markets from foreign competition. Through a variety of international institutions such as the General Agreement on Tariffs and Trade (GATT), the World Bank, and the International Monetary Fund (IMF), to be discussed below, the hope was that states could collaborate and peaceably adjust their differences to avoid the mercantilist tensions of earlier eras.

During the 1980s, a period of "stagflation" (high unemployment and high inflation) occurred that befuddled Keynesian economic planners, leading to conservative leaders coming to power—most notably, Ronald Reagan in the United States and Margaret Thatcher in the United Kingdom—who argued that the welfare state had gone too far, that people had become overtaxed and overregulated by Big Government, and that what was needed was increased privatization, deregulation, and downsizing of public sector bureaucracy; included in their prescriptions were further reductions in barriers to the free flow of goods and services across national boundaries. The 1990s were marked by continuing ideological debate over how much weight to attach to the state, as opposed to the market, as the prime basis for economic organization. A new generation of leaders, exemplified by Bill Clinton in the United States and Tony Blair in Britain, won elected office by presenting themselves as "Third Way" politicians who claimed to be forging a new consensus around the twin propositions that "the era of Big Government is over" yet government still had a critical if more modest role to play in the economic life of a country.

By the end of the cold war, imports and exports as a percentage of GNP in many countries had been restored to, and in some cases exceeded, their high pre–World War I levels. Fueled by the Internet and other technological developments, globalization in the 1990s seemed poised to take off to its next stage, permitting the integration of the world economy in a way that had not previously been possible. Markets seemed to be ascendant almost everywhere in the post–cold war era. Newspaper headlines announced the drift toward free-market economics even in the more highly statist economies of Western Europe ("The Cries of Welfare States Under the Knife [in France and Italy]," "Sweden, the World's Role Model [as a Welfare State] Now Drifting as Currents Change," and "To Spur German Economy, [Gerhard] Schroeder Offers Veer to Right") as well as the third world ("A Chilean

Socialist in the Clinton-Blair Mold [Elected President of Chile]" and "Iran's President Would Privatize Big Industries").[33] The new thinking extended even as far as the command economies of the former Soviet Union, where Mikhail Gorbachev had set in motion economic restructuring and phasing out of inefficient state-run industries under the banner of *perestroika,* and Communist China, where Marxist-Leninism was giving way to "Market-Leninism."[34]

Where does this leave us in the early twenty-first century? One of the most important storylines to be followed in coming years is the tension between economic nationalism, which remains a potent force, and world-without-borders capitalism, which has been gathering momentum—in Gilpin's words, "the clash between the integrating forces of the world economy and the centrifugal forces of the sovereign state."[35] Meanwhile, globalization is playing havoc with the "compromise of embedded liberalism" and the functioning of the welfare state, including the manipulation of Keynesian fiscal and monetary levers to stabilize one's national economy. As one observer notes, globalization threatens to undermine "the capacity of the individual . . . state to control its own economic future. At the very least, there appears to be a diminution of state autonomy."[36] Friedman calls this the "golden straightjacket"—requiring "shrinking the size of its state bureaucracy . . . eliminating and lowering tariffs on imported goods, removing restrictions on foreign investment, getting rid of quotas and domestic monopolies, increasing exports . . . opening its industries, stock and bond markets to direct foreign ownership and investment. . . . Governments . . . which deviate too far from the core rules will see their investors stampede away, interest rates rise and stock market valuations fall."[37]

He adds that, even in an age of globalization, there remains a need for well-run welfare states that collect enough revenue and have enough "capacity" to provide the kinds of public goods that undergird a thriving economy (such as good roads and other infrastructure that can facilitate commerce, an educated work force that can enhance productivity, a law enforcement system that can protect property rights and enforce contracts). Business does not want a bigger state but "a better state, a smarter state and a faster state, with bureaucrats that can regulate a free market, without either choking it or letting it get out of control."[38]

Recalling the statements quoted earlier from Charles Kindleberger, Raymond Vernon, and others about the erosion of economic sovereignty, many commentators speak of growing "loss of control" on the part of national governments.[39] Granted there has never been any "golden age of state control,"[40] nonetheless the multinational corporation and unprecedented capital mobility pose extraordinary contemporary challenges to the viability of nation-states, even the most powerful ones, which are increasingly held hostage to external economic forces.[41] Friedman says, "The symbol of the Cold War was a wall, which divided everyone. The symbol of the globalization system is a World Wide Web, which unites everyone. The defining document of the Cold War system was 'The Treaty.' The defining document of the globalization system is 'The Deal.' "[42] However, overlooked here is the fact that "deals" cannot be made without "treaties," without a larger set of rules governing international economic transactions. International law is necessarily looked to by states as a vehicle for coping with loss of control and managing the relationship between states and markets in the pursuit of expanded commerce. We discuss next the development of international economic regimes and the role they play in promoting stability in world economic affairs.

International Regimes and Economic Order

A distinction is often made between "public international law" and "private international law." The former has to do with the rules applied by nation-states in their international relations; much of what has been discussed in this book, including the concept of international regimes, falls in the category of public international law. Private international law has to do with rules that affect private individuals in their dealings across national boundaries; this can often involve a clash between different municipal legal systems over such issues as commercial contracts and sales, taxation, and intellectual property. Much of private international law, in fact, has to do with commercial relations. At times, states have entered into treaties to reconcile and harmonize rules of private international law—for example, the 1980 UN Convention on Contracts for the International Sale of Goods—in which case the distinction between public and private international law becomes blurred.

David Bederman writes, "What makes the vast and growing network of private commercial relations across national boundaries possible is the global system of trade and monetary liberalization. This system is manifestly the domain of public international law and has been the subject of treaties and custom for two centuries."[43] One can go back still further, to pre-Westphalia times, to the medieval *Lex Mercatoria* (Merchant Law) promulgated and applied by specialized tribunals, typically situated in major ports, that attempted to develop common commercial practices within and between the Italian city-states and other jurisdictions. Then, as now, the rules "were the product of expediency," as "merchants needed certainty in their operations across frontiers."[44]

The need for a degree of order in international economic relations that governments as well as business elites have felt throughout history is only growing today. Raymond Vernon articulates the added pressures for states to pool sovereignty in an age of globalization: "As governments try to apply unilateral responses to . . . [economic] problems, they stand an excellent chance of damaging both their own national interests and the interests of the multinational enterprises on which they depend. The challenge is to find the multilateral approaches that can reduce the inescapable tensions to manageable proportions."[45] Likewise, another observer notes that there are pressures to develop a broader consensus and strengthened international institutions behind a free trade system, as "the role of international economic regimes has changed from creating a framework in which each state could decide command or market economics to creating a shared regulatory framework within which a globalized market economy will function."[46] Yet another commentator remarks:

As the global system becomes more integrated, there is a demand for international public goods that neither markets nor nation-states will provide. . . . These are roughly as follows: systematic financial stability; the rule of law and dispute settlement needed for an open system of trade and investment; common standards of weights and measures; management of global communications networks like aviation, telecommunications, and sea-lanes to prevent congestion and disasters. . . . All these require some sort of institutional development, beyond the nation-state. Some of these activities are largely self-regulating, since the main commercial users have a collective interest in providing the public good, as is the case with many . . . industrial standards (the International Standards Organization). . . . In some cases, there is mixed public/private sector participation, as in the International Telecommunications Union. But, mostly, there is sovereignty pooling by governments through new institutions . . . and treaty obligations. There is a complex but rich system of governance growing up to manage globalization.[47]

Comparing regime-building in the economic sphere with that in the peace and security field, Charles Lipson comments: "Conflict and cooperation are, of course, commingled in both [sets of] issues, but . . . economic issues are characterized far more by elaborate networks of rules, norms, and institutions."[48] What had been in the nineteenth and early twentieth century mainly a loose conglomeration of customary rules and treaties (the latter often bilateral in scope, for example the "most favored nation" treaties the United States and other countries would sign in order to promote trade reciprocity) evolved after World War II into a much more expansive, formalized set of multilateral rules and institutions. We noted in the previous section that, while it was not an accident that the lead state in the international system with the most to gain from a relaxation of economic barriers (the United States) became the main champion of an open world economy, other states as well recognized the folly of the interwar period and were persuaded to adopt a liberalization ethos as long as it did not undermine their sovereignty and their ability to protect their national interests. The compromise of embedded liberalism after World War II was to be facilitated by three UN-affiliated IGOs—the World Bank, the IMF, and GATT—that together underpinned the "Bretton Woods international economic order," named after the city in New Hampshire where forty-four nations met in 1944 to draft a plan for postwar economic reconstruction.

The World Bank, IMF, and GATT

The design of the new structures reflected not only the desires of the United States as chief architect but also a widely held faith in applying the social engineering model of the national welfare state to the global level.[49] The UN Economic and Social Council (ECOSOC) was to have been the linchpin through which all the intergovernmental machinery devoted to global economic problem-solving was to be coordinated, much like the UN Security Council was conceived as playing a pivotal role in the military security field. However, for various reasons, ECOSOC has been largely ineffective in carrying out its mandate to integrate the efforts of GATT, the World Bank, the IMF, and a dozen other UN specialized agencies. Part of the problem is that each specialized agency has had its own distinct membership, headquarters secretariat, and budget, with little incentive to pursue a common set of policies. More problematic, the UN membership has been unwilling to entrust ECOSOC with any real decision-making power. Initially composed of eighteen states, including the economically most powerful ones, ECOSOC has mushroomed to fifty-four members, with its decision-making competence declining as its size has increased.

A lot of the politics of global governance in the economic issue-area can be understood in classic realist, "billiard ball" terms, that is, as a game played between nation-states, involving power, national interests, and other elements of the Westphalian culture. In particular, developing countries have long complained that the main global institutions in the UN system responsible for coordinating the world economy have been dominated by the Western, developed states belonging to the Organization for Economic Cooperation and Development (OECD), and especially in recent years by the Group of Seven (G-7) major industrialized economies, led by the United States. (The G-7 in the 1990s became known as the G-8, in recognition of the inclusion of Russia in the "club.") The so-called G-20, consisting of the finance ministers of both developed and developing countries, has played a growing role in trying to prevent global economic crises, but is overshadowed by the G-8.

Headquartered in Washington, D.C., the World Bank consists of 184 member states, each of which is represented with one seat on the Bank's Board of Governors. However, decision making is based on weighted voting. Member governments are assigned voting power according to the size of their capital contribution to the Bank; G-8 states account for almost half of the total shares in the Bank, with the United States being the largest single contributor. Although most foreign aid traditionally had been given bilaterally, the World Bank was conceived as an important new multilateral aid vehicle. The Bank was to obtain its funds mainly through soliciting government subscriptions and issuing interest-bearing bonds and notes purchased by governments as well as investors in the private sector. These funds were then supposed to be loaned to needy governments on relatively generous terms, particularly by the International Development Association, the "soft loan window" of the Bank, which was authorized to offer fifty-year repayment periods at low interest rates. Although the Bank over the years has played an indispensable role in providing capital to less developed countries, many problems have arisen, not the least of which is the servicing of the more than $1 trillion debt that borrowing countries have accumulated. The Bank also has been involved with foreign private investment issues through its International Center for Settlement of Investment Disputes (ICSID), a forum for resolution of disputes between governments and foreign investors that was established by a 1966 UN convention;

use of the ICSID is generally voluntary, although investment laws and treaties increasingly contain clauses that encourage, and in some instances mandate, submission of cases to the facility, whose arbitral award decisions are considered binding on the parties.

Also headquartered in Washington, D.C., near the World Bank, the International Monetary Fund likewise has 184 member states, a Board of Governors, and a weighted voting decision-making process based on financial clout. Due to their financial contributions to the central fund of currency reserves, the United States, Japan, and Germany account for approximately one-third of the votes, with other OECD states accounting for another one-third. The IMF was created to promote global monetary cooperation and financial stability by, first, furnishing temporary assistance to countries to ease balance of payments problems (where lack of hard currency might inhibit trade) and, secondly, providing a central forum for negotiating adjustments in currency values (where fluctuations in exchange rates might disrupt international economic activity). However, the IMF and the World Bank increasingly have found themselves with overlapping and duplicating missions, as each has competed to become the major global IGO in the field of international economic development.

There has been an informal understanding that an American would ordinarily head the World Bank, while a European would ordinarily head the IMF. Of the ten Bank presidents to date, all have been Americans, including a former U.S. secretary of defense (Robert McNamara) and deputy secretary of defense (Paul Wolfowitz). As a vivid example of the staying power of nationalism, there was a hotly contested debate in 2000 over who should be the executive head of the IMF. One writer noted: "France has long been an ardent advocate of the idea of Europe—a Europe led by Frenchmen. And Paris has been ruthless in its determination to put its nationals in charge of everything from the IMF to the European Central Bank. At some point, however, Europe's largest nation was going to demand its turn. Given that a Frenchman has headed the IMF for . . . 32 of the last 37 years . . . the Germans figured that it was about time they got a chance."[50] Indeed, a German did become managing director, until resigning the position in 2004, to be succeeded by a Spaniard. (Suffice it to say, applicants from the developing world are rarely considered.)

Initial efforts to create an International Trade Organization (ITO) alongside the World Bank and IMF foundered when the 1947 Havana Conference could not agree on how much power to permit the trade body to have in regulating commerce. Under traditional international law, based on "economic sovereignty," states were "free to discriminate in their economic dealings," deciding which states to give favored treatment to.[51] The ITO aimed to create a single, multilateral, nondiscriminatory trade regime. Although supportive of free trade, the United States (Congress, in particular) raised concerns about sovereignty. In lieu of the ITO, GATT was created in 1948 as an "interim" institution that could provide a global forum for multilateral negotiations aimed at reducing tariff and nontariff barriers. For nearly fifty years, GATT, headquartered in Geneva and consisting of over 100 member countries, remained the major international trade forum, with decision making—agenda-setting, policy formulation, and policy adoption—dominated by the United States and a few other OECD states. As usual, realism melded with liberal institutionalism. In the words of one official, "GATT . . . provided a rule of law for world trade" and represented "an attempt to banish into history the jungle of restrictions and bilateral dealings that strangled world trade in the 1930s like jungle weed."[52] It was replaced in 1995 by the World Trade Organization (WTO), a body that has occasioned a renewed debate over sovereignty, as suggested by the questions relating to international trade law raised at the outset of this chapter.

The WTO

The Marrakesh Treaty that created the WTO was the product of intense bargaining between states. A series of seven GATT negotiations had been conducted since 1948, including the Kennedy Round (1963–1967) and Tokyo Round (1973–1979), which succeeded in substantial tariff reductions, particularly on industrial goods. However, by the 1980s, it was clear that if the liberal trade regime was to be strengthened further, there was a need not only to involve more states but also to address protectionist practices in areas where GATT rules were weak or nonexistent, such as agriculture and services (insurance, information technology, etc.) and to improve dispute settlement procedures. The Uruguay Round was initiated in September 1986 in Punta del Este, where "chilling winds greeted the two thousand delegates from seventy-two countries,"[53] and culminated almost a decade later in the WTO treaty after "without question the most complex and protracted multilateral trade negotiation in history."[54]

Ernest Preeg describes the critical bargaining that went on even before the formal opening of Uruguay Round talks:

> An informal group of industrialized countries, the "Dirty Dozen," held a series of private meetings and produced the first comprehensive ministerial declaration. For tactical reasons, the three large members—the United States, the EC [the European Community], and Japan—temporarily withdrew from the group while the smaller industrialized countries joined with about twenty moderate developing countries to further develop and circulate the draft. Other developing countries joined, the big three rejoined, and the now forty-eight participants formally constituted themselves as the G-48 [co-chaired by a Swiss and a Colombian]. . . . The cohesion of the G-48 [which included the likes of Singapore, Malaysia, South Korea, Chile, and Mexico], cutting across North/South lines, put the hardliners [a group of ten developing countries, led by Brazil and India] on the defensive and forced them to produce their own G-10 draft. . . . A separate yet overlapping country realignment that took place during the summer of 1986 related to the agricultural sector. . . . [Six] agricultural exporters—Australia, Chile, Colombia, Thailand, New Zealand, and Uruguay—submitted a joint paper calling for substantial trade liberalization in this sector. The group [the so-called Cairns Group] expanded to

fourteen, adding Argentina, Brazil, Canada, Fiji, Hungary, Malaysia, the Philippines [and South Africa].[55]

Over the next eight years, "economic dichotomy between North and South would fade, between East and West disintegrate. . . . Globalization would be the catch-word for a brave new world of traders and diplomats."[56] Before that outcome, however, much bargaining remained to be done, and not just between nation-states but among a host of actors engaged in two-level and three-level games.

For example, the U.S. delegation at Punta del Este consisted of seventy-five members, including three cabinet-level officials (the U.S. trade representative, the secretary of commerce, and the secretary of agriculture), fifty-eight others from Executive Branch agencies (including State and Treasury), nine leaders of the corporate community, two labor union representatives, two farm sector leaders, and one member of Congress. U.S. negotiators had to consider foreign interests artic-ulated by their diplomatic counterparts across the table from them, while repre-senting "American" interests, at the same time looking over their shoulders trying to reconcile the diverse interests of various domestic pressure groups and bureau-cracies (for example, U.S. rice, soybean, and other growers seeking to open up Japanese and European markets, contrasted with U.S. cotton growers and the tex-tile lobby seeking to keep the American market closed to foreign competition).[57] Similar internal conflicts were played out within other delegations (such as effi-cient French multinational corporations supporting liberalization against the pro-tectionist views of the aforementioned Jose Bove and the French farm bloc).

Everywhere, coalitions of strange bedfellows formed in support of and against the treaty. In the American political system, on one side, opposing the agreement, were conservatives, such as Pat Buchanan and Ross Perot, joined by liberals, such as Ralph Nader and the representatives of various environmental and labor union groups. The conservatives were mainly concerned about the threat to U.S. sover-eignty posed by the proposed majority-rule voting procedures in the WTO and the binding nature of the dispute settlement procedures that, in the words of Buchanan, empowered "foreign bureaucrats [three-judge panels in Geneva] who will meet in secret to demand changes in U.S. laws"[58] when such laws violated WTO rules. The liberals were not concerned about a nascent world government so much as the failure of the Marrakesh Agreement to include adequate international labor and environmental standards that would protect American workers from a flood of cheap imports made in some cases by child or prison labor and would protect American consumers from tainted fruits and vegetables and other products that possibly threatened environmental harm; they predicted a "race to the bottom" if, in order to remain competitive in an open world economy, businesses and governments had to lower wages and environmental regulations.[59] On the other side, endorsing the agreement, were conservatives, such as George Bush (as Ronald Reagan's successor) and the Wall Street corporate community, along with liberals, such as Jimmy Carter and Bill Clinton. The conservatives here were driven mainly by their belief in the private sector and the promise of expanded investment opportunities, while the liberals were driven by a commitment to internationalism and a determination to promote multilateral cooperation that could avert future trade wars; this coalition argued that allowing China and other protectionist states into the WTO could provide a wedge to force their closed economies to become more laissez-faire and their closed political systems to become more democratic.

"Cobweb" trade politics included not only subnational actors but transnational actors. Although NGOs were not permitted nearly the direct access to participation in the trade talks as they were in other UN forums, they nonetheless were heard. Earlier, in 1990, 30,000 European farmers (not just French) had marched in protest against trade liberalization discussions in Brussels, which at the time was playing host to GATT meetings and where the European Union's Commission was engaged in trying to work out a common EU trade policy. (At least one scholar, citing the creation of the Euro and other supranational features of the EU, noted that "economic policy was no longer being made in national capitals in Western Europe."[60]) On the pro-free trade side, pharmaceutical companies in the United States, EU, and Japan consulted and mobilized across national boundaries to persuade governments to do away with barriers in that sector. Similarly, on the issue of strengthening intellectual property rights, "close collaboration developed between [NGOs like] the U.S. Intellectual Property Committee, the Union of Industrial and Employers' Confederation of Europe, and the Japanese Keidanren,"[61] supported by the World Intellectual Property Organization, a UN specialized agency. Among the nonstate actors that played a role in policy formulation and adoption were "epistemic communities" that provided technical data and research reports on trade issues, such as the Trade Policy Research Centre in the U.K. The GATT secretariat itself was looked to for analytic expertise, as well as relied on to chair the various working groups. According to one account, the executive head of GATT, Director-General Peter Sutherland, played an indispensable role in moving the proceedings along, developing "a detailed negotiating strategy for the complex diplomatic endgame ahead."[62]

The pro-globalization forces ultimately prevailed. The compromise of embedded liberalism survived, but tipped further toward markets. The WTO trade regime that finally was approved incorporated many of the GATT principles and extended them to agriculture, services, and other areas previously not covered, leaving a few loopholes that allowed states, as well as the EU and regional trade blocs ("preferential trading areas"), some discretion in regulating certain commodities and sectors. Among the WTO treaty provisions were the following:

(1) tariffs would be reduced on over 80 percent of the world's trade;

(2) dumping goods on another country's market at below-cost prices in order to eliminate that country's domestic producers would be banned;

(3) farm subsidies that artificially make one's domestic producers more competitive would be reduced, and quotas on imported textiles would be phased out;

(4) "piracy" of copyrighted books, films, music, and other intellectual property would be punished.[63]

The main legal innovation was the establishment of a compulsory dispute-resolution process. GATT had provided only for investigatory panels whose findings pertaining to GATT rule violations could be ignored by member states. There was ambivalence over whether dispute settlement should follow "the diplomatic model" or "the adjudicatory model." It "seems clear that the adjudicatory model prevailed in the Uruguay Round."[64] Under the WTO regime, any state accusing another state of being in violation of WTO rules can take the latter before an independent panel of trade experts, which is entrusted with investigating the complaint and rendering a judgment that may be subject to further review by a three-member appellate panel; if the defendant state is found guilty of violating free trade obligations and refuses to comply with the panel's judgment, member states can then legally impose trade sanctions against the state in question. In the first five years of the WTO's existence, there were some 160 cases brought by plaintiffs—three times the number handled by GATT.[65] By 2005, a total of over 250 challenges had been made against the trade policies of member states. Plaintiffs win in 85 percent of the cases, that is, "WTO tribunals systematically rule against domestic laws challenged as violating WTO rules."[66] Compliance has been the norm.

As of 2005, 148 states belonged to the WTO, with many other countries seeking to join but whose economies have not yet been sufficiently liberalized to meet the membership criteria. Policy decisions in the WTO are made by consensus as much as possible, but, to avoid paralysis, can be taken if necessary by majority rule based on a one-state-one-vote formula. At Marrakesh, U.S. concerns about being subjected to a possible "tyranny of the majority" (akin to the majority of third world states that often dominated the UN General Assembly in the 1970s) were offset by the assurance that in its sovereign capacity it could always withdraw from the WTO upon giving a few months notice and, also, that few WTO members would want to run the risk of destroying the organization by alienating the state with the largest, richest market in the world through constant policy rebukes and repeated adverse rulings in dispute cases. Washington was confident that, having the most open economy in the world, it would win more often than lose in the dispute-resolution process. Interestingly, the United States has brought more challenges than any other country (bringing suit in over one-quarter of all the cases in recent years) and, given the pro-plaintiff bias of the system, has won 78 percent of the time; however, the United States also has been a frequent defendant, losing in 83 percent of the cases filed against it.[67]

Has Politics Become Subservient to Law in the Governance of Economics?

We perhaps take it for granted that there is near-universal membership today in not only those IGOs with narrowly defined, relatively "apolitical" (or "low politics")

missions, such as the Universal Postal Union (UPU), but also in many IGOs operating in "higher politics" areas, such as the World Bank and the IMF; even in the
case of the WTO, most states are now clamoring to join, if only they could satisfy
the admissions criteria. To repeat, sovereign states do not have to join global IGOs.
Yet, with few exceptions, they all obviously feel a need to do so for fear of "being left
out." It should be added that, once states join these IGOs, they rarely leave,[68] and
IGOs themselves rarely "die."[69]

As with the UN proper, once a state exercises a sovereign decision to join the
UPU or some other IGO, its sovereignty then becomes circumscribed to some extent. We noted in chapter 2 that some IGOs—the ones that are assigned the most
technical, "functional" tasks—approach a supranational model more than others,
that is, are entrusted with decision-making competence that frequently compromises national sovereignty. Mark Zacher and Brent Sutton have shown how the felt
need of states to "pool sovereignty" in economic-related fields such as shipping,
telecommunications, postal service, and air transport results in international regimes that impact the powerful no less than the weak.[70] Although, as realists remind, some states such as the United States may well exercise more influence in
economic IGOs than other states, liberal institutionalists like Zacher and Sutton
point out how even the United States does not always get its way in the formulation and adoption of global public policy and has its autonomy ultimately constrained by rules in regimes it accepted reluctantly. In other words, the rule of law
often trumps politics.

The WTO, in particular, is "potentially [very] intrusive on national policies because it is now making rules . . . that override the preexisting national laws of
members."[71] As noted above, while the United States frequently has won in cases
before the WTO (for example, when it brought suit against the European ban on
U.S. hormone-treated beef products), it also frequently has lost (for example,
when Brazil accused the United States of subsidizing its cotton farmers in violation
of WTO rules). (See *EC Measures Concerning Meat and Meat Products Treated with
Hormones; US-Brazil Upland Cotton Dispute.*) The United States has seen several
congressional statutes "overturned," that is, judged by panels of WTO trade "experts" to be incompatible with WTO free trade requirements, such as laws banning the import of tuna caught with driftnets that kill dolphins and banning
petroleum products containing high-level pollutants; in these cases, the practices
authorized by Congress have been "ordered" ended, with failure to comply
inviting economic sanctions by WTO members.[72] (See *Restrictions on Imports of
Tuna; Venezuela-US Gasoline Dispute.*) It is not yet clear whether Washington's recent efforts to tighten up restrictions on food safety standards for imported fruits
and vegetables will pass muster with the WTO. The United States, of course, could
threaten to withdraw from the WTO and make good on its threat, but there would
be costs to Washington in terms of undermining the very free trade regime it, as
much as any state, helped to establish.

Even more intrusive than the WTO have been some of the "conditionality"
practices followed by the World Bank and IMF, where states seeking to avail

themselves of the latter's financial resources must agree to accept major externally-imposed reforms in their national economic life, notably promoting deregulation of publicly-owned industries and downsizing of their "big government" welfare sectors in the name of greater economic "efficiency." Although compliance in meeting IMF conditions has been a problem for many developing countries, and several have been cut some slack, the burden of outside expectations is ever-present.

One can see, therefore, the growing reach of international economic regimes, stimulated by concerns about order, stability, and efficiency aimed at promoting prosperity. But, to return to a question raised earlier in this chapter: What about "justice"—about prosperity not just for a few groups and countries but for all?

International Regimes and Economic Justice

The Internet homepage of the World Bank trumpets, "Our dream is a world free of poverty." In 2000, the UN Millennium Declaration, adopted at the largest gathering of heads of state in history, proclaimed a more modest, but still ambitious, goal: to halve, by 2015, the proportion of people whose income is less than one dollar a day and the proportion of people who suffer from hunger; additional goals included improvements in education, health care, and economic development generally.[73] Such aspirations were reaffirmed in a 2005 report issued by the UN Millennium Project, which noted that, "while the past thirty years saw dramatic improvements in the developing world," "still, human development is proceeding too slowly. . . . Some 54 countries are poorer now than in 1990. . . . [There has been a] decline in 21 countries in the human development index."[74] The report lays out a vision that some consider "utterly affordable" and others consider "utopian."[75]

It is open to question whether current international economic regimes will be able to deliver on this promise. We noted that global economic IGOs have been viewed by less developed countries (LDCs) as dominated by rich, developed states and privileging the latter's economic interests. Note, for example, the failure of the third world to transform the Bretton Woods economic order into a "New International Economic Order" (NIEO) during the 1970s, when the developing countries attempted to use their new-found majority control of the UN General Assembly to redistribute wealth from the North (the OECD states, headed by the G-7) to the South (the LDCs, represented by the so-called Group of 77).[76] It is worth examining briefly the exact nature of the NIEO demands made by the South, since many of these demands are still on the table today, even though the stridency of the rhetoric has subsided and even though the Group of 77 has found it harder to sustain itself as a cohesive bargaining group given the substantial socioeconomic improvements that have occurred since 1970 in some LDCs (notably the "newly industrializing countries," or NICs) relative to others (the "least developed countries," or fourth world).[77]

In the trade sector, the South attempted to establish the UN Conference on Trade and Development (UNCTAD) as their preferred forum for global trade negotiations, since LDCs enjoyed greater power there than in GATT. They sought better terms of exchange for their raw material and primary commodity exports that were hurt by depressed prices, along with greater market access for their manufactured, cheap-labor exports that were hampered by "voluntary export restrictions" (quotas). In the capital sector, specifically in regard to foreign aid, the South urged greater efforts by the North to meet the aid target established during the first UN Development Decade of the 1960s (i.e., at least 0.7 percent of the North's combined GNPs allocated for official development assistance), greater Northern willingness to cancel debts of Southern countries in serious balance of payments difficulties or to negotiate longer repayment schedules, and more loans at cheaper interest rates with fewer strings attached. As for foreign private investment, the South pushed for a code of conduct for multinational corporations that would limit the profits companies could repatriate to their home country, prohibit MNC interference in host country domestic politics, and strengthen host country ability to retain control over its natural resources and to regulate foreign subsidiaries. In the currency sector, the South objected to the IMF's tendency to withhold benefits from developing countries unless their governments agreed to adopt often painful "structural adjustment" policies calling for draconian cuts in their public expenditures and services aimed at enforcing sounder fiscal management. The South, above all, urged a greater LDC role in the governance of the IMF and other economic IGOs. They went so far as to propose a World Development Authority and other new bodies in which voting would be less tied to financial contributions and economic power.

An especially vigorous debate occurred over the issue of expropriation. The traditional, customary rule of international law (falling under "state responsibility for injury to aliens") was that a state could legally seize foreign assets, but only if its government made "prompt, adequate, and effective payment" to the owner.[78] During the NIEO discourse, the South, led by marxist states such as Cuba (which seized control over sugar plantations) and oil-producing states such as Libya (which seized control over petroleum pipelines), claimed that the only obligation was to pay "appropriate" compensation, as determined by the host government. The third world attempted to rewrite the rules through passage of a General Assembly resolution (the 1974 Charter of Economic Rights and Duties of States) that stated, "Every state has . . . full permanent sovereignty . . . over its wealth, natural resources, and economic activities. [This includes competence] to nationalize, expropriate, or transfer ownership of foreign property." Included in the Charter was a version of the "Calvo Doctrine" that Mexico and other Latin American countries had tried unsuccessfully to institute in the nineteenth century, whereby foreign enterprises were expected to waive their right under international law to seek the juridical protection of their home government against injury by the host state and instead had to settle for host state justice.

The South's NIEO demands largely went unmet as the United States and other G-7 members during the 1980s resisted calls for what they saw as a global welfare state being pushed by a would-be global parliament. The 1990s saw some rapprochement, with, for example, LDCs recognizing the need to tone down their militancy toward MNCs in order to attract much-needed foreign capital, and the MNCs themselves recognizing the need to reach some accommodation with third world governments in order to do business in secure environments free of the threat of expropriation of MNC assets;[79] in place of the shrill exchanges of the NIEO era, developed and less developed states entered into a series of bilateral investment treaties that restored most of the old rules.[80]

Order was restored even if justice was not wholly served. The 1995 World Summit for Social Development in Copenhagen, convened by UN Secretary General Boutros Boutros-Ghali to explore ways to alleviate global poverty and unemployment, drew government officials from 180 countries, as well as over 2,500 NGO representatives, dozens of MNC executives, and hundreds of IGO secretariat staff (from not only the World Bank and IMF but also the World Health Organization and other UN specialized agencies having a stake in economic development issues). The conference issued a non-binding declaration reiterating the plea for rich nations to spend 0.7 percent of their GNP on foreign aid and to provide debt relief for poor countries. Such entreaties have been repeated almost annually ever since, most recently in the 2005 UN Millennium Project Report, which noted that the 0.7 percent target had never been met and recommended, at the very least, a still-daunting "doubling of aid" from the current 0.25 percent of rich-country GNPs to 0.5 percent; trying to put things in perspective, project director Jeffrey Sachs said, "we're talking about rich countries committing 50 cents out of every $100 of income to help the poorest people in the world get a foothold on the ladder of development."[81]

Talk has exceeded action. When the WTO was created in 1995, there was hope that it would help create a level playing field, at least in regard to trade. While some third world spokespersons at the time saw the WTO reflecting "the recognition by world leaders from both the industrialized and developing nations that global free trade is beneficial,"[82] others saw it as just another power play, observing that "the agreement . . . was in truth an accord between the United States and the European Union [and Japan]. . . . It is not the GATT of the whole world but that of the rich and powerful."[83] The truth actually lies somewhere in between. Recall that, unlike the World Bank and the IMF, decision making in the WTO is not based on weighted voting tied to economic muscle; and, unlike the UN Security Council, no state, however powerful, enjoys a veto privilege. Recall, also, that LDCs such as Brazil at times have successfully gotten WTO tribunals to rule in their favor against the likes of the United States.[84] However, the formal WTO structures that would appear to check the power of the richest countries may be less important than the informal processes that still advantage those countries having the most human and financial resources to participate in global policy deliberations. LDCs are less able to participate fully in the WTO due to "capacity" limitations, that is, first, they are less likely to have the technical expertise and to be "able to afford an embassy in Geneva" to participate in the agenda-setting and policy formulation stages that precede formal voting, and, second, they are less likely to afford the substantial expense of bringing disputes before trade tribunals.[85]

Conflicts over "justice" are not simply interstate conflicts, but, as suggested by the strange-bedfellows coalitions that have formed around the globalization debate, pit "global civil society" against MNCs. In regulating states and markets, the WTO, along with the World Bank and the IMF, are said to suffer from a "democratic deficit," given the lack of transparency and lack of clear lines of accountability in these institutions (for example, the behind-closed-doors proceedings of WTO tribunals, where considerable power is exercised by appointed, unelected judges).[86] Accountability problems plague many IGOs, but none more than global economic organizations. Many nonstate actors, and not just states, have expressed dissatisfaction with current global economic governance. Annual gatherings of national economic ministers and international trade and finance bureaucrats often

SIPA Press/Tom Haley

The photo depicts "The Battle of Seattle" at the World Trade Organization summit meeting in 1999, when environmentalists, workers' rights advocates, and other groups engaged in violent street protests against the WTO.

have been disrupted by anti-globalization rallies organized by groups that cut across state lines. A measure of the relevance of international law and institutions is the amount of energy now being expended to influence politics in the WTO and other such global organizations, in recognition of the importance of the decisions taken by those bodies.

Grievances especially came to a head in the "Battle of Seattle" in 1999, at a summit meeting of WTO, World Bank, and IMF officials and governmental representatives that was marked by angry street demonstrations on the part of thousands of protesters—"environmentalists, human rights activists, the anti-sweatshop movement, and a whole grab bag of groups concerned about everything from saving the sea-turtles to saving teamster jobs."[87] The protesters were attacking what they saw as an elitist alliance between "GATTzilla" (their name for the WTO) and the multinational corporations, arguing that the meetings had been largely closed to NGOs and grassroots movements and were obsessed with free trade to the exclusion of other issues.[88] Interestingly, even though the protesters claimed to be speaking for the world's poor, the developing countries represented in Seattle did not see it that way. Led by Brazil, India, and Egypt, the LDC governments resisted any attempt to put global minimum wage or environmental standards on the agenda lest they be used to ban imports from developing countries. President Zedillo of Mexico spoke for other LDCs in his statement that "self-appointed representatives of civil society" (the street protesters) were "determined to save developing countries from development."[89]

Clearly, closing rich-poor gaps between and within countries involves complex political dynamics and difficult normative choices. One especially poignant example relates to the AIDS epidemic. Current international law protects MNCs from ill trade winds but does not protect masses of AIDS sufferers, insofar as WTO intellectual property rules limit the sale of cheap, "knockoff" antiretroviral drugs that violate the patents of global pharmaceutical companies; the challenge is to fashion rules that reconcile, on the one hand, the health needs of desperately sick people and, on the other hand, the need for patent protection to preserve incentives for Merck, Eli Lilly, and other firms to invest in medical research and development that might provide cures.[90]

Not surprisingly, poverty-related issues have not made their way to the top of the global agenda and resulted in major policy adoption any more than they have been given the highest priority on national, domestic agendas in the United States and elsewhere. However, they at least are on the radar screen. If the goals laid out in the 2000 UN Millennium Declaration are to be realized, it will have to come through some combination of private sector trade and investment and public sector largesse, mediated by strengthened international regimes.

Conclusion

The crusade to end world poverty is embodied in what Kofi Annan has called the "Global Compact," a proposed partnership between the United Nations and the global business community. This "compact" is not a legal document or even what could be called "soft law," even if some today speak of "a right to development." It is simply an expression of hope.

What is most intriguing about the Global Compact is that it seems almost an end-around the nation-state system. As reported by the New York Times, "big companies," in the name of good global corporate citizenship, are becoming "unlikely allies with the United Nations," as AMOCO, Cisco Systems, and other firms have been funding community projects in poor countries and relying on the UN Development Program and other IGOs to help administer the projects.[91] The Business Council for the UN is "engaging technology companies to help bridge the digital divide" and is "working with policy experts to deal with debt and financial crises in the developing world." [92] At a recent meeting of the World Congress of the International Chamber of Commerce (ICC), Kofi Annan's call for the United Nations as "the global institution" and the ICC as "the global business association" to join together to give globalization "more of a human face" met with a warm response from ICC members, who supported the concept even if they were lukewarm about any new regulations.[93] Other NGOs are also getting into the mix, as the World Bank and other aid donors are often bypassing LDC governments completely, instead channeling aid to poor countries through NGOs (feminist groups, village cooperatives, or other nongovernmental entities such as CARE), on the assumption that "NGOs can better reach the grassroots level, that NGOs . . . involve less bureaucratic red tape [and are less prone to graft]."[94]

Such IGO-NGO-MNC links are seemingly incongruous with the organizational logic of the Westphalian state system. Although one must always be careful not to inflate the importance of nonstate actors, these relationships offer a glimpse into what a post-Westphalian future might look like. Anne-Marie Slaughter notes how international regimes at the regional level, such as those associated with the EU and NAFTA, add another layer of complexity to those operating at the global level:

A radical departure from the traditional model of state-to-state relations is reflected in the 1994 North American Free Trade Agreement [signed by the United States, Canada, and Mexico]. Under its terms, individual investors can sue NAFTA member states directly for failing to live up to their treaty obligations. In one celebrated case, a Canadian funeral home conglomerate is suing the United States for $725 million over a series of Mississippi state court decisions that it claims deliberately and unfairly forced it into bankruptcy; the decisions allegedly violated NAFTA guarantees that Canadian and Mexican investors will be granted equal treatment with domestic U.S. corporations. The WTO grows out of a more traditional form of law in which only states can bring suit against one another, but even in the WTO, evidence of the new trend can be seen in the knots of lawyers who congregate outside WTO hearing rooms to represent the interests of individual corporations directly affected by the rulings of the organization's dispute resolution panels. And now nongovernmental organizations such as Environmental Defense and Human Rights Watch are fighting for the right to submit briefs directly in cases that raise important environmental or human-rights issues.[95]

Should these trends accelerate, they will only further weaken "the shell of state sovereignty."[96] The world is nowhere near to accepting some of the more idealistic, utopian proposals that have been floated at recent UN conferences, such as a world income tax or a global tax on currency exchanges that would be used to support a UN development fund, but the architecture of global economic governance is already evolving beyond what many realist, state-centric theorists could have predicted.[97] David Bederman muses that "international law may, indeed, have the greatest potential for progress and effectiveness in this [the economic] field"[98] if the kinds of problems discussed in this chapter can be overcome.

As the 2005 Millennium Project Report stressed, improved global governance will still depend importantly on improved *national* governance. That is, strengthening the "rule of law" in the state system is contingent upon strengthening it within states, particularly those political systems lacking stable, democratic, non-corrupt institutions.[99] Even in those countries in which the rule of law is highly institutionalized, questions often arise over what court is the proper forum to try a case involving violation of law. At times, competing claims of "jurisdiction" are made by more than one country's courts. One of the most basic, essential functions that international law performs is to provide a way to sort out these situations— what has been called "the allocation of legal competences." William Coplin describes what is meant by this:

> One of the primary functions of a legal system in a democratic society is to define the legal competences of the individual, that is, to provide guidelines which tell him what he can and cannot do in his everyday relationships with other citizens. In democratic societies this function is performed by civil, as distinct from criminal law. Civil law outlines the legal powers as well as responsibilities of individuals in their relations with others in the community. An analogous function is performed by international law. Through a series of rights and duties formulated by international law, the leaders of states are able to know what legal powers and responsibilities they have in relation to other states in the international community. For example, international law functions to designate which state has jurisdiction if there is a collision on the high seas or if a citizen of one state murders a citizen of another in a third state. . . . Without international law to distribute legal competences, states would find it difficult to regulate their own internal affairs and impossible to avoid frequent disputes with each other [over jurisdiction].[100]

The next chapter deals with these everyday workings of international law that are rarely reported by the media and, hence, generally go unnoticed by the average person. We will also look at some more politically charged matters. Ascertaining jurisdiction can at times be complicated enough when some infraction occurs on land. When it occurs on other "territory," such as the oceans or the skies, there are further issues to consider.

7

The Law of the Sea, Air, and Outer Space: Negotiating Troubled Waters and Other Territorial Issues

Almost three-quarters of the globe is covered with water. The oceans are sailed by approximately 50,000 large ships, which transport 80 percent of the world's traded cargo.[1] Myriad other vessels are cruise ships or smaller private boats used for fishing, recreation, or other activities. Virtually every vessel of any size is registered with and sails under the flag of a nation-state (not an MNC, NGO, or other nonstate entity). If a crime is committed somewhere at sea, under whose jurisdiction does the case fall? For example, if a German kills a Belgian on a Canadian-owned cruise ship flying the Panamanian flag in U.S. territorial waters, whose courts have jurisdiction to try the crime? Any state involved in the incident? No state? The flag state? The state on whose territory the incident occurred? The shipowner's state, the victim's state, or the defendant's state? Although most situations in international relations involve a much less tangled set of jurisdictional possibilities than this case, numerous incidents occur daily that require some determination of jurisdiction. Any one of us could conceivably find ourselves facing just such a situation—if not at sea, then in the air or somewhere else—which may not make the headlines as an international incident, but nonetheless brings international law into play.

When a state attempts to claim jurisdiction based on the fact that a crime occurred on its sovereign "soil," this assumes that its "soil" is clearly demarcated from other countries, something which itself may be contested, especially where one's "soil" refers to "territorial waters" or "national air space." Additional issues arise when the event occurs in a part of the world over which no state exercises sovereignty, such as the "high seas" or "outer space." In this chapter, we will see how the aforementioned Panamanian cruise ship case and other situations are handled, as we examine the rules governing not only how jurisdictional claims get processed but also how territorial claims are established in the first place.

ALTHOUGH SOME OBSERVERS in an age of economic globalization, cyberspace, and proliferating "boundary-spanning activities and processes" see "the end of geography,"[2] world maps continue to remind us of the importance of physical borders. Some of the world's geographical space—most of the land—is occupied by the roughly 200 nation-states, each of which claims sovereignty over the area within its boundary lines. However, far more space is taken up by what is sometimes called the "global commons"—the great oceans, the airspace over the great oceans, outer space, Antarctica, and other areas that are outside any state's sovereign territory. Contrary to the commons being a legal black hole where no law prevails, rules have been developed both to delimit where international space begins and ends and to facilitate the allocation of legal competences in this domain no less than in those zones under national control.

Before we discuss the question of *ownership* of territory, we first will examine the *bases of jurisdiction*. Although it may seem as if we are putting the cart before the horse, the "territorial principle" is only one of several bases upon which a state can attempt to exercise jurisdiction over a criminal act committed somewhere on the planet.

Bases of Jurisdiction

The Five Principles of Jurisdiction

Jurisdiction refers to the authority or power of a state to prescribe, enforce, or adjudicate rules of law. Here we are interested particularly in the competence of a state to prosecute certain acts of individuals in its courts.[3] There are five principles widely recognized as possible "bases of jurisdiction":

(1) the territorial principle

(2) the nationality principle

(3) the protective principle

(4) the universality principle

(5) the passive personality principle.[4]

The most fundamental, firmest basis for asserting jurisdiction is the *territorial* principle (see *The Schooner Exchange v. McFaddon*), whereby a state may exercise jurisdiction over the acts of anyone—nationals or aliens—committed within its territorial borders (for example, U.S. courts trying a Frenchman for a theft committed in Chicago); certain classes of aliens, however, may be exempt from host state prosecution, such as foreign diplomats who enjoy immunity under the Vienna Convention on Diplomatic Relations and foreign military personnel who are covered by a so-called Status of Forces agreement that gives the sending state primary jurisdiction over its soldiers stationed in another country (usually so long as the act in question occurred on the military base or in the line of duty).[5] (See *Wilson v. Girard*.) Also frequently invoked as a grounds for jurisdiction is the *nationality* principle, whereby

"Your Honor, my client would like to be tried offshore."

The allocation of legal competences.

a state may exercise jurisdiction over any acts perpetrated by its own nationals, no matter where they are committed in the world (for example, U.S. courts trying an American for a murder committed in Singapore)[6]; the nationality principle especially comes into play when one has committed an act abroad that may not be illegal in the host state but is a violation of one's own country's laws that are intended to apply to its citizens not only domestically but also overseas (as in the case of an American military contractor bribing a foreign official to gain a weapons contract or an American citizen or company evading U.S. tax or anti-trust laws).[7] (See *American Banana Co. v. United Fruit Co.* and *Blackmer v. United States.*)

The other three principles, only occasionally invoked, are exceptions to the general notion that states should not seek to prosecute in their national courts those acts committed by aliens abroad. The *protective* principle allows a state to claim jurisdiction over the acts of any persons—nationals or aliens (with a few exceptions)—committed anywhere in the world, if such acts threaten a state's national security or core interests (for example, U.S. courts trying a Hungarian for counterfeiting U.S. currency in Venezuela or trying a foreigner for lying to American consular officials when applying abroad for visa entry into the United States). (See *United States v. Pizzarusso.*) The *universality* principle permits a state to claim jurisdiction over the acts of any persons—nationals or aliens (with a few exceptions)—committed anywhere in the world, if such acts constitute crimes against the community of nations (for example, U.S. courts trying an Algerian for engaging in an act of piracy on the high seas by seizing a French fishing vessel, or trying a Palestinian for skyjacking an Israeli jetliner). (See *Attorney-General of Israel v. Eichmann* for "crimes against humanity.") The *passive personality* principle enables a state to claim jurisdiction over any person who has injured one of its nationals, no matter where in the world the act was committed (for example, U.S. courts trying a Syrian for killing an American in Lebanon).

Concurrent Jurisdiction

It is clearly possible for more than one state to have legitimate grounds on which to claim jurisdiction over some act. Take, for instance, the situation where a person in State A shoots across the national frontier and kills a person in State B; both states can invoke the territorial principle, State A based on the "subjective" nature of the act (insofar as the act began there) and State B based on the "objective" nature of the act (insofar as the effects were felt there). Concurrent jurisdiction can also involve two or more states invoking the nationality or passive personality principle, when the perpetrator or victim of a crime has dual or multiple nationality, a condition that is occurring more frequently as states relax restrictions on how many countries its citizens can owe "allegiance" to.[8]

At times, all five principles can be operative in a given case. For example, in 1977, eleven Japanese terrorists belonging to the Japanese Red Army hijacked a Japan Air jet and held hostage over 150 passengers and crew members during a six-day, 6,000-mile odyssey in which they threatened to kill the hostages if they did not receive a $6 million dollar ransom payment and obtain the release of several comrades from Japanese prisons. The plane, which was seized upon takeoff from Bombay, India, proceeded to touch down in Bangladesh, Kuwait, and Syria before finally landing in Algeria, where the plane and its occupants were freed. The hijackers were granted asylum by the Algerian government, although the ransom was returned to Japan. Had Japan been able to take custody of the hijackers, it could have conceivably claimed jurisdiction based on (1) the territorial principle (since technically the flag state is entitled to regulate conduct on its aircraft as an extension of its "territory"), (2) the nationality principle (since the perpetrators of the hijacking were Japanese citizens), (3) the protective principle (since the Japanese Red Army arguably threatened Japanese national security), (4) the universality principle (since piracy, whether of the air or sea variety, has long been considered an affront to the community of nations prosecutable by any state which captures the pirates), and (5) the passive personality principle (since most of the hostages were Japanese citizens). Jurisdiction could also have been claimed by India or any of the other four countries through whose airspace the plane flew and on whose territory the plane landed, by any state whose citizens were on board and were victimized by the hijackers, or for that matter by any country invoking the universality principle.

The *Achille Lauro* affair is another incident that illustrates the potential for concurrent jurisdiction to be claimed by many different states. In 1985, four armed Palestinians boarded the *Achille Lauro,* an Italian cruise ship carrying some 400 passengers, while it was in Egyptian waters near Alexandria. Their intent was to pressure Israel to free 50 Palestinian prisoners held in Israeli jails. They terrorized the ship's passengers for two days. After shooting an elderly, disabled American Jew named Leon Klinghoffer and throwing his body and wheelchair into the Mediterranean Sea, the hijackers (along with the mastermind of the plot, Abu Abbas, traveling with an Iraqi passport) persuaded Egyptian authorities to give them safe passage on an Egyptian aircraft back to Tunisia, the headquarters of the Palestinian Liberation Front. However, U.S. navy fighter jets intercepted the plane in Egyptian airspace and forced it to land in Sicily, where Italian authorities arrested the hijackers and then tried them in an Italian court. The United States conceded the jurisdiction of Italy, given the fact Italy was both the flag state on whose "territory" (the cruise ship) the act was committed as well as the final destination of the hijackers, although the United States, had it wished, could have invoked the passive personality principle (due to Klinghoffer's death) and the universality principle (due to the act of piracy) as grounds for its own jurisdictional claim. Among other states that could have staked a claim to jurisdiction were Egypt (based on the incident occurring in Egyptian waters and airspace), any state identifying any of the hijackers as its nationals, and, again, any state whose nationals were passengers victimized by the terrorists or which sought to prosecute a crime against the community of nations.

Both of the above hijacking cases show that, as a practical matter, one state—namely, the one that has the offender in custody—is normally in a position to determine whether to exercise jurisdiction itself or to *extradite* that person to another state seeking jurisdiction. I noted earlier that states ordinarily rely on bilateral extradition treaties as the basis for requesting the arrest and transfer of wanted fugitives from one country to another. The oldest such treaty on record is an extradition agreement between the Egyptians and Hittites in 1280 B.C.[9] Today, most bilateral treaties specify a mutually acceptable list of offenses—usually ones that are serious crimes in both states' legal systems—that trigger the surrender of an alleged or convicted criminal, although states are often exempt from surrendering their own nationals or persons accused of "political" crimes.[10] Some extradition rules may be found in multilateral treaties, as in the case of the Montreal Convention and other aviation conventions that obligate parties that have skyjackers or aerial saboteurs in their custody to either prosecute them or extradite them.

What happens, as in the case of the 1977 Japan Air skyjacking, when a country, in this case Algeria, is either not a party to an extradition treaty or refuses to honor an extradition request, and allows an individual to go unpunished? In our discussion of terrorism, we noted that, as a general customary rule, a state's agents cannot legally engage in what amounts to forcible extradition by entering a state's territory without that government's permission and abducting someone wanted for trial. In other words, it is understood that "one state should not encroach on another's sovereign boundaries by arresting a wanted criminal within another state."[11] Realists might note that this rule is sometimes ignored, particularly by powerful states, as in the case of U.S. fighter jets trespassing into Egyptian airspace to intercept the plane carrying the *Achille Lauro* hijackers. However, liberals and constructivists would counter that such violations are rare, as states are reluctant to undermine a norm that is critical to the smooth functioning of criminal justice systems. As one commentator says, "The perceived benefits of invoking irregular alternatives to international extradition may yield exhilaration for a moment [in bringing an offender to justice]. Such benefits, however, are not worth the long-term burdens to state sovereignty."[12]

Both the Japan Air and *Achille Lauro* hijacking cases also show the complex, overlapping jurisdictional claims that arise when incidents happen on board a foreign ship in a state's territorial waters or on a foreign aircraft in a state's national airspace. Based on long-standing customary law as well as more recent treaty law, a state that adjoins a body of water is entitled to exercise complete and exclusive sovereignty over its so-called territorial sea (including its ports and internal waters) immediately adjacent to its shoreline (see my discussion below of the 1982 UN Convention on the Law of the Sea), while a state also enjoys the same sovereignty over its skies above its land mass and territorial sea (see my discussion below of the 1944 Chicago Convention on International Civil Aviation). Foreign vessels enjoy a "right of innocent passage" to enter and navigate through a country's territorial waters, meaning that they can pass freely but only if they cause no harm to the security or well-being of the coastal state (see the *Corfu Channel Case*); the persons on board a foreign ship sailing through territorial waters are generally subject to the laws of the flag state to which a ship is registered, so that the latter has criminal jurisdiction over all acts occurring on board, except if the consequences of the crime are felt by the coastal state, which can then assert its right to exercise jurisdiction in the matter (see the *Wildenhus Case*).[13] There is no comparable "right of innocent passage" through national airspace—the right of scheduled airline traffic to fly overhead is established through bilateral agreements—although otherwise the same logic applies, that is, if a crime were to take place on board a foreign aircraft in one's airspace, the flag state would exercise jurisdiction, except in the extraordinary circumstance that the crime affects the state in whose airspace it was committed.[14]

Let's return to the hypothetical scenario cited at the start of the chapter: If a German kills a Belgian on a Canadian-owned cruise ship flying the Panamanian flag in U.S. territorial waters, *whose* courts have jurisdiction to try the crime? Applying these jurisdictional principles, it is conceivable that Germany could invoke the nationality principle, Belgium the passive personality principle, and the United States or Panama the territorial principle. As a general proposition, if the "good order" of the port of the coastal state (here, the United States) was not disturbed by the incident—if a wild shooting spree did not ensue—then the coastal state ordinarily would be willing to defer to the authority of the flag state (Panama), which in turn could decide to hand over the perpetrator to his government (Germany) for trial. In any event, it is not likely that the German would go scot-free.

It should be noted that Panama is annually ranked among the top ten countries of ship registration, owing to the fact that many shipowners shop for "flags of convenience," seeking to fly the flag of a state that can provide financial benefits in terms of granting licenses for modest fees and imposing only modest safety, environmental, and other regulations the owner must meet. The lax oversight of many flag states has complicated enforcement of anti-pollution conventions and other rules promulgated by the International Maritime Organization, a UN specialized agency with 164 members. The 1986 UN Convention on Conditions for Registration of Ships attempted to curb abuses by specifying the minimum conditions for a "genuine link" to exist between a ship and its flag state (for example, a "satisfactory part" of the crew was to consist of nationals of the flag state, and the flag state was expected to insure compliance with international standards), but the treaty has yet to come into force due to the failure of most states to ratify.

Since no state has sovereignty over the high seas—the "commons" area beyond any state's territorial waters—it follows that vessels on the high seas are subject to no authority except that of the state whose flag they fly. Should a collision occur on the high seas and criminal charges be brought against the captain and crew of either ship, the UN Law of the Sea Treaty provides that "no arrest or detention of the ship . . . shall be ordered by any authorities other than those of the flag state." (In the famous 1927 *Lotus Case* heard before the Permanent Court of International Justice, involving a collision at sea between a French steamer and a Turkish ship that resulted in the deaths of eight Turkish seamen, the court had ruled that Turkey had a right to institute manslaughter proceedings against not only the captain of the Turkish vessel but also the captain of the French vessel, a ruling so controversial that it prompted subsequent rethinking.) The UN Law of the Sea Convention contains three exceptions to exclusive flag state jurisdiction over vessels on the high seas, all of which are codifications of customary law: the ships of other nations may legally seize a foreign vessel on the high seas if (1) the latter is found to be engaged in piracy,[15] (2) if the latter is found to be engaged in the slave trade, and (3) if the latter is found to have violated the laws of the coastal state while in that state's territorial waters, in which case coastal state ships have a right of "hot pursuit" onto the high seas (see the *I'm Alone* and *United States v. F/V Taijo Maru* cases).[16]

Acquisition of Title to Territory

Sovereignty over territory presumes "title" (ownership). Traditionally, international law has recognized several possible modes whereby a state can acquire title to territory. These apply mainly to the most common form of territoriality: land.

We will first discuss these rules as they relate to adding land space and then discuss the rules governing claims to ocean space, airspace, and outer space.

Land

For much of the history of international relations, there were five possible ways in which a state could establish title to new land holdings: (1) occupation, (2) prescription, (3) voluntary cession, (4) accretion, and (5) conquest. As with the rules pertaining to the bases of jurisdiction, these rules pertaining to modes of acquiring title to territory have mostly evolved as customary law rather than having been the product of "negotiation" through a treaty-making process.

Occupation should not be confused with "military occupation." *Occupation* here refers to acquiring land through, first, discovery of an area that previously had been considered *terra nullius* (belonging to nobody) and, second, establishing at least some minimal administrative supervision over the area beyond merely planting one's flag. Whereas at one time discovery alone conferred title, by the nineteenth century it was generally understood that some sort of settlement and effective control was also necessary. This was the basis for European powers once claiming parts of the New World and Africa as colonial possessions; even though these lands were already inhabited by native populations ruled by tribal authorities, these were not viewed as states having proper title and governing capabilities.

Prescription refers to obtaining title to land that had been occupied by another state but whose claim has lapsed due to the loss of effective control, accompanied by indifference toward and tacit recognition of a takeover by the new owner. As an often-cited example, in the *Palmas Island* arbitration of 1928, the arbitrator awarded the island to the Netherlands, because Spain, the original title holder, had acquiesced in Dutch rule for over 200 years without protest; this had the effect of nullifying the ownership claim of the United States, which thought it had gained title through Spain's ceding it the Philippine Islands following the Spanish-American War. *Voluntary cession* refers to the formal transfer of title over territory from one state to another, usually through sale (as in the case of the Louisiana Purchase, for which the United States paid France $15 million in 1803) or gift (as in the case of the United States relinquishing claims to Christmas Island and nearby islands to Kiribati when that state attained independence in 1979). *Accretion* refers to acquiring title to territory through acts of nature, such as the gradual buildup of silt and other deposits from rivers; although a minor mode of territorial acquisition, accretion is still relevant at times, such as in a 1998 agreement between China, Russia, and North Korea over the changed course of the Tumen River.

Conquest, the annexation of territory by the use of armed force, is no longer a legal basis for claiming valid title, ever since the UN Charter outlawed aggression. We noted earlier, in chapter 5, the post–World War II emergence of the "territorial integrity" norm and the fact that the last successful annexation of territory by force occurred in the 1970s. Even where a state takes control over territory as a result of a war fought arguably in self-defense, there is a reluctance by the international community to confer title; hence, Israel's claims to the Arab territories of the West

Bank and the Golan Heights it captured during the 1967 Six-Day War, when it responded to the mobilization of Arab armies with a preemptive strike, have not been recognized by most states (see *Legal Consequences of the Construction of a Wall in the Occupied Palestinian Territory*). If the rules governing acquisition of title to land tended to favor powerful states in the early life of the international system, such realist principles seem much less operative today as colonization and conquest have become less normatively acceptable.

When much of international relations was about land-grabbing, peacefully or otherwise, the rules pertaining to acquisition of title were a major part of international law. Although these rules have become somewhat less important today, as there are fewer lands to be "discovered" or "transferred," boundary and other territorial disputes still exist and involve international legal skirmishing. (See *Frontier Dispute Between Benin and Niger* and *Territorial Dispute Between Libya and Chad*.) For example, in 2004, Canada sent hundreds of its troops into the mineral-rich North Pole region in order to symbolize its presence there and reinforce its claims to tens of thousands of miles of Arctic wintry wilderness, claims contested by the United States, Denmark, and other states. As one Canadian official said, "If you are going to exercise your sovereignty, you have to be able to show you can operate and be there." The so-called sovereignty patrols were not entirely successful; in the case of one in particular, "only 5 out of the 16 mostly rented snowmobiles survived the treacherous 900-mile journey through the shifting ice and howling winds in working order. The five troopers who managed to complete the patrol hammered metal plaques into the tundra declaring Canada's sovereignty over the remote Arctic archipelago off the coast of northwest Greenland."[17] It is not clear whether any were left behind to take up residence and solidify the claim.

On the opposite side of the globe, at the South Pole, the dominion over Antarctica remains somewhat unsettled as well. Numerous states at one time or another have claimed sovereignty over Antarctica and its valuable raw materials, including the United Kingdom, Argentina, Chile, Norway, Australia, New Zealand, and France, all of which have invoked the occupation principle. Other countries, such as the United States, have not asserted any official claim but have reserved the right to operate weather stations and scientific expeditions there. In 1959, the Antarctic Treaty created a regime whereby a dozen states, including the ones above, agreed to repudiate or suspend claims of sovereignty and to provide joint stewardship over Antarctica. The Antarctic Treaty System has grown to include twenty-seven "Consultative Parties" who have scientific or other operations at the South Pole and who meet periodically to review existing rules. Governance has included agreements to ban military activity, to place a moratorium on mining, and to conserve wildlife. Although the regime has been successful in managing conflict over the world's last ownerless landmass, many UN members have urged that, instead of Antarctica being regulated by a small condominium of self-appointed guardians, it be made into a "world park" administered by the General Assembly as part of the "common heritage of mankind."

The "common heritage of mankind" concept also has been invoked in connection with other commons areas, as discussed below in examining the status of territorial claims in the realms of ocean space, airspace, and outer space.

Water

Two authors comment that "the sea has always been an anarchic domain. Unlike land and air, it is barely policed, even today."[18] This is a gross understatement of the degree of law that governs ocean space. There is no Law of the Land Treaty, but, as noted above, there is a Law of the Sea Treaty. The 1982 UN Convention on the Law of the Sea (also known as the Montego Bay Convention) was the result of one of the great diplomatic conferences in history, involving virtually every country in the international system negotiating a single comprehensive text covering fishing and almost all other human activities on over 70 percent of the Earth's surface. In addition to codifying hoary customary rules governing "the right of innocent passage," "the right of hot pursuit," and other issues, the treaty added new rules, such as expanding the width of the territorial sea. In this section we will focus especially on the latter.

Let us trace briefly the law of the sea leading up to, and ultimately refined by, the Montego Bay Convention, since it is instructive of how global policy or regime-making processes operate. As mentioned in chapter 3, the "freedom of the sea" norm goes back a long way in history. Even the ancient Romans spoke of the free, public use of the oceans by all peoples. It is true that a few states in the fifteenth and sixteenth centuries made extravagant claims of ownership of large ocean areas (for example, Spain claimed possession of the Pacific Ocean). However, these claims had been generally discredited by the time Hugo Grotius initiated the notion of *mare liberum* (open seas) in his seventeenth-century international law treatises. The British and the Dutch, great seafaring and trading nations, led the way in pushing for universal acceptance of the freedom of the sea doctrine.

The basic principle that became widely accepted was that no state could exercise sovereignty over any part of the oceans except for the narrow band immediately adjacent to its coast—the *territorial sea,* in which the coastal state could regulate navigation and any other activities in the interest of its security. This area was to be distinguished from the high seas, where no such regulation was permissible. Most coastal states established territorial seas three nautical miles in width, based on the prevailing range of seventeenth-century cannon, although a few states did attempt to assert rights of up to twelve miles.[19]

For centuries, the oceans were relatively calm in terms of rule consensus. However, after World War II, the "laissez-faire" approach to ocean management came to be challenged for a variety of reasons. First, as land-based resources began to dry up, states intensified their search for ocean-based resources and discovered oil, gas, and mineral deposits in the seabed. Second, with new technologies, such as sonar fishing that could enable distant-water fleets to sweep huge expanses of the ocean clean of fish and supertankers that could spill oil over huge stretches of shoreline, humans were faced for the first time in history with the prospect of the oceans becoming depleted and even destroyed if not regulated in some fashion; coastal states suddenly had to be concerned about policing commercial activities not only within their territorial seas but in coastal waters beyond a three-mile limit.

Ironically, it was the United States, a major naval power and long-time champion of the freedom of the sea doctrine, that set a key precedent for expanded claims on the oceans. With Americans pioneering deep-sea drilling, the Truman administration proclaimed in 1945 the exclusive right of the United States to exploit the oil and other resources on its *continental shelf* to a depth of 200 meters (extending well outside three miles). This action sparked a wave of new claims to assorted segments of the oceans, with many states claiming territorial seas of twelve miles or greater (as in the case of Peru, Chile, and Ecuador in 1952 issuing the Santiago Declaration declaring sovereignty out to 200 nautical miles), others claiming 12- to 200-mile exclusive fishing zones, and still others claiming 12- to 200-mile zones in which they had a right to regulate pollution or other activities. The collapse of the existing regime threatened the oceans with chaos.

Two conferences—UNCLOS (UN Conference on the Law of the Sea) I and II, held in Geneva in 1958 and 1960—attempted to promote uniformity of state practice and produced a series of conventions representing the "first major hard codification of the law of the sea."[20] However, they failed to reach agreement on the critical territorial sea issue. Further complications arose when, in 1967, Malta's UN ambassador, Arvid Pardo, introduced the phrase "common heritage of mankind" into the debate, arguing that the *deep seabed* and its mineral wealth was not *terra nullius* (belonging to no one and, hence, free for use by anyone who had the capability to exploit those resources) but was *terra communis* (belonging to everyone and, hence, to be shared with all). In 1968, the UN Committee on the Peaceful Uses of the Seabed was created and proceeded to make preparations for UNCLOS III, which was, in the words of one observer, "the largest single international legal undertaking since the time of Grotius."[21]

Such was the setting for forging a new global ocean regime, as officials from 149 states met in Caracas, Venezuela, in 1973. There would eventually be eleven sessions convened in New York and Geneva over the next decade. The negotiations leading to the 1982 Law of the Sea Treaty reflected the dynamics of two-level games. At one level, the global policy process here could be understood as involving a dispute between those states that wished to maintain the traditional rules governing the oceans (notably, each coastal state having the right to exercise sovereignty over its territorial waters three miles out from its coastline, with the remainder of ocean space being high seas open for unrestricted navigation and exploration by any state) and those states that sought changes in the existing rules (such as extending the territorial sea to twelve miles, allowing for 200-mile exclusive economic zones in which the coastal state could regulate fishing, and creating a UN Seabed Authority to regulate mining of zinc, manganese, and other minerals on the deep seabed). Major maritime powers, including the United States, became

alarmed that twelve-mile territorial seas, especially around such vast island archi-
pelagos as Indonesia, would endanger the principle of the open sea that allowed
maximum freedom of operation for their large far-flung navies, scientific research
expeditions, and fishing fleets. Coastal states lacking such maritime prowess felt
they benefited more from an "enclosure" policy that limited other countries' access
to their offshore waters than from an "open sea" policy that gave free rein to
anyone who had the capability to exploit the oceans. Smaller, less developed
states, then, tended to advocate increased national control over their coastal waters. The latter sought to restrict certain activities on the high seas as well, urging
international regulation through the United Nations to ensure that technologically
superior states did not exploit the deep seabed for their exclusive gain, particularly
at the expense of established LDC mineral producers such as Zambia, Zimbabwe,
and Zaire ("the three Zs"). Insofar as they were calling for regime change, it was the
developing countries more than the developed ones that pushed law of the sea issues onto the global agenda. Landlocked states, some thirty in number, were also
present at the conference; they were wary of all coastal states—big and small
alike—and voiced concerns about how they too could share in the riches of the
sea, the "common heritage of mankind."

While such ocean politics could be understood at least partially in simple state-
centric, "billiard ball" terms, with each state through its leadership advancing demands that tended to favor its own national interests, beneath the surface there
was a more complex reality as the law of the sea game was played at several levels.
Subnational groups, such as U.S. fishermen, waded into the fray and muddied the
waters further, frequently disagreeing among themselves over what legal positions
best served the national interest of their country. For example, American fishermen on the East Coast, generally operating with small boats in nearby waters
and having to compete with mechanized Russian floating fish factories, favored a
200-mile exclusive fishing zone; in contrast, West Coast tuna fishermen, plying
the distant waters off the coasts of Peru and Ecuador, supported the principle of a
more limited twelve-mile zone so that they would not be excluded entirely from
Latin American waters. Various governmental agencies also often took conflicting
positions and engaged in domestic bureaucratic politics to have their particular
views accepted as official national policy. American Defense Department officials—concerned primarily about the free passage of U.S. warships on the high
seas—sought to retain the traditional narrow three-mile territorial sea, although
expressed a willingness to tolerate a twelve-mile territorial limit as long as the
principle of "unimpeded transit" applied to international straits falling in the extended band; conversely, Interior Department officials—primarily concerned
about managing U.S. coastal waters, including policing would-be polluters and
exploiting offshore oil and natural gas resources—were less supportive of the
freedom of the sea doctrine and instead wanted to expand the national zone of jurisdiction to 200 miles for certain purposes. (About one U.S. official who at first
represented the Pentagon at the conference and subsequently was shifted to the
Interior Department, it was said: "When he worked for the Pentagon, other dele-

gates would say 'Here comes Mr. Freedom of Navigation!' Then, as soon as he moved to Interior, suddenly seabed mining became the big issue.")[22] Battles between such subnational factions, both ministries and interest groups, were fought out not only in the United States but in other countries as well. Regarding the two types of games that occurred, a Canadian official noted: "The truth is that some of our delegation meetings [within the Canadian delegation itself] were far tougher than the negotiations with other states, because understandably a Newfoundland dory fisherman wanted assurance that his interests were not being sold out to protect British Columbia salmon."[23]

The story of how the Law of the Sea Treaty came to be would be incomplete without adding a third-level game to the analysis. In addition to national and subnational elements, *transnational* elements were also at work shaping agenda-setting, policy formulation, adoption, and implementation. The nonstate actors who played a role in the global policy process at Caracas and other venues where the decade-long negotiations occurred included multinational mining corporations interested in tapping the wealth of the deep seabed; scientific and environmental NGOs concerned about exploring and protecting the oceans; transgovernmental coalitions formed between ministries of different countries that at times had more in common with each other than with colleagues in their own foreign policy establishment; and IGO officials, such as the International Maritime Organization secretariat, which provided technical assistance, and the "Eurocrats" in the European Commission, who attempted to forge a common "European Community" position. Clyde Sanger provides a glimpse into the nature of NGO input into the global policy process and the way in which they helped some countries cope with their "capacity" problems:

> The Final Act of the conference lists 57 varieties of NGOs that in some way attached themselves to   the conference; they were as diverse as the World Muslim Congress and the International Hotel Association. However, it does not mention the group that did outstanding work in public education . . . for delegates whose countries lacked expertise on ocean resources, pollution problems, technology transfer, and other technical subjects. This was the *Neptune* group, a coalition of the United Methodists and the Quakers. . . . The energy of this small team of workers was phenomenal. In seven years they put out 19 issues of a lively tabloid. . . . They also sponsored press briefings and conferences . . . luncheon seminars for delegates on subjects from dispute settlement to the economics of tuna fishing, and evening panels for other NGOs and delegates. They worked with [U.S.] Senators and Congressmen on ocean legislation, and in 1982 fed their own ideas for amendments to the Convention into the conference.[24]

Few would argue that this or any other NGO was a lead player. Nonetheless, in combination with dozens of other nonstate actors and state actors, it was part of the equation that ultimately produced a global regime in 1982 that, as of 2005, 148 states had joined, including Japan, Russia, and the membership of the

European Union. (The treaty entered into force in 1994, upon the ratification of Guyana, the sixtieth state to approve.) The key provisions of the Law of the Sea Treaty include the right of a coastal state to claim up to a twelve-mile territorial sea (over which it exercises sovereignty) and a 200-mile exclusive economic zone (over which its authority is limited to regulating the conservation of living and nonliving natural resources), and the establishment of a UN Seabed Authority empowered to regulate mining on the ocean floor through the granting of licenses.[25] It is the latter provision that has kept the United States from acceding to the treaty, even though Washington accepts the rest of the convention and considers those articles binding as customary law.[26] Despite President Clinton signing the treaty in 1994, after a Modification Agreement was negotiated that addressed American concerns about legitimizing what to some smacked of "global socialism" and "world government," and the Senate Foreign Relations Committee ten years later voting unanimously to endorse the treaty, the United States has yet to become a party.

In the end, realists and liberals could both claim validation of their theories. On the one hand, realists can point out that the United States and other maritime powers were able to force compromises with developing countries that weakened many of the more radical demands LDCs had hoped to advance; and despite some misgivings about abandoning the old three-mile rule, the developed states with the largest coastlines, notably the United States, were the biggest winners, increasing their "territory" by millions of square miles as territorial seas expanded in width. As for the "common heritage" idea, forty percent of the oceans are now under state control—the largest portion ever enclosed—while the principle itself "still lacks acceptance as a customary legal norm sustained and substantiated by state practice."[27] There is erratic compliance with some of the treaty's 320 articles and nine annexes, especially those aimed at protecting the marine environment. Moreover, the effectiveness of the seabed regime has yet to be tested, since depressed prices of raw materials on the world market have put expensive deep-sea mineral extraction on hold.

On the other hand, the leading maritime power, the United States, found itself being mostly dragged along in the law-making process rather than dominating it, hardly in keeping with realist theory. Smaller states along with nonstate actors played a larger role than one might have expected based on realist precepts. More to the point, realists could not have predicted that the international community would be able to achieve such wide agreement over such a large set of issues spanning more than 70 percent of the globe, through a process that was based on "consensus voting" and allowed no reservations to be attached to the final draft. The Law of the Sea Treaty, for all its holes, remains one of the most impressive accomplishments engineered by the international legal system.

Air

Just as there is no Law of the Land Treaty, there is no Law of the Atmosphere Treaty. However, there is a regime governing use of the Earth's troposphere (the roughly ten miles of airspace above the surface) and stratosphere (the skies beyond), mainly consisting of a web of bilateral and multilateral agreements.

There was essentially no need for any rules governing airspace until the twentieth century, when the invention of aviation technology suddenly posed security and other problems for nation-states. It is true that France under Napoleon had a nascent air force of sorts in the form of hot-air balloons, and eighteenth-century visionaries like Benjamin Franklin were already speculating about the potential challenges such weapons posed for national defense: "Where is the prince that can afford so to cover his country with troops for its defense, as that ten thousand men descending from the clouds might not in many places do an infinite deal of mischief before a force could be brought together to repel them?"[28] However, the felt need to control one's airspace did not become a reality until the age of airplane travel was ushered in by the Wright Brothers in 1903. A decade later the United Kingdom was the first state to claim sovereignty over its "national airspace." After several other states unilaterally followed suit, a conference was called in 1919 to provide a common set of rules to deal not only with the perils of aerial warfare experienced during World War I but also with the emergent commercial aviation industry. The result was the Convention Relating to the Regulation of Aerial Navigation, a multilateral treaty that gave each state "complete and exclusive sovereignty over the airspace above its territory," with freedom of the skies applying elsewhere.

Ever since, there has been universal agreement that each state exercises sovereignty in its national airspace, although there has never been any certitude as to exactly how high up this area extends. Few states recognize a national air column reaching infinitely to the heavens. To the extent there is any consensus regarding the height boundary where national airspace ends, the upper limit is thought to be between fifty and one hundred miles above the ground. The rule of thumb is that national airspace extends to the highest altitude that can be navigated by an aircraft not in orbit.[29]

The core of the air regime is the 1944 Chicago Convention, signed originally by fifty-two states and amended several times since through "annexes" negotiated under the auspices of the International Civil Aviation Organization (ICAO), a UN specialized agency now having 188 member countries. The convention reaffirms a state's sovereignty over the airspace above its territory (which includes both its land area and territorial waters), prohibits the entry of foreign aircraft into a state's airspace without the latter's prior permission (although some exceptions are made for noncommercial private planes and planes in distress), and develops standards for airport and airline safety. As noted earlier, there is no right of innocent passage through airspace; instead, the world's scheduled commercial airline traffic is regulated mostly by a series of bilateral pacts between states that authorize the use of specific air routes and corridors for passenger and cargo planes. If a foreign aircraft intrudes into one's airspace, the latter's air force is permitted to bring it down, but is required to do so as peaceably as possible, first issuing a warning and following other procedures similar to those used in "hot pursuit" of ships at sea.[30]

Another important part of the international law of the air, related to the question of jurisdiction, is the 1963 Tokyo Convention on Offenses and Certain Other Acts Committed on Board Aircraft, drafted through the ICAO as a supplement to the Chicago Convention and ratified by almost the entire ICAO membership. This treaty deals with violent crimes on international flights and assigns primary jurisdiction over such acts to the flag state, no matter whether the offense is committed over international waters or in the airspace of another state.[31]

In addition, there are a host of more mundane rules that have been drafted by the ICAO, at times in conjunction with the International Air Transport Association (an NGO that includes most of the world's airlines and accounts for over 90 percent of all international scheduled air traffic), covering such matters as setting of international passenger fares, coordination of communications between airport control towers and pilots, and mandating technical specifications for aircraft. Although, as realists would have predicted, the major aerial powers have tended to dominate regime-formation in this field—for example, not surprisingly, English rather than Swahili or some other language has been established as the common language of civil aviation used in airport-pilot communications on international flights—it is mainly mutual interest in a stable aviation regime rather than raw coercion that has driven global governance of the air. It was such motivation that led the Soviet bloc finally to join ICAO in the 1970s after boycotting it for decades, and that has led the United States frequently to accept policy outcomes it did not fully support.[32]

We see in the case of the skies, as with the oceans, that global common space has been increasingly enclosed and placed under national control, although a considerable amount of "open" terrain remains. If the contemporary global aviation regime owes its origins mainly to national security concerns and "states' desire to control foreign airlines' access to their markets and hence their ability to protect their national airlines," its subsequent development owes more to liberal impulses, namely states' desire to "promote the rapid and safe international movement of goods and people."[33] Toward this end, international law has managed to create considerable order through institutions that facilitate the routinization of air transport.

Outer Space

Where airspace ends, outer space begins. Space law developed even more quickly than the law of the air, once the need for rules arose following the Soviet Union's placement of the first man-made object in orbit around the Earth, when it launched its Sputnik satellite in 1957. Almost instantly, the customary practice was established that a state's sovereignty over its national airspace did not preclude other states from over-flying the latter's territory in extraterrestrial vehicles. Within a year of Sputnik, the UN General Assembly passed a resolution (1348) calling for the peaceful use of outer space. Within two years, in 1959, around the time that the United States entered space competition, the General Assembly created the UN Committee on Peaceful Uses of Outer Space (COPUOS), which became the main agent for developing space law over the next several decades.

Five multilateral treaties, drafted and negotiated by COPUOS, constitute the main elements of the global regime governing outer space. The most important one is the 1967 Treaty on Principles Governing the Activities of States in the Exploration and Use of Outer Space, which was ratified quickly by Washington and Moscow and now counts about 100 parties. The Outer Space Treaty affirmed that space, including the moon and other celestial bodies, was part of the global commons, "not subject to national appropriation by claim of sovereignty." Hence, the Soviet Union and the United States, the two cold war rivals that inaugurated the space age, recognized from the start the folly of attempting to make territorial claims on other planets or heavenly bodies. The Outer Space Treaty also provides that exploration of space shall be open to all states and carried out for the benefit of all humankind; astronauts are to be viewed as emissaries of humanity; nuclear weapons and other weapons of mass destruction cannot be placed in space, in orbit, or on the moon; objects put into space are to be registered to the launching state and subject to that state's jurisdiction; and states shall be liable for any damage caused by their satellites or other objects. Although the treaty demilitarizes outer space, it allows for limited military activity related to "scientific research" or "other peaceful purposes," a concession made to the two superpowers, who otherwise might not have endorsed the treaty for fear of their not being able to utilize space legally for satellite reconnaissance, missile defense testing, or other such ends.

The other multilateral accords that comprise the outer space regime augment and strengthen various provisions of the Outer Space Treaty. The 1968 Agreement on the Rescue and Return of Astronauts and the Return of Objects Launched into Space (ratified by over eighty states as of 2005) obligates parties to cooperate in assisting in the rescue of astronauts and returning them to their home country along with returning space objects to the country of launch. The 1972 Convention on International Liability for Damage Caused by Space Objects (also ratified by over eighty states) spells out the responsibility of the launching state to pay compensation for any damage to persons or property resulting from falling objects or other causes; this was the basis for a successful 1979 claim by Canada against the Soviet Union, which paid the Canadian government $3 million for the cost of cleaning up radioactive debris following the crash of a Soviet nuclear-powered satellite in a remote wilderness area. The 1975 Convention on Registration of Objects Launched into Space (ratified by forty-four states) establishes a central UN registry whereby all parties are obligated to provide the UN secretary general with detailed information about any satellite or other object they put into space, including the registration number, orbital characteristics, and function. The 1979 Moon Treaty (ratified by only eleven states) reiterates that the moon and other celestial bodies are to be used only for peaceful purposes, but contains explicit language declaring them the "common heritage of mankind" and calls for an international regime regulating exploitation of natural resources found there.

Although the Moon Treaty is in force (having received the requisite fifth ratification, by Austria, in 1984), few states are bound by the agreement. In the case of the major space powers in particular, their opposition is based mainly on the treaty's treatment of outer space as *terra communis,* that is, requiring that any potential revenues derived from extraction of moon rocks, helium, or other raw materials be shared with all of humanity. Although these states agree that outer space cannot be claimed as sovereign territory, they interpret this to mean that this domain is *terra nullius,* open to free use and exploitation on a first come, first served basis.

In addition to nation-states (the roughly twenty countries currently capable of launching satellites as well as the remaining "have-nots"), the group of actors involved in space politics also includes MNCs and other enterprises that launch and rent satellites or contract for services from space (such as utilizing high-resolution photographic images of natural resource deposits and other data gained from remote sensing devices above the Earth), as well as IGOs such as the International Telecommunication Union (ITU), a UN specialized agency with 189 members that regulates the satellite uses of space, including the all-important allocation of radio frequencies used by everyone from TV broadcasters to weather forecasters, and promotes uniform standards in the operation of transborder telephone and other communications systems.

ITU, which traces its roots back to the International Telegraphic Union created in 1865, is the chief forum for global bargaining and rule-making in the telecommunications field. Its formal structure consists of the Plenipotentiary Conference, the plenary body and supreme authority that sets general policy and meets every four years to review the ITU Convention; the ITU Council, the smaller board of directors that meets annually; and the Secretary General and Secretariat, the administrative arm headquartered in Geneva. The very technical, seemingly "low politics" nature of telecommunications can lead one to overlook the high political stakes potentially involved in ITU deliberations, which occur in the meetings of its Plenipotentiary Conference, World Radiocommunication Conferences, and World Conferences on International Telecommunications.[34] ITU reserves specific segments of the radio spectrum for specific categories of users, maintains a registry of frequency assignments with an International Frequency Registration Board, and requires states to notify the ITU secretariat in Geneva of any future satellite placements in space and to obtain clearance for those so as to minimize signal interference, orbital overcrowding, and other problems.

Of special concern is the geostationary orbit, located 22,300 miles above the equator, where satellites move in synch with the Earth's rotation, making the orbit a preferred spot for television, telephone, remote sensing, and other transmission links. In 1986, the equatorial nations, raising concerns about remote sensing as an invasion of their national privacy and a threat to their national security, and also questioning the fairness of space-faring states co-opting the geostationary orbit for themselves, declared in the Bogota Declaration that their sovereignty extended straight upward into space, that any states seeking to occupy an earth-stationary position above the equator would have to pay an orbiting fee owed to the country below, and that any wishing to engage in remote sensing would have to get prior consent from the countries being "spied on" and be willing to share the data.

As realists could forecast, these demands of less developed countries have gone unheeded. Yet, from a liberal (or perhaps constructivist) perspective, the Outer Space Treaty, in repudiating any claims to sovereignty over space, is a visionary document representing considerable normative progress compared to the discovery-based titles to ownership staked out by the explorers sent to distant reaches of the Earth by great-power states in earlier ages. It can probably be said that there has been greater law compliance in space than down below, granted there are fewer rules to violate and occasions to break them, although the record in space is not perfect either (for example, U.S. efforts to deploy a space-based anti-missile system, known as the Strategic Defense Initiative or "Star Wars," are seemingly at odds with the Outer Space Treaty). Despite the huge economic and other barriers to space exploration, there is reason to expect further need for, and development of, space law in the twenty-first century. There are now more than 500 satellites in space, hundreds more are expected to be in orbit in the next decade or so, and "people likely will inhabit space stations and other planets for extended periods of time, if not permanently."[35] Jurisdictional and other rules will need to be articulated beyond the presently skimpy body of law, perhaps creating a growing niche specialty for "astrolawyers."[36]

Conclusion

Space law and politics raise profound questions and challenges that seem far off in both geography and time, yet are already upon us. Consider that planning is proceeding for space stations that are intended to be "international" projects jointly developed, operated, and governed by several states. Consider also, closer to home, here on Earth, we are still trying to come to grips with the governance of cyberspace that knows no borders, practically defies national regulation, and poses extraordinarily difficult problems for international regulation as well.[37] The nascent global governance of electronic information flows thus far has included ICANN (the Internet Corporation for Assigned Names and Numbers), which is a private body that manages the Internet domain system; a network of NGOs and epistemic communities seeking to shape norms in the digital world; the UN World Summit on the Information Society (WSIS) conferences of 2003 and 2005 organized by ITU in an effort to develop uniform rules and standards for using the Internet and World Wide Web; and numerous other international gatherings, all of which have produced up until now what amounts to, at best, "soft law."

The WSIS conference held in Geneva in 2003, attended by government officials and civil society representatives from 175 countries, produced a Declaration of Principles promoting the "idea of universal, accessible, equitable, and affordable ICT [Information and Communications Technology] infrastructure" and "an enabling environment at the national and international level based on the rule of law with a transparent, predictable policy and regulatory framework." However, much work remains to be done not only in addressing the many complex technical challenges associated with coordinating Internet usage across boundaries but also in dealing with issues relating to closing the digital divide, accommodating cultural diversity, promoting freedom of speech and artistic expression, and other matters that divide peoples and states, including the perceived dominance of the United States over the information highway.[38]

It was thought in 1948 that "once a photograph of the Earth, taken from the outside is available . . . a new idea as powerful as any other in history will be let loose."[39] Yet neither Sputnik's orbiting of the planet in 1957, nor the Apollo moon landing in 1969, nor thousands of satellite photos taken since have fundamentally altered our image of the human species as organized around a state system, no matter how many exhortations about Spaceship Earth have been uttered. Typical of this mindset is the recent billing of Brazil as "a developing nation on the frontiers of space" whose "equatorial location gives it a competitive edge in launching rockets [that are] faster and carry heavier payloads" than "temperate zone competitors." Brazil is building its own Cape Canaveral, at Alcantara on the eastern edge of the Amazon basin—in a tropical rainforest region some assert to be part of the "common heritage of mankind."[40]

Partly because of its importance of tropical rainforests to global ecology, Rio de Janeiro, Brazil, was selected as the site for the 1992 UN Conference on Environment and Development (the so-called Earth Summit). The report of the Brundtland Commission, the study group formed by the United Nations that provided the intellectual impetus for the Earth Summit, opened with the observation that "the Earth is one but the world is not,"[41] denoting the reality that the biosphere may represent a single interdependent ecosystem, where pollution and other environmental hazards transcend national boundaries, but the sociosphere still consists of separate political-legal jurisdictions. The next chapter examines the development of international environmental law and how nation-states are coping with the challenge of global governance in this area.

8

International Environmental Law:
Protecting the Biosphere

In 1973, the United States passed the Endangered Species Act, aimed at protecting various creatures ranging from the bald eagle to the spotted owl to the grizzly bear. What happens if these critters should wander across the border into Canada or Mexico or go even further astray, as wildlife is wont to do? What good is U.S. municipal legislation if protection stops at the border? Likewise, the U.S. Congress has passed Clean Air legislation and Clean Water legislation, but how effective can this be when air currents carry pollutants thousands of miles across national boundaries (as happened in 1998, when uncontrolled fires in Mexico produced a long blanket of smoke that necessitated a health alert throughout Texas) and water currents also carry contaminants across borders (as in the case of the Rio Grande River shared by the United States and Mexico and the Great Lakes shared by the United States and Canada). The United States, Canada, and Mexico all complain about each other's environmental negligence. So, for that matter, do New York and other Eastern seaboard states in the U.S. complain about pollution from Illinois and other Midwestern states, although here at least there is a central authority in Washington that can compel cooperation, something that is lacking at the international level. If it is hard to get neighboring nation-states to cooperate fully on environmental matters, it is that much harder to forge cooperation on a global scale. Still, there have been some successes, along with failures.

In chapter 1, I cited a recent newspaper headline that read "Biological Treaty, With the Goal of Saving Species, Becomes Law," referring to the 1992 Convention on Biological Diversity that requires countries to protect forests and other habitats rich in biodiversity. The Biodiversity Treaty is only one of several multilateral treaties on the books that attempt to curb species extinction. There are 1.75 million known plant and animal species on Earth, although the total number thought to exist may be as high as 100 million.[1] At least 1,000 species a year (50,000 a year and one every hour, according to some accounts) are being lost worldwide due to habitat destruction and other causes—a trend described by Peter Raven as "the greatest mass extinction since the die-off of the dinosaurs."[2] Hence, existing treaties thus far are proving unable to slow this phenomenon.

Of special concern are the tropical rainforests, since over half of all species are found there; as one illustration, famed biologist E. O. Wilson once identified forty-three different species of ants on a single tree in a Peruvian rainforest.[3] The rainforests, located in equatorial regions of South America, Africa, and Southeast Asia, are being cleared at the rate of 15 million hectares (40 million acres) a year—an area almost twice the size of Austria—owing to logging, farming, cattle-ranching, road-building, and other "development" activities.[4] At the present rate of destruction, unless the rules in place are strengthened and enforced, virtually all the rainforests will be gone by the middle of this century.[5] The possible elimination of such a pristinely beautiful biome would be not only an aesthetic disaster but a much larger calamity. Many species housed in the rainforests have important medical and other applications—for example, almost three-fourths of the 3,000 plants identified by the American National Cancer Institute as containing cancer-fighting chemicals come from the rainforests, and one-quarter of all prescription drugs are derived from this source[6]—so that the loss of such biodiversity could have catastrophic consequences for human beings.

An even greater, more direct threat potentially facing the human species is global warming, which has been traced to the steady increase in atmospheric levels of carbon dioxide and other "greenhouse" gases that are produced by the burning of fossil fuels and other man-made sources and that have resulted in an alarming rise in the Earth's temperature in recent decades. There are fears of the polar ice caps melting and flooding dozens of coastal cities such as Miami and New York or entire island countries such as the Maldives, scorched croplands adding to food supply concerns, and wildly erratic weather patterns causing substantial loss of life as well as massive economic losses. Although scientists are not in full agreement about the magnitude of the threat, there are many warning signs, including annual news headlines reading "1995, the Hottest Year on Record," "1998 and 1999 Are the Warmest Years on Record," "2004 Is Fourth-Hottest on Record," and the like.[7] All told, the fifteen warmest years since recordkeeping began in 1867 have occurred since 1980, with the ten hottest registered since 1990.[8] Other occurrences that have been attributed to global warming include: Mt. Kilimanjaro in Africa has lost three-fourths of its ice cap since 1912; the cherry blossoms in Washington, D.C., now bloom seven days earlier in the spring than they did in 1970; in 2002, an iceberg 40 miles long and 53 miles wide broke away from Antarctica.[9] Some observers even attributed Hurricane Katrina, the unusual Category 5 hurricane that produced the catastrophic flooding of New Orleans in 2005, to global warming. The main international legal response to this problem is the

1997 Kyoto Protocol, which attempts to set limits on CO_2 and other emissions that countries are allowed, but which is widely viewed as inadequate to the task of combating global warming.

Homo sapiens would seem to be on the list of "endangered species" if one takes into account all the environmental problems that presently confront us, not only loss of biodiversity and global warming but also ozone layer deterioration, acid rain, desertification, water shortages, hazardous waste disposal, energy crises, overpopulation, and other concerns.[10] While environmentally-friendly technology may offer potential remedies, law, too, will have to play an important role if the worst is to be averted. Not all of the above problems are equally threatening and not all have sparked global responses in the form of international regimes, but most have attracted enough attention to involve state and nonstate actors in the development of new rules aimed at managing planetary resources. It is impossible to cover all of these problems and attempted solutions here. Instead, I will try to summarize the general features of global governance in the environmental field—providing a brief overview of the landmark conferences and major policy outputs produced by these meetings, the range and nature of environmental regimes and the extent of their effectiveness, and the political dynamics at work in creating and implementing international environmental law. How do issues such as biodiversity and global warming get on the global agenda, what kinds of international legal norms and rules emerge as a result, and what is the record of compliance? And what are the prospects for improving governance in this area? In other words, as one commentator started his Inquiry Into the Human Prospect, "Is there hope for man?"[11]

IN THE ENVIRONMENTAL FIELD AS ELSEWHERE, we find cooperation intermingling with conflict. Although environmental issues tend to be quite technical in nature, they often overlap with economic and security concerns and, hence, can trigger high-politics as much as low-politics. In relation to economics, there are considerable tensions between the laissez-faire, free-trade principles of the WTO regime and the regulative desiderata of environmental regimes (for example, the contradiction between, on the one hand, WTO rules prohibiting the boycott of tuna caught with dolphin-killing driftnets and, on the other hand, the obligations contained in several environmental agreements to protect marine life). Regarding security, one observer has gone so far as to call the environment

the national security issue of the early twenty-first century. The political and strategic impact of surging populations, spreading disease, deforestation and soil erosion, water depletion, and, possibly, rising seas levels in critical, overcrowded regions like the Nile Delta and Bangladesh—developments that will prompt mass migrations and, in turn, incite group conflicts—will be the core

National Archives (306-PSD-69-3083)

This is a satellite photo of the Earth, taken on November 10, 1967, from geostationary orbit, 22,300 miles in space.

foreign policy challenges from which most others will ultimately emanate.[12]

While the latter statement may overstate the importance of environmental issues, it does seem safe to predict that global ecology will become a growing topic of discussion in global governance affairs. It is also safe to say that there will be growing pressures for states to pool sovereignty in addressing environmental problems, since so many of these problems transcend borders and defy unilateral and, in many cases, even regional solutions. But, as in other issue-areas, it remains to be seen whether the "need" will find a "way." In exploring this question, it is helpful to start with some historical perspective on how environmental consciousness and legal thinking have evolved.

Environmental Politics and Law in Historical Perspective

Pre-1972: From Ancient Rome to the Club of Rome

Environmental concerns are not new. One can read accounts of air pollution as far back as ancient times, in Seneca's references to "the heavy air of Rome." In 1659, John Evelyn wrote that London was covered in "such a cloud of sea-coal, as if there be a resemblance of hell on earth." It was an English chemist, Angus Smith, who in 1872 first coined the term "acid rain," in his book *Air and Rain*. A Swedish scientist named Svante Arrhenius in 1897 predicted potentially devastating global warming as a result of growing CO_2 concentrations in the atmosphere. In 1798, the most famous doomsayer of all, Thomas Malthus, predicted massive world famine as population growth outstripped increases in food production.[13] The term "ecology" itself is credited to a German scientist, Ernst Haeckel, writing in 1866. Environmental consciousness had appeared in colonial America as early as 1680, when William Penn decreed that for every five acres of land cleared, one had to be preserved as virgin forest. By the late nineteenth and early twentieth centuries, the U.S. government had already set aside great national parks such as Yellowstone, while Theodore Roosevelt and Progressive Era leaders, such as those in the newly formed Sierra Club, had pushed for a variety of conservation measures. Similar efforts at national-level policy making were underway in other countries as well.

Regarding international conservation efforts, according to one source "the first distinct period in the greening process began with nineteenth-century bilateral fisheries treaties and the Pacific Fur Seal Arbitration [involving an American-British dispute in the 1880s over British exploitation of seals in the Bering Sea]."[14] Even earlier, there were the Rhine and Danube river commissions, created in 1815 by Central European states to foster cooperation in riparian usage—the first modern IGOs to appear on the world scene. In 1900, several European states concluded the Convention Designed to Ensure the Conservation of Various Species of Wild Animals in Africa, Which Are Useful to Man or Inoffensive, aimed at regulating wildlife in colonial Africa. Countless other examples can be cited of historical interest in environmental concerns.

However, with a few exceptions, "before the 1920s or 1930s, there was simply no law on this subject. One would have looked in vain for state practice, treaties, case law, or even academic writings."[15] The reason was that the dominant paradigm at the time assumed that the Earth's bounty of resources was infinite, requiring little regulation. For example, the oceans were thought to be vast sinks impervious to overfishing, pollution or other human impacts, seen in T. H. Huxley's observation that the storehouses of cod and other fish "were inexhaustible because the multitude of those fishes are so inconceivably great that the number we catch is relatively insignificant."[16] When the UN Charter was drafted in 1945, it was silent on environmental matters, reflecting the fact that the environment had not yet made it onto national and international agendas as a major public policy concern.

Although there were some steps taken in the immediate post–World War II period to address environmental problems (for example, the creation of the International Whaling Commission in 1946, a 1949 UN-sponsored Conference on the Conservation and Utilization of Resources, and the establishment of the International Geophysical Year in 1957), it was not until the 1960s and 1970s that the modern environmental movement took off in the United States and elsewhere, grabbing public and elite attention to a degree heretofore unseen. Rachel Carson's 1962 book *Silent Spring,* on the dangers of pesticides, as much as any other work popularized ecology as a topic worthy of expanded governmental action and of increased study by K–12 schoolchildren and Ph.D. scientists. The first U.S. Clean Air Act was passed in 1963. The U.S. Environmental Protection Agency (EPA) was created in 1970 as an independent agency, apart from the Department of the Interior, to focus solely on ecological concerns; it was among the first such agencies in the world, and by the end of the century would have counterparts in almost every country on the planet. The first Earth Day was observed in 1970 as well, the brainstorm of U.S. Senator Gaylord Nelson of Wisconsin, at the time a relatively small celebration (with 20 million participants, mostly from the United States, compared with 500 million celebrants worldwide in 2005).

It is commonly noted that, in the typical polity, public support for clean air and other environmental goods is a mile wide and an inch deep. That is, almost all people want to see an improved environmental quality of life, but environmental issues still tend to possess not as high a level of salience as leaders and publics attach to pocketbook and other issues.[17] This complicates efforts at environmental problem-solving at both the national and international levels. It often takes a huge natural disaster and media event to sensitize people to environmental problems and provide the necessary catalyst for action, if only momentarily until the crisis has passed. Such was the massive *Torrey Canyon* oil spill in the English Channel in 1967. In what was described by one observer as the "Hiroshima of the environmental age,"[18] the third largest supertanker of the day ran aground and leaked 30 million gallons of oil, despoiling over 100 miles of shoreline, killing 15,000 birds, and prompting the International Maritime Organization to draft two treaties regulating dumping and discharges at sea.

On other occasions, it takes the work of "epistemic communities" of scientific experts to mobilize interest and place issues on the political agenda. In 1972, a small book entitled *The Limits to Growth*, written by a team of researchers calling themselves the Club of Rome, attracted wide-scale attention and began to fundamentally alter prevailing views about the relationship between humans and nature. Using elaborate computer models, the authors painted a grim portrait of a future in which unbridled economic growth and population growth worldwide would result in overconsumption and exhaustion of petroleum and other finite, nonrenewable raw materials, leading ultimately to the collapse of human civilization sometime in the twenty-first century; the only way out of this scenario, according to the authors, was a radical change in lifestyles and an acceptance of a less materialistic, "small is beautiful," no-growth model.[19] Although dismissed by some critics as unduly alarmist and "globaloney,"[20] the study provided the backdrop for the first global gathering devoted to a comprehensive examination of the environment, the 1972 UN Conference on the Human Environment, held in Stockholm, Sweden, which ushered in a new era in global environmental governance.

Post-1972: Stockholm and Beyond

The first UN conference on the environment in 1972 did not produce a single treaty, but nonetheless is considered a landmark event. One of the most important outputs of the meeting was the Stockholm Declaration of Twenty-Six Guiding Principles, a normative, hortatory statement rather than a statement of explicit, binding legal obligations. However, the Declaration gave written expression to a fundamental principle that had received only cursory treatment previously. In 1941, in the *Trail Smelter* case, an international tribunal was asked by the United States to consider whether Canada should be held liable for damages caused by a British Columbia smelter spewing sulfur dioxide across the border into the state of Washington; in what was the first statement of its kind on transboundary air pollution, the panel of judges found in favor of the United States, arguing that "no state has the right to use its territory in such a manner as to cause injury . . . to the territory of another." This principle was reaffirmed in Article 21 of the Stockholm Declaration, which acknowledged "the sovereign right of states to exploit their resources in accordance with their environmental policies" but urged states to "insure that activities within their own jurisdiction do not cause damage to the environment of other states or areas beyond the limits of national jurisdiction [i.e., the global commons]." Other outputs of the Stockholm meeting included an Action Plan containing 109 recommendations to be taken by governments to deal with environmental problems, as well as the creation of the UN Environmental Program (UNEP), the first global IGO focused on the environment.

The Stockholm conference, particularly the creation of UNEP, provided tremendous impetus for the development of international environmental regimes. Of the hundreds of international environmental agreements that currently exist, the vast majority were initiated after 1972.[21] The 1992 Earth Summit, held in Rio de Janeiro, added further impetus to the growth of environmental regimes. Since neither developed nor less developed countries had enthusiastically embraced the no-growth message of the Club of Rome, the Rio conference attempted to take a somewhat more positive approach, based on the 1986 UN-sponsored study by the Brundtland Commission, entitled *Our Common Future*.[22] The full, official name of the Rio meeting was the UN Conference on Environment and Development, reflecting the view that economic growth was compatible with ecological quality so long as it was achieved in a way that was sensitive to environmental concerns. The new concept "sustainable development" was much more acceptable to both the North and the South than "limits to growth" insofar as it seemed to imply less need for retrenchment and sacrifice. Rejecting the notion held by some environmentalists that "as the Dow Jones [stock market average] goes up, the Earth's health goes down,"[23] the Brundtland Commission argued that it was often the *lack* of economic growth that was responsible for environmental degradation—as in the Sahel region of sub-Saharan Africa, where attempts by peasant farmers to eke out a living by cultivating marginal lands were only destroying the landscape—and that economic development was critical to improving human well-being, assuming it could be done in a sustainable fashion.

The conference itself produced the Rio Declaration and the Agenda 21 Action Plan (two soft law outputs that refined and expanded upon the earlier versions produced in Stockholm twenty years earlier) as well as two treaties, the Framework Convention on Climate Change and the Convention on Biological Diversity. A follow-up conference, the 2002 World Summit on Sustainable Development, held in Johannesburg, South Africa, was mainly a stock-taking event that produced only another declaration (the Johannesburg Declaration) and a "Plan of Implementation," which set timetables for achieving various environmental and development goals (for example, by 2010, reducing the rate of biodiversity loss significantly; by 2015, reducing by half the proportion of people without access to clean water). Johannesburg seemed to reflect growing fatigue over the gap between aspirations and accomplishments, with a sense that sustainable development had become a "buzzword largely devoid of content."[24]

There is general recognition today that, much like human rights, the challenge in the environmental field is not so much the establishment of new rules but rather better enforcement of existing rules. The current era has been called "the era of implementation and compliance," as "the sheer number of MEAs [multilateral environmental agreements] has become an increasing problem. In addition to the staff and money needed to design and carry out meaningful action plans, the day-to-day logistics of servicing so many agreements is daunting."[25]

Although the global environmental movement in some respects has stalled, one should not underestimate the progress that has occurred. Margaret Karns and Karen Mingst remind that "the ad hoc conference process over the course of three decades . . . put the issue [of the environment] on the international agenda, forced states to adopt national agendas, [and] socialized states to accept new norms of behavior. . . . As constructivists argue, this process led to significant shifts in perceptions and behaviors that are the foundations of global environmental governance."[26] Although constructivists are right to point out the influence of "epistemic communities" in generating new ideas that have infused environmental diplomacy, realist and liberal perspectives offer further insights in helping us to understand how international environmental norms and rules develop. Before examining "ecopolitics," we need to survey the existing body of international environmental law.

The Range and Nature of Environmental Regimes

Our discussion of the Stockholm, Rio, and Johannesburg conferences reveals how global policy outputs in the environmental field can take the form not only of "hard law" treaties but also "soft law" declarations, principles, norms, action plans, and other such regime elements, along with the creation of IGOs and other institutions for facilitating further regime development.[27] It is difficult to distinguish at times between these various categories, since many of these approximate the status of customary law or at least have quasi-legal status.

Among the generally accepted principles or norms that are considered by many scholars to be part of the "governing arrangements" in the environmental field are:

(1) "good neighborliness" (the notion that one state has a responsibility not to do environmental harm to others);

(2) "the duty to inform and cooperate" (the notion that states should provide prior notice and consultation before undertaking actions that might possibly harm others);

(3) "the precautionary principle" (the notion that policies that could threaten the environment should be avoided even if there is not absolute scientific certainty regarding the potential harm);

(4) "intergenerational equity" (the notion that policies must consider not only the needs of the current generation but succeeding ones).[28]

Treaties have been the main instrument used to advance environmental protection. Commenting on the stimulus provided by the Stockholm Conference, one study notes that "before 1972 only a dozen international treaties with relevance to the environment were in force; twenty-five years later more than a thousand such instruments could be counted."[29] Counting only multilateral treaties, there are now over 500 such international agreements, "325 of which are regional in scope and 302 of which were promulgated [since] 1972."[30] The UNEP register itself lists some 200 MEAs (multilateral environmental agreements) of broad global significance.[31]

Most of these multilateral treaties each have their very own governance structure, although one finds a similar institutional apparatus across MEAs that includes a conference of the parties, which is the ultimate governing body that reviews implementation and arranges for negotiation and adoption of amendments; a secretariat responsible for providing administrative support, including gathering and dissemination of technical data; and various working groups and committees charged with monitoring and analysis tasks. The myriad treaties tend to fall into four categories: the atmosphere, water, land and biodiversity, and chemical and hazardous wastes.

The Atmosphere

Although air quality in many industrialized countries has improved somewhat in recent years because of environmental measures taken by governments, pollution in the North remains a serious problem. The problem is worsening in most developing countries of the South as they add automobiles and other trappings of industrialization. In India, for example, breathing the air in Bombay is said to be equivalent to smoking ten cigarettes a day, while inhaling in Mexico City has been compared to smoking two packs a day.[32] UNEP and the World Health Organization (WHO) administer a Global Environmental Monitoring System (GEMS) that collects data on urban air quality from some eighty cities in over fifty countries in order to determine to what extent pollutants are increasing or not. Atmospheric pollutants become an international problem when, as so often happens, they cross national borders. A recent reminder was the thick plume of smog that covered Malaysia, Singapore, and much of Southeast Asia in the late 1990s, which was traced to peasant farmers burning heavily forested areas in Indonesia to clear land for crops.

Acid rain, caused mainly by coal-burning and the release of sulfur dioxide and nitrogen dioxide into the atmosphere, has resulted in damage to forests and lakes as well as bridges and infrastructure. Since acid rain tends to be a transborder problem confined to a particular geographic locale rather than global in its reach, international regimes in this area have been bilateral or regional in scope. For example, the United States and Canada have attempted to forge agreements, even though Canada continues to find American responses inadequate. The most ambitious efforts to combat acid rain have been undertaken in Europe. In 1979, thirty-three European countries including the Soviet Union (as well as the United

States and Canada) signed the Framework Convention on Long-Range Trans-boundary Air Pollution, which committed the parties to study and assess acid rain damage and to explore what steps could be taken to reduce sulfur dioxide emissions. This was followed by the 1985 Helsinki Protocol, which required the same European parties to go beyond the framework convention and actually commit to reducing their SO_2 emissions by at least 30 percent from the 1980 level. More than twenty of the parties, notably Germany (a major net exporter of such pollutants), agreed to join the "30 percent club," and have since made considerable progress in cutting sulfur emissions, although the regime's effectiveness has been hampered by the fact that the United Kingdom and some other states have refused to join the protocol and by the complication that sulfur reductions have been offset by growing emissions of other harmful pollutants not covered by the treaty.[33]

European acid rain diplomacy illustrates what has become a common pattern in environmental regime-making, namely starting with a "framework convention" (sometimes called a "mother" treaty) that contains fairly vague language and modest obligations calling for little more than further study of a problem, and then following up with a "protocol" that contains explicit requirements, including specific targets and timetables, and entails real costs. It is easy to dismiss framework conventions as mostly empty, preachy documents, but they have been shown to play a strategic role in greasing the regime process by getting states to overcome initial resistance to cooperation and setting the stage for more robust collaboration down the road

This same process was at work in the global effort to address the climate change problem caused by the buildup of carbon dioxide and other greenhouse gases in the Earth's atmosphere. The Framework Convention on Climate Change that came out of the 1992 Earth Summit contained a nonbinding set of principles that acknowledged global warming was a serious concern requiring continued monitoring, that called upon countries to try to reduce their greenhouse gas emissions to 1990 levels by 2000, and that urged industrialized countries in particular to take immediate steps to curb their emissions and to help developing countries do likewise. The convention was signed and quickly ratified by almost the entire UN membership present at the conference, including the three biggest CO_2 emitters in the developed world—the United States (responsible for almost 25 percent of the worldwide total), Russia (7 percent), and Japan (5 percent). The Kyoto Conference in 1997 produced a follow-up Kyoto Protocol that obligated industrialized countries to meet specific targets (averaging approximately 5 percent below their 1990 levels) by 2008–2012, while less developed countries for the most part were exempted from any obligations.

The Kyoto Protocol, which required the ratification of at least fifty-five states accounting for at least 55 percent of developed-country CO_2 emissions before it could take effect, finally came into force when Russia ratified the agreement in 2005. Since the United States has refused to join (due to concerns about sovereignty, economic costs, the uncertainty of scientific evidence, and the free ride given to China and India, which are among the world's top five CO_2 emitters),

Russia's participation was needed in order to meet the 55 percent threshold. As of 2005, there are 146 parties representing over 60 percent of CO_2 emissions. There is fear that the treaty is too weak to remedy global warming, given not only the absence of the United States and several other major sources of carbon emissions, but also the fact that many parties themselves are not on track to meet their commitments. Meanwhile, each year sees record carbon emissions and more ominous warnings of the sort noted at the outset of this chapter, with the UN's Intergovernmental Panel on Climate Change estimating that, without vigorous action, temperatures could rise as much as 11 degrees Fahrenheit by the end of the century.[34]

One of the greenhouse gases, chlorofluorocarbons (CFCs), has also been blamed for contributing to the depletion of the ozone layer, which shields us from the sun's ultraviolet rays and helps to prevent skin cancer. By the 1950s, CFCs were being produced in large quantities by chemical companies as coolants in refrigeration systems, propellants in aerosol spray cans, styrofoam packaging in fast food restaurants, and for other purposes. When, in the 1970s, scientists established the link between CFCs and ozone layer depletion, the international community responded with a meeting in 1985 in Vienna that produced the Framework Convention for the Protection of the Ozone Layer. Ratified by virtually all the major CFC-producing industrialized states, the treaty was a modest instrument that merely obligated the parties to take "appropriate measures" to protect the ozone layer and to monitor the problem and exchange data. However, it paved the way for the subsequent protocol produced in Montreal two years later that would set explicit, mandatory CFC phase-out targets and timetables.

As described by Richard Benedick, the chief U.S. negotiator in Montreal, "On September 16, 1987, representatives of countries from every region of the world reached an agreement unique in the annals of international diplomacy."[35] The Montreal Protocol on Substances that Deplete the Ozone Layer has been hailed as "the most significant international agreement in history" and "unparalleled as a global effort."[36] The protocol called for CFCs to be cut by 50 percent from 1986 levels by 1998, with developing countries given a grace period of an additional ten years to phase out their CFCs, along with financial aid in weaning themselves off of CFCs. In addition, the agreement contained an unusual provision for periodic review whereby fast-track revisions of the protocol could occur without lengthy negotiations if the scientific evidence revealed the necessity for amendments.

By the late 1990s, both the Vienna Framework Convention and the Montreal Protocol had attained nearly universal adherence, including acceptance by the United States, the EU membership, India, and China. Ultimately, in the face of increasingly alarming scientific data about the widening of the ozone "hole," the parties agreed to a total ban on all CFC production by 1996. There generally has been good compliance with the treaty, notwithstanding foot-dragging by a few states and the existence of a "black market" for CFCs in some places.[37] Despite the success of the ozone regime, there remain concerns about its effectiveness, given gaps in the regime (in particular, the harm caused by methyl bromide as well as chemicals substituted for CFCs) and the fact that CFCs already deposited in the upper atmosphere may not be inert for another fifty years.

Water

Some eighty countries, mostly in the Middle East, Africa, and Asia, are now facing water shortages due to weather factors and expanded agricultural and industrial usage.[38] The potential for international conflict over water is heightened by the fact that 40 percent of the world's population depends for drinking water and irrigation on 215 river systems shared by at least two states; twelve of these are shared by at least five different states.[39] Mutual dependence can create cooperation as well as conflict. For example, the UNEP-sponsored Zambesi River Action Plan has coordinated riparian rights and obligations among eight different countries that depend on the waterway for drinking water for 20 million people in southern Africa.

Aside from water availability concerns, there is the problem of water quality. Lakes, rivers, and other freshwater sources are being subjected to increased pollution, which in turn eventually impacts the world's oceans and seas. From inland wetlands to coral reefs, water habitats worldwide are at risk. (The main global regime covering water space, the UN Convention on the Law of the Sea, was discussed in chapter 7.) Overfishing remains a problem despite the fishing regulations contained in the treaty, while the extensive provisions aimed at protecting the marine environment have also proven inadequate. Among several other global regimes that deal with ocean pollution are the 1972 London Dumping Convention (ratified by 81 states) that prohibits the dumping of high-level radioactive and toxic wastes overboard and regulates other waste disposal through a permit system, and the 1973 MARPOL Convention (ratified by 130 parties) that limits oil, plastic, and other discharges from ships at sea. There has been some progress made in reducing oil spills and other oceanic hazards; at the very least, these treaties have prevented the oceans from becoming an open sewer.[40] However, compliance with the reporting and related requirements of the conventions has been hampered by the "flags of convenience" problem noted in chapter 7.

Ocean governance also suffers from the fact that two-thirds of all ocean pollution is land-based. Precisely for that reason, UNEP during the 1970s established over a dozen Regional Seas Programs in areas where neighboring states shared a common resource and had a mutual interest in reducing pollution not only at sea but also originating from on-shore industrial and other activities. The Mediterranean Action Plan is the most well known of these. It involves eighteen countries that border the Mediterranean—including such traditional, bitter rivals as Israel, Syria, and Libya, as well as Greece and Turkey—in cooperation on research, monitoring, and pollution control. Member countries have established a protocol that bans ("blacklists") or regulates ("greylists") various categories of effluents into the Mediterranean. Although many pollution problems persist, along with disputes over who is to blame, considerable cooperation has occurred.[41]

Land and Biodiversity

Land degradation can take several forms, including soil erosion, desertification, deforestation, and other environmental harms. It is estimated that over one-fourth of the world's land area is arid or semi-arid desert and that the deserts in sub-Saharan Africa and elsewhere are gradually expanding at an annual rate of 81,000 square miles (an area the size of Kansas).⁴² The only global regime addressing desertification is the 1994 Convention to Combat Desertification, resulting from a promise that developed countries made at the 1992 Earth Summit to assist African countries experiencing arid conditions in return for their support on other issues. The treaty, which as of 2005 had been ratified by 191 states, thus far has failed to generate the necessary financial resources to support technical assistance for irrigation and land rehabilitation programs to slow the advance of drylands.

Deforestation has attracted more attention on the global environmental agenda than desertification, mainly because more valuable resources are thought to be at risk, particularly the rainforests' biodiversity described at the beginning of this chapter.⁴³ Building upon a previous Tropical Forest Action Plan that the UN Food and Agriculture Organization had initiated in the 1980s, the Earth Summit succeeded in issuing a Statement of Forest Principles along with the Convention on Biodiversity that affirmed the sovereign right of states to exploit their forest resources for purposes of economic development, albeit with the understanding that they were also obligated to do so in a sustainable fashion in order to protect these ecosystems and the biodiversity housed in them. The Biodiversity Treaty, now ratified by 188 states, requires less developed countries to formulate plans for preserving rainforests and other biomes, while obligating developed states to provide financial assistance and to ensure "fair and equitable sharing of the benefits" (for example, profits from pharmaceutical sales) with species-rich but cash-poor countries—a provision that has caused the United States to remain outside the treaty.⁴⁴ Neither North nor South has kept its end of the bargain to preserve what members of the UN have called "the common heritage of mankind." The treaty has been widely criticized, not only because of its failure to stop deforestation but also because, in limiting drug-company "bioprospecting" (theft of valuable plant and animal species), it has limited access to scientific researchers as well. The 2000 Cartagena Protocol on Biosafety was added to the Biodiversity Treaty to regulate genetically modified foods, and likewise pits economic and other considerations against ecological concerns.

Considerably more effective has been the 1973 Convention on International Trade in Endangered Species (CITES), which bans or restricts trade in hundreds of animal and flora species thought to be endangered. Ratified by 167 countries, CITES contains a list (in its first appendix) of species threatened with extinction, whose trade is totally forbidden (except for scientific or cultural purposes, such as zoos), as well as a list (in its second appendix) of species at least marginally threatened, whose trade is restricted through a system of quotas and export permits. CITES has been credited with saving the African elephant (which, before it was added to the first appendix in 1989, was being killed at the rate of 200 a day by hunters, mostly poachers, seeking to profit from the $60 million a year ivory trade), the black rhino (whose horn can fetch $25,000 for its aphrodisiac qualities), and other species, although "capacity" problems continue to limit the ability of many less developed countries to meet fully their treaty obligations.[45]

In another effort at species preservation, the International Whaling Commission has imposed a moratorium on commercial whaling since 1985 that has been mostly observed except for some recent transgressions by Japan and a few other leading whaling states.[46] (As a striking example of how far environmental consciousness has come, in the 1960s the U.S. Navy still used whales for target practice.)[47]

Chemical and Hazardous Wastes

It is estimated that 300 to 500 million tons of nuclear and other hazardous wastes are generated annually, with roughly 10 percent shipped across national boundaries.[48] Prior to the 1990s, many less developed countries were dumping grounds for toxic wastes exported from industrialized countries; less developed countries' (LDCs) governments often accepted the wastes (despite lack of safe disposal facilities) out of desperate revenue needs, but at times were victimized by covert waste trafficking companies. David Downie notes that "in one of the most notorious examples [of covert toxic waste disposal], the cargo ship *Khian Sea* left port in 1986, in search of a disposal for 14,000 tons of incinerator ash, originally from Philadelphia, that contained lead and cadmium. The ship spent almost two years at sea, during which it changed its name twice, dumping 4,000 tons of ash on a beach in Haiti and the remaining 10,000 tons somewhere between the Suez Canal and Singapore."[49]

Such practices have been significantly curtailed by the 1989 Basel Convention on the Control of Transboundary Movements of Hazardous Wastes and Their Disposal (ratified by over 160 states), which is the core hazardous waste regime. The Basel Convention limits the export of hazardous wastes, based on an informed consent regime that requires receiving states to agree to such imports and sending states to certify that adequate disposal sites exist in the country of destination. There are still lingering disputes, however, over the treaty's coverage of recyclables (one of several reasons why the United States has refused to join).[50]

There are several other treaties dealing with hazardous wastes, such as the 2001 Stockholm Convention on Persistent Organic Pollutants (POPs), which restricts the production and use of dioxin, polychlorinated biphenyls (PCBs), and ten other highly toxic, long-lasting chemicals.[51] The POPs treaty has almost 100 parties. Numerous other environmental regimes exist, not only in the area of hazardous wastes but also population and other areas as well.

Compliance and Effectiveness

Lynton Caldwell has commented that "the record of organized international cooperation in environmental affairs is superficially impressive. Tangible results . . . although significant, fall far behind [what is needed]."[52] I have noted that there is general recognition that environmental law-making is less of a problem than law-enforcement. Even where the compliance record is good, regimes may still be ineffective in making a dent in a particular environmental concern because of overly modest provisions. However, better compliance makes effectiveness more likely.[53]

Paul Wapner points out compliance failures even in the case of the relatively successful CITES and International Whaling Commission (IWC) regimes:

> For years, Iceland violated the International Whaling Commission moratorium by engaging in commercial whaling under the guise of scientific research. (In 1992, Iceland quit the IWC.) In 1993, Norway openly defied the IWC ban, commercially killing 226 minke whales in the northeastern Atlantic and in 1994 repeated its intention to breach the ban. The Cayman Islands have been in violation of [CITES] for exporting endangered turtle skins to CITES signatories England, France, and Australia, and Mexico has been cited in violation of CITES also for exporting endangered sea turtles to a number of other countries. These represent only the most flagrant infractions. Noncompliance is a broader issue in that many states lack the resources to implement accords or choose not to abide by them because the international system lacks a strong mechanism of enforcement.[54]

Wapner adds:

> Monitoring and verification of domestic implementation of international accords are carried out predominantly by states themselves. Self-monitoring and verification is a problem because it creates the possibility of lax implementation with no verifiable way to gauge effectiveness. According to studies carried out by the United Nations, most signatories to most international agreements fail to submit timely, accurate reports on their relevant activities. For example, only 30 percent of signatories to the MARPOL Convention for the Prevention of Pollution from Ships have submitted monitoring reports, and only 60 percent of parties to the 1972 London Dumping Convention have submitted reports on their dumping activities.[55]

In the words of another writer, "in large part, environmental treaties rely on an 'honor system' with little, if any, accountability other than the public pressure that NGO watchdog groups can apply. . . . Only a small number of environmental treaties include robust enforcement mechanisms, such as trade sanctions, fines, or withdrawal of technical or financial aid."[56]

In addition to the "capacity" and other explanations cited by Wapner for poor compliance, additional factors can include lack of specificity of targets and timetables, lack of international funding (for example, the entire UNEP annual budget is only $100 million), lack of transparency in confirming and publicizing noncompliance, and "gaps in international policy, fragmentation of effort, and competing or incoherent decision making structures."[57] While "many developing nations simply lack the technical capacity and financial resources to fully carry out their responsibilities,"[58] developed states have no such excuses, yet often have been delinquent themselves, reflected in the comments of a member of the European Parliament, who remarked that "we have now reached the point in the EC [EU] where, if we do not tackle implementation and enforcement properly, there seems very little point in producing new environmental law."[59]

Naturally, underlying much of the enforcement problem and environmental in-action are *political* differences. We need to look more closely at "ecopolitics."

Ecopolitics

At times it is possible to explain global environmental regimes by relying simply on "billiard ball" lenses.[60] Certainly the billiard ball paradigm provides at least a partial explanation of what happened at the first UN conference on the environment in Stockholm. Delegations from 114 states attended the 1972 Stockholm conference, representing governments drawn from both North and South. The Soviet Union and most states in Eastern Europe boycotted the meeting in protest over the non-recognition of East Germany, their Warsaw Pact ally. The United States and other developed states to varying degrees were advancing an environmental agenda calling upon less developed countries to control their population growth and to take other measures to address ecological concerns. The LDCs in turn crit-icized the rich industrialized states for failing to take responsibility for causing the bulk of the planet's environmental problems and for failing to provide adequate technical and financial aid transfers that might enable third world governments to respond properly to their own national needs. Partly as a symbolic gesture to co-opt the South into buying into the North's agenda, the major UN donors agreed to put the headquarters of UNEP in a third world capital, in Nairobi, Kenya.

Although the 1992 Rio conference was considerably larger—176 states attended, more than 110 of which were represented by their head of state—and although it was much more receptive than the Stockholm conference to the coequal priorities of the environment and economic development, in many respects it was a replay of 1972. Less developed states in a self-serving way reiterated their NIEO demands for more "green" in the form of money, while developed states in an equally self-serving way reiterated their call for "green" policies in Brazil, China, and other parts of the South to curb the latter's growing contribution to deforestation, global warming, and other such trends. To be sure, there were splits within the North and the South that made for shifting coalitions across different sets of issues. For example, the United States joined with Saudi Arabia and other members of the Organization of Petroleum Exporting Countries (OPEC) to block any provisions in the Climate Change Convention that would adversely affect major oil-producing or oil-consuming economies, while Germany, Japan, Sweden and some other industrial-ized states joined with the thirty-two nation Alliance of Small Island States (the Maldives and others that were especially vulnerable to the sea-level rise effects of global warming) to press for tougher measures. Each country sought to have others make the greater sacrifice. In the end, some delicate compromises were reached, including pledges by LDCs to pursue sustainable development and pledges by developed countries (DCs) to help bring that about through the infusion of additional funds channeled through the Global Environmental Facility that had just been created by UNEP, UNDP, and the World Bank, although differences persisted between DCs and LDCs over voting power in the Facility.[61]

Within the G-7, there remains a split between EU countries and Japan on the one hand and the United States on the other over whether to support the Kyoto Protocol along with a global carbon tax on fossil fuel use. This is based largely on national interest calculations. Germany has been a lead state in support of sizeable CO_2 reductions, since it can easily meet its Kyoto obligations by simply closing down heavily polluting factories in the former East Germany, which it would be inclined to do anyway. France relies on nuclear energy for 65 percent of its electricity while Japan also heavily utilizes nuclear energy; hence, they are more supportive of carbon taxes and other anti-fossil fuel measures than the United States, which not only has a more fossil fuel–driven economy, but also is more automobile-dependent and less able to shift to mass transit given its vast continent-wide highway system. Not surprisingly, China, which depends on coal for three-quarters of its total energy use as the basis for fueling its high-octane economic growth, was opposed to developing countries being saddled with obligations under the Kyoto Protocol and continues to resist any such demands. It is also not surprising, in regard to the European acid rain problem, that it was Sweden, a net importer of SO_2 emissions, and not the United Kingdom, a net exporter, which put the issue on the agenda and pressed for solutions that resulted in the Helsinki Protocol. Likewise, it is understandable why the United States, once its own chemical industry developed a substitute for CFCs, pushed for a total ban on CFCs to combat the ozone problem, only to be rebuffed initially by many European states reluctant to give the United States a competitive edge.[62]

Describing ecopolitics in traditional billiard ball, state-centric terms, Lawrence Susskind comments that "a few powerful nations play [a] . . . dominant role in most treaty negotiations, forcing other countries and nongovernmental interests to accept secondary roles or to sit on the sidelines."[63] Just as Germany has been a lead state on the global warming issue, the United States and China have been referred to as "veto states" whose cooperation is crucial to the success of any global warming regime since they are the two leading emitters of greenhouse gases. Japan is a veto state with regard to the IWC whaling moratorium and the CITES protection of the African elephant, since it has accounted for a very large percentage of whale kills and ivory imports.[64] Susskind adds that, for developed and developing states alike, there is "the stubborn persistence of national sovereignty as an important goal unto itself."[65] The UN membership was unresponsive when, in 1989, twenty-four states, led by the Netherlands, France and Norway, proposed a new supranational UN body in the environmental field that would be empowered to make "nonunanimous" binding decisions "for the good of the world community" and proposed, also, that the International Court of Justice in the Hague would be given jurisdiction over rule compliance.[66]

Although billiard ball dynamics are clearly evident in ecopolitics, so, too, are "cobweb" dynamics, as there is a growing role played by nonstate actors in agenda-setting, policy formulation, adoption, and implementation in the environmental arena.[67] As an example of how nonstate actors have increased their involvement in global environmental governance, compare the NGO presence at the 1972 UN Stockholm conference with their presence twenty years later at the 1992 UN Rio conference. In 1972, there were some 500 representatives from 250 NGOs. In 1992, there were over 25,000 representatives from 1,400 NGOs.[68] Many of the delegates at Rio were representing NGOs that had been officially invited to participate directly in the proceedings (e.g., Greenpeace and the International Union for the Conservation of Nature), while others participated in an informal, parallel nongovernmental Global Forum. Although 70 percent of the accredited NGOs were based in industrialized countries, some developing countries, such as India, the Philippines, and Kenya, also were heavily represented.[69] Not all NGOs at Rio were environmental groups. Some were business and other groups lobbying against excessive new governmental and intergovernmental regulations, although at least one corporate NGO—the Business Council for Sustainable Development, an alliance of Volkswagen, Dow Chemical, Nippon Steel, and a few other MNCs—took a pro-environmental stance.[70] James Speth describes this "global civil society" phenomenon as follows:

> Rio signaled the rise of an increasingly powerful group in international diplomacy: nongovernmental organizations (NGOs). The Earth Summit brought together an international community of scientists, policy experts, business groups, and activists representing a wide array of interests. Although far from cohesive themselves, NGOs worked together surprisingly well throughout the summit process, lobbying and educating delegates, helping draft agreements, and communicating with the 9,000 journalists who covered Rio.[71]

Echoing Speth, other observers note that efforts were made by the conference organizers to give NGOs "unprecedented" access both to the preparatory (PREPCOM) meetings as well as to the Rio sessions themselves,[72] and that Rio "represented a new level of NGO participation in global environmental politics."[73] In addition, there were numerous IGO representatives, drawn not only from UNEP, which helped to sponsor the conference, but also from UNCED's own secretariat, which was responsible for running the conference, as well as from FAO, WHO, IMO, and other UN specialized agencies involved in environmental regimes. Then, too, below this transnational layer, there were quite complicated domestic politics at work within national delegations (for example, in the U.S. delegation, there were conflicting positions to be reconciled among the Environmental Protection Agency, the Commerce Department, and other government agencies as well as among environmentalists, oil companies, utilities, and other interest groups). Rio, in short, saw a rich set of two- and three-level games being played by a variety of state and nonstate actors. So did the 2002 World Summit on Sustainable Development in Johannesburg, where almost 3,000 officially accredited NGOs and dozens of IGOs joined the 191 states that participated.[74]

Susskind is more cautious than Speth in evaluating the importance of nonstate actors. He argues that, while there is general agreement that in the environmental area as a whole "NGOs have been given substantial roles . . . up to and including shared responsibility for managing working sessions, and speaking (although not voting) at formal plenary meetings at which final decisions are made," "the rights accorded to NGOs, however, are unpredictable."[75] Obviously, not all nonstate actors have had equal impacts on global environmental governance at Rio or in other forums, but many have had input at various points in the global policy process. At the front end, "most multilateral environmental treaty negotiations have been initiated by international organizations,"[76] with UNEP in particular serving as a catalyst for convening dozens of conferences since 1972. Even before IGOs, activist NGOs have frequently succeeded in attracting world attention to certain environmental causes, notably Greenpeace, with its over 3 million members in twenty countries, which has raised global awareness of everything from the plight of whales in the Pacific facing extinction by harpoonists to the plight of "oil communities" in Nigeria facing land degradation by oil drillers.

Scientific NGOs ("epistemic communities") have played a special role in the agenda-setting stage. For example, in the case of the ozone layer, it was a 1974 article in *Nature* that first alerted the world to the link between CFCs and ozone layer deterioration; and it was a series of alarming findings about the widening "hole" reported by transnational scientific teams that prompted accelerated action at Montreal and thereafter.[77] Epistemic communities generally have been given a far greater consultative role in the policy process at Rio and other such environmental conclaves than they have enjoyed in such venues as the Uruguay Round trade talks or global arms control talks, where nation-state officials have been less likely to defer to "technical experts."

Such actors affect global environmental governance not only in contributing to agenda-setting but also in subsequent phases of the policy process, at times helping to craft treaty language, to mobilize mass publics to support governmental action, and—especially in the case of LDCs—to supplement national capacity to carry out regime obligations and perform policy evaluation. For example, an NGO named FIELD provided critical expertise to the member governments in the Alliance of Small Island States that enabled the latter to participate more fully in the Rio climate negotiations.[78] In the view of one commentator, "NGOs [at Rio] set the original goal of negotiating an agreement to control greenhouse gases long before governments were ready to do so, proposed most of its structure and content, and lobbied public pressure to force through a pact [the Framework Convention on Climate Change] that virtually no one else thought possible when the talks began."[79] Similarly, the World Wildlife Fund has been instrumental in compiling statistics on endangered species and putting pressure on governments to add various animals and plants to the protected list of the CITES treaty, while the International Union for the Conservation of Nature was called upon to draft the treaty itself, and TRAFFIC and other NGOs have been relied upon by governments to monitor treaty implementation and compliance.

It should be added that the more neutral and professional that scientific NGOs are perceived to be by national governments, the greater access they are likely to be accorded to the regime process; such perceptions are enhanced when the epistemic community is composed of participants from many diverse countries. Of course, as the global warming issue demonstrates, experts may be able to put certain issues on the global agenda and may help to propose solutions and foster initial action, but meaningful policy adoption and implementation may lag if the scientific community itself appears to lack consensus or, more importantly, if there are no politically palatable "cheap fixes" to the problem. The sounding of alarm bells about global temperature increases by many of the world's leading climatologists on the UN Intergovernmental Panel on Climate Change has been met more by a kill-the-messenger mentality than by a serious response to the message. As Susskind reminds, "independent scientific investigations may play a role in environmental treaty making, but they are intertwined with, not separate from, political considerations."[80]

It may yet be politics—national and other interests—that will move the climate change agenda forward. One writer asks: "What does it mean that top European insurance executives have begun consulting with Greenpeace about global warming?"[81] referring to the concerns of the insurance industry about the potential financial costs associated with floods and other disasters that might be caused by rising temperatures. This may produce little regime change in the foreseeable future, but—as with the Global Compact in the economic arena—it may nonetheless signal the beginning of a new kind of post-Westphalian politics that features a web of NGO-MNC-IGO interactions that often bypass nation-state capitals.[82] Jennifer Clapp, in a study of the politics surrounding amendments to the 1989 UNEP-sponsored Basel Convention that restricted the export of hazardous wastes, comments that "the attempt by business leaders to influence global environmental matters has traditionally been via lobbying the state at the domestic level. . . . While this is an important aspect of industry's efforts to insure that treaties which states enter into are in accordance with industry's desires, business actors are increasingly focusing their lobby efforts at the global level as well."[83] She analyzes the two- and three-level games played over the issue of whether scrap metal and other recyclables should be included in the waste ban—a highly technical, yet multi-million dollar controversy involving not only developed and developing states but also the Bureau International de la Recuperation (composed of some 600 firms and national recycling federations in over fifty countries), the International Chamber of Commerce, and other industry groups, pitted against Greenpeace and environmental NGOs.

Conclusion

There remains a lively debate over the "carrying capacity" of the planet in terms of how many people it can handle, how much consumption of resources it can manage, and how much further ecological decay it can stand. Just as important is the question of the capacity of the international system to develop improved governance arrangements to address these issues, along with security, economic, and other concerns discussed in Part Two of this book. Richard Benedick frames the problem as follows:

> The ozone treaty reflects a realization that nations must work together in the face of global threats and that if some major actors do not participate, the efforts of others will be vitiated. . . . The Montreal Protocol can be a hopeful paradigm of an evolving global diplomacy, one wherein sovereign nations find ways to accept common responsibility for stewardship of the planet and for the security of generations to come.[84]

Benedick has suggested that the governance structure of the Montreal Protocol might serve as a model for future environmental regimes and perhaps global regimes generally:

> At the top of the structure is the Meeting of the Parties to the Montreal Protocol, which combines executive, legislative, and judicial functions in a single supreme decision-making body. The parties, which had numbered only 35 states at the First Meeting of parties in Helsinki in 1989, grew to 157 by the eighth assembly in San Jose, Costa Rica, in 1996. (Meetings of parties were also open to nonparty states, UN agencies, and other intergovernmental institutions and nongovernmental organizations, which could all participate in discussions but did not have decision-making privileges.) . . . The main job of the assembly is to debate and decide on adjustments or amendments to the protocol. . . . Decisions [are to be] adopted by a two-thirds majority of parties present, representing at least separate simple majorities of both industrialized and developing-country parties. . . . An Open-Ended Working Group . . . is a less formal negotiating body . . . that prepares detailed options for decisions by the Meeting of Parties [based on review of scientific, financial, and other data]. . . . The Ozone Secretariat, located at UNEP headquarters in Nairobi . . . is responsible for convening meetings, assembling reports, [and carrying out other administrative tasks]. . . . Assessment Panels . . . [comprised of] hundreds of experts from around the world, coming from universities, governments, industry, and research institutes but serving in their personal capacities [perform policy evaluation in assessing regime effects]. . . . The Implementation Committee, comprising 10 members from the state parties, has assumed a central role in a unique process of monitoring compliance.[85]

Elegant as this governance model appears, questions abound. Despite the reference to "supreme" authority, is it not the case that ultimately each state retains its sovereign right to join or not join and to remain in or leave the regime? As the number of state parties belonging to the regime approaches 200, how easy or hard will it be to forge a global consensus and reach meaningful global agreements with so many actors crowding around the global bargaining table, including many that barely have enough state capacity to pay the airfare of their delegation? Does the participation of a myriad of IGO officials and NGO representatives, some representing private industry and some representing competing interests—all claiming to speak for "global civil society"—further complicate regime-making, and how exactly will they be accommodated? On ozone and other issues, to the extent that the locus of decision making shifts to international institutions—where MNCs and other transnational actors are peculiarly well-organized for lobbying and where unelected bureaucrats ("Eurocrats" and the like) can often wield considerable influence in the political process—how does one avoid a "democratic deficit"? Will major state players, such as the United States, tolerate enhanced participation of these nonstate actors, and will they accept a decision-making formula where they are not assured of veto power? If compliance is found lacking, what means exist for regime enforcement? Is the ozone case "unusual"[86] in the stress placed on technical expertise, or can we expect global problem-solving in all fields to rely increasingly on "an intimate collaboration between scientists and policymakers."[87] Will high and low politics imperceptibly blend into one another as the concepts of "security" and "welfare" broaden to include environmental threats? And will people in the United States and elsewhere be willing to accept global regulation of their behavior, when even now they often complain that their national capital is too far away and unresponsive to their concerns?

All of these uncertainties bring us back to where we began in chapter 1—to the search for, at the very least, a "more mature anarchy." In the concluding chapter, I will consider what lessons can be drawn from our examination of humanity's efforts to "pool sovereignty" and will offer some final thoughts on the constraints and opportunities surrounding global institution-building in the contemporary state system. As throughout the book, the focus will be particularly on international law and its relationship to international politics. Where might international law fit in an emergent architecture of a new world order in the twenty-first century? Where, between peril and promise, might we end up?

III

Conclusion

A Summation of the Argument

Things fall apart; the centre cannot hold;
Mere anarchy is loosed upon the world.

—W. B. Yeats, "The Second Coming," 1922

In relations between nations, the progress of civilization
may be seen as movement from force to diplomacy, from
diplomacy to law.

—Louis Henkin, How Nations Behave, 1979

Two roads converged in a wood, and I—
I took the one less traveled by,
And that has made all the difference.

—Robert Frost, "The Road Not Taken," 1915

An opportunity for rejuvenating the international legal
system—a new "Grotian moment"—is at hand.

—*Richard Falk, Friedrich Kratochwil, and Saul H. Mendlovitz,*
International Law: A Contemporary Perspective, *1985*

The least likely future is the present.

—*Anonymous*

9

The Future of International Politics, International Law, and Global Governance

LOUIS HENKIN HAS WRITTEN that "in relations between nations, the progress of civilization may be seen as movement from force to diplomacy, from diplomacy to law."[1] The reader will have to judge for himself or herself how much progress has occurred. It should be apparent from my movement through the previous eight chapters that, in the author's judgment, the verdict is mixed. International law does matter, both in the latent functions it performs—in allocating legal competences, setting parameters that constrain, if not restrain, state behavior, providing at times a surrogate for violence by serving as a medium of communication and bargaining, and otherwise subtly shaping international interactions—and in its more direct effects of dictating the actions taken by governments and their citizenry in various arenas. Yet, it does not matter as much as Henkin implores.

In this closing chapter, I will revisit some of the themes sounded at the start, distill what generalizations can be gleaned from this study (for example, why international law is somewhat more developed and successful in certain issue-areas than others), and weigh what role international law might play in future world politics.

It has been said that "four times in the modern age, men have sat down to reorder the world—at the Peace of Westphalia in 1648 after the Thirty Years War, at the Congress of Vienna in 1815 after the Napoleonic Wars, in Paris in 1919 after World War I, and in San Francisco in 1945 after World War II."[2] Neither men nor women "sat down" in 1989 to attempt to fashion a new order after the end of the cold war, since it ended so peaceably—something we should be thankful for, except for the fact that it left the world somewhat rudderless. As John Mearsheimer has noted, the cold war gave "a kind of order to the anarchy of international relations."[3] Similarly, Abba Eban has written that "the Cold War, with all its perils, expressed a certain bleak stability: alignments, fidelities, and rivalries were sharply defined."[4]

I have written elsewhere that "like the passengers on a large ship, humanity currently seems to be undergoing passage through unfamiliar and somewhat treacherous straits. We have left one international system [the cold war system] behind and are seeking to establish our bearings in a new system."[5] One could add to this imagery that the waters are choppy, the currents are swift, and our compass is malfunctioning. Reflective of how frenetic the pace of change has been lately, no

Malcolm Hancock

Between peril and promise.

sooner did we start referring to "the post–cold war era" in the 1990s than that designation gave way to "the post–9/11 era" in the 2000s. By the time this book is published or shortly thereafter, the post–9/11 era may well have given way to still another system transformation. The one thing we have been able to count on—the one constant over the past several centuries that has served to anchor our understanding of how the world works—has been the centrality of the nation-state and the state system. Although states and the state system remain lodestars on the planet, even this fixture is now being uprooted a bit, as the nation-state as an institution is being buffeted from above and below by the winds of "McWorld" and "Jihad" that appear to be stronger than the centripetal and centrifugal forces of the past. Could it be that we are on the brink of a change not just *in* the state system but *of* the state system? We may, in fact, be living in a time of a great transition between two epochs—a Westphalian world struggling to survive and a post-Westphalian world struggling to be born. Such traditional concepts as sovereignty, national interests and national security, citizenship, and the like remain fundamental to understanding world politics, yet in some respects are becoming increasingly problematical, if not anachronistic, in an age of economic globalization, cyberspace, "super-powered individuals"[6] in networks of terrorist cells, and other developments we have discussed.

It is easy to get carried away with the rhetoric of a brave new world, and to allow our normative judgments to cloud our empirical judgments, as the following statement from a leading scholar of interdependence suggests: "Boundaries between states are of decreasing legal and moral significance. States are no longer regarded as discrete political worlds. . . . [Any] assumption that sovereignty is an indivisible, illimitable, exclusive and perpetual form of public power—entrenched within an individual state—is now defunct. Within the wider international community, rules governing war, weapon systems, war crimes, human rights, and the environment, among other areas, have transformed and delimited the order of states, embedding national polities in new forms and layers of accountability and governance."[7]

Consider another statement, this one from a former president of the American Society of International Law:

> Stop imagining the international system as a system of states—unitary entities like billiard balls or black boxes. . . . [Instead,] imagine a genuinely new set of possibilities for a future world order. The building blocks of this order would not be states but parts of states: courts, regulatory agencies, ministries, legislatures. The government officials within these various institutions would participate in many different types of networks, creating links across national borders and between national and supranational institutions. The result could be a world that looks like the globe hoisted by Atlas at Rockefeller Center, crisscrossed by an increasingly dense web of networks . . . for collecting and sharing information, for policy coordination, for enforcement cooperation, for technical assistance and training, perhaps ultimately for rule-making. They would be bilateral, plurilateral, regional, or global.[8]

The latter author goes so far as to say that the foundation for this new system is already in place, that "not only *should* we have a new world order but that we already *do*."[9]

Although one can find lots of bytes of data that may indicate we have entered a "post-international politics" era marked by "a new feudalism"[10] or some other governance model (for example, the recent selection of Howard Stringer as the new CEO of Sony, bringing a non-Japanese-speaking American of British birth to the leadership of a company that had epitomized the insular Japanese style of economic management), there are more numerous bytes of data that indicate otherwise (for example, the classic state-centric politics at work today in the area of UN Security Council reform, where the United Kingdom and France have been unwilling to surrender their seats to an EU actor and where, when Germany is mentioned as a possible new permanent member, fellow EU member Italy complains that such proposals would create "a train with 175 nations crowded into third class").[11]

There are two simple truths about the global condition that cannot escape attention today. A few people may dispute these facts of international life, but the supporting evidence is overwhelming. On the one hand, notwithstanding a rising tide of transnational and transgovernmental activity, elites and attentive publics almost universally remain wedded to the traditional state system culture, with its emphasis on nationalism; and it is difficult to imagine the international organization movement or any other development undermining this condition anytime soon. It would seem quite premature to write off the nation-state, as there are now more such units than ever and the range of concerns their governments are expected to deal with has never been greater. In some respects, 9/11 and the war on terrorism have only strengthened the regulatory authority of the state. On the other hand, given technological imperatives that are incessantly reducing travel, communications, and other distances between states, and concomitantly increasing interdependence in terms of "sensitivity" and "vulnerability,"[12] it is equally difficult to imagine these same elites and publics—except the most isolationist-oriented—experiencing in the foreseeable future any diminution in their felt need for improved, more elaborate ways to manage interstate relations.

These thoughts, of course, are not new or profound. They have been uttered so often in one manner or another as to border on cliché, which is perhaps why their implications have been so blithely ignored. Nonetheless, however small the window of opportunity, this situation would seem to provide some opening—a "portal"—for the growth of global governance, particularly in the form of international law. Is it possible that, in the wake of various pressures operating on states to adapt to a rapidly changing international environment, this might be a "Grotian moment"[13]—an occasion for some creative thinking about international legal arrangements? If we are to seize the moment, we have to go beyond mere musing and think in more concrete terms, fully cognizant of the realities around us. What does experience tell us about the possibilities and the limits of international law?

A Few Observations about the Observance of International Law

From our previous discussion, the following "rules" of international politics, as they relate to international law, can be deduced:

1. *One can talk of "the international community," but there is none; what we have is an international political system, not an international community.* Many states themselves lack community, given ethnic and other divisions that prevent a true sense of nationhood. In these states, and even more so in the international polity, the "rule of law" is not highly developed, since the latter requires, among other things, trust that the legal institutions will treat individuals and groups—whatever their "identity"—roughly equal. In those municipal legal systems where the rule of law is deeply embedded, the application of the law approaches the "justice is blind" ideal (expressed in John Adams's famous definition of a republic as "a government of laws, and not men"). The international legal system, in contrast, is characterized

by blinders when it comes to the administration of law, as one's legal views are heavily colored by one's nationality.

This can be seen most vividly on the World Court. Borrowing from Mr. Dooley (the late nineteenth century American humorist), if U.S. Supreme Court justices tend to "follow the election returns," ICJ judges tend to "follow the flag." Unlike the Supreme Court justices, who are chosen independent of their home state and whose decisions ordinarily do not ride on whether they hail from Missouri, Alabama, or any other part of the Union, ICJ judges are nominated by their government and rarely if ever vote against the position taken by their own country's leadership, particularly when their country is a defendant. Indeed, the assumption that justice is not blind is built into the system, in the provision in the ICJ Statute that, if a state involved in a dispute before the Court does not have a seat on the Court, it is entitled to be represented by one of its own as an ad hoc judge in that case.

2. *Adding to the often arbitrary nature of international law, the scales of justice are heavily tilted toward the powerful.* The golden rule—"whoever has the gold rules"— applies to both municipal systems and the international system, but it is especially endemic to the latter. For starters, the Big Five members of the UN Security Council have permanent seats not only on the council (formally) but also on the Court (informally), and the richest countries dominate those IGOs that make decisions regarding the distribution of wealth. It is instructive that UNEP, and not the IMF or World Bank, was the bone thrown to third world countries as the only UN agency of any significance to be headquartered in the South. Power suffuses the entire global policy process, from agenda-setting (determining what issues are "problems" worthy of global attention and law development), to policy formulation and adoption (law-making), to policy implementation (law-enforcement and adjudication). Note, for example, how hard it has been to get the poverty concerns of less developed countries high on the global agenda and, even when they appear on the agenda (as with the decades-long target of DCs contributing 0.7 percent of their GNP to foreign aid), to produce meaningful policy outputs. Note the ability of the United States to impose its will in creating new rules through the Truman Proclamation in 1945 that gave the U.S. control over its continental shelf, compared with the failure of the 1986 Bogota Declaration to assert the right of equatorial states to collect fees for use of the geostationary orbit. Note, also, the failure of LDCs to achieve the adoption of new rules during the New International Economic Order (NIEO) debate in the 1970s, as well as the difficulty in implementing adopted rules that lack DC acceptance, such as the Moon Treaty declaring the moon the "common heritage of mankind" (*terra communis*). Note, too, the designation of English, as opposed to, say, Swahili, as the language of international aviation mandated by ICAO's air transport regime. Most egregiously, even in regard to rules of international law that are enshrined in the UN Charter, the most powerful states in the world often are above the law. To cite just a couple illustrations, witness the U.S. violation of the law, with impunity, in mining Nicaraguan harbors in the 1980s, and in the invasion and occupation of Iraq in the 2000s.

Even where the formal arrangements in international regimes seem to play down the role of power, as with the majority-rule or consensus-based voting procedures in such IGOs as the WTO and the UPU, the lack of "state capacity" to participate fully in agenda-setting and other stages of the policy process hinders LDC influence. It is a challenge for highly developed states themselves to marshal the human and financial resources needed to attend the myriad conferences sponsored by IGOs and to monitor the various secretariats, committees, and other bodies that constitute the governance structure of so many different regimes.

The exercise of power sometimes takes the form of a "veto state" or "veto coalition" whose importance in a specific issue-area is such that its lack of cooperation may be enough to frustrate the development of international law in that particular area (for example, Japan's pivotal position regarding both the CITES ban on ivory exports derived from the killing of African elephants and, with Russia and a handful of other states, the IWC whaling moratorium). During the cold war, in addition to the two superpowers being "veto states" across many issues, when they worked together out of mutual interests they could often push through major new rules of international law, such as limiting the nuclear club through the 1968 Nuclear Non-Proliferation Treaty. In the 1990s, U.S. hegemony, particularly market dominance, enabled Washington to move the international system to accept the World Trade Organization. Today, the ultimate power that the United States has is, through its abstinence, to deny any newly emergent international regime full legitimacy and effectiveness. It is questionable, for example, how the International Criminal Court can remotely come close to reaching its potential to deter and punish war crimes, crimes against humanity, and genocide without Washington's participation.

3. *As powerful as power is as a determinant and explanation of international legal happenings, it is not the only variable that counts; power has its limits.* Thucydides' dictum that "the strong do what they will and the weak suffer what they must" is not entirely borne out by events, particularly of late. After all, small, seemingly powerless states at times are also "above the law," not only failing to endorse treaties supported by the biggest states (e.g., the refusal of small maritime countries like Panama and Liberia to give up "flags of convenience") but frequently ignoring, without penalty, laws to which they have subscribed; in some cases, the violations may be quite conscious and intentional (e.g.., many human rights conventions), while in other cases they may have more to do with "capacity" problems (e.g., environmental treaties). It is debatable which is a bigger drag on the international legal system—strong states whose heavy-handed wielding of power and frequent flouting of the law damage respect for the law, or weak states and failed states whose dysfunctional character makes it impossible to honor obligations, whether submitting reports to the United Nations on their anti-terrorism efforts as required by the Convention for the Suppression of the Financing of Terrorism, filing reports with the IMO on their ocean pollution control efforts as required by the London Dumping Convention, or performing other obligations.

Just as we should not exaggerate the impotence of some states, we should not exaggerate the power of others. It is well understood by political scientists that hegemony is not omnipotence. A hegemon may be able to render treaties ineffectual by withholding its imprimatur, but may not be able to block adoption. For instance, many human rights treaties went into force during the cold war without U.S. approval, including the 1966 Covenant on Civil and Political Rights (which Washington did not ratify until 1992) and the 1966 Covenant on Economic, Social, and Cultural Rights (which Washington has yet to ratify). Indeed, since 1990, the United States has "lost" time and again at the bargaining table in failing to shape multilateral treaties to its liking, hence rejecting the treaties, and in the process suffering the embarrassment of being cast as an international pariah, as other states, including U.S. allies, have passed what amounts to international legislation. The list of multilateral treaties that have taken effect recently without U.S. participation includes not only the Rome Statute that established the International Criminal Court but also the Biodiversity Treaty, the Kyoto Protocol on Climate Change, the Basel Convention on Hazardous Wastes, the Convention on the Rights of the Child, the Ottawa Anti-Personnel Landmine Treaty, and the Convention on Illicit Trade in Small Arms, among others.

The American record of failure to impact international law since the end of the cold war demonstrates that even a unipolar system dominated by a single state, as some observers characterize the contemporary international system, can be difficult to manage. The United States arguably was more successful in influencing the international system between 1945 and 1990, when it had to share center stage with another superpower, than in the years since, when it has had no equal. Many commentators have noted the almost unprecedented power superiority the United States has enjoyed, at least on paper, in the post–cold war era. For example, Paul Kennedy notes that "nothing has ever existed like this disparity of power. . . . No other nation comes close. . . . Charlemagne's empire was merely western European in its reach. The Roman Empire stretched further afield, but there was another great empire in Persia, and a larger one in China. There is, therefore, no comparison."[14] Joseph Nye: "Not since Rome has one nation loomed so large above the others. In the words of The Economist, 'the United States bestrides the globe like a colossus. It dominates business, commerce, and communications; its economy is the world's most successful, its military might second to none.' "[15] Stephen Walt: "The end of the Cold War left the United States in a position of power unseen since the Roman Empire."[16] Timothy Garton Ash: "Not since Rome has a single power enjoyed such superiority."[17] Josef Joffe: "Its power is more overwhelming than that of any previous hegemon since the Roman Empire."[18] Stephen Brooks and William Wohlforth: "If today's American primacy does not constitute unipolarity, then nothing ever will. . . . In the military arena, the United States is poised to spend more on defense than the next 15–20 biggest spenders combined. . . . There has never been a system of sovereign states that contained one state with this degree of dominance."[19]

Left unsaid here, but a common thread running through all these writings, is the growing unreliability, even disutility, of power in international relations, reflected in the travails Gulliver has experienced in getting the Lilliputians (including ministates, such as Monaco, no larger than Washington's Capital Mall) to follow its lead. One could already begin to see superpower slippage during the second half of the cold war (recalling Lyndon Johnson's failure to understand how "the greatest power in the world" could be defeated by "a band of night-riders in black pajamas" in Vietnam[20]), but that was just a harbinger of further humiliations that would follow in Somalia and elsewhere. The main threat to American core interests today, in the age of "the long peace," comes not from great powers but not-so-great powers. As with Rome, the United States failure may reside less in its hard power than in its "soft power," that is, the power to lead through the force of one's ideas and one's status as an exemplar to be emulated (what Nye refers to as "getting others to want what you want," co-opting people rather than coercing them).[21]

Though always envied, and therefore only grudgingly liked, by many countries over the past half-century, the United States nonetheless for many years was widely admired and respected for the values it seemed to project, not only democracy and economic vitality but also a commitment to global institution-building and multilateralism. Washington led the way after World War II in creating the United Nations and the UN system of IGOs, partly through sheer dominance and partly through the art of compromise in various negotiations on air transport regimes (for example, the 1946 Bermuda Agreement accommodated Britain's desire to limit access of American carriers into the British market), trade regimes (for example, the United States allowed GATT rules to operate in a way that opened up the U.S. market to the exports of Japan and other cold war allies while not insisting on strict reciprocity from them), and other rule-making projects. Carrots were used as much as sticks, in recognition that some concessions had to be made in pursuit of larger American national interests; U.S. policy makers grasped that the United States, in providing the lion's share of collective goods that Americans benefited from, sometimes had to tolerate free riders.[22]

However, since the Reagan years, and especially in the post–cold war era, there has been a greater hesitance to go the extra mile to craft whatever compromises are needed to nudge international law forward in a way that meshes the interests of the United States with those of its allies and others in the international system. This unilateralist turn has been due to a variety of factors—a changing domestic American political scene (e.g., the election of a more conservative Congress) and a changing international political scene (e.g., the declining cohesion of the Western alliance in a post-Soviet world)—and has involved both petty concerns (e.g., rejecting the treaty on the rights of the child and the small arms treaty because of concerns about usurping parental rights and infringing on the constitutional right to bear arms) and more weighty concerns (e.g., the worries over the ICC undermining American sovereignty). The result has been a huge public relations disaster for the United States, whose soft power has declined substantially as Washington has acquired the image of a bully, if not outlaw state.[23]

The central challenge for the United States is, as former U.S. Secretary of State Henry Kissinger once remarked, to define a role for itself in a world which, "for the first time in her history . . . she cannot dominate, but from which she also cannot withdraw."[24] Kissinger, himself a classic realist, by the 1990s had gravitated reluctantly in the direction of multilateralism. If it was true before 9/11 that America could ill afford to "run off into the future all by ourselves,"[25] it is all the more evident after 9/11. An isolationist United States tried "running off" in the interwar period, when the failed effort at global governance produced a great depression and world war because "the United Kingdom could not [lead]" and "the United States would not."[26] Should current efforts at global governance—at cultivating shared norms, rules, and institutions—fail, there could be far worse consequences for the world and for the United States. Nye has put it most succinctly, noting that the United States cannot be the Lone Ranger but, at best, must settle for the role of "sheriff of the posse," with an emphasis on the need for Washington to recruit others to join it in combating terrorism and other problems.[27] In trying to convince the "posse" to put its opposition and fears aside and act when necessary to confront aggression,[28] it would help if the "sheriff" showed "a decent respect for the opinions of mankind"[29] on security, economic, environmental, and other Issues. The bottom line here is that the United States needs international law as much as international law needs the United States.[30]

4. *Politics at times is subservient to law in international affairs, as the strong frequently come to rely on norms and rules as much as the weak.* Realists maintain that "efforts to improve international cooperation [through law] must bow to the logic of state self-interest and state power."[31] We have seen that the logic of state power is not quite what it is cracked up to be, as—to repeat Rousseau's caution—"the strong are never so strong that they can be master of all." What about self-interest? The realist argument that "the best explanation for when and why states comply with international law is not that states have internalized international law, or have a habit of complying with it, or are drawn by its moral pull, but simply that states act out of self-interest"[32] is a valid one. However, it fails to address the distinction between short-term interests and long-term interests, including the "shadow of the future" that liberals contend hovers over international institutions. Notwithstanding the considerable law-breaking that occurs in international relations by both strong and weak states, there is evidence that some norms and rules do take hold and are able to compel obedience in many instances even when they are at odds with a state's immediate interest, since the long-term interest in sustaining a norm or rule often overrides the short-term, expedient advantage to be gained from violating it.

How else can one explain U.S. behavior in enduring a huge beating in the court of world public opinion by refusing to ratify the Convention on the Rights of the Child and other widely accepted treaties, when, if such documents were merely "scraps of paper,"[33] the path of least resistance would seem to be to go along? The

American long-term interest in sustaining *pacta sunt servanda* as a cornerstone of international law arguably has trumped the American short-term interest in deflecting global criticism as a pariah. How else, also, can we account for the willingness of the United States and other states to accept the binding decision-making authority of the WTO dispute settlement tribunals and to comply with adverse decisions? And how can we account for the willingness to concede almost supranational authority to the World Health Organization and some other IGOs on a number of issues, and, almost without exception, to remain in IGOs even when the latter do not always act in accordance with one's preferences? It is one thing for a state to leave UNESCO or the International Labor Organization, as the United States has done (only to return); but it is another matter to leave an organization like the Universal Postal Union, from which "exit is generally not a feasible option"[34] if one wishes to engage in international mail transactions.

Although it is true that "habits of compliance" and "internalization of norms" are not well-developed in the international system, some principles become so institutionalized that it is almost unthinkable to depart from them. For example, the understandings about diplomatic immunity are so ingrained in the international body politic that even the Soviet judge on the World Court could not bring himself to vote against the United States in the 1979 Iranian hostage case; likewise, the "territorial integrity norm" has become so entrenched that there has been no successful forced annexation of territory in 30 years (since Morocco's seizure of the Spanish Sahara in 1976) and the one attempt to eliminate a UN member sparked a near-global collective security operation that defeated it (Desert Storm's rollback of Iraqi aggression against Kuwait in 1991). Even regarding morality, international law in a few instances seems to owe more to a reflectivist, constructivist instinct to "do the right thing" than to any identifiable rationalist, instrumental motivation, as with the development of anti-slavery conventions, the decolonialization norm, the ban on hazardous wastes exports to poor countries, and the agreement of states not to claim real estate in outer space as national territory.

5. *International law more closely resembles municipal law, in terms of the existence of a law-giver and the expectation of law-enforcement, in low-politics issue-areas than high-politics issue-areas.* It may be true that there is no "sheltered area of concordant interests" in which "we are vouchsafed the privilege of warming up the motors of institutional collaboration . . . getting off to an easy start and building up momentum for crashing the barriers of conflicting interests that interpose between us and the ideal of world order."[35] However, some issue domains are far more amenable to *robust* cooperation—a "maturer" anarchy—than others. We would expect states to more readily agree to something approximating hierarchical governance when it comes to sharing cancer research data than sharing data on armaments. Low-politics issues, by definition, involve relatively narrow or technical problems, which often are significant but tend to be not quite as politicized in that they do not bear on the survival of the state. Not only do all states gain from the routinization of, say, transborder mail flows or civilian air traffic control on international routes, but there is less worry over absolute versus relative gains from

such cooperation. In these circumstances, states are more willing not only to pool sovereignty but also to surrender some of it to other bodies. Highly detailed regulations governing state behavior tend to be the form international law takes in these areas, with the drafting often left to IGO technocrats. Compliance is the rule, not the exception.

That "planes land, packages are delivered, and phone calls go through"—all in a prescribed, predictable fashion—"does not mean that the international legal order is operating as it should,"[36] but neither should it be taken for granted. Of course, what are low-politics concerns one moment may become elevated subsequently. Aviation, telecommunications, and other "functional" fields have the potential to become more embroiled in controversy in the future as welfare concerns increase and overlap with security concerns.

6. *International law changes not only due to shifts in the power structure of the state system and redefinitions of national interests, but also in response to technology, scientific discovery, and other developments, with nonstate actors often leading the way.* The international law of airspace and outer space did not exist—and was not anywhere on the global agenda—until the invention of airplanes and rocket ships necessitated the introduction of rules into those bailiwicks, just as the centuries-old law of the sea did not change substantially until supertankers, floating fish factories, offshore oil rigs, and other innovations created pressures against the three-mile, freedom of the sea regime.

As in the case of the global environment, "epistemic communities" often are instrumental in getting issues on the global agenda. That the UN Charter was silent on ecology but was followed by hundreds of environmental treaties after World War II owed mainly to the work of environmental scientists. Although scientific experts may succeed at agenda-setting, they may not succeed beyond that, in influencing subsequent stages of the global policy process, unless certain conditions obtain. The wider the agreement ("consensual knowledge")[37] among scientists regarding the nature and magnitude of a problem, and the greater the availability of a solution that is economically cheap and politically palatable, the more likely that expertise will translate into public policy outputs, including hard law. This can be seen most clearly in comparing the success of the ozone layer regime and the failure of the climate change regime. Scientific and other NGOs can play an important role in agenda-setting and policy formulation and adoption when they effectively marshal empirical data and are able to get the attention of the mass media, as with the International Campaign to Ban Landmines, which is largely credited with the Ottawa Treaty.

Just as states have proliferated, so have nonstate actors. The more actors—states and nonstates—that clamor to be at the global bargaining table, the more difficult it can be to forge agreements; it is generally easier to reach bilateral agreements than multilateral ones. Still, there are any number of near-universal treaties, demonstrating what is possible when the will to collaborate is present. Nonstate actors, either transnational or subnational, increasingly are agents of change. Any attempt to strengthen international law must take into account the complex two- and three-level games that are played in producing rules on everything from food safety to chemical weapons. While multiple layers of complexity can be an obstacle to the development of international law, they also present new opportunities to create links across national boundaries in support of international regimes.[38]

7. *There seems to be a feedback, "learning" process at work that moves international law along incrementally.* Nobody "decided" that custom should be superseded by treaties as the primary source of international law. Such a development occurred over time as a common-sense reaction in many national capitals to the growing size and complexity of the state system. The pattern of using framework conventions to grease the global policy process and promote adoption of protocols evolved from experiences with problem-solving on acid rain and the ozone layer. Peacekeeping was a creative response to the realization that collective security was not working and that conflict management could be enhanced through a less conflict-generating, more consent-based set of practices. The human rights regime, because of different definitions of rights held by different countries and the possibility of separating out various categories of rights, evolved through "salami tactics" that sliced up the problem into individual treaties covering specific concerns (race, gender, political and civil, economic and social, and so forth), while the Law of the Sea Treaty, given the nature of ocean space, was conceived as a single comprehensive package. The compromise of embedded liberalism managed to attract broad support in its artful ability to avoid the "beggar thy neighbor" economic nationalism of the interwar period while accommodating the needs of the Keynesian welfare state after World War II. Likewise, sustainable development became the "prominent solution"[39] in the game played over limits to growth, maximizing acceptance of the global environmental project. IGOs themselves, as halfway houses between nation-states and world government, represent the ultimate novel adaptation of the state system to its environs.

Although international law grows partly through a kind of "invisible hand" not unlike Adam Smith's invisible hand of the market, it often requires an actual, purposeful human hand—a great power or concert of great powers or a larger set of actors—to produce forward motion. How might international law be strengthened through human engineering?

Strengthening the Rule of Law in International Politics

Order, we have noted, is not the only value to be served by law. Justice is another desirable value, not only in itself but also because a just order is likely to be a more stable order. On issues of justice and morality, Barbara Ward Jackson has written: "We have been more or less brought up to believe that the bonds of community, responsibility, and obligation run only to the [national] frontiers. Should we extend our vision to include all the people of our planet?"[40] Justice can be difficult enough to define in a national context; it is that much harder to operationalize internationally much less globally. One problem here is whether to adopt a Grotian "society of states" morality, which stresses obligations states have toward each other (for example, the obligation not to intervene in each other's affairs, and the obligation to try to narrow the rich-poor gap between states), or a "cosmopolitan" morality, which takes a more holistic view of humanity and the obligations individuals have toward each other (for example, the obligation to promote human rights and democracy, including supporting humanitarian intervention in civil wars where genocide is occurring, and closing the rich-poor gap within states).[41] As normatively compelling as the cosmopolitan view may be, it may make more sense at this juncture to promote a society-of-states morality, given the fact that sovereignty is one of the few principles that has universal appeal among national elites and mass publics.

Jack Goldsmith and Eric Posner have raised another normative problem. They argue that it is anti-democratic (and, hence, contradicts the cosmopolitan theory of morality) to put "other-regarding" international law, which takes into account the interests of other states and peoples, above the wishes of a democratic state whose policies "reflect the usually self-regarding interests of voters."[42] While waiting to remedy the "democratic deficit" associated with the World Trade Organization and other international institutions, we would do well to remind ourselves that, if the current anarchy and weakness of international law should prevent adequate governance of WMDs and other worrisome aspects of contemporary world politics, there may not be any voters left anywhere to exercise their franchise.

Henry Kissinger, whose central challenge for the United States was cited earlier, also poses the central challenge for humanity:

> Opportunity for world order presents itself to each generation disguised as a set of problems. The dilemma of our age was perhaps best summed up by the philosopher Immanuel Kant over two hundred years ago. In his essay "Perpetual Peace," he wrote that the world was destined for perpetual peace. It would come about either by human foresight or by a series of catastrophes that leave no other choice.[43]

Realistically, strengthening the rule of law in international affairs would seem to require reform at two levels. At one level, there is a need and, as Anne-Marie Slaughter argues, opportunity to build on the already "dense web of networks" across national boundaries for "collecting and sharing information, for policy coordination, for enforcement cooperation, for technical assistance and training."[44] Much of this will be unglamorous work, building nitty-gritty institutional infrastructure in relatively "low-politics" areas; the importance of these efforts, however, is that they not only can help develop habits of cooperation but also can facilitate more effective rule-making, implementation, and adjudication. This is along the lines of what Richard Gardner not long ago called "practical internationalism" aimed at problem-solving bilaterally, regionally, and globally.[45]

There remains the greater challenge of achieving reform at another level—in the macro-level, "high-politics" governance bodies at the United Nations. Difficult

This is a photo of the United Nations Secretariat building at night, around the time of the UN Millennium Summit in New York City in 2000. As world leaders gathered, there was both hope and skepticism over whether the twenty-first century would mark a new age in global institution-building.

as this will be, the challenge is no greater than that which faced those who founded the United Nations in the first place. A useful starting point would be Kofi Annan's 2004 report, "In Larger Freedom: Towards Development, Security and Human Rights for All," which was based on the recommendations of both the High-Level Panel on Threats, Challenges, and Change and the UN Millennium Project whose ideas the Secretary General had elicited, and which was discussed at a UN summit of world leaders in the fall of 2005. Among the many ideas contained in the report are: an expansion of the UN Security Council from fifteen to twenty-four members, with six to eight permanent seats added, drawn mainly from among the top financial or peacekeeping-troop contributors from various regions; the creation of a Human Rights Council to replace the Human Rights Commission, which would have an elevated status and would be designed to lessen the influence of non-democratic members; a comprehensive anti-terrorism regime that would ban attacks on civilians; the empowerment of the Security Council to authorize what amounts to a "preventive" use of armed force in those circumstances where a major security threat may be in the process of materializing; closing the current loophole in the Nuclear Non-Proliferation Treaty that permits member states to, in effect, go to the brink of nuclear weapons development through exploiting peaceful uses of nuclear energy; and rethinking of ways to deliver foreign aid and improve economic development.[46]

There are few more daunting undertakings one can imagine than attempting to get Israel, Iran, and others in "our global neighborhood"[47] to agree to the "mother" of all regimes that would be a next-generation central guidance system. However, if a critical mass of states, accounting for much of the international system's hard and soft power—the industrialized democracies led by the United States, the EU, and Japan, joined by the likes of Russia, India, and China, each with growing economies in need of a stable world order—can somehow forge a coalition in support of UN reform, it may be possible to achieve some strengthening of the rule of law. As with the compromise of embedded liberalism and sustainable development, perhaps a "prominent solution" might emerge around United Nations reform that can take the organization to the next stage of global institution-building.

Between Peril and Promise

It may seem a fool's errand to talk of central guidance systems in world politics, when the planet has been unable even to reach agreement on a standard "world plug and socket system" that would enable any of 6 billion people to get their electric shavers or hair dryers to work while abroad.[48] Granted, this is a rather trivial matter compared with halving the number of poor people who have no access to electricity, but it still can make life miserable for the overseas traveler. More than one global meeting has been held to produce global policy on this issue, without any success up to now. That global conferences would be convened to address such a concern shows how far the world has come in terms of the range of problems now being treated at the global level. That no politically acceptable outcome has yet been found for such a miniscule matter shows how far the world still has to go to become a true global community with effective rule-making machinery.

Is Henkin's vision of human progress an impossible dream? Possibly, but possibly not. We already have seen some such progress, including a multilateral treaty that has been more than 50 percent effective in governing 70 percent of the Earth's surface. Besides, the seemingly "impossible" occasionally happens. Witness the virtual elimination of the millennia-old institution of slavery, the termination of centuries-old rivalries in Europe and their replacement by a common currency and drafting of a European constitution, and the sudden end of the decades-old cold war and transformation of the post–WWII bipolar system without a shot being fired.

John Herz, who as early as the 1950s was predicting the "demise of the territorial state" and the need for leaders to develop coping mechanisms, once said: "It is not wishful thinking that leads us on, but an ever so faint ray of hope that

that which is not entirely impossible will emerge as real."[49] At a time when we have the potential to take the human race to an unprecedented level of well-being or to extinguish it, one might ask: who is the *realist*—one who believes that our prosperity and survival are possible with a lawless politics, or one who believes that politics through law is the only path conceivable? If asked whether we are on the right road, I can only conclude by borrowing Chou En-Lai's reply, when Secretary of State Kissinger asked the Chinese leader in the 1970s what he thought of the 1789 French Revolution: "Too soon to tell." Although we may not have the luxury of waiting 200 years for a final verdict about the convergence of international politics and international law, we may take heart in the old saw that most revolutions on their eve seem unimaginable, and on the morning after seem to have been inevitable.

The shadowy outline of a new dawn can be seen just over the horizon if one looks hard enough.

Endnotes

Chapter 1

1. On the failure of international relations theory to anticipate and account for the end of the Cold War, see John Lewis Gaddis, "International Relations Theory and the End of the Cold War," *International Security* 17 (winter 1992–1993), pp. 5–58; and Charles W. Kegley Jr., "How Did the Cold War Die: Principles for an Autopsy," *Mershon International Studies Review* 38 (April 1994), pp. 11–41.

2. Zbigniew Brzezinski, *Game Plan: A Geostrategic Framework for the Conduct of the US-Soviet Contest* (Boston: Atlantic Monthly Press, 1986), p. xiii.

3. Francis Fukuyama, "The End of History?" *The National Interest* 16 (summer 1989), pp. 3–16. Among those questioning Fukuyama's assumptions were, most notably, Samuel P. Huntington, who hypothesized about the "clash of civilizations" pitting "the West vs. the rest" as the successor to the East-West axis of conflict between communist and noncommunist ideologies. See "The Clash of Civilizations," *Foreign Affairs* 72 (summer 1993), pp. 22–49. John Mearsheimer also saw things more pessimistically, in "Why We Will Soon Miss the Cold War," *The Atlantic Monthly* (August 1990), pp. 35–50.

4. The "holiday from history" line is attributed to Charles Krauthammer, "The *Real* New World Order," *Jewish World Review,* November 7, 2001.

5. Some observers had foreseen the "disorder" long before 9/11. See Ted Galen Carpenter, "The New World Disorder," *Foreign Policy* 84 (fall 1991), pp. 24–39.

6. This classic definition of international law is adapted from J. L. Brierly, *The Law of Nations,* 6th ed. (Oxford: Oxford University Press, 1963), p. 1. Similarly, William R. Slomanson, in *Fundamental Perspectives on International Law,* 3rd ed. (Belmont, Calif.: Wadsworth, 2000), p. 3, defines international law as "the body of rules by which nations are bound in their mutual relations." As the author will discuss later, nonstate actors, such as international organizations, increasingly have gained "international legal personality" alongside states.

7. "What Good Is International Law?" *The Wilson Quarterly* (autumn 2003).

8. The first headline appeared in the *New York Times,* January 2, 1994, p. 4. The second headline appeared on the front page of the *New York Times,* May 20, 2001. The third headline appeared on the front page of the *New York Times,* July 10, 2004. The fourth headline appeared in the *St. Louis Post-Dispatch,* August 7, 2004, p. 25.

9. On the issue of relevance, see Karl W. Deutsch and Stanley Hoffmann, eds., *The Relevance of International Law* (Cambridge: Schenkman, 1968); and Christopher C. Joyner, "The Reality and Relevance of International Law," in Charles W. Kegley and Eugene R.

Wittkopf, eds., *The Global Agenda,* 3rd ed. (New York: McGraw-Hill, 1992), pp. 202–215.

10. Charles Tilly, "Violence, Terror, and Politics as Usual," *Boston Review* (summer 2002) http://www.bostonreview.net/BR27.3/tilly.html (cited February 20, 2004).

11. Jonathan Schell, *The Fate of the Earth* (New York: Knopf, 1982), pp. 181–182. More recently, Schell has written *The Unconquerable World* (New York: Metropolitan Books, 2003).

12. *The War Game* is a 1965 British BBC TV documentary that depicted what a nuclear war might look like.

13. Cited in the *Christian Science Monitor,* April 24, 1985, p. 5.

14. World Bank, *World Development Report 2003* (New York: Oxford University Press, 2003), p.1. Also, see Shoahua Chen and Martin Ravallion, "How Did the World's Poorest Fare in the 1990s?" World Bank Policy Research Working Paper 2409 (Washington, D.C.: World Bank, 2000); and Worldwatch Institute, *Vital Signs 2003* (New York: W. W. Norton, 2003), pp.88–89.

15. David Victor, *Climate Change* (New York: Council on Foreign Relations, 2004), p.10; Worldwatch Institute, *Vital Signs 2003,* pp. 40–41; and *St. Louis Post-Dispatch,* December 16, 2004.

16. World Bank,*World Development Report 2003,* p. 1.

17. Dave Whitman, "It's a Breath of Fresh Air," *U.S. News and World Report,* April 17, 2000, pp. 16–19.

18. Freedom House, *Freedom in the World 2003,* accessed on August 5, 2004 at http://www.freedomhouse.org/research/freeworld/2003/ak. Also see Samuel Huntington, *The Third Wave: Democratization in the Late Twentieth Century* (Norman: University of Oklahoma Press, 1991).

19. Thomas Friedman, *The Lexus and the Olive Tree,* rev. edition (New York: Anchor Books, 2000), p. xviii.

20. John Lewis Gaddis, "The Long Peace: Elements of Stability in the Postwar International System," *International Security* 10 (1986), pp. 99–142.

21. Stephen D. Krasner, "Structural Causes and Regime Consequences: Regimes as Intervening Variables," in Krasner, ed., *International Regimes* (Ithaca: Cornell University Press, 1983), p. 1.

22. Robert O. Keohane and Joseph S. Nye, *Power and Interdependence,* 3rd ed. (New York: Longman, 2001), p. 17.

23. Stanley Hoffmann, *Primacy or World Order* (New York: McGraw-Hill, 1978), p. 193.

Chapter 2

1. Thomas S. Kuhn, *The Structure of Scientific Revolutions,* 2nd ed., (Chicago: University of Chicago Press, 1970), p. 4.

2. James N. Rosenau and Mary Durfee, *Thinking Theory Thoroughly* (Boulder: Westview Press, 1995), p. 6.

3. Ibid., pp. 2 and 7.

4. The realist-idealist debate is discussed in Charles W. Kegley, ed., *Controversies in International Relations Theory: Realism and the Neoliberal Challenge* (New York: St. Martin's Press, 1995); and David A. Baldwin, "Neoliberalism, Neorealism, and World Politics," in David A. Baldwin, ed., *Neorealism and Neoliberalism* (New York: Columbia University Press, 1993), pp. 3–25.

5. The idealist tradition is discussed in Louis Beres and Harry Targ, *Reordering the Planet: Constructing Alternative World Futures* (Boston: Allyn and Bacon, 1974).

6. E. H. Carr, *The Twenty Years' Crisis 1919-1939* (London: Macmillan, 1939); and Hans J. Morgenthau, *Politics Among Nations* (New York: Knopf, 1948). As John Vasquez has noted, *Politics Among Nations* so dominated international relations scholarship for decades after World War II that one could characterize the entire field as "Color It Morgenthau." John Vasquez, "Coloring It Morgenthau: New Evidence for an Old Thesis on Quantitative International Politics," *British Journal of International Studies* (1979), pp. 210–228.

7. There are a few exceptions. Recent efforts to ameliorate this situation can be seen in works such as Jack L. Goldsmith and Eric A. Posner, *The Limits of International Law* (New York: Oxford University Press, 2005); Christopher C. Joyner, *International Law in the 21st Century* (New York: Rowman and Littlefield, 2005); and Christian Reus-Smit, *The Politics of International Law* (Cambridge: Cambridge University Press, 2004). Also, see Anne-Marie Slaughter et al., "International Law and International Relations Theory: A New Generation of Interdisciplinary Scholarship," *American Journal of International Law*, vol. 92 (3), 1998, pp. 367–397; and the special issue of *International Organization*, 54 (summer 2000).

8. Leo Gross, "The Peace of Westphalia, 1648–1948,"*American Journal of International Law* 42 (January 1948), p.28. Stephen Krasner, Bruce Bueno de Mesquita, and others have argued that the significance of Westphalia as marking the origin of the state system has been exaggerated, in that one could already see the emergence of the modern state and state system well before 1648, for example in the Concordat of Worms in 1122, when the pope surrendered to local princes the right to appoint bishops in their territories; and one could find relics of the feudal era, such as the Holy Roman Empire, persisting into the 19th century long after Westphalia. See Bruce Bueno de Mesquita, "The Concordat of Worms and Westphalia," paper presented at the annual meeting of the International Studies Association, Washington, D.C., February 18, 1999; Stephen D. Krasner, "Westphalia and All That," in Judith Goldstein and Robert O. Keohane, eds., *Ideas and Foreign Policy* (Ithaca: Cornell University Press, 1993), pp. 240–246.

9. On the origins of nation-states in Europe, see Charles Tilly, *Coercion, Capital, and European States, A.D. 900–1990* (Cambridge: Basil Blackwell, 1990); and Tilly, ed., *The Formation of National States in Western Europe* (Princeton: Princeton University Press, 1975).

10. K.J. Holsti, *Peace and War: Armed Conflicts and International Order, 1648–1989* (Cambridge: Cambridge University Press, 1991), p. 25.

11. The extension of the Westphalian state system into Asia, Africa, and other parts of the globe is discussed in Hedley Bull and Adam Watson, eds., *The Expansion of International Society* (Oxford: Oxford University Press, 1985).

12. Oran R. Young, "The Actors in World Politics," in James N. Rosenau et al., eds., *The Analysis of International Politics* (New York: Free Press, 1972), p. 125.

13. Hedley Bull, *The Anarchical Society* (New York: Columbia University Press, 1977), p. 8. On the primacy of states, see Robert H. Jackson and Alan James, eds., *States in a Changing World* (Oxford: Clarendon Press, 1993).

14. Alexander Wendt, *Social Theory of International Politics* (Cambridge: Cambridge University Press, 1999), p. 9.

15. Stephen D. Krasner, in *Sovereignty: Organized Hypocrisy* (Princeton: Princeton University Press, 1999), argues that sovereignty has always been a problematical concept, with

great powers historically often ignoring the sovereignty of members of the international community.

16. John Mearsheimer, "The False Promise of International Institutions," *International Security* (winter 1994), pp. 5–49.

17. The definition is attributed to David Lilienthal; cited in Yair Aharoni, "On the Definition of a Multinational Corporation," in Ashok Kapur and Phillip D. Grub, eds., *The Multinational Enterprise in Transition* (Princeton: Darwin Press, 1972).

18. See Robert Gilpin, *The Political Economy of International Relations* (Princeton: Princeton University Press, 1987).

19. The "states as billiard balls" metaphor is credited to Arnold Wolfers's discussion in *Discord and Collaboration* (Baltimore: Johns Hopkins University Press, 1962).

20. Rosenau and Durfee, *Thinking Theory Thoroughly,* p. 12. This is the "rational actor" model discussed by Graham Allison as one explanation for the U.S. naval blockade decision during the 1962 Cuban missile crisis, in *Essence of Decision,* 2nd ed. (New York: Longman, 1999).

21. This is consistent with Aaron Wildavsky's "The Two Presidencies" article, which argued that in the American political system the U.S. president enjoys far more decision latitude and power to act in the area of foreign policy than in the area of domestic policy. Aaron Wildavsky, "The Two Presidencies," *Transaction* 4 (December 1966), pp. 7–14.

22. Hans J. Morgenthau, *Politics Among Nations,* 5th ed. (New York: Knopf, 1973), p. 27.

23. Thucydides, *The Peloponnesian War,* ed. T. E. Wick (Columbus, Ohio: McGraw-Hill, 1982), p. 5.89.

24. This definition of peace comes from Ambrose Bierce's *The Devil's Dictionary*; cited in Charles Krauthammer, "An American Foreign Policy for a Unipolar World," speech given to the American Enterprise Institute, February 10, 2004.

25. Among the major neorealist works is Kenneth N. Waltz, *Theory of International Politics* (Reading: Addison-Wesley, 1979).

26. Ibid., p. 105; also, see Joseph Grieco, "Anarchy and the Limits of Cooperation: A Realist Critique of the Newest Liberal Institutionalism," *International Organization* 42 (summer 1988), pp. 486–507.

27. Morton A. Kaplan and Nicholas de B. Katzenbach, *The Strategy of World Order: International Law* (New York: World Law Fund, 1966). Also, see their *The Political Foundations of International Law* (New York: Wiley, 1961); and William D. Coplin, "International Law and Assumptions about the State System," *World Politics* 17 (July 1965), pp. 615–634.

28. Depending on the criteria used, the number of IGOs may exceed 1,000, the number of NGOs may exceed 28,000, and the number of MNCs may exceed 50,000. On IGOs, see Harold Jacobson et al., "National Entanglements in International Governmental Organizations," *American Political Science Review* 80 (March 1986), pp. 141–159; and the Union of International Associations, *Yearbook of International Organizations 2003* (Brussels: UIA, 2003). On NGOs, see the Commission on Global Governance, *Our Global Neighborhood* (Oxford: Oxford University Press, 1995), p. 32; and John Boli and George M. Thomas, "INGOs and the Organization of World Culture," in Paul F. Diehl, ed., *The Politics of Global Governance,* 2nd ed. (Boulder: Lynne Rienner, 2001), pp. 62–96. On MNCs, see David Held et al., *Global Transformations* (Stanford: Stanford University Press, 1999), p. 236.

29. Kjell Skjelsbaek, "The Growth of International Nongovernmental Organization in the Twentieth Century," *International Organization* 25 (summer 1971), pp. 435–436.

30. On the growing role of NGOs, see Jessica Matthews, "Power Shift," *Foreign Affairs* (January/February 1997), pp. 50–66; and Thomas G. Weiss and Leon Gordenker, eds., *NGOs, the UN, and Global Governance* (Boulder: Lynne Rienner, 1996). On IGOs, see A. Leroy Bennett and James K. Oliver, *International Organizations,* 7th ed. (Upper Saddle River, N.J: Prentice-Hall, 2002). On IGOs and NGOs, see Margaret P. Karns and Karen A. Mingst, *International Organizations: The Politics and Processes of Global Governance* (Boulder: Lynne Rienner, 2004).

31. Maryann Cusimano, *Beyond Sovereignty* (New York: St. Martin's Press, 2000), p. 217.

32. Inis L. Claude, "The Record of International Organizations in the Twentieth Century," Tamkang Lecture Series #64 (1986), p. 25.

33. The "functionalist" explanation for the growth of IGOs is discussed in Jacobson et al., "National Entanglements." Also, see Craig N. Murphy, *International Organization and Industrial Change: Global Governance Since 1850* (New York: Oxford University Press, 1994).

34. See Thomas L. Friedman, *The Lexus and the Olive Tree* (New York: Farrar, Straus, Giroux, 1999), pp. xiv–xvi; and Robert O. Keohane and Joseph S. Nye, "Introduction," in Nye and John D. Donahue, eds., *Governance in a Globalizing World* (Washington, D.C.: Brookings Institution Press, 2000), pp. 7–11. On the various dimensions of interdependence, see Held et al., *Global Transformations.*

35. For an in-depth discussion of why states form IGOs, see Kenneth Abbott and Duncan Snidal, "Why States Act Through Formal International Organizations," *Journal of Conflict Resolution* 42 (February 1998), pp. 3–32.

36. By the 1970s, the international role of "domestic" bureaucracies had grown to the point where "of 19,000 Americans abroad on diplomatic missions, only 3,400 were from the State Department and less than half of the governmental delegates accredited to international conferences came from the State Department." Joseph S. Nye, "Independence and Interdependence," *Foreign Policy* 22 (1976), p. 138. Also, see Raymond F. Hopkins, "The International Role of 'Domestic' Bureaucracy," *International Organization* 30 (1976), pp. 405–432.

37. The "cobweb" model was first suggested by John Burton et al., *The Study of World Society* (Pittsburgh: International Studies Association, 1974).

38. Robert O. Keohane and Joseph S. Nye, *Power and Interdependence,* 3rd ed. (New York: Longman, 2001), p. 21.

39. Stanley Hoffmann, "Choices," *Foreign Policy* (fall 1973), p. 5.

40. Robert D. Putnam, "Diplomacy and Domestic Politics: The Logic of Two-Level Games," *International Organization* 42 (summer 1988), p. 434.

41. Ibid., p. 433.

42. Anne-Marie Slaughter, *A New World Order* (Princeton: Princeton University Press, 2004), pp. 1 and 12–15.

43. On the complex politics involving states and various kinds of subnational and transnational actors, see Margaret E. Keck and Kathryn Sikkink, *Activists Beyond Borders: Advocacy Networks in International Politics* (Ithaca: Cornell University Press, 1998); also, Maria Cowles, "Multinationals, Two-Level Games, and the European Community," paper presented at the annual meeting of the International Studies Association, Chicago, 1995.

44. See Kenneth Oye, ed., *Cooperation Under Anarchy* (Princeton: Princeton University Press, 1986); and Arthur A. Stein, *Why Nations Cooperate* (Ithaca: Cornell University Press, 1990).

45. Examples of neoliberal writings are Robert O. Keohane, *After Hegemony: Cooperation and Discord in the World Political Economy* (Princeton: Princeton University Press, 1984); Joseph S. Nye, "Neorealism and Neoliberalism," *World Politics* 40 (January 1988), pp. 235–251; and Mark W. Zacher and Brent A. Sutton, *Governing Global Networks* (Cambridge: Cambridge University Press, 1996).

46. See Robert Axelrod, *The Evolution of Cooperation* (New York: Basic Books, 1984).

47. The classic functionalist work is David Mitrany, *A Working Peace System: An Argument for the Functional Development of International Organization* (London: Royal Institute of International Affairs, 1943); also, see Ernst B. Haas, "International Integration: The European and the Universal Process," in *International Political Communities* (New York: Doubleday Anchor, 1966), pp. 93–130.

48. Robert O. Keohane, "International Institutions: Can Interdependence Work?" *Foreign Policy* 110 (1998), p. 82.

49. Harold K. Jacobson, *Networks of Interdependence,* 2nd ed, (New York: Knopf, 1984), p. 14.

50. Alexander Wendt, "Why a World State Is Inevitable: Revisiting the Logic of Anarchy," paper delivered at the annual meeting of the International Studies Association, New Orleans, March 2002.

51. On this point, see Yale H. Ferguson and Richard W. Mansbach, *Polities, Authority, Identities, and Change* (Columbia, S.C.: University of South Carolina Press, 1996).

52. Benjamin Barber, *Jihad vs. McWorld* (New York: Times Books, 1995). Also, see James Rosenau's discussion of "fragmegration" in *Turbulence in World Politics* (Princeton: Princeton University Press, 1990).

53. Susan Strange, "The Defective State," *Daedalus* 124 (spring 1995), pp. 56–57. See Paul Kennedy, "The Future of the Nation-State," chapter 7 in *Preparing for the Twenty-First Century* (New York: Random House, 1993).

54. On the "new feudalism" and "new medievalism," see Bull, *Anarchical Society,* p. 254; James Nathan, "The New Feudalism," *Foreign Policy,* no. 42 (spring 1981), pp. 156–166; and Strange, "Defective State." On the "post-international politics" paradigm, see Rosenau, *Turbulence in World Politics,* chapter 1.

55. Boutros Boutros-Ghali, *An Agenda for Peace,* UN Doc A/47/277 and S/24111, June 17, 1992, p. 3.

56. Ibid., p. 5.

57. Kennedy, "Future of the Nation-State," p. 134.

58. Ibid.

59. John G. Stoessinger, *The Might of Nations,* 10th ed. (New York: McGraw-Hill, 1993), p. 4.

60. Karns and Mingst, *International Organizations,* p. 4. The Commission on Global Governance, *Our Global Neighborhood,* p. 2, defines "global governance" more broadly, as "the sum of the many ways individuals and institutions, public and private, manage their common affairs." Also, see James N. Rosenau and Ernst-Otto Czempiel, eds., *Governance Without Government* (Cambridge: Lexington, 1992).

61. Marvin S. Soroos, *Beyond Sovereignty: The Challenge of Global Policy* (Columbia, S.C.: University of South Carolina Press, 1986), p. 20. Also, see J. Martin Rochester, "The Future of the United Nations and Global Policy," *Journal of Peace Research* 27 (May 1990), pp. 141–154.

62. Claude, "Record of International Organizations," pp. 4–5.

63. Barry Buzan, *People, States and Fear* (Chapel Hill: University of North Carolina Press, 1983), p. 97.

64. The terms "bad idealism" and "bad realism" come from Giovanni Sartori, *Democratic Theory* (New York: Praeger, 1965).

65. For a discussion of constructivism and where it fits into the "paradigm debate," see Ken Booth and Steve Smith, eds., *International Relations Theory Today* (State College, Pa: Penn State University Press, 1995), pp. 13–20; Andreas Hasenclever et al., *Theories of International Regimes* (Cambridge: Cambridge University Press, 1997), chapter 5; and "Bridging the Gap: Toward a Realist-Constructivist Dialogue," forum in *International Studies Review* 6 (June 2004), pp. 337–352.

66. Among writings that take a constructivist approach, see John Ruggie, ed., *Constructing the World Polity* (London: Routledge, 1998); Alexander Wendt, "Constructing International Politics," *International Security* 20 (summer 1995), pp. 71–81; Martha Finnemore, "Norms, Culture, and World Politics: Insights from Sociology's Institutionalism," *International Organization* 50 (spring 1996), pp. 347–360; and Peter M. Haas and Ernst B. Haas, "Learning to Learn: Improving International Governance," *Global Governance* 1 (Sept.–Dec. 1995), pp 255–285.

67. Ruggie, *Constructing the World Polity,* p. 11.

68. Martha Finnemore, "Constructing Norms of Humanitarian Intervention," in Peter J. Katzenstein, ed., *The Culture of National Security: Norms and Identity in World Politics* (New York: Columbia University Press, 1996), pp. 153–185.

69. On the end of slavery and colonialism, see James Lee Ray, "The Abolition of Slavery and the End of International War," *International Organization* 43 (summer 1989), pp. 405–439.

70. On "free trade" as an idea, see Judith Goldstein and Robert O. Keohane, eds., *Ideas and Foreign Policy: Beliefs, Institutions, and Political Change* (Ithaca: Cornell University Press, 1993).

71. See note 32.

72. Martha Finnemore, *National Interests in International Society* (Ithaca: Cornell University Press, 1996), p. 5.

73. For example, see Peter M. Haas, *Saving the Mediterranean: The Politics of International Environmental Cooperation* (New York: Columbia University Press, 1990).

74. Stephen A. Kocs, "Explaining the Strategic Behavior of States: International Law as System Structure," *International Studies Quarterly* 38 (December 1994), p. 538.

75. A good critique of constructivism and its application to the study of international law is provided by Anthony Clark Arend, *Legal Rules and International Society* (New York: Oxford University Press, 1999), pp. 124–147.

76. V. Spike Peterson and Anne Sisson Runyan, *Global Gender Issues* (Boulder: Westview Press, 1993); Cynthia Enloe, *Bananas, Beaches, and Bases: Making Feminist Sense of International Politics* (Berkeley: University of California Press, 1990). Also, see David Boucher, *Political Theories of International Relations* (Oxford: Oxford University Press, 1998), chapter 16.

77. See Robert W. Cox, "Social Forces, States, and World Orders: Beyond International Relations Theory," in Robert O. Keohane, ed., *Neorealism and Its Critics* (New York: Columbia University Press, 1986), pp. 204–254; and Boucher, *Political Theories,* chapter 15.

Chapter 3

1. *UN Chronicle* (March 1990), p. 77.
2. The Court handed down its judgment on the merits on May 24, 1980. See *United States v. Iran, International Court of Justice Reports,* 1980, p. 3. Also, see *International Legal Materials,* 1980, p. 553; and Ted Stein, "Contempt, Crisis, and the Court: The World Court and the Hostage Rescue Attempt," *American Journal of International Law* 76 (1982), pp. 499–531.
3. The vote was 14–1, with the lone dissenting vote cast by the U.S. judge, Thomas Buergenthal. Buergenthal, with Harold G. Maier, has written *Public International Law in a Nutshell,* 2nd ed. (St. Paul: West, 1990).
4. The figure is cited on the Web site of the U.S. Department of State's Office of the Legal Advisor at http://www.state.gov/s/1/3190.htm (cited August 22, 2004).
5. Paul Martin, Canadian Secretary of State for External Affairs, cited in *External Affairs* 16 (1964).
6. The skeptical view is represented by Jack L. Goldsmith and Eric A. Posner, *The Limits of International Law* (New York: Oxford University Press, 2004), whose theory of international law "gives pride of place to . . . state power and state interests" (p. 3). They use rational choice theory to show that what idealists take to be law compliance is merely behavior conforming to self-interest that would occur even in the absence of law. See p. 28.
7. *Nicaragua v. United States, International Court of Justice Reports,* 1986, p. 14; *International Legal Materials,* 1986, p. 1023.
8. This definition is based on William D. Coplin, *The Functions of International Law* (Chicago: Rand McNally, 1966), pp. 1–3.
9. *The Random House College Dictionary,* revised ed. (New York: Random House, 1984), p. 759.
10. Here I am indebted to Anthony Clark Arend, *Legal Rules and International Society* (New York: Oxford University Press, 1999), p. 29. Arend himself credits the "Five C's" terminology to lectures he heard Inis Claude give. Neither Arend nor Claude subscribe to the view that international law's failure to meet the "Five C's" test means that it cannot be law; both were merely articulating the common assumptions surrounding law.
11. This is the traditional notion of law attributed to John Austin, a nineteenth century British writer, cited in Edward Collins, ed., *International Law in a Changing World* (New York: Random House, 1970), p. 2.
12. George Will, "The Perils of 'Legality'," *Newsweek,* September 10, 1990, p. 66.
13. Marvin S. Soroos, *Beyond Sovereignty: The Challenge of Global Policy* (Columbia, S.C.: University of South Carolina Press, 1986), p. 82.
14. Harold K. Jacobson et al., "National Entanglements in International Governmental Organizations," *American Political Science Review* 80 (March 1986), pp. 157–158.
15. Under the UN Charter, so-called important decisions require a two-thirds majority of the entire General Assembly membership. There are a very few decisions taken by the General Assembly, mostly "housekeeping" in nature (for example, involving budget assessments), that are binding on all members. States, of course, are always free not to join the UN or to leave it when they are unhappy with the organization, but virtually all states have joined and virtually none have left.
16. Frederic L. Kirgis, "Specialized Law-Making Processes," in Christopher C. Joyner, ed., *The United Nations and International Law* (Cambridge: Cambridge University Press,

1997), p. 74. Kirgis also discusses rule-making in other specialized agencies such as the International Labor Organization and the International Maritime Organization.

17. "WHO Expected to Gain Broad Powers," *New York Times* May 28, 2003.

18. Lawrence Ziring, Robert Riggs, and Jack Plano, *The United Nations,* 3rd ed. (New York: Harcourt Brace, 2000), p. 346.

19. Ithiel de Sola Pool, *Technologies Without Borders* (Cambridge: Cambridge University Press, 1990), p. 71; cited in Mark W. Zacher, "The Decaying Pillars of the Westphalian Temple: Implications for International Order and Governance," in James N. Rosenau and Ernst-Otto Czempiel, eds., *Governance Without Government* (Cambridge: Cambridge University Press, 1992), p. 65.

20. The rules governing diplomats and embassies were admittedly somewhat vague in Grotius's day, and were to be refined further after the Congress of Vienna in 1815, and still further in codified agreements in the twentieth century.

21. Arend, *Legal Rules and International Society,* p. 73. One should add, however, that there are also such things as "regional" customs in international law. See the discussion of *The Asylum Case* in Ray August, *Public International Law* (Englewood Cliffs, N.J.: Prentice-Hall, 1995), pp. 65–66; and William R. Slomanson, *Fundamental Perspectives on International Law,* 3rd ed. (Belmont, Calif.: Wadsworth, 2000), p. 16.

22. Martin Dixon, *Textbook on International Law,* 3rd ed. (London: Blackstone, 1996), p. 29. On the relationship between power and law in international relations, see Morton A. Kaplan and Nicholas de B. Katzenbach, *The Political Foundations of International Law* (New York: Wiley, 1961).

23. Dixon, *International Law,* p. 29. There are some legal scholars who go so far as to argue that customary rules are binding on "all members of the world community." See Antonio Cassese, *International Law* (Oxford: Oxford University Press, 2001), p. 119. Controversies surrounding customary law are discussed in Anthea Elizabeth Roberts, "Traditional and Modern Approaches to Customary Law: A Reconciliation," *American Journal of International Law* 95, no. 4 (2001), pp. 757–791.

24. The "evidences" of customary law can include "statements by government officials, actions and decisions taken by government officials, domestic legislation, activities of diplomatic personnel, behavior of military commanders, decisions of domestic courts, and the like." Arend, *Legal Rules and International Society,* p. 73. A classic international law case often cited for its treatment of the issue of "evidence" of customary law is *The Paquete Habana and The Lola* heard by the U.S. Supreme Court in 1900. See Slomanson, *Perspectives on International Law,* pp. 17–19.

25. Richard Bilder, *Managing the Risks of International Agreement* (Madison: University of Wisconsin Press, 1981), p. 5.

26. Some international agreements take the form of "executive agreements" rather than treaties. These have the same binding character in international law as treaties but are not subject to the same ratification procedures domestically. The United States, in particular, has relied heavily on executive agreements, requiring only presidential signature, in recent years. Under the U.S. Constitution, "treaties" require the approval of two-thirds of the U.S. Senate. These are to be distinguished not only from executive agreements, which require no congressional action, but also from "congressional-executive agreements," which are presidential agreements that require approval by a majority of both the House of Representatives and the Senate.

27. Shirley V. Scott reports the figure of 4,065 multilateral treaties in *International Law in World Politics: An Introduction* (Boulder: Lynne Rienner, 2004), p. 5; she credits the

source of the data as Christian L. Wiktor, *Multilateral Treaty Calendar 1648–1995* (The Hague: Martinus Nijhoff, 1998). Bilder, *Risks of International Agreement,* pp. 6 and 233, notes that of more than 15,000 treaties in force in the 1980s, bilateral agreements far exceeded multilateral ones. The same can be said for the 1990s. For data on the growth of multilateral treaty-making, see John King Gamble, "Reservations to Multilateral Treaties: A Macroscopic View of State Practice," *American Journal of International Law* 74 (April 1980), pp. 372–394; and James P. Muldoon, *The Architecture of Global Governance* (Boulder: Westview, 2004), pp. 155–157.

28. Charlotte Ku, "Global Governance and the Changing Face of International Law," *ACUNS Reports and Papers No. 2* (New Haven: Academic Council on the United Nations System, 2001), p. 5.

29. Iran was also in violation of the 1963 Vienna Convention on Consular Relations and the 1973 UN Convention on the Prevention of Crimes Against Internationally Protected Persons, Including Diplomatic Agents.

30. See Clyde Haberman, "Diplomatic or Not, Mayor Gets Results With His War on Scofflaws," *New York Times,* March 30, 2000; and, also, Elaine Sciolino, "When Citizens of the World Break the Laws of New York," *New York Times,* June 8, 1986. Although Mayor Rudolph Giuliani managed to reduce traffic violations by the diplomatic community in New York City in the 1990s, diplomats could not be forced to pay fines or towing fees.

31. Based on University of Washington Treaty Research Center Studies, reported in Bilder, *Risks of International Agreement,* p. 232.

32. Michael Akehurst, *A Modern Introduction to International Law,* 6th ed. (London: Allen and Unwin, 1987), p. 25.

33. Mark W. Janis, *An Introduction to International Law* (Boston: Little, Brown, 1988), p. 11.

34. Michael J. Glennon, "Sometimes a Great Notion," *The Wilson Quarterly* (autumn 2003), p. 45.

35. This point is nicely made in ibid., p.49 and Arend, *Legal Rules and International Society,* p. 123.

36. Louis Henkin, *How Nations Behave* (New York: Columbia University Press, 1979), p. 4.

37. Ibid., p. 47.

38. Abram Chayes and Antonia Chayes, "On Compliance," *International Organization* 47 (spring 1993), pp. 175–206; and their *The New Sovereignty: Compliance With International Regulatory Agreements* (Cambridge: Harvard University Press, 1995).

39. Geraldine Brooks, "It's UN Protocol: No Chair, No Office for Tajikistan's Man," *Wall Street Journal,* September 20, 1993, p. 1.

40. Corey Kilgannon, "Landlords Around UN Find Diplomacy Doesn't Pay," *New York Times,* December 25, 1999, p. 5.

41. David V. Edwards, *The American Political Experience,* 4th ed. (Englewood Cliffs, N.J.: Prentice-Hall, 1988), pp. 372–373. In 1996, there were an estimated 25 million serious crimes committed in the United States, with only some 500,000 resulting in punishment. "Firing Line," KETC-TV, January 19, 1997. Law enforcement is not much better in the British criminal justice system, with only 22 percent of the robberies committed in England and Wales solved by the police according to a recent survey. Akehurst, *Modern Introduction to International Law,* p. 2.

42. The data are from the U.S. Federal Bureau of Investigation's Uniform Crime Statistics; accessed on August 31, 2004, at http://www.fbi.gov/ucr/cius_02/pdf.
43. Abram Chayes, *The Cuban Missile Crisis: International Crises and the Role of Law* (New York: Oxford University Press, 1974).
44. In recent years, countries have been reluctant to take a case to the World Court on behalf of individual citizens, such as the famous *Nottebohm Case* in 1955, in which Liechtenstein brought suit against Guatemala on behalf of someone who had attempted to switch his nationality from Germany to Liechtenstein.
45. Data on trends in the caseload of the Court can be found in A. Leroy Bennett, *International Organizations,* 6th ed. (Englewood Cliffs, N.J.: Prentice-Hall, 1995), pp. 188–194; also, see *UN Chronicle,* 20, no. 11 (1983), pp. 47–53.
46. J. Alan Beesley, *New Frontiers of Multilateralism* (Hanover, N.H.: Academic Council on the UN, 1989), p. 9.
47. The current caseload of the Court is reported on the ICJ homepage on the Web, at http://www.icj-cij.org/icjwww/decisions.htm.
48. For example, see Eric A. Posner, "All Justice, Too, Is Local," *New York Times,* December 30, 2004; and Goldsmith and Posner, *Limits of International Law.*
49. Slomanson, *Perspectives on International Law,* p. 378.
50. Ibid., p. 376.
51. These are the words of Benjamin Civiletti, former U.S. Attorney-General, in his oral argument presented before the World Court on December 10, 1979, during the proceedings of the *US Diplomatic and Consular Staff in Tehran* case; cited in U.S. Department of State, Bureau of Public Affairs, Current Policy No. 118 (December 1989), p. 1.
52. Based on a 2003 article in the *Atlanta Journal-Constitution;* accessed on November 1, 2003 on http://www.washtimes.com/national/20031030-120613-3167r.htm.
53. Goldsmith and Posner, *Limits of International Law,* p. 3.
54. This statement appears as a template on the inside back cover of the journal.

Chapter 4

1. *New York Times,* September 26, 1977.
2. This squares with the conceptual definition of a nation-state that I provided in chapter 2.
3. Multinational corporations will be discussed in chapter 6. The legal personality of IGOs, such as the UN, was noted in chapter 2. Regarding NGOs, the European Convention on the Recognition of the Legal Personality of International Non-Governmental Organizations, drafted by the Council of Europe, entered into force in 1991. See Paul Ghils, "International Civil Society: International Non-Governmental Organizations in the International System," *International Social Science Journal* 133 (1992), p. 420.
4. Anne-Marie Slaughter, "Leading Through Law," *The Wilson Quarterly* (autumn 2003), pp. 42–43.
5. On the tensions between sovereignty and human rights, see Gene M. Lyons and Michael Mastanduno, eds., *Beyond Westphalia? State Sovereignty and International Intervention* (Baltimore: Johns Hopkins University Press, 1995). Humanitarian intervention will be discussed in chapter 5.
6. On state responsibility, see William R. Slomanson, *Fundamental Perspectives on International Law,* 3rd ed. (Belmont, Calif.: Wadsworth, 2000), pp. 191–196; David J. Bederman, *International Law Frameworks* (New York: Foundation Press, 2001), chapter 8;

and Gerhard von Glahn, *Law Among Nations*, 7th ed. (New York: Longman, 1996), chapter 11.

7. "Public Beheadings Carried Out Weekly, Rights Group Says," Amnesty Report on Saudi Arabia by Alan Philips, accessed at http://www.ukar.org/philps01.html and "Human Rights Watch World Report 2001: Saudi Arabia Human Rights Developments," accessed at http://www.hrw.org/wr2k1/mideast/saudi.html. Data on enforcement of Islamic law are reported in "A World of Ways to Say 'Islamic Law,' " *New York Times*, March 13, 2005.

8. "Texas Woman Gets 80 Lashes in Iran," *St. Louis Post-Dispatch*, May 6, 1994; and "The Noose for an American?" *Newsweek*, October 15, 1990. The hangings of the two Australians in 1986 were the first cases of Westerners being subjected to that penalty under Malaysian drug laws.

9. In addition to the 1998 case discussed below, there has also been the 1999 *LaGrand Case* (*Germany v. United States*), involving Arizona's execution of two German nationals, and the 2004 *Avena and Other Mexican Nationals* case (*United States v. Mexico*), in which the World Court ordered the United States to review the death sentences of 51 Mexican prisoners on death row in American prisons. See "World Court Rules U.S. Should Review 51 Death Sentences," *New York Times*, April 1, 2004.

10. "International Court of Justice Orders United States to Stay Execution of Paraguayan National in Virginia," *ASIL Insights* (April 1998), accessed on September 13, 2004, at http://www.asil.org/insights/insigh17.htm. On the steps taken by various state and local jurisdictions to improve compliance with the Vienna Convention, see http://www.lightmillennium.org/spring01. For example, California has passed legislation requiring police officers to notify foreign nationals of their consular rights within two hours of detention.

11. Judge Stephen Schwebel, quoted in Margaret Jacobs, "World Court Orders U.S. to Stay Virginia Execution of Paraguayan," *Wall Street Journal*, April 10, 1998.

12. Rhoda E. Howard and Jack Donnelly, eds., *International Handbook of Human Rights* (New York: Greenwood Press, 1987), p. 1. An excellent compendium on the law of human rights, containing synopses of many cases, is Louis Henkin et al, *Human Rights* (New York: Foundation Press, 1999).

13. Stephen D. Krasner, "Sovereignty," *Foreign Policy* (January/February 2001), p.22. On the early history of human rights, also see Slomanson, *Perspectives on International Law*, pp. 495–498; and Paul Gordon Lauren, *The Evolution of International Human Rights: Visions Seen* (Philadelphia: University of Pennsylvania Press, 1998).

14. On the politics of ending slavery in the United States and elsewhere, see Margaret E. Keck and Kathryn Sikkink, *Activists Beyond Borders: Advocacy Networks in International Politics* (Ithaca: Cornell University Press, 1998), chapter 2.

15. On the problematizing of sovereignty, see Krasner, ed., *Problematic Sovereignty: Contested Rules and Political Possibilities* (New York: Columbia University Press, 2001); and David A. Lake, "The New Sovereignty in International Relations," *International Studies Review* 5 (September 2003), pp. 303–323.

16. Bederman, *International Law Frameworks*, p. 95.

17. Similar proceedings were held in Tokyo, where Japanese officials were tried for war crimes, although not crimes against humanity. Although there had been a few instances of "war crimes" trials previously, as discussed in Slomanson, *Perspectives on International Law*, p. 391, these lacked the full judicial quality of the Nuremberg Trials.

18. See David P. Forsythe, "The United Nations and Human Rights, 1945–1985," *Political Science Quarterly* 100 (summer 1985), pp. 249–270. Forsythe examines the politics of human rights in his *Human Rights and World Politics*, 2nd ed. (Lincoln: University of Nebraska Press, 1989). A comprehensive list of conventions and accompanying protocols can be found on the homepage of the UN Office of the High Commissioner for Human Rights, accessed at http://www.unhchr.ch/html/intlinst.htm. Also see "A Summary of United Nations Agreements on Human Rights" at http:www.hrweb.org/legal/undocs.html.

19. As of 2005, 70 percent of the UN membership had ratified the convention on genocide, 88 percent the convention on racial discrimination, 78 percent the convention on civil and political rights, 77 percent the convention on economic and social rights, 91 percent the convention on discrimination against women, 70 percent the convention on torture, and 99 percent the convention on the rights of children, reflecting wide endorsement of these treaties even if adherence by many members has been spotty. Data are reported in Jack L. Goldsmith and Eric A. Posner, *The Limits of International Law* (New York: Oxford University Press, 2005), p. 108.

20. Michael Ignatieff, "Human Rights: The Midlife Crisis," *New York Review of Books*, May 20, 1999, p. 61.

21. Cited in "U.S. Bans Child Soldiers," CBS News, accessed on September 19, 2004, at http://www.cbsnews.com/stories/2002/12/24/national. Also, see Jill M. Gerschutz and Margaret P. Karns, "Transforming Visions into Reality: Actors and Strategies in the Implementation of the Convention on the Rights of the Child," in Mark Ensalaco and Linda Majka, eds., *Children's Human Rights: Progress and Challenges* (Lanham, Md.: Rowman and Littlefield, 2005).

22. Oona Hathaway, "Do Human Rights Treaties Make a Difference?" *Yale Law Journal* 111, no. 8 (June 2002).

23. *Freedom in the World* (London: Freedom House, 1993), p. 4.

24. "Freedom in the World 2004," accessed on September 19, 2004, at http://www.freedomhouse.org/research/survey2004.htm.

25. *Freedom in the World*, p. 4.

26. For an overview of enforcement mechanisms and the degree of success in achieving compliance with human rights treaties, see Jack Donnelly, *International Human Rights* (Boulder: Westview, 1993), chapter 4. Also, see W. B. Ofuatey-Kodjoe, "Human Rights and Humanitarian Intervention," in Albert Legault et al., *The State of the United Nations: 1992* (Providence: Academic Council on the United Nations System, 1992), pp. 33–47.

27. Donnelly, *International Human Rights*, pp. 80–81.

28. "New Thai Tourist Sight: Burmese 'Giraffe Women'," *New York Times*, October 19, 1996; "Africa's Culture Wars," *New York Times*, February 2, 1997; and "Account of Punjab Rape Tells of a Brutal Society," *New York Times*, August 17, 2002.

29. Margaret P. Karns and Karen A. Mingst, *International Organizations* (Boulder: Lynne Rienner, 2004), pp. 452–453.

30. Martha Alter Chen, "Engendering World Conferences: The International Women's Movement and the UN," in Thomas G. Weiss and Leon Gordenker, eds., *NGOs, the UN, and Global Governance* (Boulder: Lynne Rienner, 1996), p 140. On the politics of the global women's movement, see V. Spike Peterson and Anne Sisson Runyan, *Global Gender Issues*, 2nd ed. (Boulder: Westview Press, 1999).

31. Henkin et al., *Human Rights*, pp. 1210–1211.

32. Ibid., p. xi.

33. See Nicholas Kristof, "China Sees 'Market-Leninism' as Way to Future," *New York Times,* September 6, 1993; Mark T. Berger, "The End of the 'Third World'?" *Third World Quarterly* 15 (June 1994), pp. 257–275; and the special issue of *Third World Quarterly* entitled "The South in the New World (Dis) Order," 15 (March 1994).

34. The countries of the developing world had already become quite diverse toward the end of the cold war, making collective action by their governments difficult. For categorization problems, see Christopher Clapham, *Third World Politics* (London: Routledge, 1985); also, see Paul Kennedy, *Preparing for the Twenty-First Century* (New York: Random House, 1993), chapter 10. Seven distinct economic groupings of nation-states are identified in Richard J. Barnet and John Cavanaugh, *Global Dreams* (New York: Simon and Schuster, 1994), pp. 284–287.

35. Gideon Gottlieb, *Nation Against State* (New York: Council on Foreign Relations, 1993), p. 21.

36. Samuel P. Huntington, "The Clash of Civilizations?" *Foreign Affairs* 72 (summer 1993), p. 48. The article was later expanded into a book-length work, *The Clash of Civilizations and the Remaking of World Order* (New York: Simon and Schuster, 1996).

37. Bilahari Kausikan, "Asia's Different Standard," *Foreign Policy* (fall 1993), pp. 28–34; cited in Samuel P. Huntington, "If Not Civilizations, What?" *Foreign Affairs* 72 (November/December 1993), p. 193. On cultural relativism, also see R.J. Vincent, *Human Rights and International Relations* (Cambridge: Cambridge University Press, 1986).

38. Slomanson, *Perspectives on International Law,* p. 504.

39. Thomas M. Franck, "Are Human Rights Universal?" *Foreign Affairs* (January/February 2001), p. 191. Franck answered in the affirmative.

40. Michael Ignatieff, "Is the Human Rights Era Ending?" *New York Times,* February 5, 2002, p. A29. Also, see Ignatieff's "The Attack on Human Rights," *Foreign Affairs* 80 (November/December 2001), pp. 102–116.

41. "European Court Orders Britain to Restrict Beatings by Parents," *New York Times,* September 24, 1998; and "European Identity: Nation-State Losing Ground," *New York Times,* January 14, 2000.

42. Mark Janis and Richard Kay, *European Human Rights Law* (Hartford: University of Connecticut Law School Foundation Press, 1990), p. vii; cited in Slomanson, *Perspectives on International Law,* p. 511.

43. See Fareed Zakaria, "Don't Shut Turkey Out of Europe," *Newsweek,* September 27, 2004, p. 39. The change in Cyprus's treatment of women resulting from EU pressure is discussed in Chrystalla Ellina, *Promoting Women's Rights: The Politics of Gender in the European Union* (London: Routledge, 2002). On regional human rights regimes in Europe and elsewhere, see Donnelly, *International Human Rights,* pp. 82–97.

44. "Pinochet Is Ruled Unfit to Be Tried and May Be Freed," *New York Times,* January 12, 2000.

45. U.S. courts also recently have increased their involvement in domestic enforcement of human rights norms, through the application of the Alien Tort Claims Act, which enables foreigners to use American courts to bring civil suits against their own government for violations of humanitarian law or other international law. This trend began with *Filartiga v. Pena-Irala* in 1980. See Bederman, *International Law Frameworks,* pp. 107–108. See "U.S. Courts Become Arbiters of Global Rights and Wrongs," *New York Times,* June 21, 2001.

46. A 1993 Belgian law had empowered "Belgian judges to hear war crimes and genocide cases regardless of where they occurred or who committed them." However, in 2002, the International Court of Justice ruled that, based on the laws governing diplomatic immunity, Belgium could not try former and current world leaders for such actions. Belgium had instituted criminal proceedings against Fidel Castro of Cuba, Ariel Sharon of Israel, and Saddam Hussein of Iraq, among others. "UN Court Rules Belgium Can't Hold War Crimes Trials," *Baltimore Sun*, February 15, 2002. See ASIL Insights, "World Court Orders Belgium to Cancel Arrest Warrant Issued Against the Congolese Foreign Minister" (February 2002).

47. See William A. Schabas, *An Introduction to the International Criminal Court* (Cambridge: Cambridge University Press, 2001); and Bruce Broomhall, *International Criminal Justice and the International Criminal Court* (New York: Oxford University Press, 2003).

48. In 2002, President Bush formally nullified his predecessor's signature, while the U.S. Congress was drafting legislation threatening to withhold American forces from UN peacekeeping operations unless they were exempted from any possible ICC prosecution. On the pros and cons of the U.S. joining the ICC, see John Washburn, "Tyrants Beware: The International Criminal Court Is Born," *The Interdependent* (summer 1998), pp. 5–7; and Ruth Wedgewood, "An International Criminal Court Is Still a Bad Idea," *Wall Street Journal*, April 15, 2002. Also, see the statements by the Lawyers Committee for Human Rights and by John Bolton (former U.S. assistant secretary of state) before the hearings of the International Relations Committee of the U.S. House of Representatives on July 25, 2000 (Washington, D.C.: U.S. Government Printing Office, 2000).

49. "UN Espouses Animal's Lib," *St. Louis Post-Dispatch*, October 16, 1978.

50. Slaughter, "Leading Through Law," p. 38.

51. Jarat Chopra and Thomas G. Weiss, "Sovereignty Is No Longer Sacrosanct: Codifying Humanitarian Intervention," in Steven Spiegel and Daniel Pervin, eds., *At Issue: Politics in the World Arena*, 7th ed. (New York: St. Martins Press, 1994), p. 397.

52. Slaughter, "Leading Through Law," p. 38.

Chapter 5

1. David Kinsella, *Regime Change* (Belmont, Calif.: Wadsworth, 2004) discusses the "origins, execution, and aftermath of the Iraq War." Also, see the articles by Adam Roberts and Pascal Teixeira da Silva in David M. Malone, *The UN Security Council: From the Cold War to the 21st Century* (Boulder: Lynne Rienner, 2004), dealing with both the Afghanistan and Iraq wars; and Yutaka Arai-Takahashi, "Shifting Boundaries of the Right of Self-Defense: Appraising the Impact of the September 11 Attacks on Jus Ad Bellum," *International Lawyer* 36 (winter 2002), pp. 1082–1083 and 1101–1102.

2. Anthony Clark Arend, *Legal Rules and International Society* (New York: Oxford University Press, 1999), p. 139.

3. William D. Coplin, *The Functions of International Law* (Chicago: Rand McNally, 1966), p. 97.

4. "The conduct of war . . . is policy itself which takes up the sword in place of the pen." Karl von Clausewitz, *On War*, edited by Anatol Rapoport (Baltimore: Penguin, 1968), p. 410.

5. See note 10 in chapter 1.

6. See the quotation at the start of Part Two.

7. James Chace and Caleb Carr, *America Invulnerable: The Quest for Absolute Security from 1812 to Star Wars* (New York: Summit Books, 1988), p. 12.

8. See U.S. Department of State, *World Military Expenditures and Arms Transfers, 2003* (Washington, D.C.: U.S. State Department, 2003); and the *SIPRI Yearbook, 2004* (Stockholm, Sweden: Stockholm International Peace Research Institute, 2004), chapter 10.

9. Robert H. Jackson, "Continuity and Change in the State System," in Robert H. Jackson and Alan James, eds., *States in a Changing World* (Oxford: Clarendon Press, 1993), pp. 354–355 and 358.

10. Mark W. Zacher, "The Territorial Integrity Norm: International Boundaries and the Use of Armed Force," *International Organization* 55 (spring 2001), pp. 215–250.

11. As noted by Jack S. Levy in "War and Peace," in Walter Carlsnaes et al., eds., *Handbook of International Relations* (London: Sage, 2002), p. 351, "the twentieth century, and the second half-century in particular, marked a significant shift in warfare from the major powers to the minor powers, from Europe to other regions, and from inter-state warfare to intra-state wars." Also, see Mary Kaldor, *New and Old Wars: Organized Violence in a Global Era* (Cambridge: Polity, 2001); and Meredith Sarkees et al., "Inter-State, Intra-State, and Extra-State Wars: A Comprehensive Look at Their Distribution Over Time, 1816–1997," *International Studies Quarterly* 47 (March 2003), pp. 49–70. For the view that "new wars" have been exaggerated, see Edward Newman, "The 'New Wars' Debate: A Historical Perspective Is Needed," *Security Dialogue* 35 (June 2004), pp. 173–189.

12. *The Defense Monitor,* XXVII, no.1 (1998), p.1.

13. *The Defense Monitor,* XXXII, no.1 (2003), pp. 1 and 3.

14. See Michael Renner, "Violent Conflicts Continue to Decline," in Worldwatch Institute, *Vital Signs 2003* (New York: W. W. Norton, 2003), pp. 74–75.

15. Measurement problems are discussed in ibid. It should be noted that there have been more than 230 instances since 1789 in which an American president has sent U.S. troops into harm's way, only 5 of which were preceded by a formal declaration of war by Congress as required by the U.S. Constitution; but it was commonly assumed throughout much of American history that major wars entailed such formal authorization.

16. Barry M. Blechman and Stephen S. Kaplan, *Force Without War: U.S. Armed Forces as a Political Instrument* (Washington, D.C.: Brookings Institution, 1979); and Kaplan, *Diplomacy of Power: Soviet Armed Forces as a Political Instrument* (Washington, D.C.: Brookings Institution, 1981).

17. The Chinese case is an example of what has been called "coercive diplomacy," that is, the use of armed force in a highly limited, surgical, mostly threatening fashion, rather than as a raw military instrument, in order to persuade an adversary to refrain from some undesired behavior. See Alexander L. George et al., *The Limits of Coercive Diplomacy* (Boston: Little, Brown, 1971). Also, see a discussion of "diplomacy of violence" in Thomas C. Schelling, *Arms and Influence* (New Haven: Yale University Press, 1966).

18. Evan Luard, *War in International Society* (London: I. B. Taurus, 1986), p. 396.

19. James Lee Ray, "The Abolition of Slavery and the End of International War," *International Organization* 43 (summer 1989), pp. 405–439. Also, see Michael C. Desch, "War and Strong States, Peace and Weak States?" *International Organization* 50 (spring 1996), pp. 237–268.

20. Ray, "Abolition of Slavery," pp. 405–439; and John Mueller, *Retreat from Doomsday: The Obsolescence of Major War* (New York: Basic Books, 1989).

21. See Max Singer and Aaron Wildavsky, *The Real World Order,* revised ed. (Chatham, N.J.: Chatham House, 1996), p.3.

22. See Bruce Russett, *Grasping the Democratic Peace* (Princeton: Princeton University Press, 1993); and Russett and John R. Oneal, *Triangulating Peace* (New York: W. W. Norton, 2001), chapters 2 and 3. For another view of the "democratic peace," see Zeev Maoz, "The Controversy Over the Democratic Peace," *International Security* 22 (summer 1997), pp. 162–198.

23. Charles Krauthammer, "B-2 Is Weapon for Our Times," *St. Louis Post-Dispatch,* November 1, 1995. Also, see Edward Luttwak, "Toward Post-Heroic Warfare," *Foreign Affairs* 74 (May/June 1995), pp. 109–122, which argues that demographic trends (toward smaller family size) make families less willing to face potential loss of children in war.

24. One has to be careful in making this argument. Recall that Norman Angell's *The Great Illusion,* published in 1910 on the eve of World War I, claimed that war had become an anachronism insofar as it was no longer profitable even to the victors and predicted that the trade ties among the European powers made war highly unlikely. However, empirical support for the hypothesis is found in Russett and Oneal, *Triangulating Peace,* chapter 4.

25. Thomas L. Friedman, *The Lexus and the Olive Tree,* expanded ed. (New York: Anchor Books, 1999), chapter 12. Friedman acknowledges that his theory becomes more questionable if one includes civil wars and not merely interstate wars. Friedman has updated the "golden arches theory of conflict prevention" with the "Dell theory of conflict prevention," that is, "no two countries that are both part of a major global supply chain [like those which supply Dell Computer] will ever fight a war against each other." *The World Is Flat* (New York: Farrar, Straus, and Giroux, 2005), p. 421.

26. Thomas Friedman, "Was Kosovo World War III?" *New York Times,* July 2, 1999.

27. For example, see Josef Joffe, "Three Unwritten Rules of the Serbian War," *New York Times,* July 25, 1999; and Donald G. McNeil, "Bombing Won in Kosovo. Africa Is a Tougher Case," *New York Times,* July 25, 1999.

28. K. J. Holsti, "War, Peace, and the State of the State," *International Political Science Review* 16 (October 1995), p. 320.

29. Lester Brown, Michael Renner, and Brian Halwell, *Vital Signs 1999* (New York: W. W. Norton, 1999), p. 112. The authors were reporting on the Conflict Data Project at the University of Uppsala in Sweden, which used a relatively loose definition of war.

30. International Commission on Intervention and State Sovereignty, *The Responsibility to Protect* (Ottawa: International Development Research Centre, 2001), p. 4.

31. "The World's Wars," *The Economist,* March 12, 1988, pp. 19–20.

32. Melvin Small and J. David Singer, "Conflict in the International System, 1816–1977: Historical Trends and Policy Futures," in Charles W. Kegley and Patrick J. McGowan, eds., *Challenges to America: United States Foreign Policy in the 1980s* (Beverly Hills: Sage, 1979), p. 100.

33. On ethnopolitical conflict, see Ted Robert Gurr and Barbara Harff, *Ethnic Conflict in World Politics* (Boulder: Westview, 1994). The authors argue that the "explosion" of ethnopolitical conflict in the post–cold war era is actually an extension of a trend they trace to the 1960s.

34. On "failed states," see Gerald B. Hellman and Steve R. Ratner, "Saving Failed States," *Foreign Policy* (winter 1992–1993), pp. 3–20; William Zartman, ed., *Collapsed States* (Boulder: Lynne Rienner, 1995); and Tonya Langford, "Things Fall Apart: State Failure

and the Politics of Intervention," *International Studies Review* 1 (spring 1999), pp. 59–79.

35. Walter Laqueur notes that terrorism was high on the foreign policy agenda of world leaders in 1900 as one of the most serious security threats. Walter Laqueur, "Postmodern Terrorism," *Foreign Affairs* (September/October 1996), pp. 24–36.

36. Based on a study by Alex Schmid, cited in Anthony Clark Arend and Robert J. Beck, *International Law and the Use of Force* (New York: Routledge, 1993), p. 140. In December 9, 1985, the UN General Assembly adopted a resolution that attempted to define terrorism but left the term rather vague, as any acts that "endanger or take innocent human lives, jeopardize fundamental freedoms, and seriously impair the dignity of human beings." The 2004 Report of the Secretary-General's High-Level Panel on Threats, Challenges, and Change defined terrorism as "any action . . . that is intended to cause death or serious bodily harm to civilians or non-combatants, when the purpose of such an act . . . is to intimidate a population, or to compel a government or an international organization to do or to abstain from doing any act."

37. Cited in Schmid, *International Law and Use of Force,* p. 140.

38. *Patterns of Global Terrorism 2001* (Washington, D.C.: U.S. Department of State, 2002), p. xvi. A similar definition can be found in Arend and Beck, *International Law and Use of Force,* p. 140.

39. See Claire Sterling, *The Terror Network* (New York: Holt, Rinehart, and Winston, 1981).

40. During the 1980s, there was an average of 500 terrorist incidents reported annually, with the 856 incidents recorded in 1988 marking the peak year. *Patterns of Global Terrorism 1988,* pp. 1–2. In the 1990s, there was a downward trend, with 273 incidents reported in 1998: "the lowest annual total since 1971." *Patterns of Global Terrorism 1998,* p. 1. The latest report shows 208 incidents occurring in 2003. *Patterns of Global Terrorism 2003,* p. 1.

41. On the changing nature of the terrorist threat, see Laqueur, "Postmodern Terrorism," pp. 24–36; and Bruce Hoffman, *Inside Terrorism* (New York: Columbia University Press, 1998).

42. Thomas C. Schelling, "Thinking about Nuclear Terrorism," *International Security* 6 (spring 1982), p. 76.

43. From http://www.acda.gov/factshee/conwpn/small.htm; accessed on November 24, 1999.

44. "Messy War, Messy Peace," *The Economist,* June 12, 1999, pp. 15–16, referring to the Kosovo War.

45. See Michael Walzer, *Just and Unjust Wars* (New York: Basic Books, 1977); and William V. O'Brien, *The Conduct of Just and Limited War* (New York: Praeger, 1981).

46. For historical treatment of international legal restrictions on the resort to armed force, see Anthony Clark Arend and Robert J. Beck, *International Law and the Use of Force,* (New York: Routledge, 1993), chapter 2; and John Norton Moore, "Development of the International Law of Conflict Management," in *National Security Law* 47 (1990), pp. 51–83.

47. William R. Slomanson, *Fundamental Perspectives on International Law,* 3rd ed. (Belmont, Calif.: Wadsworth, 2000), p. 119.

48. On the rules governing the resort to armed force under the Charter, see Arend and Beck, *International Law and Use of Force;* John F. Murphy, "Force and Arms," in Christopher C. Joyner, ed., *The United Nations and International Law* (Cambridge: Cambridge University Press, 1997), pp. 97–130; Gerhard von Glahn, *Law Among Nations,* 7th ed. (New York: Longman, 1996), chapter 20; Oscar Schachter, "The Right of States To Use

Armed Force," *Michigan Law Review* 82 (1984), pp. 1620 ff; and Mary Ellen O'Connell, *International Law and the Use of Force* (New York: Foundation Press, 2004).

49. Quoted in Stephen C. Schlesinger, *Act of Creation* (Boulder: Westview, 2003), p. 171.

50. Slomanson, *Perspectives on International Law*, p. 119.

51. See John G. Ruggie, "Multilateralism: The Anatomy of an Institution," *International Organization* 46 (summer 1992), p. 584. Ruggie is responding here to questions posed by David Kennedy's examination of IGO growth in the twentieth century in "The Move to Institutions," *Cardozo Law Review* 8 (April 1987), pp. 841–988.

52. See note 32 in chapter 2.

53. By 1970, Thomas Franck was lamenting that "national self-interest, particularly the self-interest of the super-powers, has usually won out over treaty obligations." Thomas M. Franck, "Who Killed Article 2 (4)?" *American Journal of International Law* 64 (1970), p. 809.

54. Depending on the criteria used, the first peacekeeping mission is considered by some to be the UN Truce Supervision Organization (UNTSO), created in 1948 to supervise the truce between Israel and its Arab neighbors following the creation of the State of Israel. UNTSO still operates in the Middle East today.

55. Ernst Haas examined 123 disputes submitted to the UN for settlement between 1945 and 1981 and concluded that the organization helped to resolve or at least manage ("ameliorate") conflict, through reducing hostilities, in 51 percent of the cases. Ernst B. Haas, "Regime Decay, Conflict Management and International Organizations, 1945–1981," *International Organization* 37 (spring 1983), pp. 189–256.

56. Even the UN's strongest supporters expressed concern. Ernst Haas found that the early 1980s marked a low point in the life of the UN, with the "lowest share" of "all disputes involving military operations and fighting" being referred to that body "in the history of the organization." Ernst B. Haas, *Why We Still Need the UN* (Berkeley: University of California Press, 1986), p. 20. A former UN secretary general worried that the organization was becoming "irrelevant." Kurt Waldheim, "The United Nations: The Tarnished Image," *Foreign Affairs* 63 (fall 1984), p. 106.

57. For an overview of UN peacekeeping, see *The Blue Helmets*, 3rd ed. (New York: United Nations, 1997).

58. In his 1992 *Agenda for Peace* proposal, prepared at the behest of the Security Council, UN Secretary General Boutros Boutros-Ghali suggested a number of conflict management roles the UN might play, ranging from peace maintenance (where disputes had not yet erupted into actual hostilities and the UN might engage in "preventive deployment" of troops to quiet the situation) to peacemaking (where hostilities had begun and the UN might dispatch mediators to arrange a ceasefire) to peacekeeping (where UN personnel would be used to sustain the ceasefire) to peacebuilding (where the UN might foster conditions for a long-term, durable peace through promoting postwar reconstruction) to peace enforcement (where peacekeepers or other UN personnel were being prevented from doing their job by various governmental or rebel groups, necessitating stronger UN action against those forces). See *Agenda for Peace*, UN Doc. A/47/277 and S/24111, 1992.

59. Margaret P. Karns and Karen A. Mingst, *International Organizations: The Politics and Processes of Global Governance* (Boulder: Lynne Rienner, 2004), p. 297.

60. See ibid. p. 303 for a "selected list" of cases involving UN sanctions. The effectiveness of economic and other sanctions is discussed in David Cortright and George A. Lopez, *Sanctions and the Search for Security* (Boulder: Lynne Rienner, 2002).

61. See note 55. An empirical analysis of UN successes and failures, particularly in the case of civil wars, which finds that peacekeeping "does indeed make an important contribution to the stability of peace," is provided in Virginia Fortna, "Does Peacekeeping Keep Peace?" *International Studies Quarterly* 48 (June 2004), pp. 269–292.

62. Michael J. Glennon, *Limits of Law, Prerogatives of Power* (New York: Palgrave, 2001), p. 84. Glennon (p. 69) cites several empirical studies showing numerous military interventions since 1945, including a study by Herbert Tillema that counted 690 "overt foreign military interventions" between 1945 and 1996.

63. Louis Henkin, *How Nations Behave,* 2nd ed. (New York: Columbia University Press, 1979), p. 146. Murphy, "Force and Arms," p. 102, supports Henkin.

64. Joseph S. Nye, "What New World Order?" *Foreign Affairs* (spring 1992), p. 90. Another commentator similarly notes that the institutional "machinery we have to combat [security] problems are (sic) wired for the sovereign military confrontations of a bygone era." Maryann K. Cusimano, ed., *Beyond Sovereignty: Issues for a Global Agenda* (New York: St. Martin's Press, 2000), p., 2.

65. Arend and Beck, *International Law and Use of Force.*

66. See ibid.; Lori Fisler Damrosch, ed., *Enforcing Restraints: Collective Intervention in Internal Conflicts* (New York: Council on Foreign Relations, 1993); and Glennon, *Limits of Law,* chapter 4.

67. The UN General Assembly adopted the "Declaration on the Inadmissibility of Intervention in the Domestic Affairs of States and the Protection of Their Individual Sovereignty" on December 19, 1966 (UN Doc. GA 2225), but, at best, this represents "soft law."

68. On the rules governing intervention in civil wars, see von Glahn, *Law Among Nations,* chapter 21.

69. Quoted in Walter McDougall, "America and the World at the Dawn of a New Century," *WIRE* (December 1999).

70. Cited in Judith Miller, "Sovereignty Isn't So Sacred Anymore," *New York Times,* April 18, 1999. In 1999, according to Miller, "Kofi Annan unveiled a doctrine with profound implications for international relations in the new millennium. The air strikes against Yugoslavia [in the Kosovo War]. . .showed that the world would no longer permit nations to 'hide' behind the United Nations charter, which had traditionally safeguarded national sovereignty."

71. David J. Scheffer, "Use of Force after the Cold War," in Louis Henkin et al., *Right v. Might* (New York: Council on Foreign Relations Press, 1991), p. 144.

72. Martha Finnemore, "Constructing Norms of Humanitarian Intervention," in Peter J. Katzenstein, ed., *The Culture of National Security: Norms and Identity in World Politics* (New York: Columbia University Press, 1996), p. 170.

73. Slomanson, *Perspectives on International Law,* p. 463.

74. See Mark S. Stein, "Unauthorized Humanitarian Intervention," *Social Philosophy and Policy* 21 (winter 2004), p. 14.

75. On the Article 2 (7) controversy and other aspects of humanitarian intervention, see Abiodun Williams et al., *Article 2 (7) Revisited* (Providence: Academic Council on the United Nations System, 1994); Sean D. Murphy, *Humanitarian Intervention: The United Nations in an Evolving World Order* (Philadelphia: University of Pennsylvania Press, 1996); J.L. Holzgrefe and Robert O. Keohane, eds., *Humanitarian Intervention: Ethical, Legal, and Political Dilemmas* (Cambridge: Cambridge University Press, 2005); and Arend and Beck, *International Law and Use of Force,* chapter 8.

76. On "unauthorized humanitarian intervention," see Stein, *Social Philosophy and Policy,* p. 14.

77. Cited in Glennon, *Limits of Law* p. 158. Glennon (pp. 159–160) provides quoted statements representing the official positions of many different states objecting to unilateral humanitarian intervention.

78. As one illustration, the United States in the 1990s, after the first Gulf War, enforced a "no-fly" zone against Iraqi aircraft intimidating Kurdish villages in Northern Iraq, thereby providing a safe haven for Kurds that protected them from their own government. This action was based on no more than indirect UN authorization. At the same time, Washington looked the other way when Turkey, an American ally facing calls for self-determination by its own Kurdish population, strafed Kurdish camps inside Iraq's boundaries in retaliation for those camps supporting Kurdish rebels operating within Turkey. On the unclear mandate from the UN regarding the "no-fly zones," see Scheffer, "Force after the Cold War."

79. Donna M. Schlagheck, *International Terrorism* (Lexington: Lexington Books, 1988), pp. 125–126.

80. A similar case was the 1990 kidnapping of a Mexican physician named Alvarez-Machain in Mexico by bounty hunters hired by the U.S. government to bring the doctor to the United States to stand trial for allegedly participating in the torture and murder of a U.S. Drug Enforcement Administration agent. Washington had despaired of getting the Mexican government to extradite the man, so it took matters into its own hands. The U.S. Supreme Court ultimately ruled, in *United States v. Alvarez-Machain,* that, even if the abduction was a violation of international law, American courts could nonetheless try such cases, although Alvarez-Machain was acquitted of the charges. President Clinton later issued an apology to Mexico.

81. For a discussion of international law pertaining to terrorism, see Arend and Beck, *International Law and Use of Force,* chapter 9.

82. Article 51 of the UN Charter refers to both individual self-defense and collective self-defense. Technically what was at issue was the latter, as NATO for the first time in its history invoked Article 5 of the NATO Treaty, declaring the attack on the United States an attack on the entire alliance. Two weeks after 9/11, the UN Security Council passed Resolution 1373 imposing global financial sanctions, travel restrictions, and other sanctions on terrorists and their sponsors, and created a Counter-Terrorism Committee that was to receive annual reports from member states that indicated the measures they were taking to combat terrorism.

83. Patrick Tyler, "UN Chief Ignites Firestorm by Calling Iraq War 'Illegal'," *New York Times,* September 17, 2004. Also, see the front page of the *New York Times,* September 22, 2004.

84. Following 9/11, a group of sixty prominent American scholars released a statement, entitled "What We're Fighting For," supporting the war on terrorism as consistent with the "just war" tradition. See Jennifer K. Ruark, "Scholars' Statement Says Fight Against Terrorism is Consistent with Idea of 'Just War,'" *Chronicle of Higher Education,* February 12, 2002. It remained open to question whether the statement might apply to not only the Afghanistan War but also the Iraq War.

85. Hugo Grotius, *The Law of War and Peace,* chapter 22, trans. by R. Kelsey et al. (1925).

86. On anticipatory self-defense, see Arend and Beck, *International Law and Use of Force,* chapter 5; Anthony Clark Arend, "International Law and the Preemptive Use of

Military Force," *The Washington Quarterly* (spring 2003), pp. 89–103; and Antonio Cassese, *International Law* (Oxford: Oxford University Press, 2001), pp. 307–311.

87. George W. Bush, "The National Security Strategy of the United States of America," annual report to the U.S. Congress pursuant to the National Security Act of 1947 (Washington, D.C., September 2002). See note 1 for sources that discuss the U.S. legal position in regard to the Iraq War. Some supporters of the Bush Doctrine noted that President Kennedy had essentially used the same logic to justify the U.S. naval blockade during the 1962 Cuban missile crisis.

88. The laws of war are discussed in von Glahn, *Law Among Nations,* chapter 22.

89. Seymour Hersh, "The Gray Zone," *The New Yorker* (May 24, 2004).

90. Scheffer, "Force after the Cold War," pp. 141–142.

91. Ibid., pp. 142–143.

92. "How Precise Is Our Bombing?" editorial, *New York Times,* March 31, 2003. The *Times* added that "the allies deserve credit for conducting the most surgically precise bombing effort in the history of warfare."

93. There have been reports of other instances in which lethal chemical agents may have been used, such as Japan against China during World War II, but these are not fully documented. See J. P. Perry Robinson, "Origins of CWC," in Benoit Morel and Kyle Olson, eds., *Shadows and Substance: The CWC* (Boulder: Westview, 1993), pp. 40–45. Not included here are cases of non-lethal chemicals being used, such as the use of herbicides as defoliants by the United States in Vietnam.

94. Virginia Nesmith, "Landmines Are a Lingering Killer," *St. Louis Post-Dispatch,* December 31, 1995.

95. Robert J. Mathews and Timothy L. H. McCormack, "Entry into Force of the Chemical Weapons Convention," *Security Dialogue* 26, no. 1 (1995), p. 93.

96. Data are from "Chemical and Biological Weapons at a Glance," Arms Control Association Fact Sheet, accessed at http://www.armscontrol.org/factsheets/cbwprolif.asp on October 13, 2004.

97. See the Carnegie Endowment for International Peace, "Chemical Weapons Status 2004" map at http://www.ceip.org/files/projects/npp/resources/Deadly Arsenals/maps; accessed on October 13, 2004.

98. See the Carnegie Endowment for International Peace, "Biological Weapons Status 2004" map at http://www.ceip.org/files/projects/npp/resources/DeadlyArsenals/maps/; accessed on October 12, 2004.

99. As with chemical weapons, there are sketchy reports of biological weapons having been used on rare occasions, such as Soviet germ warfare in Afghanistan in the 1980s, but these, too, are not fully documented. See John Barry, "Planning a Plague?" *Newsweek,* February 1, 1993, pp. 40–41.

100. The Partial Test Ban Treaty of 1963 prohibited atmospheric testing of nuclear weapons but permitted underground testing, and was followed up in 1996 with a Comprehensive Nuclear Test Ban Treaty that was slated to take effect upon ratification by not only the members of the nuclear club but all forty-four countries possessing nuclear energy reactors; this treaty has been called "the longest-sought, hardest-fought prize in the history of arms control," since a stoppage of all nuclear testing might effectively put the nuclear genie back in the bottle. However, the United States, India and some other states have yet to sign on, with the U.S. in particular expressing concerns about adequate verification mechanisms as well as adequate alternative technologies for determining whether the existing nuclear arsenals were in working order

should they be needed. See U.S. Arms Control and Disarmament Agency discussion at http://www.acda.gov/ctbtpage/quotes.htm; accessed on November 24, 1999.

101. See the Carnegie Endowment for International Peace, "Nuclear Weapons Status 2004" map at http://www.ceip.org/files/projects/npp/resources/DeadlyArsenals/maps/; accessed on October 13, 2004.

102. Ibid.

103. See David Bederman, *International Law Frameworks*, (New York: Foundation Press, 2001), pp. 229–230; Burns H. Weston, "Nuclear Weapons and the World Court: Ambiguity's Consensus," *Transnational Law and Contemporary Problems* 7, no. 2 (1996); and Ved P. Nanda and David Krieger, *Nuclear Weapons and the World Court* (Ardsley, N.Y.: Transnational Publishers, 1998).

104. Abram Chayes and Antonio Chayes, "On Compliance," *International Organization* 47 (spring 1993), p. 180.

105. The quotation is attributed to Will Carpenter, a Monsanto Company executive who headed the Chemical Manufacturers Association during the 1980s and 1990s, based on an interview I conducted on November 1, 1999. Also, see Will Carpenter, "The Perspective of the Western Chemical Industry," in Morel and Kyle, *Shadows and Substance,* pp. 115–120.

106. The quote is from Daniel Bell in the fall 1990 issue of *Dissent,* cited in Samuel P. Huntington, "Why International Primacy Matters," *International Security* 17 (spring 1993), p. 81.

Chapter 6

1. James Bennet, "President Wants F.D.A. to Regulate Foreign Produce," *New York Times,* October 3, 1997.

2. Ibid.

3. For a critical view of how the WTO and the Codex tend to permit "trade to trump public health," see Lori Wallach and Patrick Woodall, *Whose Trade Organization?* (New York: The New Press, 2004), chapter 2.

4. CNN's "Allpolitics," October 2, 1997.

5. Thomas Friedman, *The Lexus and the Olive Tree* (New York: Farrar Straus Giroux, 1999), p. 221.

6. These statistics can be found on the home pages of these companies on the World Wide Web, itself now reaching over 200 million people in over 100 countries. Also, see Richard Barnet and John Cavanaugh, *Global Dreams* (Simon and Schuster, 1994), pp. 169 and 184–185; and David Held et al., *Global Transformations* (Stanford: Stanford University Press, 1999), chapter 7.

7. Richard O'Brien, *Global Financial Integration: The End of Geography* (London: Pinter, 1992). Also, see John Agnew, "The Territorial Trap: The Geographical Assumptions of International Relations Theory," *Review of International Political Economy* 1 (spring 1994), pp. 60–65; and Stephen J. Kobrin, "Strategic Alliances and State Control of Economic Actors," paper presented at the annual meeting of the International Studies Association, Chicago, February 24, 1995.

8. Charles P. Kindleberger, *American Business Abroad* (New Haven: Yale University Press, 1969), p. 207.

9. Raymond Vernon, *Sovereignty at Bay* (New York: Basic Books, 1971).

10. George W. Ball, "The Promise of the Multinational Corporation," *Fortune*, June 1, 1967, p. 80.

11. Hans J. Morgenthau, "The New Diplomacy of Movement," *Encounter* 43 (August 1974), p. 57.

12. Walter Wriston, *The Twilight of Sovereignty* (New York: Scribner's, 1992); and Robert B. Reich, *The Work of Nations* (New York: Knopf, 1991).

13. UN Development Program, *Human Development Report 2005* (New York: UNDP, 2005). Not all countries are included in the rankings, since in some cases there are inadequate data.

14. FAQs on the Human Development Indices, found on the web at http://www.undp.org/ hdr2000/english/FAQs.html#15; accessed on January 17, 2005.

15. Paul Lewis, "UN Lists 4 Lands at Risk Over Income Gaps," *New York Times*, June 2, 1994, p. A7. On disparities within countries based on cultural groupings, see the *Human Development Report 2004*, (New York: UNDP, 2004), p. 36.

16. Viviana Jimenez, "World Economic Growth Fastest in Nearly Three Decades," Earth Policy Institute, accessed on April 19, 2005, at http://www.earthpolicy.org/Indicators/ Econ/2005.htm.

17. The $1 a day figure is from *New York Times*, June 3, 1999, citing World Bank data. The billionaire figure for Mexico is from Norman Lewis, "Globalization and the End of the Nation-State," paper presented at the annual meeting of the International Studies Association, San Diego, April 16, 1996. The U.S. figure is cited in Friedman, *Lexus and Olive Tree*, p. 250.

18. UNDP, *Human Development Report 2004*, p. 30.

19. Jeffrey Sachs, *Investing in Development: A Practical Plan to Achieve the Millennium Development Goals*, A Report of the UN Millennium Project (London: Earthscan, 2005), p. 13. The report offers some hopeful statistics on the developing world, noting that, between 1990 and 2001, "the rate of undernourishment declined by 3 percentage points, and . . . life expectancy rose from 63 years to nearly 65 years [despite the AIDS epidemic]. An additional 8 percent of the developing world's population gained access to improved drinking water supply, and 15 percent more to basic sanitation services."

20. Robert Gilpin, *The Political Economy of International Relations* (Princeton: Princeton University Press, 1987), p. 31.

21. Jacob Viner, "Power versus Plenty as Objectives of Foreign Policy in the Seventeenth and Eighteenth Centuries," *World Politics* 1 (October 1948), p.10.

22. Cited in Gilpin, *Political Economy*, p. 180.

23. Ibid., pp. 181–182.

24. Cited in Kenneth N. Waltz, *Theory of International Politics* (Reading, Mass. Addison-Wesley, 1979), p. 140.

25. Cited in Geoffrey Barraclough, *An Introduction to Contemporary History* (Baltimore: Penguin, 1967), p. 53.

26. See Gilpin, *Political Economy*, chapter 2, for an excellent summary of these three international political economy "ideologies."

27. John Toye and Richard Toye, *The UN and Global Political Economy* (Bloomington: Indiana University Press, 2004). This volume takes a constructivist approach to the study of international political economy, examining particularly the intellectual currents that have affected the North-South conflict.

28. See note 70 in chapter 2.

29. Charles P. Kindelberger, *The World in Depression, 1929–1938* (Berkeley, Calif.: University of California Press, 1973). Kindleberger pointed out that the United Kingdom "couldn't lead" and the United States "wouldn't lead," the former due to diminished power and the latter due to isolationist tendencies.

30. By 1990, the Western industrialized democracies of the first world accounted for roughly 70 percent of all exports worldwide, selling mostly to each other. Regarding East-West trade, roughly 30 percent of Soviet trade was with the West, 10 percent with developing countries, and the largest share with fellow East bloc members. As for North-South trade, roughly one-third of the exports of first world countries went to third world countries, while 70 percent of the exports of the latter went to the former, with relatively little South-South trade occurring, due mainly to lack of purchasing power. For trade, and also investment, patterns, see Joan E. Spero, *The Politics of International Economic Relations,* 4th ed. (New York: St. Martins Press, 1990), chapters 3, 7, and 10; and *Handbook of Economic Statistics 1989* (Washington, D.C.: U.S. Central Intelligence Agency, 1989), tables, section 12 and pp. 180–181.

31. Lewis, "End of the Nation-State," p. 24.

32. John Gerard Ruggie, "International Regimes, Transactions, and Change: Embedded Liberalism in the Postwar Economic Order," in Stephen D. Krasner, ed., *International Regimes* (Ithaca: Cornell University Press, 1983), pp. 195–231.

33. For the headlines from Western Europe, see *New York Times,* September 19, 1997; *New York Times,* August 10, 1998; *New York Times,* July 25, 1999. For the third world headlines, see *New York Times,* January 18, 2000; and *New York Times,* September 16, 1999.

34. Nicholas Kristof, "China Sees 'Market-Leninism' as Way to Future," *New York Times,* September 6, 1993. Kristof said that what remained of marxism in China resembled "Groucho more than Karl."

35. Gilpin, *Political Economy,* p. 379. This relates to my discussion of "Jihad vs. McWorld" in chapter 2.

36. D. Held and A. McGrew, "Globalization and the Liberal Democratic State," in Y. Sakamoto, ed., *Global Transformation: Challenges to the State System* (New York: United Nations Press, 1994), p. 66.

37. Friedman, *Lexus and Olive Tree,* pp. 86–88.

38. Ibid., p. 134. In *The World Is Flat* (New York: Farrar, Straus and Giroux, 2005), p. 320, Friedman says that the most economically successful countries will be those that have a government regulatory environment that makes it easy to obtain a license to start a business, has flexible labor laws, and places minimal restrictions on operating a business. Some analysts have argued that, ultimately, there is a point at which the downsizing of the welfare state can become counterproductive in terms of attracting and keeping business within one's borders. That is, investors are not just attracted to states where there are low wages, low taxes, and low regulations. If the latter were the key magnets for capital, then states such as Somalia and Haiti would be booming economically. Clearly, firms in many instances are looking for states that offer, among other things, internal political stability that reduces the risk of violent upheaval (which itself ordinarily requires that rich-poor gaps not become excessively wide). Geoffrey Garrett, "Global Markets and National Politics: Collision Course or Virtuous Circle?" *International Organization* 52 (autumn 1998), pp. 787–824.

39. For example, see Robert O. Keohane and Joseph N. Nye, eds., *Transnational Relations and World Politics* (Cambridge: Harvard University Press, 1971), p. 392; and Vincent

Cable, "The Diminished Nation-State: A Study in the Loss of Economic Power," *Daedalus* (spring 1995), pp. 23–53.

40. Janice E. Thomson and Stephen D. Krasner, "Global Transactions and The Consolidation of Sovereignty," in Ernst-Otto Czempiel and James N. Rosenau, eds., *Global Changes and Theoretical Challenges* (Lexington: Lexington Books, 1989), p. 198.

41. On capital mobility, see Kenneth P. Thomas, *Capital Beyond Borders* (New York: Macmillan, 1997). Stephen Krasner disputes loss of control, arguing that "large, highly developed states" are better able than ever to "mitigate or adjust to pressures emanating from the international environment [such as dependence on foreign capital]," while "small underdeveloped states" have always been vulnerable and "remain extremely vulnerable." Stephen D. Krasner, "Economic Interdependence and Independent Statehood, in Robert H. Jackson and Alan James, eds., *States in a Changing World* (Oxford: Clarendon Press, 1993), p. 303.

42. Friedman, *Lexus and Olive Tree,* p. 8.

43. David J. Bederman, *International Law Frameworks* (New York: Foundation Press, 2001), pp.142–143.

44. Ibid., p. 141.

45. Raymond Vernon, "Sovereignty at Bay: 20 Years After," *Millennium* 20 (summer 1991), p. 195.

46. These are remarks made by an anonymous reviewer.

47. Cable, "Diminished Nation-State," p. 37.

48. Charles Lipson, "International Cooperation in Economic and Security Affairs," *World Politics* 37 (October 1984), p. 12. A similar observation is made by Robert Jervis in "Security Regimes," *International Organization* 36 (spring 1982), pp. 357–378.

49. On the subject of American hegemony, see note 51 in chapter 5. On social engineering and a faith in applying scientific principles of public management to the solution of global problems through IGOs, see Craig Murphy, *International Organization and Industrial Change* (New York: Oxford University Press, 1994).

50. Paul Krugman, "DOA at IMF," *New York Times,* March 1, 2000, p. A31.

51. William E. Slomanson, *Fundamental Perspectives on International Law,* 3rd ed. (Belmont, Calif.: Wadsworth, 2000), p. 585.

52. Sir Roy Denman, head of the European Community mission to the United States; cited in *Washington Post National Weekly* edition, September 22, 1986, p. 19, upon the opening of GATT's Uruguay Round trade talks.

53. Ernest H. Preeg, *Traders in a Brave New World* (Chicago: University of Chicago Press, 1995), p. 2.

54. Ibid., p. 185.

55. Ibid., p. 58.

56. Ibid., p. 10.

57. On two-level games in trade negotiations, see note 41 in chapter 2.

58. Quoted in Robert Dodge, "Grappling With GATT," *Dallas Morning News,* August 8, 1994; cited in Bruce Moon, *Dilemmas of International Trade* (Boulder: Westview Press, 1996), p. 91. On the strange-bedfellows coalitions generally, see Friedman, *Lexus and Olive Tree,* chapter 18.

59. For example, Teamsters president James Hoffa asked how American truckers could be expected to compete when "a fifteen-year old sitting on an orange crate may be driving an eight-wheeler truck from Mexico into the U.S. now that trucking safety rules at the

border were being relaxed." A remark made on "Both Sides," a TV show hosted by Jesse Jackson on April 4, 1999.

60. Remarks by Jeffry Frieden of Harvard University, in a talk given at the University of Missouri-St. Louis on March 26, 1998.

61. Preeg, *Traders in a Brave New World,* p. 65.

62. Ibid., p. 161.

63. See Slomanson, *Perspectives on International Law,* pp. 579–587. Slomanson (p. 580) notes that "the shift from GATT to WTO was a significant change. The GATT thus shifted from a *de facto* arrangement to a truly international organization intended to become the treaty-based centerpiece of International Trade Law."

64. Ibid., p. 583. Similarly, Toye and Toye, *Global Political Economy,* p. 288, state that the WTO treaty provisions "further 'judicialize' the process of trade cooperation."

65. Toye and Toye, *Global Political Economy,* p. 288.

66. Wallach and Woodall, *Whose Trade Organization?* p. 10. Also see pp. 244–245.

67. Ibid., pp. 244–245.

68. The United States left the International Labor Organization in 1977 and the UN Educational, Scientific and Cultural Organization (UNESCO) in 1984—both times over what it viewed as excessive "politicization" of these UN specialized agencies—but eventually returned to the organizations. Other states also on occasion have withdrawn from global IGOs, usually to return later.

69. "The death rate for IGOs . . . is remarkably low." Richard Cupitt, Rodney Whitlock, and Lynn Williams Whitlock, "The (Im)mortality of International Governmental Organizations," in Paul F. Diehl, ed., *The Politics of Global Governance,* 2nd ed. (Boulder: Lynne Rienner, 2001), p. 58

70. Mark W. Zacher and Brent A. Sutton, *Governing Global Networks* (Cambridge: Cambridge University Press, 1996).

71. Toye and Toye, *Global Political Economy,* pp. 287–288. A contrary view is expressed in Jack L. Goldsmith and Eric A. Posner, *The Limits of International Law* (New York: Oxford University Press, 2005), pp. 158–160.

72. A recent ruling by a WTO appellate body suggested that sanctions could be triggered not only by national laws that violated WTO strictures but even by policy "statements" made by a national government that were at odds with free trade norms. See Eliza Patterson, "WTO Appellate Body Places Government Policy Statements at Risk," *ASIL (American Society of International Law) Insight,* January 2005.

73. "Millennium Development Goals: A Compact Among Nations to End Human Poverty," in UN Development Program, *Human Development Report 2003* (New York: UNDP, 2003), pp. 1–2.

74. Sachs, *Investing in Development,* p. 2. On economic progress in the developing world, see note 19 in this chapter and note 16 in chapter 1.

75. Jeffrey Sachs, the director of the UN Millennium Project and author of the 2005 report, said that the doubling of aid to reduce poverty was "utterly affordable." Critics called it "utopian." See "UN Proposes Doubling of Aid to Cut Poverty," *New York Times,* January 18, 2005.

76. A realist, state-centric analysis of the NIEO debate is provided by Stephen N. Krasner in *Structural Conflict: The Third World Against Global Liberalism* (Berkeley: University of California Press, 1985). For a somewhat different perspective, see Roger D. Hansen, *Beyond the North-South Stalemate* (New York: McGraw-Hill, 1979); and Toye and Toye, *Global Political Economy.*

77. Gilpin, *Political Economy,* p. 304 has argued that the third world "no longer exists as a meaningful entity." Likewise, Louise Fawcett says "the Third World has lost much of the homogeneity it once appeared to possess" and is now "of little use as an analytical category." See "Regionalism in Historical Perspective," in Fawcett and Andrew Hurrell, eds., *Regionalism in World Politics* (New York: Oxford University Press, 1995), pp. 26–27. See note 33 in chapter 4.

78. On the rules governing expropriation, as well as contracts, see Gerhard von Glahn, *Law Among Nations,* 6th ed. (New York: Macmillan, 1992), pp. 263–280.

79. On the bargain struck between MNCs and LDCs, see Charles Lipson, *Standing Guard: Protecting Foreign Capital in the Nineteenth and Twentieth Centuries* (Berkeley: University of California Press, 1985).

80. Expropriation problems still occur on occasion, for example the recent seizure by Venezuela's leftist government of the land holdings of foreigners, allowing peasants to occupy those properties. See, for example, *Sunday Telegraph* (London), January 9, 2005.

81. Sachs is quoted in "UN Proposes Doubling of Aid To Cut Poverty," *New York Times,* January 18, 2005.

82. This was a statement made in an Indonesian newspaper; cited in Preeg, *Traders in a Brave New World,* p. 175.

83. Ibid., p. 176.

84. "Global Trade Body Rules Against U.S. on Cotton Subsidies," *New York Times,* April 27, 2004. The WTO supported "Brazil's contention that the subsidies paid to American cotton farmers violate international trade rules." Brazil and India have been among the top five plaintiffs. See Wallach and Woodall, *Whose Trade Organization?* p. 245.

85. See Toye and Toye, *Global Political Economy,* pp. 288–293; Richard H. Steinberg, "In the Shadow of Law or Power? Consensus-Based Bargaining and Outcomes in the GATT/WTO," *International Organization* 56 (spring 2002), pp. 339–374; and Wallach and Woodall, *Whose Trade Organization?* pp. 244–245. Wallach and Woodall argue that, although larger LDCs such as Brazil and India have made use of WTO tribunals as plaintiffs, "to the extent smaller countries have been involved, it has been mainly as a defendant." They note that nearly 25 percent of the cases brought to the WTO have been brought by developed countries against LDCs, with the plaintiff normally winning. They conclude (p. 10) that, because "they generally do not have the money and expertise to either bring cases to the WTO or defend themselves before the WTO," "developing countries are among the biggest losers in the system."

86. A number of concerns were addressed in *The Future of the WTO: Addressing Institutional Challenges in the New Millennium,* a high-level report issued in 2005. On "justice" and the "democratic deficit," see Anne-Marie Slaughter, *A New World Order* (Princeton: Princeton University Press, 2004).

87. This was the image painted by Molly Ivins in "Time to Begin Building Labor, Human, and Environmental Rights on a Global Scale," *St. Louis Post-Dispatch,* November 30, 1999.

88. On "GATTzilla," see Wallach and Woodall, *Whose Trade Organization?* p. 242.

89. Quoted in "Clinton Gives a Pass to 'Globaphobia,'" *Wall Street Journal,* January 31, 2000. Also see "Seattle Talks on Trade End," *New York Times,* December 5, 1999.

90. "For an AIDS patient in a poor country lucky enough to get antiretroviral treatment, chances are that the pills that stave off death come from India. Generic knockoffs of

AIDS drugs made by Indian manufacturers—now treating patients in 200 countries—have brought the price . . . down to $140 a year from $12,000. . . . [Due to WTO pressures] India's government has issued rules that will effectively end the copycat industry." "India's Choice," editorial in the *New York Times,* January 18, 2005.

91. Claudia Deutsch, "Unlikely Allies with the United Nations," *New York Times,* December 10, 1999. By 2004, over 1,000 MNCs were members of the Compact, although not all were equally committed to fighting poverty. See "Will 2004 Be the Defining Year for UN's Global Compact?" *The Interdependent* (spring 2004), p. 26.

92. "In Shadow of Iraq, UN's Development Agenda Evolves, Expands," *The Interdependent* (spring 2003), p. 25.

93. The meeting occurred on May 4, 2000. "Business Supports Kofi Annan's Global Compact But Rejects 'Prescriptive Rules," cited at http://www.iccwbo.org/home/news_archives/2000/buda_global.asp; accessed on January 28, 2005.

94. Maryann Cusimano, *Beyond Sovereignty* (New York: St. Martin's Press, 2000), p. 262. Also, see Julie Fisher, *NGOs and the Political Development of the Third World* (West Hartford: Kumarian Press, 1998).

95. Anne-Marie Slaughter, "Leading Through Law," *The Wilson Quarterly* (autumn 2003), p. 43.

96. Ibid., p. 44. In *A New World Order* (Princeton: Princeton University Press, 2004), p. 5, Anne-Marie Slaughter stresses that, obviously, "states still exist in this world . . . [and] indeed, they are crucial actors"; but she devotes the bulk of her attention to states as "disaggregated" actors enmeshed in transgovernmental networks. See note 42 in chapter 2.

97. The idea for a tax on currency transactions is credited to Nobel laureate economist James Tobin of Yale, who first proposed it in 1978. See Hilary French, "Reshaping Global Governance," in Christopher Flavin et al., eds., *State of the World 2002* (New York: W. W. Norton, 2002), pp. 188–189. On the world income tax, proposed by Nobel laureate Jan Tinbergen in the *Human Development Report 1994* (p. 88), see "World Income Tax: Report Floats Idea," *New York Times,* June 12, 1994. Also, see UN Development Program, *Human Development Report 1999* (New York: UNDP, 1999), pp. 110–111.

98. Bederman, *International Law Frameworks,* p.148.

99. Sachs, *Investing in Development,* chapter 7.

100. See William D. Coplin, *The Functions of International Law* (Chicago: Rand McNally, 1966), p. 26.

Chapter 7

1. Gall Luft and Anne Korin, "Terrorism Goes to Sea," *Foreign Affairs* (November/December 2004), p. 62.

2. On "the end of geography," see note 7 in chapter 6. The "boundary-spanning" phrase is from James N. Rosenau, "Declaration of Interdependence," *International Studies Perspectives* 6 (February 2005), inside back cover.

3. See Oscar Schachter, "The Jurisdiction of States," *International Law in Theory and Practice* (Dordrecht, Neth.: Martinus Nijhoff, 1991).

4. See William R. Slomanson, *Fundamental Perspectives on International Law,* 3rd ed. (Belmont, Calif.: Wadsworth, 2000), pp. 208–214.

5. The Vienna Convention on Diplomatic Relations is discussed in chapter 3 under "Treaties." Status of Forces agreements are discussed in Gerhard Von Glahn, *Law Among Nations,* 7th ed. (New York: Longman, 1996), pp. 165–167.
6. In the *Nottebohm* case, the International Court of Justice argued that the legal bond between a state and someone it claims as a citizen must be based on a "genuine link." *Liechtenstein v. Guatemala, International Court of Justice Reports,* 1955, p. 4.
7. In the *American Banana Co. v. United Fruit Co.* case, the U.S. Supreme Court argued that the matter of whether U.S. laws applied to American citizens abroad depended on the intent of the specific legislation in question. *U.S. Supreme Court Reports,* 1909, p. 347. The Anglo-Saxon legal tradition accords somewhat less importance to the nationality principle than does the continental European legal tradition.
8. Acquisition of nationality was discussed in chapter 4. In the past, countries such as the United States were reluctant to permit their citizens to vote in foreign elections, to obtain passports from foreign governments, and to engage in other actions that threw into question their national "allegiance," all of which could result in Washington revoking one's U.S. citizenship. However, loss of citizenship is rare today. See Mark Fritz, "Pledging Multiple Allegiances," *Los Angeles Times,* April 6, 1998.
9. Slomanson, *Perspectives on International Law,* p. 215.
10. For example, the constitutions of Columbia and Honduras prohibit their governments from extraditing their citizens to a foreign country, leaving it to the country's municipal courts to prosecute the case, if there is to be any trial. France and Germany are also among those countries that tend not to honor requests to extradite their citizens to stand trial abroad.
11. Slomanson, *Perspectives on International Law,* p. 205.
12. Ibid.
13. The classic case here is *Mali v. Keeper of the Common Jail (The Wildenhus Case),* where local authorities in Jersey City, N.J., arrested a Belgian crew member of a Belgian steamer for killing a fellow sailor while the ship was docked in the harbor. The U.S. Supreme Court ruled that the effects of the murder disturbed the "tranquility" of the port, permitting U.S. courts to try the case. *U.S. Supreme Court Reports,* 1887, p. 1. The Anglo-American legal tradition is more sympathetic than the European tradition to coastal state jurisdictional rights trumping flag state rights in such situations.
14. The 1963 Tokyo Convention on Offenses and Certain Other Acts Committed on Board Aircraft, ratified by most countries, cedes primary jurisdiction to the aircraft's state of registration rather than the state in whose airspace the offense was committed. See Note 31.
15. On continued problems with piracy at sea, see Luft and Korin, "Terrorism Goes to Sea."
16. Certain rules have to be followed by the pursuing vessels in order for hot pursuit to be legal (for example, pursuit can begin only after a clear visual or auditory signal has been given for the offending vessel to stop, and pursuit must cease when the vessel has entered the territorial waters of its own state or a third state unless permission is granted to continue the chase). See Nicholas Poulantzas, *The Right of Hot Pursuit in International Law* (Leyden, Neth.: A.W. Sijthoff, 1969).
17. Clifford Krauss, "Canada Reinforces Its Disputed Claims in the Arctic," *New York Times,* August 29, 2004.
18. Luft and Korin, "Terrorism Goes to Sea," p. 62.
19. Jack L. Goldsmith and Eric A. Posner, *The Limits of International Law* (New York: Oxford University Press, 2005), pp. 59–65, question the "traditional account" of state

practice largely conforming to the three-mile rule. Although they point to some variation among states, even they acknowledge general acceptance of the basic precept of the "territorial sea" as an international legal category.

20. Christopher C. Joyner, *International Law in the 21st Century* (New York: Rowman and Littlefield, 2005), p. 229. Four conventions, drafted by the International Law Commission, came out of UNCLOS I. These were the Convention on the Territorial Sea and Contiguous Zone, the Convention on Fishing and Conservation of Living Resources, the Convention on the High Seas, and the Convention on the Continental Shelf.

21. David L. Larson, ed., *Major Issues of the Law of the Sea* (Durham, N.H.: University of New Hampshire, 1976), p. 10.

22. Clyde Sanger, *Ordering the Oceans* (Toronto: Toronto University Press, 1987), p. 25.

23. Ibid., p. 28.

24. Ibid., p. 33.

25. In addition, the treaty clarified the outer limits of the continental shelf and created a 24-mile contiguous zone, which enables coastal states to regulate smuggling, immigration, and pollution.

26. The United States officially proclaimed a 200-mile exclusive fishing zone as early as 1977, and adopted a 12-mile territorial sea by 1990. The United States did ratify the 1995 UN Convention on Straddling Fish Stocks, which attempted to address concerns about overfishing of migratory species that had not been adequately covered by the Law of the Sea Treaty.

27. Joyner, *International Law in the 21st Century*, p. 226.

28. Cited in Jeremy Rifkin, *Biosphere Politics* (San Francisco: Harper Collins, 1991), p. 59.

29. See Joyner, *International Law in the 21st Century*, p. 239; Slomanson, *Perspectives on International Law*, p. 275; and Antonio Cassese, *International Law* (Oxford: Oxford University Press, 2001), p. 56.

30. Although violence is permitted only as a last resort, there have been incidents in which states have not exhausted peaceful means to end a foreign aircraft's trespass into one's airspace, such as the 1983 shooting down of a Korean Air Line 007 plane by Russian jets that had supposedly spotted the airliner flying over sensitive military installations in the Soviet Union.

31. The Tokyo Convention replaced the provision of the 1944 Chicago Convention that had ceded primary jurisdiction to the state in whose airspace the offense was committed. There may still be possibilities for concurrent jurisdiction involving the nationality principle and other jurisdictional principles.

32. On some "losses" suffered by the United States in multilateral negotiations over aviation agreements, see Mark W. Zacher and Brent A. Sutton, *Governing Global Networks* (Cambridge: Cambridge University Press, 1996), pp. 110–115.

33. Ibid., p. 125.

34. The global politics of regime-making in the telecommunications area are discussed in ibid., chapter 5.

35. Slomanson, *Perspectives on International Law*, p. 279.

36. See Mark Zieman, "Lack of Law May Slow the Use of Outer Space by Private Enterprise," *Wall Street Journal*, August 20, 1985.

37. See "Symposium on Jurisdiction and the Internet," *International Lawyer* 32 (1998), pp. 959–1191; Slomanson, *Perspectives on International Law*, pp. 223–225; and Roland Paris, "The Globalization of Taxation? Electronic Commerce and the Transformation of the State," *International Studies Quarterly* 47 (June 2003), pp. 153–182.

38. On the politics of developing a global information regime covering the Internet, see Marcus Franda, *Launching Into Cyberspace: Internet Development in Five World Regions* (Boulder: Lynne Rienner, 2002); Derrick Cogburn, "Partners or Pawns?: The Impact of Elite Decision-Making and Epistemic Communities in Global Information Policy on Developing Countries and Transnational Civil Society," paper presented at the annual meeting of the International Studies Association, Montreal, March 17, 2004; and Cogburn, "Global Idea Networks and the World Summit on the Information Society," paper presented at the annual meeting of the International Studies Association, Honolulu, March 4, 2005. Cogburn raises concerns about developed country domination of the global policy process.

39. The quote is attributed to Fred Hoyle.

40. *New York Times,* May 23, 2000, pp. C1 and C4. Brazil is also "the only developing country to be invited to join the 15-nation group building the international space station."

41. The World Commission on Environment and Development (Brundtland Commission), *Our Common Future* (New York: Oxford University Press, 1987), p. 27.

Chapter 8

1. The 1.75 million figure refers to the number of species catalogued by scientists. See David Hosansky, "Mass Extinction," *CQ Researcher,* September 15, 2000, pp. 715–726; and United Nations Environment Program, *Global Biodiversity Assessment* (Cambridge: Cambridge University Press, 1995), p. 118.

2. Peter Raven, "A Time of Catastrophic Extinction," *The Futurist* (September/October 1995), p. 38. Extinction rates can be found in John Tuxill and Chris Bright, "Losing Strands in the Web of Life," in Lester Brown et al., *State of the World 1998* (New York: W. W. Norton, 1998), p. 41; and *Environment on File* (Washington, D.C.: World Resources Institute, 1995).

3. On the richness of biodiversity, particularly in the tropical rainforests, see Edward O. Wilson, *The Diversity of Life* (New York: W.W. Norton, 1992); and Norman Myers, *The Primary Source* (New York: W.W. Norton, 1992).

4. Lester Brown et al., *Vital Signs 1995* (New York: W.W. Norton, 1995), p. 116.

5. G. Tyler Miller, *Living in the Environment,* 10th ed. (Belmont, Calif.: Wadsworth, 1998), p. 183. Myers, *The Primary Source* p. xx, estimates that as many as 5,000 to 10,000 species are being lost each year due to rainforest destruction.

6. G. Tyler Miller, *Environmental Science,* 4th ed. (Belmont, Calif.: Wadsworth, 1993), p. 326.

7. The first headline appeared in the *New York Times,* January 4, 1996; the second is from the *New York Times,* December 19, 1999; and the third is from the *St. Louis Post-Dispatch,* December 16, 2004.

8. See *St. Louis Post-Dispatch,* December 16, 2004; *Vital Signs 2003* (New York: W. W. Norton, 2003), pp. 40–41; and Seth Dunn and Christopher Flavin, "Moving the Climate Change Agenda Forward," in *State of the World 2002* (New York: W. W. Norton, 2002), pp. 24–50.

9. These and other data can be gleaned from *Time,* April 9, 2001; and the *New York Times,* May 10, 2002.

10. An overview of current global environmental problems, as well as a regional assessment, is provided in UN Environmental Program, *Global Environment Outlook 2000* (New York: Earthscan, 1999).

11. Robert Heilbroner, *An Inquiry into the Human Prospect: Looked at Again for the 1990s* (New York: W. W. Norton, 1991), p. 11.

12. Robert Kaplan, "The Coming Anarchy," *Atlantic Monthly* (February 1994), p. 58.

13. These and other historical examples of early environmental consciousness are found in Adam Markham, *A Brief History of Pollution* (New York: St. Martin's Press, 1994).

14. Phillippe Sands and Jacqueline Peel, "Environmental Protection in the Twenty-First Century," in Axelrod et al., eds., *The Global Environment: Institutions, Law, and Policy,* (Washington, D.C.: CQ Press, 2005), p. 46.

15. David J. Bederman, *International Law Frameworks* (New York: Foundation Press, 2001), p. 46.

16. The statement was made in 1883; cited in Jeremy Rifkin, *Biosphere Politics* (San Francisco: Harper Collins, 1991), p. 56.

17. See Everett Carl Ladd and Kathryn H. Bowman, *Attitudes Toward the Environment* (Washington, D.C.: American Enterprise Institute, 1995).

18. Richard A. Falk, *This Endangered Planet* (New York: Vintage Books, 1971), p. 284.

19. Report of the Club of Rome, *The Limits to Growth* (New York: Universe Books, 1972).

20. For example, see Julian L. Simon, *The Ultimate Resource* (Princeton: Princeton University Press, 1981). On the other hand, the Carter Commission that issued the *Global 2000 Report to the President* in 1979 echoed many of the findings and warnings of the Club of Rome.

21. *World Resources 2002–2004* (Washington, D.C.: World Resources Institute, 2004), p. 145, puts the figure at 60 percent. Statistics vary on the number of environmental treaties in existence, depending on how one defines the scope and content of such instruments. See notes 29–31 below.

22. See note 41 in chapter 7.

23. Lester Brown et al., *State of the World 2000* (New York: W. W. Norton, 2000), p. 4.

24. Daniel C. Esty, "A Term's Limits," *Foreign Policy* 126 (September–October 2001), p. 74.

25. *World Resources 2002–2004,* pp. 149 and 151.

26. Margaret P. Karns and Karen A. Mingst, *International Organizations: The Politics and Processes of Global Governance* (Boulder: Lynne Rienner, 2004), p. 468.

27. For a comprehensive treatment of customary and treaty law in the environmental field, along with discussion of historical and other aspects, see David Hunter, James Salzman, and Durwood Zaelke, *International Environmental Law and Policy,* 2nd ed. (New York: Foundation Press, 2002).

28. See Sands and Peel, "Environmental Protection," pp. 52–56; Christopher C. Joyner, *International Law in the 21st Century* (New York: Rowman and Littlefield, 2005), pp. 206–209; Bederman, *International Law Frameworks,* pp.46–48; and Nancy K. Kubasek and Gary S. Silverman, *Environmental Law,* 5th ed. (Upper Saddle River, N.J.: Prentice-Hall, 2005), pp. 409–412.

29. Michael Faure and Jorgen Lefevere, "Compliance with Global Environmental Policy," in Axelrod et al., eds., *The Global Environment,* p 163.

30. Joyner, *International Law,* p. 210. According to another source, "by one count, there are more than 900 international agreements with some environmental provisions." See Norman Vig, "Introduction: Governing the International Environment," in Axelrod et al., eds., *The Global Environment,,* p. 2., citing the work of Edith Brown Weiss.

31. Ibid., p. 9.

32. The figure for Bombay is from Hilary F. French, "Clearing the Air," in Lester Brown et al., *State of the World 1990* (New York: W. W. Norton, 1990), p. 98, while the figure for Mexico City is from Miller, *Living in the Environment*, p. 314.

33. The 1988 Sofia Protocol tried to deal with nitrogen oxides. On the European acid rain regime, see Marc A. Levy, "European Acid Rain: The Power of Tote-Board Diplomacy," in Peter M. Haas et al., *Institutions for the Earth* (Cambridge: MIT Press, 1993), pp. 75–132. Levy argues that, although the United Kingdom did not formally sign the Helsinki Protocol, it was shamed by adverse European-wide publicity into reducing its SO_2 emissions.

34. Intergovernmental Panel on Climate Change, "Climate Change 2001: The Scientific Basis" (2001). On climate change, see Dunn and Flavin, "Moving the Climate Change Agenda Forward"; David G. Victor, *Climate Change* (New York: Council on Foreign Relations, 2004); and John Browne, "Beyond Kyoto," *Foreign Affairs* 83 (July/August 2004), pp. 20–32.

35. Richard E. Benedick, "Ozone Diplomacy," *Issues in Science and Technology* (fall 1989), p. 43. Also, see Benedick, *Ozone Diplomacy*, enlarged ed. (Cambridge: Harvard University Press, 1998); and Edward A. Parson, "Protecting the Ozone Layer," in Peter M. Haas, *Institutions for the Earth* (Cambridge: MIT Press, 1993), pp. 27–74.

36. Comments made by Lee Thomas in testimony before the U.S. Senate, Committee on Foreign Relations Hearings, February 19, 1988; and George Mitchell, statement in U.S. Senate, 1988; cited in Benedick, *Ozone Diplomacy*, p. 1.

37. Dunn and Flavin, "Moving the Climate Change Agenda Forward," p. 48, note that use of ozone-depleting chemicals has declined 90 percent since 1987.

38. "Next, Wars Over Water," *World Press Review* (November 1995), p. 8; Mark W. Rosegrant et al., "Global Water Outlook to 2025: Averting an Impending Crisis," a report of the International Water Management Institute (2002); and Sandra Postel, "Facing a Future of Water Scarcity," in John Allen, ed., *Environment 1995/1996* (Guilford, Conn.: Dushkin, 1996), pp. 170–180.

39. Michael G. Renner, "Shared Problems, Common Security," in Charles W. Kegley and Eugene Wittkopf, eds., *Global Agenda* (New York: St. Martin's Press, 1992), p. 337.

40. See Ronald Mitchell, "Intentional Oil Pollution of the Oceans," in Peter M. Haas et al., *Institutions for the Earth* (Cambridge: MIT Press, 1993), pp. 183–248.

41. See Peter M. Haas, *Saving the Mediterranean: The Politics of International Environmental Cooperation* (New York: Columbia University Press, 1990).

42. Miller, *Living in the Environment*, pp. 555–556.

43. Between 1960 and 1990, one-fifth of the tropical rainforests on the globe disappeared. Based on satellite data, estimates of how much tropical deforestation is occurring range from the equivalent of fourteen city blocks per minute to sixty-eight city blocks per minute. See Janet N. Abramowitz, "Sustaining the World's Forests," in Lester Brown et al., *State of the World 1998* (New York: W. W. Norton, 1998), p. 22; and Miller, *Living in the Environment*, p. 342.

44. Kal Raustiala and David Victor, "The Future of the Convention on Biological Diversity," *Environment* (May 1996), pp. 17–20 and 37–45.

45. Gareth Porter, Janet Welsh Brown, and Pamela S. Chasek, *Global Environmental Politics*, 3rd ed. (Boulder: Westview Press, 2000), pp. 98–103.

46. On the IWC, see ibid., pp. 93–98.

47. Paul Wapner, *Environmental Activism and World Civic Politics* (Albany: State University of New York Press), p. 65.

48. Porter et al., *Global Environmental Politics,* p. 103.
49. David Downie et al., "Global Policy for Hazardous Chemicals," in Axelrod et al., eds., *The Global Environment,* pp. 128–129.
50. See ibid., pp. 128–131.
51. See ibid., pp. 133–136.
52. Lynton Caldwell, *International Environmental Policy* (Durham, N.C.: Duke University Press, 1992), p.18.
53. On distinctions between such terms as implementation, compliance, and effectiveness, see Harold K. Jacobson and Edith Brown Weiss, "Strengthening Compliance with International Environmental Accords," *Global Governance,* 1 (May–August 1995), pp. 119–148; and Faure and Lefevere, "Global Environmental Policy."
54. Wapner, *Environmental Activism,* p. 22.
55. Ibid., p. 23. Also, see U.S. Government Accounting Office, *International Environment: International Agreements Are Not Well Monitored,* GAO/RCED (January 1992); and Peter H. Sand, ed., *The Effectiveness of International Environmental Agreements* (Cambridge, Eng.: Grotius, 1992).
56. *World Resources 2002–2004,* p. 151.
57. Ibid., p. 144. A survey of factors is offered by Faure and Lefevere, "Global Environmental Policy."
58. *World Resources 2002–2004,* p. 150.
59. Cited in Faure and Lefevere, "Global Environmental Policy," p. 163.
60. See Detlef Sprinz and Tapani Vaahtorana, "The Interest-Based Explanation of International Environmental Policy," *International Organization* 48 (winter 1994), pp. 77–105.
61. See Michael Grubb et al., *The Earth Summit Agreements* (London: Earthscan, 1993); and James Speth, "A Post-Rio Compact," *Foreign Policy* 88 (fall 1992), pp. 145–161. On the politics of the Global Environmental Facility, see Lawrence E. Susskind, *Environmental Diplomacy* (New York: Oxford University Press, 1994), pp. 37–41.
62. In 1983, Norway, Sweden, Finland, and Switzerland, with the United States and Canada, formed the "Toronto Group" to take action, while the European Community was opposed to strong measures. The story of how the initially ambivalent Reagan administration came around to supporting a CFC ban and how the EC was persuaded to join the effort is told in Benedick, *Ozone Diplomacy.*
63. Susskind, *Environmental Diplomacy,* p. 8.
64. Japan in the past has accounted for 80 percent of all ivory imports. Japan, Norway, Peru and Russia have accounted for 75 percent of the whale kills. See Porter et al., *Global Environmental Politics,* pp. 93–95.
65. Susskind, *Environmental Diplomacy,* p. 18.
66. Ibid., p. 107.
67. On nonstate actors and global environmental governance, see Hilary F. French, "Coping with Ecological Globalization," in Lester Brown et al., *State of the World 2000* (New York: W. W. Norton, 2000), pp.184–202; and Porter et al., *Global Environmental Politics.*
68. Statistics are from Jacqueline V. Switzer, *Environmental Politics: Domestic and Global Dimensions* (New York: St. Martin's Press, 1994), p. xv.
69. Peter Haas, "The Future of International Environmental Governance," paper delivered at the annual meeting of the International Studies Association, San Diego, April 17, 1996, p. 16. *World Resources 2002–2004,* p. 166, notes that "in Stockholm, only 10 percent of registered NGOs came from developing countries. By the Rio Earth Summit,

that had risen to about one-third. By 2002 [at Johannesburg], at least 40 percent . . . were from developing countries."

70. Following Rio, the Business Council for Sustainable Development expanded to become the World Business Council for Sustainable Development, which included many of the largest MNCs in the world. Although not all were equally committed to improving the environment, all felt a need to improve their image as environmental stewards.

71. Speth, "Post-Rio Compact," p. 146.

72. Grubb et al., *Earth Summit Agreements*, p. 44.

73. Gareth Porter and Janet Welsh Brown, *Global Environmental Politics*, 2nd ed. (Boulder: Westview Press, 1996), p. 58.

74. See *World Resources 2002–2004*, p. 74. Again, not all NGOs present were environmental ones. The *World Directory of Environmental Organizations* lists 2,500 environmental organizations. For an overview, see John McCormick, "The Role of Environmental NGOs in International Regimes," in Axelrod et al., eds., *The Global Environment*, pp. 83–102; Ken Conca, "Greening the UN: Environmental Organizations and the UN System" in Thomas G. Weiss and Leon Gordenker, eds., *NGOs, The UN, and Global Governance* (Boulder: Lynne Rienner, 1996), pp. 103–119; Thomas Princen and Mathias Finger, eds., *Environmental NGOs in World Politics* (London: Routledge, 1994); and chapter 4, "Awakening Civil Society," in *World Resources 2002–2004*.

75. Susskind, *Environmental Diplomacy*, p. 48. Also see Kal Raustiala, "States, NGOs, and International Environmental Institutions," *International Studies Quarterly* 41 (December 1997), pp. 719–740.

76. Susskind, *Environmental Diplomacy*, p. 24.

77. The 1974 study was done by Mario Molina and Sherwood Rowland. In 1986, an international research team of 150 scientists from the United States, Brazil, Canada, Australia, Japan, and several other countries, under the leadership of NASA and auspices of UNEP and WMO, finalized their data collection and published their findings showing that the accumulation of CFCs in the atmosphere had doubled between 1975 and 1985 and was steadily eroding the ozone layer. In April 1987, a well publicized meeting of scientists was held in Wurzburg, West Germany, that reinforced earlier warnings about the ozone layer problem. Also in April 1987, a preparatory meeting for Montreal Protocol deliberations was held in Geneva, where UNEP Executive Director Mostafa Tolba told the diplomatic gathering that the latest research made it "no longer possible to oppose action to regulate CFC release on the grounds of scientific dissent." Parson, "Protecting the Ozone Layer," p. 43. Similar scientific warnings continued to be reported subsequent to Montreal that accelerated the adoption of amendments to strengthen the Protocol.

78. Raustiala, "States, NGOs, and International Environmental Institutions," p. 728.

79. Jessica Mathews, "Power Shift," *Foreign Affairs* 76 (January/February 1997), p. 55.

80. Susskind, *Environmental Diplomacy*, p. 62.

81. Bill McKibben, "A Special Moment in History," *Atlantic Monthly* (May 1998), p. 72.

82. See Peter Newell, "Environmental NGOs, TNCs, and the Question of Governance," paper presented at the annual meeting of the International Studies Association, Washington, D.C., February 17, 1999.

83. Jennifer Clapp, "The Global Recycling Industry and Hazardous Waste Trade Politics," paper presented at the annual meeting of the International Studies Association, Washington, D.C., February 16, 1999.

84. Benedick, "Ozone Diplomacy," p. 50.

85. Benedick, *Ozone Diplomacy*, pp. 220–223.

86. Susskind, *Environmental Diplomacy*, p. 71, says that "in two decades of debate over ozone depletion, the focus was on scientific rather than political issues. . . . All of this was unusual."

87. Benedick, "Ozone Diplomacy," p. 43.

Chapter 9

1. Louis Henkin, *How Nations Behave*, 2nd ed. (New York: Columbia University Press, 1979), p. 1.

2. English historian John Keegan, cited in Stephen C. Schlesinger, *Act of Creation* (Boulder: Westview, 2003), p. xv.

3. John Mearsheimer, "Why We Will Soon Miss the Cold War," *Atlantic Monthly* (August 1990), p. 35.

4. Abba Eban, "The UN Idea Revisited," *Foreign Affairs* 74 (September/October 1995), p. 50.

5. Frederic S. Pearson and J. Martin Rochester, *International Relations in the Twenty-First Century*, 4th ed. (New York: McGraw-Hill, 1998), p. 80. I have drawn heavily in this work from both the latter book as well as my *Between Two Epochs* (Upper Saddle River, N.J.: Prentice-Hall, 2002).

6. Thomas L. Friedman, *The Lexus and the Olive Tree* (New York: Farrar, Straus, Giroux, 1999), p. 13.

7. David Held, *Global Covenant* (Cambridge: Polity Press, 2004), p. 139.

8. Anne-Marie Slaughter, *A New World Order* (Princeton: Princeton University Press, 2004), pp. 5–6.

9. Ibid. These words are on the book jacket. In fairness, Slaughter is careful to add, on p. 30, that "the state is not disappearing; it is disaggregating. . . . The conception of the unitary state is a fiction, but it has been a useful fiction. . . . It still holds for some critical activity such as decisions to go to war, to engage in a new round of trade negotiations, or to establish new international institutions. . . . But it hides as much as it helps."

10. See note 54 in chapter 2.

11. Paul Lewis, "UN Panel Proposes Expanding Security Council to 24 Members," *New York Times*, March 21, 1997.

12. Robert O. Keohane and Joseph S. Nye, *Power and Interdependence*, 3rd ed. (New York: Longman, 2001), p. 10.

13. The "Grotian moment" phrase is taken from Richard Falk, Friedrich Kratochwil, and Saul H. Mendlovits, eds., *International Law: A Contemporary Perspective* (Boulder: Westview Press, 1985), p. 7.

14. Quoted in Charles Krauthammer, "An American Foreign Policy for a Unipolar World," speech given to the American Enterprise Institute, February 10, 2004.

15. Joseph S. Nye, *The Paradox of American Power* (New York: Oxford University Press, 2002), p. 1.

16. Stephen M. Walt, "American Primacy: Its Prospects and Pitfalls," *Naval War College Review* (spring 2002), p. 1.

17. Timothy Garton Ash, "The Peril of Too Much Power," *New York Times*, April 9, 2002.

18. Josef Joffe, "Bismarck's Lessons for Bush," *New York Times*, May 29, 2002.

19. Stephen Brooks and William Wohlforth, "American Primacy in Perspective," *Foreign Affairs* 81 (July/August 2002), pp. 21 and 23.

20. "I still believe he [President Johnson] found it viscerally inconceivable that what Walt Rostow [Johnson's chief national security advisor] kept telling him was the 'greatest power in the world' could not dispose of a band of night-riders in black pajamas." Quoted from Arthur Schlesinger Jr., "The Quagmire Papers," *New York Review of Books,* December 16, 1971, p. 41. Although the United States has had a number of military victories since Vietnam, including in the First Gulf War, Afghanistan, and the Second Gulf War, these have not translated as easily into political successes.

21. Nye, *Paradox of American Power,* pp.8–9.

22. On the need for hegemons to blend carrots and sticks, soft and hard power, see G. John Ikenberry and Charles A. Kupchan, "Socialization and Hegemonic Power," *International Organization* 44 (summer 1990), p. 284.

23. The image of the United States as a law-abiding country was not helped by the statement made by John Bolton, President Bush's nominee for UN ambassador, during his 2005 Senate confirmation hearings, when he said that international treaties are not "legally binding." He reiterated this view in "The Global Prosecutors: Hunting War Criminals in the Name of Utopia," *Foreign Affairs* (January/February 1999), pp. 157–164; also, see David Bosco, "The World According to John Bolton," *Bulletin of the Atomic Scientists* (July/August 2005), pp. 24–31.

24. Henry A. Kissinger, "Clinton and the World," *Newsweek,* February 1, 1993, p. 45.

25. Remarks by President Bill Clinton, in a 1997 speech.

26. Charles Kindleberger, "Hierarchy Versus Inertial Cooperation," *International Organization* 40 (autumn 1986), p. 841.

27. Joseph S. Nye, "Conflicts After the Cold War," Washington Quarterly (winter 1996), p.2. Also, see Nye, *Paradox of American Power*; and Richard Haass, *The Reluctant Sheriff: The United States After the Cold War* (New York: Council on Foreign Relations, 1997).

28. In *Of Paradise and Power* (New York: Knopf, Vintage Books, 2003), p. 95, Robert Kagan likens the United States to the sheriff's role played by Gary Cooper in the movie *High Noon,* where the town marshal tried unsuccessfully to mobilize a posse against some ruthless outlaws; he likens America's European allies to the town's saloonkeepers, who wanted to give the outlaws a few drinks in the hope they would go away.

29. James Madison, in *The Federalist Papers.*

30. On U.S. foreign policy and international law, see John F. Murphy, *The United States and the Role of Law in International Affairs* (Cambridge: Cambridge University Press, 2004).

31. Jack L. Goldsmith and Eric A. Posner, *The Limits of International Law* (New York: Oxford University Press, 2005), p. 203.

32. Ibid., p. 225.

33. This was German Chancellor Theobald von Bethmann-Hollweg's reference to the German-Belgian neutrality treaty that Germany violated when it invaded Belgium in World War I. Quoted in Robert W. Tucker and David C. Hendrickson, "The Sources of American Legitimacy," *Foreign Affairs* 83 (November/December 2004), p. 20.

34. Mark W. Zacher, "The Decaying Pillars of the Westphalian Temple: Implications for International Order and Global Governance," in James N. Rosenau and Ernst-Otto Czempiel, eds., *Governance Without Government* (Cambridge, Eng.: Cambridge University Press, 1992), p. 60.

35. Inis Claude Jr., *Swords Into Plowshares,* 4th ed. (New York: Random House, 1984), p. 399.

36. Michael J. Glennon, "Sometimes a Great Notion," *The Wilson Quarterly* (autumn 2003), p. 49.

37. See Ernst B. Haas, *When Knowledge Is Power: Three Models of Change in International Organizations* (Berkeley: University of California Press, 1990).

38. This is one of the main themes in Slaughter, *New World Order.*

39. The term "prominent solution" is taken from Thomas Schelling. See his *The Strategy of Conflict* (New York: Oxford University Press, 1960), pp. 55–56.

40. Barbara Ward Jackson, *The Lopsided World* (New York: W.W. Norton, 1968), p. 1.

41. On "cosmopolitan" and other perspectives on morality, see Charles Beitz, *Political Theory and International Relations* (Princeton: Princeton University Press, 1979); and Terry Nardin, *Law, Morality, and the Relations of States* (Princeton: Princeton University Press, 1983).

42. Goldsmith and Posner, *Limits of International Law,* pp. 165–166. U.S. Supreme Court Justice Anthony Kennedy has sparked controversy in suggesting that American judges take into account the values held by other democratic systems in terms of defining, for example, what constitutes "cruel and inhuman punishment." See Jeffrey Toobin, "Swing Shift," *New Yorker,* September 12, 2005, pp. 42–51. Also, see note 52 in chapter 3 for Justice Sandra Day O'Conner's views on this subject.

43. Henry A. Kissinger, "America's Assignment," *Newsweek,* November 8, 2004, p. 38. See note 24, where Kissinger posed the challenge facing incoming President Bill Clinton. Here he posed the challenge facing the just reelected President George W. Bush.

44. See note 9.

45. Richard Gardner, "Practical Internationalism," *Foreign Affairs* 66 (spring, 1988).

46. See Kofi Annan, "In Larger Freedom: Decision Time at the UN," *Foreign Affairs* (May/June 2005). Also, see Rochester, *Between Two Epochs,* pp. 249–253.

47. The Commission on Global Governance, *Our Global Neighborhood* (New York: Oxford University Press, 1995).

48. See John Calcott, "A World-Wide Plug Faces Disconnection After 74-Year Effort," *Wall Street Journal,* April 1, 1982.

49. John Herz, *International Politics in the Atomic Age* (New York: Columbia University Press, 1959), p. 305. Herz later retracted his statement that the nation-state was facing extinction, arguing that it might be able to withstand the challenges posed by nuclear weapons, economic interdependence, and communications technology that were making national borders increasingly "permeable."

Appendix A

Questions for Study and Discussion

Chapter 1

1. In evaluating the overall state of the world today, is it the best of times, the worst of times, or somewhere in-between?

2. Looking at specific problem-areas (war and peace, economic well-being, etc.), in what respects has humanity been witnessing progress, and in what respects retrogression, in recent years?

3. What is your general impression of how "relevant" you think international law is in influencing the behavior of states and their leaders?

4. Can human progress move forward without progress in the development of international law?

Chapter 2

1. How can you reconcile the traditional, ingrained way of thinking about international relations—that is, as a "game" played by nation-states, revolving around such concepts as national power, national interests, and national sovereignty—with the growing contemporary reality of cyberspace, a globalized world economy of multinational corporations, and other phenomena that seem to be blurring national boundaries and national identities and rendering the traditional conceptions increasingly problematical, if not anachronistic?

2. If you had to choose, which paradigm do you think makes more sense as an accurate representation of contemporary world politics—the billiard ball paradigm (which stresses the continued primacy of sovereign nation-states as the dominant actors, concerned mainly about their physical security and survival in an anarchic environment) or the cobweb paradigm (which assumes a more complex, richer set of actors and issues, including IGOs, NGOs, and other nonstate actors competing with national governments and economic and other issues competing equally with security issues for attention)? What is the evidence to support one or the other?

3. What is the dominant planetary trend today—integration or disintegration? Neither? Are current conditions in the contemporary international system very hospitable, or not very hospitable, for improved global institution-building and for promoting at the very least what Barry Buzan has called "a more mature anarchy"?

4. Would you characterize yourself as a "realist" or an "idealist" ("liberal") in terms of your general orientation toward world politics and the potential role that international law might play in the future? Do you believe, as Thucydides argued, that "the strong do what they will and the weak suffer what they must" or, as Rousseau argued, that "the strong are never so strong that they can be master of all"? Or are you a "constructivist," or subscribe to some other school of thought?

Chapter 3

1. Is international law really law, creating binding obligations on nation-states? If so, how are the law-making, law-enforcement, and law-adjudication functions performed in the absence of a world government? If not, why do statesmen labor so long over the fine print in treaties, and why do foreign ministries and multinational corporations bother hiring international lawyers?

2. To the extent that international law gets obeyed, why is that so? How does one explain compliance with international law when there is no authoritative "traffic "cop" to enforce the rules and punish violators?

3. Is there such a thing as a "global policy process" whereby international regimes (agreements) are created and implemented? If so, how do the agenda-setting stage and other stages operate? How do problems (e.g., the proliferation of land-mines) become widely perceived as global concerns and elicit global responses?

4. What is the relationship between international law and international organization?

5. How does international law function in "high-politics" issue-areas as opposed to "low-politics" issue-areas?

Chapter 4

1. If sovereignty refers to the exclusive authority of the central government of a nation-state to regulate all activity within its borders, and the refusal to recognize any higher authority outside its borders, how does that square with the concepts of "human rights" and "humanitarian intervention"?

2. How does the treatment that a national government accords "aliens" within its borders differ from the treatment it accords its own "nationals" (citizens)? Do aliens tend to get better treatment, or worse, in terms of due process of law and other standards of justice?

3. Did the Nuremberg Trials of Nazi officials after World War II represent a triumph of human rights and a watershed moment in holding individual leaders accountable for crimes against humanity, or was it merely victor's justice?

4. How should one assess the record of human rights law since World War II—very successful, very unsuccessful, or modest but not insignificant? What rules have worked the best? What rules have worked the least?

5. The cold war divided the world into Western, communist, and third world blocs. With the end of the cold war, are we likely to see greater acceptance of universal human rights, or greater dissension due to the "clash of civilizations," post–9/11 security concerns, and other factors?

6. Can the new International Criminal Court succeed, particularly without American participation?

7. In the human rights issue-area, how does politics shape law, and law shape politics?

Chapter 5

1. Is the world becoming more war-prone, or less? What are the major trends in the use of armed force?

2. Was the decision of the United States to bomb Afghanistan and engage in "regime change" after the September 11, 2001 attacks a violation of international law or was it a legal action? How about the decision of the United States to invade Iraq and overturn its government in 2003? What specific rules of international law apply in these cases?

3. The United Nations Charter prohibits the use of armed force except in individual or collective self-defense and in the service of the United Nations (under the collective security provisions of the Charter). There is some allowance for the right of "anticipatory" self-defense, that is, firing the first shot before one's adversary if one can demonstrate that the latter's aggression is imminent. However, there can be a fine line between what precisely constitutes a "preemptive" use of armed force against a known immediate threat (which is generally permitted by the Charter) as opposed to a "preventive" use of armed force against a suspected longer-term threat (which is not permitted). In an age of WMDs, can a leader such as George Bush afford to honor these distinctions and wait to absorb the first blow—which could potentially be a radioactive "dirty bomb" attack on New York City that could render the city uninhabitable—before acting? The Bush Doctrine would appear to be clearly contrary to the UN Charter, but do we need new rules of international law to cover these situations?

4. What does international law have to say about the circumstances under which one state can punish another state for warlike actions committed by nonstate actors (say, al Qaeda or Hamas) based in the latter's territory?

5. It is sometimes said that one person's terrorist is another's national liberation hero. How does international law handle this problem?

6. Under what circumstances is "humanitarian intervention" legal?

7. Given the fact that the UN Charter was designed to deal mainly with the traditional problem of interstate war, and that the most common forms of violence today are intrastate (civil war) and extrastate (terrorism), should there be a major overhaul of the Charter provisions relating to war and peace?

8. Can we still have confidence in arms control treaties, given the recent problems with transparency, verification, and enforcement in the case of chemical and nuclear weapons in Iraq, North Korea, and Iran, or do arms control treaties remain vital elements in regulating warfare?

9. In the war and peace issue-area, how does politics shape law, and law shape politics?

Chapter 6

1. What challenges does economic globalization pose for international law? What opportunities?

2. How has international law evolved in response to changed thinking about states (mercantilism) and markets (free trade)? Can the "compromise of embedded liberalism" be sustained in an age of globalization, and how might international law play a role?

3. What are the key international regimes in the areas of trade, capital, and monetary affairs? How much economic order, prosperity, and justice have these produced since World War II?

4. How have international regimes in relatively "low-politics," "functional" areas, such as the regulation of cross-border mail and air traffic, contributed to the growth of the world economy? Is compliance in these domains routinized, or are these domains frequently politicized and characterized by erratic rule observance?

5. Has politics become subservient to law in the governance of international economics, particularly in the case of the World Trade Organization? In the economic realm, how does politics shape law, and law shape politics?

Chapter 7

1. How easy or hard is it to sort out which country is likely to be in a position to claim "jurisdiction" over some act committed by somebody somewhere on the planet? Do the rules governing jurisdiction appear to work reasonably well?

2. What are the key features of the law of the sea? If the world has been able to get fairly wide acceptance of a set of rules governing virtually every human activity on over 70 percent of the Earth's surface, what, if anything, does that tell us about the prospects for further development of international law and global institution-building?

3. What are the key features of the international regimes governing airspace and outer space? What explains the fact that "the common heritage of mankind" concept has been generally accepted in the realm of outer space but has gotten a somewhat mixed reception regarding Antarctica?

4. Do the traditional rules of international law governing the acquisition of title to territory still matter in an age when territorial annexation, particularly by great powers, is no longer a major feature of world politics, or do they still have relevance?

5. In the law of the sea, airspace, and outer space, how does politics shape law, and law shape politics?

Chapter 8

1. How effective have global environmental regimes been in addressing ecological problems? What have been major successes and failures? How does one explain the successes?

2. What accounts for the fact that there was not a single mention of the environment in the UN Charter when it was drafted in 1945, and relatively little attention paid to the development of international environmental regimes in the next two decades, until the 1972 UN Conference on the Human Environment triggered a wave of subsequent conferences and treaties?

3. Under what circumstances do "epistemic communities" exercise the most influence in affecting international environmental regimes?

4. When countries enter into agreements to, say, eliminate all ozone-depleting chemicals or reduce CO_2 emissions by a certain date, how is compliance monitored and enforced? Does each party trust the other to report honestly whether it has fulfilled its treaty obligation and met the prescribed target, which can involve complex measuring procedures, or are there neutral third parties that can be relied on for verification? In the case of less developed countries, even if they are well-intentioned, do they have the necessary economic and technological "capacity" to carry out their treaty obligations?

5. In the environmental issue-area, how does politics shape law, and law shape politics?

Chapter 9

1. Is it a "Westphalian moment," that is, with all the complex subnational and transnational forces at work today, are we witnessing not merely a change in the Westphalian state system but *of* the Westphalian state system? For better or worse, are we possibly seeing the beginning of the end of the nation-state as the primary basis for human political organization? Is this also a "Grotian moment"? What are the implications of current trends for the growth of international law in the twenty-first century?

2. Should we be promoting a "society of states" morality that mainly aims to improve relations between states (for example, honoring the obligation not to interfere in any state's internal affairs), or a "cosmopolitan" morality that focuses on the obligations people have toward each other (for example, insisting that all governments observe human rights)?

3. What kinds of reforms in global institution-building in general, and the United Nations in particular, do you believe are desirable and feasible?

4. The United States has been widely criticized for failing to ratify many multilateral treaties in recent years and failing to provide leadership in support of multilateral institutions. What stance should the United States, as the lead power today, take in the world? Can the United States succeed without international law? Can international law succeed without the United States?

5. Alan Goodman, in *A Brief History of the Future,* predicts that "the twenty-first century will encompass the longest period of peace, democracy, and economic development in history." What is the basis for such a rosy forecast? Are you optimistic or pessimistic about the future of the planet? *Your* future? Do you think the world will be a better place, say, in the year 2048 (the 400th anniversary of the Peace of Westphalia), than it is today?

Appendix B

Table of Cases

THE CASES LISTED BELOW have been adjudicated by various national and international courts and are frequently discussed in international law textbooks as principal illustrations of how international law is applied. Several of these are mentioned in this book, either in the body of the text or in the endnotes; page references are noted below. For excerpted opinions and legal commentaries relating to these cases, along with full citations of original sources, consult the casebooks listed in Appendix C, Resources for Researching International Law, on page 253. For the full text of the opinions issued in these cases, see www.cqpress.com/cs/rochester, which contains links to the homepages of the International Court of Justice (ICJ), the Permanent Court of International Justice (PCIJ), the European Court of Human Rights, the World Trade Organization (WTO), and the U.S. Supreme Court and other federal courts. You can access most of the cases below using those links and other links provided.

Cases (Subject Matter Listing)

A. *Sources of International Law*

B. *Relationship Between International and Municipal Law*

C. *Subjects of International Law (States and International Organizations)*

D. Human Rights and Humanitarian Law

E. Nationality of Individuals and Corporations

F. State Responsibility and Injury to Aliens

G. Jurisdiction

H. The Use of Armed Force and the Laws of War

I. Title to Territory

J. Law of the Sea

North Sea Continental Shelf Cases (ICJ)
Gulf of Maine Case (ICJ)
United States v. F/V Taijo Maru (U.S. District Court)   145

K. International Economic Law

Restrictions on Imports of Tuna (GATT panel)   131
Import Prohibition of Certain Shrimp and Shrimp Products (WTO panel)
EC Measures Concerning Meat and Meat Products Treated With Hormones (WTO
    panel)   131
Measures Affecting Imports of Fresh, Chilled, and Frozen Beef (WTO panel)
Regime for the Importation, Sale, and Distribution of Bananas (WTO panel)
Patent Protection for Pharmaceutical and Agricultural Chemical Products (WTO
    panel)
Venezuela-US Gasoline Dispute (WTO panel)   131
US-Brazil Upland Cotton Dispute (WTO panel)   131
(Also, see cases listed under "State Responsibility and Injury to Aliens,"
involving expropriation of property and other economic matters.)

L. Environmental Law

Trail Smelter Case (heard by U.S.-Canadian arbitration tribunal)   164
Gabcikovo-Nagymaros Project (ICJ)
(Also, see cases listed under International Economic Law above, involving GATT
    and WTO decisions relating to conflicts between environmental and eco-
    nomic concerns.)

Cases (Alphabetical Listing)

American Banana Co. v. United Fruit Co. (U.S. Supreme Court)   141, 228
Anglo-Norwegian Fisheries Case (ICJ)
Armed Activities on the Territory of the Congo (ICJ)
Asakura v. City of Seattle (U.S. Supreme Court)
The Asylum Case (ICJ)   207
Attorney-General of Israel v. Eichmann (Israel, District Court of Jerusalem)   97, 142
Avena and Other Mexican Nationals (ICJ)   210

Banco Nacionale de Cuba v. Sabbatino (U.S. Supreme Court)
Blackmer v. United States (U.S. Supreme Court)
Brown Claim (United States v. Great Britain, heard before an arbitrator)

Caroline Case   98
*Case Concerning Application of the Convention on the Prevention and Punishment of
    the Crime of Genocide* (ICJ)   72
Case Concerning the Barcelona Traction, Light and Power Co. (ICJ)

Appendix C

Resources for Researching International Law: Web Sites, Casebooks and Reference Works, and Readings

I. Web Sites

www.asil.org

This is the homepage of the American Society of International Law, which contains a wide variety of links to all aspects of international law.

www.eisil.org

This is the Electronic Information System for International Law (EISIL) maintained by the American Society of International Law. It provides access to on-line sources of information about states, international organizations, and basic documents in various issue-areas, including international economic law, environmental law, human rights law, laws governing the use of armed force, and air, space, and ocean law.

www.un.org

This is the homepage of the United Nations, which contains links to the entire UN system, not only the main organs such as the UN Security Council and the General Assembly but also to the specialized agencies such as the World Bank, IMF, the World Health Organization, the World Trade Organization, and other IGOs.

www.un.org./law/

This can be accessed through the UN homepage or accessed directly on the Internet. It is the UN Web site that focuses on international law, and contains links to the International Court of Justice, the International Criminal Court, the law of the sea, treaties, and research guides.

www.icj-cij.org

This is the homepage of the International Court of Justice (the ICJ, or World Court). The ICJ was created in 1945 in conjunction with the UN. You can access all ICJ cases (click "Decisions," and you will see a list of the cases heard by the Court since 1946, including the full text of judgments and opinions issued).

www.worldcourts.com/pcij/eng/

This is the homepage of the Permanent Court of International Justice (the PCIJ). The PCIJ was created in 1921 in conjunction with the League of Nations, and is the predecessor to the ICJ. You can access all PCIJ cases (click "Decisions" and you will see a list of the cases heard by the Court between 1921 and 1939, including the full text of judgments and opinions issued).

www.echr.coe.int/echr
   This is the homepage of the European Court of Human Rights (ECHR). You
   can access all ECHR cases (click "Case Law" and then click "Lists of Judgments" to review the full text of the judgments and opinions issued).

www.wto.org/english/tratop_e/dispu_e/dispu_e.htm
   This is the homepage of the World Trade Organization (WTO) "Dispute Settlement" Locator. It provides access to summaries of trade disputes heard by
   WTO panels. You can search for cases by name, country (litigants), subject
   matter (e.g., bananas), or chronology.

www.supremecourtus.gov/opinions/opinions.html
   This is the homepage of the U.S. Supreme Court that provides access to all
   cases heard by the Court, including the full text of the Court's opinions.

www.findlaw.com/casecode/supreme.html
   This is the Findlaw service that quickly enables you to find U.S. Supreme
   Court decisions in cases you are researching. Simply type in one of the party's
   names (e.g., Sabbatino) in the "Party Name Search" box, and you can then access the full text opinion. Findlaw only has cases since 1893. For earlier cases,
   use http://web.lexis-nexis.com/universe, which is available on almost all university computers.

www.people.virginia.edu/~rjb3v/rjb.html
   This is Foreign Affairs Online, perhaps the best comprehensive Web site on
   international affairs—international politics, law, and organization. It enables
   you to access the CIA World Factbook and other sources of information on
   every country in the world, plus has a link on international organizations that
   provides information on both IGOs (the UN, the European Union, and other
   intergovernmental organizations) and NGOs, and has an international law
   link that connects you to the ICJ, regional courts, major international law
   journals, and other resources.

fletcher.tufts.edu/multilaterals.html
   This is the site of the Multilaterals Project maintained by the Fletcher School
   of Law and Diplomacy at Tufts University. It is a comprehensive survey of
   multilateral treaties in various issue-areas, including trade and commercial relations, atmosphere and space, marine and coastal, biodiversity, diplomatic relations, and rules of warfare. It also contains links relating to "treaty research
   resources" and is a good place to begin locating the text of any multilateral
   treaty.

www.law.ecel.uwa.edu.au/intlaw
   This is an excellent Web site on international law maintained by the University of Western Australia. It has a collection of international law links.

www.lib.uchicago.edu/~llou/intlaw.html
   This is the "Key Resources on the Internet for International Law Research" site
   maintained by the University of Chicago (Lyonette Louis-Jacques). It provides
   access to international organization links (including the UN, the WTO, EU,

Organization of American States, and other IGOs) as well as various databases on international law.

www.ppl.nl

This is the Web site for the Peace Palace Library in The Hague and provides access to their large online catalog as well as current reference information.

www.jstor.org/journals/00029300.html

This is the homepage of the *American Journal of International Law* (*AJIL*) published by the American Society of International Law. The *AJIL* contains a wealth of articles that include commentaries on important court cases as well as general discussion of contemporary international legal issues.

www.state.gov/www/publications/dispatch/index.html

This is the homepage of the U.S. Department of State *Dispatch* magazine, which is the successor publication to the U.S. Department of State *Bulletin*. These publications contain a record of U.S. official diplomatic practice and views of customary international law, in the form of speeches and other evidences.

home.att.net/~slomansonb/txtcsesite.html

This is the Web site maintained by William Slomanson in connection with his book *Fundamental Perspectives on International Law,* 3rd ed. It contains useful tips on researching international law along with links to various sources of information.

II. Casebooks and Reference Works

Bishop, William. *International Law: Cases and Materials,* 3rd ed. Boston: Little, Brown, 1971.

Blakseley, Christopher L., Edwin B. Firmage, Richard F. Scott, and Sharon A. Williams. *The International Legal System: Cases and Materials,* 5th ed. New York: Foundation Press, 2001. Also see earlier editions by Noyes E. Leech, Covey T. Oliver, and Joseph Sweeney (1973 and 1988).

Bledsoe, Robert L. and Boleslaw A. Boczek. *The International Law Dictionary.* Santa Barbara, Calif.: ABC-Clio, 1987.

Brownlie, Ian, ed., *Basic Documents in International Law,* 5th ed.. Oxford, Eng.: Oxford University Press, 2002.

Buergenthal, Thomas, Sean D. Murphy, and Harold G. Maier. *Public International Law in a Nutshell,* 3rd ed. St. Paul: West, 2002.

Carter, Barry E., Phillip R. Trimble, and Curtis A. Bradley. *International Law,* 4th ed. New York: Aspen Publishers, 2003.

Damrosch, Lori F., Louis Henkin, Richard C. Pugh, Oscar Schachter, and Hans Smit. *International Law: Cases and Materials,* 4th ed. St. Paul: West, 2001.

Damrosch, Lori F., Louis Henkin, Richard C. Pugh, Oscar Schachter, and Hans Smit. *Basic Documents Supplement to International Law: Cases and Materials,* 4th ed. St.Paul: West, 2001.

Dunoff, Jeffrey L., Steven R. Ratner, and David Wippman. *International Law: Norms, Actors, Process.* New York: Aspen Publishers, 2002.

Janis, Mark W. and John E. Noyes. *Cases and Commentary on International Law,* 2nd ed. St.Paul: West, 2001.

III. Readings

Arend, Anthony Clark and Robert J. Beck, *International Law and the Use of Armed Force.* London: Routledge, 1993.

Bederman, David J. *International Law Frameworks.* New York: Foundation Press, 2001.

Benedick, Richard. *Ozone Diplomacy.* Cambridge, Mass.: Harvard University Press, 1998.

Boyle, Francis. *World Politics and International Law.* Durham, N.C.: Duke University Press, 1985.

Brown, Edith Weiss. *In Fairness to Future Generations: International Law, Common Patrimony, and Intergenerational Equity.* New York: Transnational Publishers, 1989.

Brown, Edith Weiss and Harold K. Jacobson, eds., *Engaging Countries: Strengthening Compliance with International Environmental Accords.* Cambridge, Mass.: MIT Press, 1998.

Chayes, Abram. *The Cuban Missile Crisis: International Crises and the Role of Law.* New York: Oxford University Press, 1974.

Chayes, Abram and Antonia H. Chayes. *The New Sovereignty: Compliance With International Regulatory Agreements.* Cambridge, Mass.: Harvard University Press, 1995.

Christol, Carl Q. *Space Law: Past, Present, and Future.* Neth.: Kluwer, 1991.

D'Amato, Anthony A. *The Concept of Custom in International Law.* Ithaca, N.Y.: Cornell University Press, 1971.

Damrosch, Lori F. and David J. Scheffer, eds., *Law and Force in the New International Order.* Boulder, Colo.: Westview, 1991.

Dinstein, Yoram. *War, Aggression, and Self-Defense,* 3rd ed. Cambridge, Eng.: Cambridge University Press, 2001.

Donnelly, Jack. *International Human Rights.* Boulder, Colo.: Westview, 1993.

Forsythe, David P. *The Politics of International Law: U.S. Foreign Policy Reconsidered.* Boulder: Lynne Rienner, 1990.

Franck, Thomas M. *The Power of Legitimacy Among Nations.* New York: Oxford University Press, 1990.

Glennon, Michael J. *Limits of Law, Prerogatives of Power: Interventionism After Kosovo.* New York: Palgrave, 2001.

Goldsmith, Jack L. and Eric A. Posner. *The Limits of International Law.* New York: Oxford University Press, 2005.

Haas, Peter M. *Saving the Mediterranean: The Politics of International Environmental Cooperation.* New York: Columbia University Press, 1990.

Haas, Peter M., Robert O. Keohane, and Marc A. Levy, eds., *Institutions for the Earth.* Cambridge, Mass.: MIT Press, 1995.

Henkin, Louis. *How Nations Behave,* 2nd ed. New York: Columbia University Press, 1979.

Henkin, Louis et al. *Right v. Might: International Law and the Use of Force,* 2nd ed. New York: Council on Foreign Relations Press, 1991.

Higgins, Rosalyn. *Problems and Process: International Law and How We Use It.* Oxford, Eng.: Clarendon Press, 1994.

Ignatieff, Michael. *Human Rights as Politics and Idolatry.* Princeton: Princeton University Press, 2001.

Joyner, Christopher C. *International Law in the 21st Century.* Lanham, Md.: Rowman and Littlefield, 2005.

Joyner, Christopher C., ed., *The United Nations and International Law.* Cambridge, Eng.: Cambridge University Press, 1997.

Karns, Margaret P. and Karen A. Mingst. *International Organizations: The Politics and Processes of Global Governance.* Boulder, Colo.: Lynne Rienner, 2004.

Krasner, Stephen D. *Sovereignty: Organized Hypocrisy.* Princeton: Princeton University Press, 1999.

Ku, Charlotte and Paul F. Diehl, eds., *International Law: Classic and Contemporary Readings,* 2nd ed. Boulder, Colo.: Lynne Rienner, 2003.

Murphy, Sean D. *Humanitarian Intervention: The United Nations in an Evolving World Order.* Philadelphia: University of Pennsylvania Press, 1996.

Porter, Tony. *States, Markets, and Regimes in Global Finance.* New York: St. Martins Press, 1993.

Reisman, W. Michael and Andrew R. Willard, eds., *International Incidents: The Law That Counts in World Politics.* Princeton: Princeton University Press, 1988.

Sands, Phillippe. *Principles of International Environmental Law,* 2nd ed. Cambridge, Eng.: Cambridge University Press, 2005.

Sanger, Clyde. *Ordering the Oceans: The Making of the Law of the Sea.* Toronto: University of Toronto Press, 1987.

Sassen, Saskia. *Losing Control? Sovereignty in an Age of Globalization.* New York: Columbia University Press, 1996.

Slaughter, Anne-Marie. *A New World Order.* Princeton: Princeton University Press, 2004.

Slomanson, William R. *Fundamental Perspectives on International Law,* 3rd ed. Belmont, Calif.: Wadsworth, 2000.

Von Glahn, Gerhard. *Law Among Nations,* 7th ed.. New York: Longman, 1996.

Wallach, Lori and Patrick Woodall. *Whose World Trade Organization?* New York: The New Press, 2004.

Zacher, Mark W. and Brent A. Sutton. *Governing Global Networks: International Regimes for Transportation and Communications.* Cambridge, Eng.: Cambridge University Press, 1996.

Index